WARSHIP 2015

WARSHIP **2015**

Editor: John Jordan

Assistant Editor: Stephen Dent

NAVAL INSTITUTE PRESS
Annapolis, Maryland

Frontispiece:
*The Japanese aircraft carrier Shôkaku photographed on 30 May
1939 at berth no.2 of Yokosuka NY, the day before she was
launched in the presence of Prince Fushimi and other members of
the Imperial family. The bulbous bow – the first to be fitted in an
IJN warship – is particularly prominent. The naval officers and
engineers are in working dress. The ship's principal designer,
Cdr. Inagawa Seiichi, is in the front row, fourth from the left.
The launch weight of Shôkaku was 18,315 tonnes. She was the
last big ship launched from this berth before the beginning of the
Pacific War; Fukui Shizuo states that the launch ceremony was
attended by many spectators. (Fukui Shizuo collection)*

Conway
An imprint of Bloomsbury Publishing Plc

50 Bedford Square
London
WC1B 3DP
UK

1385 Broadway
New York
NY 10018
USA

www.bloomsbury.com

CONWAY™ is a trademark and imprint of Bloomsbury Publishing Plc

First published 2015

Published and distributed in the United States of America and Canada by
the Naval Institute Press, 291 Wood Road, Annapolis, Maryland 21402-5043
www.nip.org

British Library Cataloguing-in-Publication Data
A catalogue record for this book is available from the British Library.

LOC number 2015937611

ISBN: 978-1-59114-600-1

2 4 6 8 10 9 7 5 3 1

Typeset by Stephen Dent
Printed and bound in Great Britain by CPI Group (UK) Ltd, Croydon CR0 4YY

To find out more about our authors and books visit www.bloomsbury.com. Here you will find extracts,
author interviews, details of forthcoming events and the option to sign up for our newsletters.

CONTENTS

EDITORIAL

In his chapter 'A *Majestic* Fleet, 1893-1904' (*Warrior to Dreadnought*, Chatham Publishing 1997), the late David K Brown regretted the common use of the term 'pre-Dreadnought', which he considered 'derogatory', to describe the battleships of that period. As he correctly pointed out, until Dreadnoughts were at sea in numbers these ships commanded the sea. He might also have pointed out that not everyone was initially convinced by the 'all-big-gun' ship. The year 1905, which saw the remarkably rapid construction of the revolutionary battle-ship HMS *Dreadnought*, was also the year of Tsushima, the only major battle involving modern steam-powered battleships prior to 1914. The major navies all spent a considerable amount of effort analysing the lessons of this battle, but there were significant disagreements in their respective conclusions.

For the French Tsushima confirmed the power of the quick-firing medium gun batteries, which at the current battle ranges of 2000-3000m could batter a ship into submission, leaving it to be finished off at even closer range by the slow-firing big guns or the torpedo. This effectively validated the design of the ships already on the stocks, the six fleet battleships of the *Patrie* class (see the Editor's article which fronts this annual). The calibre of the French medium guns would see a steady progression but the primacy of these guns, which were capable of firing up to three rounds per minute, went unchallenged. The French laid down their first pair of all-big-gun ships only in late 1910, and they were barely worked up by August 1914. Thus, whereas in the Royal Navy the contemporaries of the *Patrie*, the *King Edward VII* class, were relegated to second-line duties shortly after the outbreak of war, the five surviving ships of the *Patrie* class, together with the six 'semi-dreadnoughts' of the *Danton* class, continued to constitute the core of the French fleet in the Mediterranean. Despite their theoretical obsolescence these ships remained formidable gunnery platforms, particularly at the shorter battle ranges for which they had been designed.

Re-evaluation is something of a theme in this year's annual. For many years Western commentators have speculated on the reason for the port-side location of the island in the IJN carriers *Akagi* and *Hiryu*, with elaborate theories being put forward relating to command and control (when these two ships were operating with their half-sisters *Kaga* and *Soryu*, both with islands to starboard) and aircraft landing circuits. Hans Lengerer, in his article on the carriers of the *Shôkaku* class, finally puts the matter to rest. He details the rationale for the port-side island, located at the mid-point of the flight deck, the trials of the concept which took place during the late 1930s, and the final decision to revert to a starboard-side island forward for *Shôkaku* and *Zuikaku*, which meant significant modifications to the former ship while under construction and left her with the vestigial support structure on the port side. Herr Lengerer's article also provides new insights into the 'passive' protection features developed specifically for these ships, including 'blow-out plates' in the sides of the hangar to vent explosions and an underwater protection system which used a liquid/air 'sandwich'.

Stephen McLaughlin's article on the circular ironclads *Novgorod* and *Vitse-admiral Popov*, often referred to as the 'popovkas', also takes a new look at these unusual vessels, and in the process targets some of the more extreme mythologies surrounding them. He concludes that, while these ships had their faults, both the ships and their designer have suffered unjust and exaggerated criticism, and that the 'popovkas' were relatively effective coast defence vessels for their size.

Michele Cosentino in turn addresses another myth: the Italian Navy's apparent total lack of interest in carrier aviation between the wars. Although the Italian admiralty was itself ambivalent about the need for aircraft carriers in the Mediterranean theatre, it did promote a serious design for a purpose-built carrier of 15,000 tons by Lieutenant-General Filippo Bonfiglietti to serve as a naval aviation demonstrator. Bonfiglietti's original plans for the ship, together with a model, were preserved by the naval engineer's family and have only recently come to light. They were the result of detailed studies by Bonfiglietti of foreign designs and reflect contemporary thinking about carrier aviation. In the end the carrier was not built due to political opposition, mainly from the *Regia Aeronautica*, but Bonfiglietti continued to produce alternative designs up to his retirement from the service in 1931.

In the second of his articles on Royal Navy weapons and electronics of the post-war era, Peter Marland provides a detailed account of the gun and missile projects undertaken from 1945 to the present, and in the process evaluates the relative success of the various weapons and their associated 'platform' technology, including launcher and replenishment systems. His description of the launcher and handling arrangements for the Sea Slug surface-to-air missile and the Ikara antisubmarine missile are particularly complete, and feature illustrations which have not previously been published.

The current plethora of naval books marking the centenary of the Great War have tended to focus on the North Sea and North Atlantic, with some coverage of the eastern Mediterranean (Dardanelles campaign); the conflict in the Adriatic between Austria-Hungary and the allied Italian, French and British navies has received less attention, and has often been viewed as an irrelevant 'side-show'. However, the progress of the naval war in this narrow sea had a major impact on the war in the Mediterranean as a whole. It was also a very different type of conflict from that being waged in the North Sea, with light surface craft, submarines and mine warfare to the fore. In the first instalment of a two-part article, Vincent O'Hara and Enrico Cernushi aim to provide a complete

Next year's Warship *will feature two major articles on IJN destroyers: a technical study of the* Asashio *class by Hans Lengerer, and one on the war career of the destroyer* Amatsukaze *(Kagero class) by Michael Williams. Seen here is the* Asashio *running her speed trials in July 1937. (Fukui Shizuo collection)*

account and analysis of the naval war in this much-neglected theatre.

The Mediterranean 1914-15 is also the setting for Philippe Caresse's article on the French submarine *Mariotte*, whose unusual configuration gave her the nickname 'The Toothbrush'. Having covered her design and early career, the author recounts her loss while attempting to penetrate the Dardanelles in July 1915.

The 'historical' part of the annual concludes with two major features. In 'The Incredible Hulks' Aidan Dodson describes the after-life of a series of Victorian big ships, as constituents of the *Fisgard* boy artificers' training establishment in Portsmouth harbour. The Royal Navy of the Victorian era hated to throw anything away which could usefully be recycled, and the large fleet of training hulks, specially adapted to the purpose, was instrumental in producing the skilled seamen who manned the Grand Fleet during the First World War.

And in his second major article for *Warship*, Peter Cannon looks at the Royal Navy's first surface engagement of the Pacific War, when the veteran destroyers HMAS *Vampire* and HMS *Thanet* attempted to evade a screen of no fewer than 21 Japanese warships and auxiliaries to attack two amphibious transports off the Malayan town of Endau during the early hours of 27 January 1942. The author's article, which is based on recent research in the British, Australian and Japanese archives, is much more than a straightforward 'blow-by-blow' account of this little-known action: it investigates Royal Navy and IJN tactical and communications procedures and provides a detailed description of RN gun and torpedo fire control practices of the period. It also reveals how different perceptions of this comparatively brief and confused night action on the two sides coloured the respective official reports, thereby raising questions which the author endeavours to answer.

The remainder of this year's annual has the usual regular features. After a year's break, Conrad Waters resumes his series of articles on the latest naval developments with a detailed look at trends in carrier aviation: he focuses in particular on the *Gerald R. Ford* (CVN-78) and *America* (LHA-6) classes on order for the US Navy, the two *Queen Elizabeth* class carriers being assembled for Britain's Royal Navy, and India's *Vikrant*. There are major 'Warship Notes' by Ian Johnston on the capital ship orders placed with the former Fairfield Shipbuilding & Engineering Co. Ltd., by Mike Williams on the little-known *Operation Rei*, the naval action off San José (Mindoro, The Philippines) on the night of 26-27 December 1944, and by Assistant Editor Stephen Dent on the standard acronyms (such as HMS) which regularly precede ship names. Finally, this year's 'Warship Gallery' features the museum ship USS *North Carolina*; Brooks Rowlett, who has a close association with the ship, has provided a series of superb on-board photographs together with detailed, informative captions.

Some readers may be aware that in the autumn of last year Conway Publishing, formerly owned by Pavilion Books, was purchased by Bloomsbury Publishing to sit alongside its own maritime imprint Adlard Coles. Shortly afterwards the *Warship* editorial team met with the Adlard Coles team in their London office, and it was agreed that *Warship* would continue in its current form for the foreseeable future. It was an extremely supportive meeting, and it was agreed that, despite the lateness of the day – we were on the point of beginning page layouts for the *Warship 2015* when the takeover took place – Adlard Coles would make every effort to make room in their busy schedule for publication in June of this year.

Preparations for *Warship 2016* are already well underway. Major articles will include a technical study of the IJN destroyers of the *Asashio* class by Hans Lengerer, a complementary historical feature by Michael Williams on the chequered service career of the IJN destroyer *Amatsukaze*, a study of the French 'colonial sloops' of the interwar period by the Editor, a superbly-illustrated article on the French coast defence battleship *Tempête* by Philippe Caresse, and the second part of 'War in the Adriatic' by Vincent O'Hara and Enrico Cernuschi.

John Jordan
April 2015

THE BATTLESHIPS OF THE *PATRIE* CLASS

Together with the 'semi-dreadnoughts' of the *Danton* class, the five surviving battleships of the *Patrie* and *Démocratie* classes formed the core of the *1re Armée Navale* in the Mediterranean at the outbreak of the Great War. **John Jordan** examines the origins of these ships and their subsequent entry into service with the *Marine Nationale*.

The *Patrie* class broke with previous practice in a number of respects. They were the first French battleships to be designed for a load displacement exceeding 12,000 tonnes; they were the first to have a deep armour belt backed by a cellular layer, a concept pioneered by the prominent naval architect Emile Bertin; and there were six ships in the programme, the original intention being that they would be built to an identical configuration.

From the time that the theories of Admiral Hyacinthe Aube and the *Jeune Ecole* took hold during the 1880s until the turn of the century, any proposal for a large battleship met with resolute political opposition. France had no chance of matching Britain's fleet ship for ship, given the need for expenditure on the army and land fortifications. The naval strategy adopted during this period was therefore essentially 'asymmetric': flotillas of small, inexpensive torpedo craft (*la poussière navale*) to defend French ports, and fast cruisers capable of escaping a British blockade and attacking her trade routes, with logistical support being provided by France's extensive overseas territories. Any large battleship submitted to parliament for approval was subject to derisive dismissal as a 'mastodon': large, ungainly and, above all, obsolescent. Even those navy ministers who were prepared to put forward such a proposal had always to be mindful of the political mood; they therefore impressed on the designers the importance of keeping displacement to 12,000 tonnes maximum. The result was a handful of ships with powerful main and secondary batteries but limited protection and sea-keeping performance, which increasingly lagged behind their British contemporaries. During the period 1893-1900, when Britain laid down 32 first class battleships of 13,200-14,500 tons with a standardised modern armament of four 12-inch guns in twin trainable turrets and twelve 6-inch QF guns in casemates (see table), the French authorised only the three *Charlemagnes* of 11,000 tonnes and the one-off *Iéna* and *Suffren* of 12,000 tonnes.

Two factors were responsible for the change of policy which occurred during the late 1890s. The first was the appointment of Emile Bertin as chief constructor in 1896.[1] The second was Admiral Tirpitz' First Fleet Act of 1898, which decreed that imperial Germany, France's

TABLE 1: FIRST CLASS BATTLESHIPS 1893-1900

Britain:

Majestic	6 ships 1893/4	*Displacement:*
	6 ships 1894/5	13,200-14,500 tons
Canopus	5 ships 1896/7	*Speed:* 17-19 knots
	1 ship 1897/8	*Armament:* 4 – 305mm,
Formidable	3 ships 1897/8	12 – 152mm QF
London	3 ships 1898/9	*Armour belt:* 155-230mm
	2 ships 1900/1	HC/KC
Duncan	4 ships 1898/9 suppl.	
	2 ships 1899/1900	
Total:	**32 ships**	

France:

Charlemagne	3 ships 1894	11,100t/18kts/
		4 -305, 10 – 138/400mm HC
Iéna	1 ship 1897	11,850t/18kts/
		4 – 305, 8 – 164/320mm HC
Suffren	1 ship 1898	12,530t/18kts/
		4 – 305, 10 – 164/300mm HC
Total:	**5 ships**	

major potential military foe, would within a few years possess a fleet of sixteen battleships (plus a flagship). The impact of this measure on the future balance of naval power in Europe made the French parliament far more receptive towards an increase in expenditure on the battle fleet.

Having spent several years in Japan, Bertin had returned to France in 1890 when the new naval programme was being prepared. In a study presented in October of that year he convincingly demonstrated that the armour plating in current use would be unable to resist penetration by the latest AP shell if fired by major-calibre guns with high initial velocity, and that current protection systems, which featured a heavy but shallow belt topped by a relatively thin protective deck, left battleships vulnerable to loss by a single shell because of the extensive flooding which would result. The merit of his proposals for a deeper armour belt backed by a cellular layer comprising multiple watertight compartments, and for torpedo bulkheads inboard of the lower hull, was

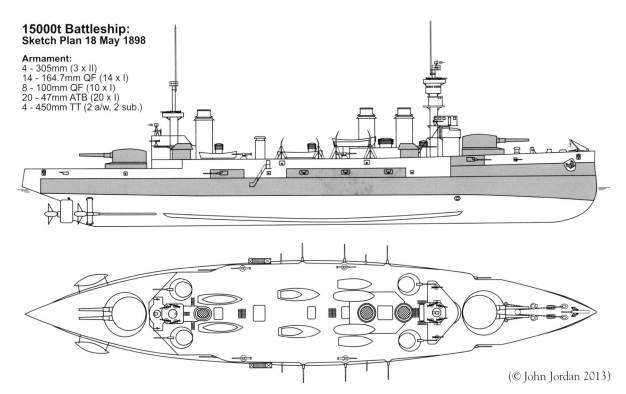

15000t Battleship:
Sketch Plan 18 May 1898

Armament:
4 - 305mm (3 x II)
14 - 164.7mm QF (14 x I)
8 - 100mm QF (10 x I)
20 - 47mm ATB (20 x I)
4 - 450mm TT (2 a/w, 2 sub.)

(© John Jordan 2013)

recognised, but the implications of these measures for the size of future battleships were deemed politically unacceptable, despite the support of the C-in-C Fleet.

Bertin persisted, and following his appointment as chief constructor was invited by the Navy Minister to give a complete and detailed presentation of his ideas. Bertin responded on 16 November 1897 with a proposal for a ship displacing 13,600 tonnes. This time his ideas met with a more favourable response, and the following year the Council of Works (*Conseil des travaux*) fully endorsed the principle of a ship with a deep belt backed by a *caisson cellulaire* extending almost the entire length of the ship, a flat upper protective deck (*pont blindé supérieur* or PBS) resting on the top edge of the belt, and a lower protective deck (*pont blindé inférieur* or PBI) over the ship's vitals, the sides being angled down to meet the lower edge of the belt. The belt itself, which was to extend up to the Main Deck (PBS), was to be of uniform thickness to a point 0.5 metres below the waterline, where it was tapered.

However, acceptance of these general principles was only a first step. It would be a further two years before the design of a new battleship was approved, the initial proposal being subject to the usual objections and counter-proposals. Concern centred primarily on the secondary battery of quick-firing guns, which still constituted in many respects the 'main armament' of the ships. While the slow-firing 305mm guns were capable of the occasional 'lucky hit' at long range, and were expected to deliver the *coup de grâce* to a disabled ship, it was anticipated that the QF guns would be primarily responsible for the disabling, subjecting the enemy upperworks to a hail of fire using high-capacity shell at the relatively close range of 2000 metres still anticipated in a fleet engagement. The number, height and disposition of these guns were therefore seen as crucial.

The First Proposal

On 20 April 1898 the STCN submitted a proposal for a battleship of 15,000 tons, a figure comparable to the latest British construction; draught was fixed at 8.4 metres to allow passage of the Suez Canal. Besides the four 305mm guns in twin turrets, which were to be provided with sufficient ammunition for four hours' fire, there were to be no fewer than fourteen 164.7mm QF guns (ammunition for three hours' firing), of which four were to be in single turrets with the remaining guns in casemates, and eight 100mm QF guns distributed between the First and Upper Decks (see sketch plan). The armament was completed by twenty 4.7mm anti-torpedo boat (ATB) guns, of which eight were to be mounted in fighting tops, and four 450mm torpedo tubes: two fixed submerged, and two trainable above-water tubes.

Protection featured a 300mm belt of cemented armour backed by a deep cellular layer, an upper protective deck 50mm thick (30mm steel on a double layer of 10mm plating), and a lower deck 60mm thick (40mm steel on a double layer of 10mm plating) which inclined downwards at the sides to meet the bottom edge of the belt. The belt was tapered to 200mm towards the bow and the stern, and was closed at the stern by a 240mm transverse bulkhead. A 140mm partial transverse bulkhead between the forward casemates protected against enfilading fire. The main turrets had 320mm faces with 280mm sides and ring bulkheads, while the 164.7mm secondary guns had a uniform protection of 140mm for the turrets, casemates and hoists.

There were to be two military masts and a straight stem. Maximum designed speed was 18 knots, and endurance was to be 5000nm at 10 knots at normal loading. Accommodation was provided for 800 officers and men, including an admiral and his staff; provisions were 45 days' food and 20 days' water.

The proposal met with the general approval of the *Conseil des travaux*, which had previously rejected other competing proposals by the constructors Thibaudier and Maugas. However, dissatisfaction was expressed with certain aspects of the design. The council wanted the straight stem replaced by a sturdy ram. It wanted six (vs. four) of the fourteen 164.7mm guns to be in turrets, with at least six (preferably eight) guns capable of end-on fire, and it wanted the floor of the mid-ship casemates to be raised from 3.6m above the waterline to 3.8m, with increased protection for the inner walls of the casemates. A fifth (above-water) torpedo tube was to be added at the stern.

The STCN did its best to respond to these requests, but the demands relating to the secondary armament were difficult to fulfil. The additional topweight implied had to be compensated by a reduction in the thickness of the belt, which was opposed by the council. The council then threw two new spanners into the works: the respective thicknesses of the protective decks were to be reversed, so that the upper was strengthened at the expense of the lower; and serious consideration was to be given to mounting a greater number of 164.7mm guns in a new twin turret. Both of these measures would tend to increase topweight – although the council was prepared to see a reduction in thickness in the light upper belt (the *cuirasse mince*) from 120mm to 80mm in part-compensation.

The design was reworked by the STCN and the stability calculations redone, but there remained a large question mark over the layout of the secondary battery. Bertin now favoured mounting no fewer than twelve of the 164.7mm guns in twin turrets on the upper deck, with four single guns in casemates – a solution he considered possible provided the upper protective deck was reduced in thickness from 60mm to 53mm. Alternative solutions he proposed were six guns in single turrets and eight in casemates (the same number of guns as in the original proposal), and twelve 194mm guns in twin turrets backed up by ten unshielded 100mm QF guns in a battery. The latter suggestion would have involved some reductions in armour thicknesses. It was not liked, in part because of the reduction in protection for the hull, but also because it would have meant the ship would have been armed exclusively with large-calibre weapons. The Naval General Staff felt that such a drastic move was unnecessary and that the 164.7mm QF more than matched the secondary guns on contemporary foreign battleships (British ships of the period were armed with 6-inch/152mm secondary guns). It expressed the view that the number of guns and the rate of fire were the crucial factors in a naval engagement, and was reluctant to sacrifice these in order to accommodate a relatively slow-firing gun with a heavier projectile.

The irony of this rejection would be highlighted within four years, when the desire to respond to the British *King Edward VII* class (see below) necessitated a *volte-face* which required a major redesign of the later ships of the *Patrie* class while they were still on the slipway. Bertin's all-big-gun proposal also anticipated the *Dantons*, with their twelve 240mm guns in turrets mounted on the beam (see the author's article in *Warship 2013*).

Competing proposals from Schneider/Creusot and from

the DCAN for a twin 164.7mm turret were duly considered on 23 December 1898. The in-house DCAN proposal, which had independent loading for the guns and declutching for the individual guns in the event of damage, won the day. The various sections then expressed a preference for twelve guns in twin turrets and four singles in casemates. This was duly approved by the *Conseil des travaux*, which on 28 February 1899 submitted a request to the STCN for further modifications which included better protection for the 164.7mm hoists, the suppression of the second military mast, and the elimination of the 100mm QF battery in favour of additional 47mm ATB guns.

The Final Design

There was a further meeting on 28 April at which the final parameters of the design were determined, and on 29 May 1899 Bertin was formally requested to make the necessary revisions. These took a further two months, but the plans completed on 8 August met all the council's requirements: there would now be eighteen 164.7mm guns, of which twelve would be in twin turrets, and protection of the ammunition trunks was increased to

TABLE 2: *FORMIDABLE* (GB) vs. *PATRIE*

	Formidable	Patrie
No. in class:	three	two
Built:	1898-1902	1901-07
Displacement:	14,500t	14,865t
Dimensions:	122m x 23m[1]	134m x 24m
Propulsion:		
Engines	2-shaft VTE	3-shaft VTE
Horsepower	15,000ihp	17,500ihp
Speed[2]	18 knots	18 knots
Armament:		
Main guns	4 x 305mm (2xII)	4 x 305mm (2xII)
2ndary guns	12 x 152mm (12xI)	18 x 164.7mm (6xII, 6xI)
ATB guns	12 x 76mm (12xI)	24 x 47mm (24xI)[2]
	6 x 47mm (6xI)	
TT	4 x 450mm	5 x 450mm (3 a/w)[2]
Protection:		
Belt	230mm KC	280mm HC[3]
Main turrets	305mm	360/280mm
2ndary guns	150mm	140mm
Conning tower	355mm	266mm
Decks	25 + 75/50mm	54 + 70/51mm[4]

Notes:

1. Metric equivalents have been supplied for *Formidable* to provide a comparison. The equivalents for gun calibres are exact; those for armour thicknesses are to the nearest 5mm.
2. Sixteen of the 47mm ATB guns were replaced by 13 x 65mm during construction; the three above-water torpedo tubes were also suppressed.
3. Thickness of armour only; this was generally secured to a double thickness of 8-20mm plating.
4. Figures for upper and lower armoured decks respectively; for the lower armoured deck, the first figure given relates to the inclined section at the sides, the second to the central (horizontal) section.

An early view of Patrie *at Toulon, probably dating from 1907. She is painted in the then-standard livery of black hull with buff upper-works; the funnel caps are painted black, and there is a narrow white line above the boot-topping.* (Philippe Caresse collection)

80mm; the 100mm QF guns were suppressed altogether, and the only other cost was a reduction in the thickness of the upper protective deck to 55mm.

The plans were approved by the Minister on 10 July 1900, and on 9 December of the same year the French parliament passed a new naval law authorising the order of six first class battleships (*cuirassés d'escadre*) of 14,865 tonnes at a cost of 243m FF. In the same programme were five powerful armoured cruisers (the *Léon Gambetta* class), 28 destroyers, 112 torpedo-boats and 26 submarines. This was the largest series of battleships to be authorised since the ten *Flandres* of 1861, and marked a break with the previous two decades. In the past French naval programmes had often been the victim of changes of

On-board view of Patrie, *showing the twin 164.7mm turrets and the relatively uncluttered upper deck amidships. Two other ships of the class are in the background.* (Philippe Caresse collection)

government or minister, but this one was followed through, despite attempts by Camille Pelletan (Navy Minister June 1902 to January 1905 and an adherent of the *Jeune Ecole*) to derail it; Pelletan's efforts to cancel the last three units and to replace them by torpedo-boats and submarines failed, although he succeeded in delaying their completion.

The first ship, to be named *République*, was ordered from Brest Naval Dockyard on 28 June 1901; the second, *Patrie*, which gave her name the class, was ordered on 9 September from Forges et Chantiers de la Méditerranée, La Seyne. In March 1902 it was announced that *Démocratie* would also be allocated to Brest, and two months later her

sisters *Liberté*, *Justice* and *Vérité*[2] were allocated to the private shipyards of AC Loire (Saint-Nazaire), FC Méditerranée and AC Gironde (Bordeaux) respectively.

Hull & Superstructures

The hull-form and construction of the *Patrie* class was modelled on the armoured cruisers of the *Gloire* class, which had been designed personally by Bertin and laid down in 1899-1900.

The plates used for the hull, which were of 50kg mild steel, were 8.4 metres long and varied in thickness from

Patrie: *profile*

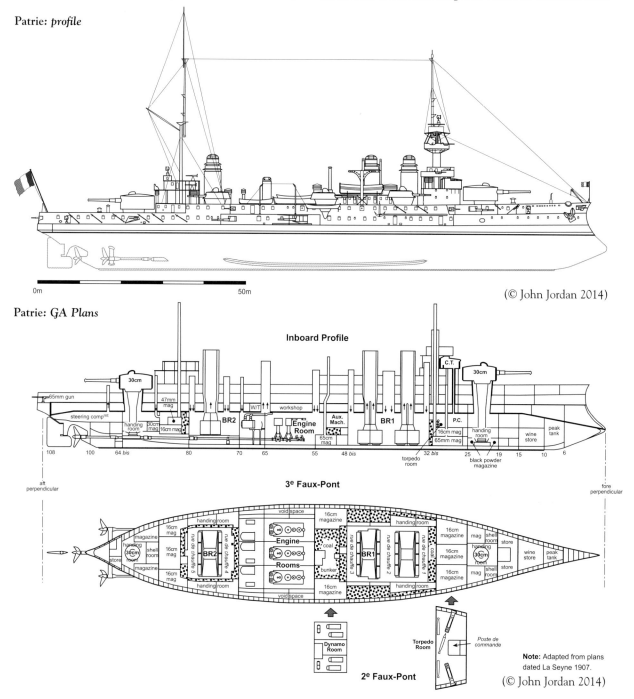

(© John Jordan 2014)

Patrie: GA Plans

Note: Adapted from plans dated La Seyne 1907.

(© John Jordan 2014)

Patrie *in company with a cruiser of the* Léon Gambetta *class; the two white funnel bands on the third funnel suggest the photo was taken in early 1915, when* Patrie *was serving as the third ship of the 2nd Division, Second Battle Squadron. The armoured cruisers of the* Gambetta *class were of the same vintage as the* Patrie *class, and were similarly armed, the principal difference being the substitution of twin 194mm guns for the 305mm end turrets.* (Philippe Caresse collection)

10mm to18mm, the thickest plates being at the bottom and centre sections of the hull. The prominent ram spur, which was of forged steel, was 4 metres long and was 3 metres beneath the waterline.

There were 107 frames at intervals of 1.2m plus three double frames of 1.7m at the stern. The double bottom (between Frames 6 and 93 *bis*) was 0.85m high and was extended at the sides up to the lower armoured deck; it was divided into 158 compartments, of which some were watertight.

Beneath the lower armoured deck, the hull was divided into fifteen compartments by fourteen main transverse watertight bulkheads. The two large boiler rooms were surrounded by transverse and lateral coal bunkers; those outboard of the boiler rooms were divided by partial transverse bulkheads.

Compared with earlier ships, the *Patrie* class had a simplified silhouette. The foremast was a military mast with an outer tube 1.8m in diameter which extended down to the upper protective deck. An inner tube 0.65m in diameter housed the hoist for the guns in the fighting top; it extended down to the 47mm magazine in the bowels of ship. The lower platform was 20m above the waterline and carried four 47mm ATB guns; the upper platform, 24m above the waterline, housed the Germain rangefinder apparatus[3] and the secondary fire control position. Above it was a platform for the forward searchlight projector.

There was a four-deck superstructure around the foremast. The second deck provided access to the conning tower; the third deck housed the bridge, the chart room

and the CO's sea cabin; the fourth, formed by the roof of the bridge, accommodated a bearing compass and the searchlight controls. At the base of the forward superstructure a semi-circular bulkhead served as a blast screen for the forward guns.

The mainmast was a simple steel signal mast; it carried the W/T antennae and was seated on the lower protective deck. There was a two-deck structure around its base on which the after 47mm ATB guns were mounted. The lower level housed the admiral's appartments, the searchlight controls and a compass (course); the upper level a compass for bearing and the after searchlight.

Between these two structures were three cylindrical funnels 3.77m in diameter, of which the first two were grouped together and served the forward boiler room, with the after funnel serving the after boiler room. The boat deck was between the second and third funnels.

Hull Protection

The protection system was a major advance on *Suffren*, particularly with respect to the secondary guns and the cellular *caisson*, the height of which was increased from 1.2m to 2.2m. The total weight of protection was 5400 tonnes (36% of load displacement), of which two thirds was for the hull and one third for the main and secondary guns. Although 'passive' protection against shell was particularly well-developed in this class, the same could not be said for underwater protection, which was little better than in previous French battleships.

Patrie in 1912-13, when she was serving as the flagship of the Second Battle Squadron, comprising the five surviving ships of the class. Note the single broad white band on the first funnel, and the vice-admiral's flag at the foremast. (Marius Bar, courtesy of Philippe Caresse)

Vertical protection

The plates of the main belt (*cuirasse épaisse*) were of cemented armour. Improvements in metallurgy – the French had adopted the Harvey face-hardening process during the late 1890s – meant that the maximum thickness could be reduced from 400mm in *Charlemagne* to 300mm in *Suffren* and now to 280mm in the *Patrie* class. The first three plates on either side of the bow and the fourteen plates of the light upper belt forward (*cuirasse mince*) were of machined special steel.

The 114 plates of the main belt were backed by an 80mm teak mattress and were secured by armour bolts to a double layer of 10mm plating; each plate was 4.8m (ie four frames) long. There were two strakes of armour plates. The lower strake extended to 70mm above the waterline and 1.5m below; the plates were of constant 280mm thickness down to 0.5m below the waterline, then tapered to 100mm amidships. The upper strake took the height of the belt to 2.3m above the waterline. Where it met the lower strake it was 280mm thick (180mm at the ends); it was then tapered to 240mm (140mm) at its upper edge.

The total weight of the main belt was 1840 tonnes. It extended to the bows of the ship, albeit at a reduced thickness and with special steel plates, and was closed at its after end by a transverse armoured bulkhead at Frame 108. The armoured bulkhead was composed of cemented plates 200mm thick on a 80mm teak mattress secured to a double layer of 10mm plating.

A light upper belt, termed the *cuirasse mince*, extended from Frame 29 to the bow above the main deck (PBS). It was composed of seven plates of 64mm special steel on a 58mm teak mattress secured to a double layer of 8mm plating. Its upper edge was 4.75m above the waterline, rising to 5.2m at the bow. Towards the after end of this belt, extending from the outer sides of the barbette for the forward 305mm turret and forming the forward wall of the

first two casemates (see below), there was a transverse bulkhead of 120mm special steel on a double thickness of 10mm plating to protect against enfilading fire.

Decks

Given the comparatively short battle ranges anticipated and the flat trajectories of the major-calibre shell, the protective decks were not intended to resist direct hits,[4] but to provide a back-stop for shell fragments which penetrated the main armour belt. The lower protective deck (PBI) was flat over the machinery spaces, and had inclined sides which joined the lower edge of belt; the central section was 0.35mm above the waterline and was angled down at the bow and the stern. The PBI was composed of a double layer of 17mm mild steel plating topped by a layer of special steel plating 17mm thick (for a total of 51mm) over the flat section and 36mm (total thickness: 70mm) on the inclined sides.

The upper protective deck (PBS), which was also the Main Deck, was flat and extended from the bow to the after transverse bulkhead; it comprised a double layer of 18mm mild steel plating topped by a layer of special steel plating of the same thickness.

Cellular Layer

Directly behind the main belt, and extending from the lower to the upper protective deck, was Bertin's *entrepont cellulaire*, the primary purpose of which was to limit flooding in the event of the belt being penetrated by shell. The outer section, which extended from the bow to the after transverse armoured bulkhead, comprised a cofferdam of watertight cells each 0.6m (ie one half-frame) long, with a passageway inboard. The cofferdam cells were to have been filled up to a height of one metre by 60 tonnes of water-excluding cork or *ébonite*, but this was never embarked. The inboard passageway was divided at intervals of four frames by partial bulkheads with water-tight doors. There was also a central passageway divided into seven compartments by eight transverse bulkheads, and four continuous longitudinal bulkheads ran from bow to stern. The number of watertight compartments thereby created between the two protective decks was 586.

Conning tower

The conning tower was supported on an elliptical base seated on the upper armoured deck. Rear access to the conning tower was protected by a bulkhead of 174mm special steel on a double layer of 13mm plating. The face and side walls of the conning tower were formed by 266mm cemented plates on a double layer of 17mm, and the rear wall by 216mm plates secured to a similar backing; the roof and floor had only light protection (see drawing). The communications tube linking the conning tower to the transmitting station (*Poste Central Artillerie*) had an internal diameter of 0.3m. It was formed by 200mm hoops (without a backing) down to the upper armoured deck, reducing to 20mm on a double layer of 10mm plating in the *entrepont cellulaire*, where additional protection was provided by the belt and the upper protective deck.

Armament

There were four 305mm Mle 1893-1896M in twin turrets fore and aft; the forward guns were 10.25m above the waterline, the after guns 7.8m. Twelve of the eighteen 164.7mm guns (also Mle 1893-1896M – the same model fitted in *Suffren* and the French armoured cruisers) were disposed in six wing twin turrets on the same level as the forward 305mm turret. The remaining six guns were in individual casemates: the forward pair were on the First Deck just abaft the forward 305mm turret; the others were disposed aft and amidships on the Main Deck between the after pair of 164.7mm turrets. All the guns were installed at the naval dockyards.

The 305mm turrets had 270-degree arcs. The firing arcs of the beam-mounted 164.7mm turrets were restricted by their closeness to the fore and after superstructures: 145° arcs for the end turrets, 180° for the centre turrets. The casemate guns were restricted to arcs of 120°. All except the midship casemate-mounted guns could fire on the ship's axis; in theory two 305mm guns, eight 164.7mm in turrets and two 164.7mm in casemates (total 12 guns) could fire on forward and after bearings, and four 305mm, six 164.7mm in turrets and three 164.7mm in casemates (total 13 guns) on the beam. This was a major improvement on earlier battleships, and was primarily due to the adoption of twin turrets for a large part of the secondary armament; the adoption of the twin turret also made possible a weight saving of 25% compared to mounting the guns individually.

Main armament

The 305mm Mle 1893-1896M was a 40-calibre weapon which fired a 349kg shell with an initial velocity of 815m/s;[5] the firing cycle was one round per minute, and range was 12,500m at the maximum elevation of 12°.

The turrets for the main guns were 'pivot'-type mount-

ings in which a tapering trunk housing the side-by-side ammunition hoists was suspended beneath the gunhouse platform and seated on a roller path with 28 rollers in the depths of the ship. The upper section was guided by 24 rollers in the vertical path to ensure that the turret could be trained with an 8° roll. The turret was trained electrically via motors in the working chamber which acted on a toothed wheel fixed to the mounting. There were four possible training speeds; the highest enabled the turret to be trained 270° in one minute. Manual back-up, using a purely mechanical linkage, required 16 men and delivered only one degree per second. For maintenance of the roller path, the entire turret structure could be lifted several centimetres hydraulically by a three-man pump.

Single-stage electric dredger-type hoists were run up from the handing room to the outside of the guns; each cage carried a shell with three bagged charges beneath. On arrival in the turret the complete charge was shunted into inclined waiting trays, using rammers operated by a hand winch. The projectile was pushed by hand into a rotating tray (*basculeur*) which was swung into line with the breech, ready for loading using a hand rammer. The three bagged charges, each of which weighed 43kg, were loaded manually. The gun had to be loaded at a depression of −5°20, which inevitably slowed the rate of fire; however,

The after 305mm turret of Patrie. *Unusually, on three ships of this class (Patrie, Vérité and Justice) the name of the ship was on a curved plaque at the end of the after superstructure, not on the sides of the hull.* (Philippe Caresse collection)

as in earlier ships the guns could be loaded at all angles of train. Behind the guns were ready-use racks (*parc d'attente*) which could hold a total of eight full rounds.

There were four glycerine-filled recoil cylinders which limited recoil to 80cm, and four spring-operated run-out cylinders. For the first time in a French battleship, elevation was electric, using switches and handwheels at control positions outside the guns. The guns were elevated together, but each gun could be declutched from the transverse shaft linking the guns and the sights for depression to the loading position; it was then brought back to the same elevation as the sights (which were left undisturbed by the loading sequence) and re-clutched to the shaft.

The turret had a single sighting hood for the turret commander in the centre of the gunhouse roof. The main sighting position inside the turret was just to the rear of, and well above, the trunnions for the guns. There was a secondary position below and forward of the main position. Both were fully equipped with the necessary 'follow-the-pointer' (FtP) dials and controls for gunlaying. Firing was mechanical, the guns being fired independently.

The faces and walls of the 305mm gunhouses were protected by ten plates of cemented armour secured to a double layer of 20mm plating. The single face plate was 360mm thick, while the plates on the sides and rear wall had a uniform thickness of 280mm. The roof and floor of the gunhouse were of special steel (see drawing for details), the raised central cupola for the sights of 80mm armour-quality steel.

Fixed protection for the ring bulkheads was formed by hoops of graduated thickness. The hoops above the upper protective deck were of 246mm cemented plates secured to a double layer of 17mm plating, reduced to 166mm behind the 64mm upper belt (forward turret only). Beneath the upper protective deck (and therefore behind the main side belt) the hoops were of 66mm special steel.

Secondary armament: turrets

The 164.7mm Mle 1893-1896M was a 45-calibre weapon which fired a 52-55kg shell with an initial velocity of 865m/s; the firing cycle was three rounds per minute, and range was 10,800m for the turret-mounted guns and 9000m for the guns in casemates at their maximum elevation of 15°.

The six 164mm turrets were of the 'balanced' type fitted in contemporary French armoured cruisers. The turret was electrically trained by a single motor acting on a toothed wheel beneath the gunhouse. The training mechanism could cope with a 5° heel/list, and there were three possible speeds, the slowest being 2.5° per second and the fastest 6.3°/sec; as the turret was balanced and significantly lighter than the 305mm turret, it could be turned at 1.7°/s manually by only two men. Directly beneath the turret there was a fixed cylindrical working chamber which served as the reception post for the fixed axial ammunition hoist.

Each turret was replenished by a single electrical bucket-type hoist. Each of the two linked 'buckets' held two shells with four half-charges below (ie two complete rounds), stowed vertically. On arrival in the working chamber the shells and charges were tipped onto waiting trays. The shells were raised to the gunhouse by manual

Starboard quarter view of République. *Note the collimator on the quarterdeck, used to bore-sight and to line up the mechanical components of the gun mountings. The opening in the upper stern was to have housed a single trainable above-water torpedo tube, but this was replaced before completion by a 65mm ATB gun.* (Philippe Caresse collection)

clip hoists each holding a single shell. The hoists emerged outside the guns abreast the sighting position, and the shells were manhandled onto the rotating loading tray or to ready-use racks on the side and rear walls of the gunhouse. Charges were passed into the gunhouse by hand via hatches in the gunhouse floor. Each turret had ready-use stowage for 40 complete rounds (40 shells + 16 half-charges charges in the gunhouse, 64 half-charges in the working chamber). In the event of a breakdown of the hoist motors, hand gear could supply two rounds per minute to the guns.

The guns were elevated by hand via an arc and pinion, and loading was possible at all angles of train and elevation. The turret commander and the gunlayer were both behind a sighting port in the armoured hood atop the turret. The telescopic sights set elevation for the guns remotely, and the guns were fired together using a mechanical firing pin.

The armour on the gunhouse was inclined at 27°, and comprised five plates: three cemented plates 138mm thick on a double layer of 10mm plating on the face and sides, and two thicker plates of 246mm mild steel (also on a double layer of 10mm plating) to counter-balance the weight of the guns. The roof of the gunhouse had only light protection, increased to 39mm (including backing) for the cupola housing the sights.

Fixed protection was in the form of a truncated cone inclined outboard at 20° (*parapet tronconnique*) made up of 140mm plates of special steel on a double 10mm backing layer which protected the working chamber and roller path. The tubular ammunition trunk below was protected by 64mm plating above the main deck, reducing to 14mm behind the side belt. It was housed within a ring bulkhead formed by a double layer of 10mm plating which supported the armoured 'parapet' and roller path and extended down to the upper protective deck; it was closed by two 20mm plates as splinter protection at its upper end.

Secondary armament: casemates

The six casemate guns were on central pivot mountings with a circular track at the rear of the gun. Each gun was trained and elevated manually and was fitted with its own sights. It was served by an electrically-powered hoist with two linked buckets each accommodating one shell and two half-charges (ie one complete round), which raised the ammunition directly from handing room to the rear of the gun. The gun could be loaded manually at all angles of bearing and elevation. Each casemate had ready-use stowage for 24 shells and 48 half-charges.

The casemates were 2.24m high, and had faces of 140mm cemented plates secured to a double layer of 10mm steel plating, with 140mm hinged masks of special steel. The inner walls were of 84mm special steel on a double layer of 8mm, and the ammunition trunks had 20mm + 2 x 10mm protection down to the lower armoured deck. The forward wall of the casemates for the first two guns was formed by the 120mm transverse bulkhead which protected against enfilading fire.

Main & secondary magazines

The magazines and shell rooms for the main 305mm guns, together with their handing rooms, were disposed around the bases of the pivot mountings fore and aft. The regulation provision was 65 rounds per gun,[6] for a total of 260 combat rounds plus 28 exercise rounds. Of the 260 combat projectiles, 104 were armour piercing (AP) shells and 156 semi-armour piercing (SAP). The total provision of charges was 780 combat and 72 exercise charges. The three bagged charges required for each round were stowed in a cylindrical welded case.

There were three groups of magazines and shell rooms for the 164.7mm guns. The layout reflected that of the turrets and casemates. There was a forward magazine group abaft the magazines and shell rooms for the main guns, an after group forward of the main magazines aft, and magazines to port and starboard which served the mid-ship guns. The handing rooms for the forward and after groups were directly beneath their respective turrets and casemates (see inboard plan). Provision was 220 rounds per gun, for a total of 3960 combat rounds plus 180 exercise rounds. The propellant was in half-charges each weighing 10.35kg; a total of 7920 combat and 744 exercise charges was provided, the charges being stowed in rectangular cases each holding six half-charges.

ATB Guns, Searchlights & Torpedo Tubes

As designed, the *Patrie* class were to have been armed with no fewer than 24 47mm Mle 1902 anti-torpedo boat guns, of which sixteen were to have been mounted behind hinged doors in the upper hull, six on the fore and after superstructures, and two in the fighting top. The 47mm, equivalent to the British 3-pdr, was a useful weapon with an exceptionally high rate of fire. However, it was quickly realised that it had insufficient range and weight of shell against the latest torpedo boats – contemporary British battleships mounted the 12-pdr (3in/76mm), and German battleships the even heavier 88mm. On 22 Aug 1905, by which time all six ships were at a relatively advanced stage of construction, it was decreed that the sixteen hull-mounted guns be replaced by thirteen 65mm: ten on the First Deck, two on the Main Deck aft with a third in place of the after above-water torpedo tube. The remaining eight 47mm ATB guns were mounted in the fighting top and on the forward and after superstructures.

There were three magazines for the light guns: the forward and midships magazines were in the Hold, the after magazine on the Second Platform Deck, above the after 164.7mm magazines. Each of the magazines had two electrically-powered hoists with manual back-up. For the forward magazine one hoist was inside the tubular mast and served the 47mm guns in the fighting top; the other was housed within the support structure for the conning tower; it emerged on the First Deck, where it served the four forward 65mm guns. The hoist arrangements for the after magazine were similar, while the port and starboard hoists for the midship (65mm) magazine exited on the First Deck and served the six guns on this level.

Ammunition provision was 450rpg for the 65mm guns, and 550rpg for the 47mm guns. The hoists for the 65mm guns could lift eight boxes each containing three fixed 4kg rounds; the hoists for the 47mm guns had a capacity of six/eight boxes each containing six 2kg rounds. Each of the guns was served by three men, and there was ready-use stowage for 24rpg for each of the 65mm guns and 36rpg for the 47mm guns.

Searchlights

Initially there were to have been six 60cm searchlight projectors, and these were fitted in *République* on completion. However, an instruction dated 23 February 1904 amended this to two 75cm (90A) projectors and four 60cm (50-75A) projectors. The two 75cm projectors were mounted in the foretop and on the after superstructure structure respectively, and were controlled remotely. The four 60cm projectors were on rails, and could be moved inside when not in use; two were on the First Deck forward, the remaining two on the Main Deck aft.

Torpedo tubes & mines

In the initial plans there were to have been five torpedo tubes for 450mm torpedoes. The three above-water tubes, which could be trained, were on the First Deck forward and on the centre-line at the stern. The two submerged torpedo tubes were located on the Second Platform Deck, just above the forward 164.7mm magazines (see GA plans). The tubes were mounted at a fixed angle of 19° forward of the beam.

The torpedo outfit was originally to have comprised fourteen Mle 1892 torpedoes (length 5.05m, weight 530kg; range 800m at 27.5 knots). However, the after above-water tube was replaced by a 65mm gun following the instruction of August 1905, and the remaining two a/w tubes were removed shortly afterwards and reallocated to torpedo boats. Torpedo stowage was now reduced to six, and these were of the latest Mle 1904, which had a length of 5.07m, a weight of 630kg with a 100kg warhead, and a range of 1000 metres at 32.5 knots.

The sights for the torpedo tubes were in the conning tower, which was connected to the torpedo compartment by a bell and voice tube.

Justice: *Profile & Plan*

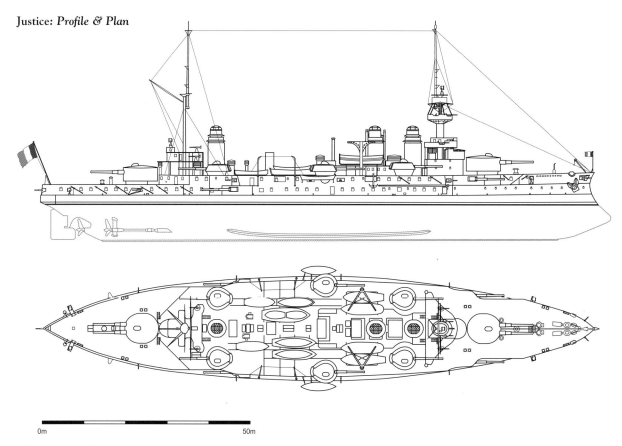

0m   50m

Liberté: *GA Plans*

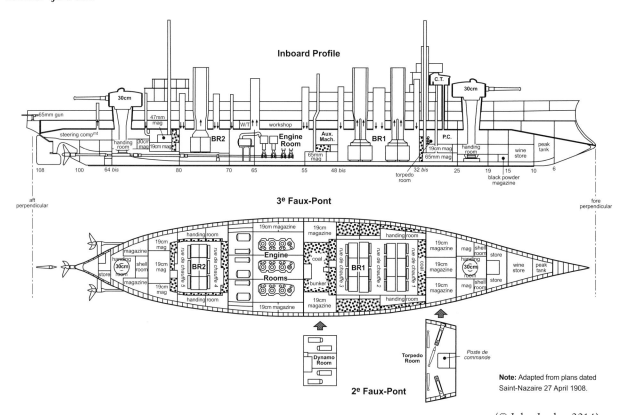

Note: Adapted from plans dated Saint-Nazaire 27 April 1908.

(© John Jordan 2014)

Liberté: *Sections*

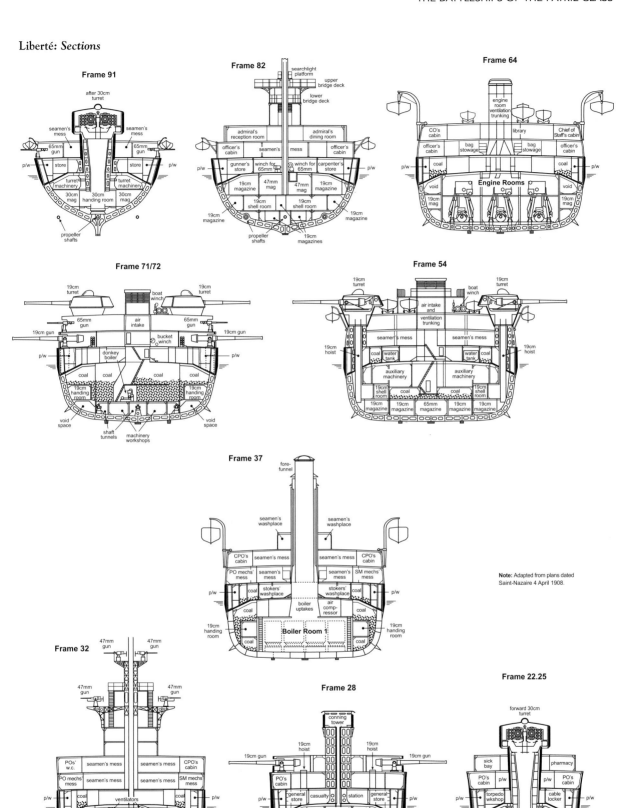

Note: Adapted from plans dated Saint-Nazaire 4 April 1908.

(© John Jordan 2014)

Ten Mle 1892 (182kg) and ten Harlé No.2 (400kg) mines were carried on the First Platform Deck around the after 305mm ammunition trunk. These were to be laid by other, smaller craft.

The Démocratie Class

Despite the best intentions of the Naval General Staff, the six ships of the *Patrie* class would not be identical in their characteristics. From conception to final design had taken more than two years. It would be six months before the programme was authorised by the French parliament and a further twelve months before the first of class was laid down. During this same period technology was continuing to advance apace. With the advent of more sophisticated fire control methods, greater battle ranges were envisaged on both sides of the Channel.[7] During 1902 the British laid down the first four ships of the *King Edward VII* class, which in addition to their main armament of four 12-inch (305mm) guns and their QF battery of ten 6-inch (152mm) guns, were armed with four 9.2-inch (234mm) guns in turrets mounted at the four corners of the ship (and therefore capable of end-on fire).

The French responded by putting the orders for 164.7mm turrets and casemates on hold (ministerial instruction dated 3 December 1902) to allow time for further discussions. Two proposals were considered:

– The substitution of a new 164.7mm Mle 1902 gun with improved performance characteristics for the Mle 1893/96M;
– The replacement of all the 164.7mm guns by ten 194mm guns, six of which would be in single turrets – a twin turret was not considered feasible because of the implications for topweight and ammunition provision.

The 194mm gun was found to have a significant advantage in accuracy and hitting power at longer range (2500m-3000m); 164.7mm shell which struck at an angle of 30 degrees was less capable of penetrating even relatively thin armour. A commission was duly set up by the Minister on 20 February 1903 to investigate the issue.

The arguments in favour of the heavier weapon were by no means decisive. Serious concerns were expressed concerning the slower rate of fire and the significant reduction in the number of guns. The theoretical weight of fire per minute for the five 194mm guns able to fire on the beam was little more than half that of the nine 164.7mm guns (see table). There were also concerns regarding magazine capacity and ease of handling of the heavier projectile, which had a more powerful propellant charge divided into three bags. The Service Technique was able to demonstrate that a total of 2000 194mm rounds could be accommodated, giving a satisfactory figure of 200 rounds per gun. Even so, the vote of the commission was a close-run thing: five (including Bertin and the Minister) voted in favour, four against.

It was in any case recognised that the construction of *Patrie* and *République* was too far advanced for such radical changes to be practical or affordable. Modified plans were approved only on 14 October 1903, and completion of the last four ships – which in most reference sources are listed as the *Démocratie* class – would be delayed by approximately twelve months.

The 194mm Mle 1902 gun was a 50-calibre weapon which fired an 86-88kg shell with an initial velocity of 875m/s; the firing cycle was two rounds per minute, and range was 12,000m at the maximum elevation of 15°. The six single turrets replaced the six twins of *Patrie* and *République*, and the four guns in casemates replaced the outer casemated guns of the first two ships, the mid-ship

An impressive stern view of Démocratie, with the after 194mm single turrets particularly prominent. (Philippe Caresse collection)

TABLE 3: *KING EDWARD VII* (GB) vs. *DÉMOCRATIE*

	King Edward VII	*Démocratie*
No. in class:	eight	four
Built:	1898-1902	1903-08
Displacement:	15,585t	14,900t
Dimensions:	130m x 24m	134m x 24m
Propulsion:		
Engines	2-shaft VTE	3-shaft VTE
Horsepower	18,000ihp	17,500ihp
Speed[2]	18.5 knots	18 knots
Armament:		
Main guns	4 x 305mm (2xII)	4 x 305mm (2xII)
2ndary guns	4 x 234mm (4xI)	10 x 194mm (10xI)
	10 x 152mm (10xI)	
ATB guns	12 x 76mm (12xI)	13 x 65mm (13xI)
	6 x 47mm (6xI)	8 x 47mm (8xI)
TT	4 x 450mm	2 x 450mm
Protection:		
Belt	230mm KC	280mm HC
Main turrets	305mm	360/280mm
2ndary guns	230mm/180mm	156/174mm
Conning tower	305mm	266mm
Decks	50 + 50/25mm	54 + 70/51mm

An impressive view of Liberté *during her full power trials. The black hull and buff upperworks would be repainted in medium blue-grey during 1908. Note the derrick on the forecastle, which was used to handle the sheet anchor in these ships.* (Philippe Caresse collection)

casemates of the latter being suppressed altogether. The weight thereby saved was put into increasing protection of the turrets and casemate walls to a level commensurate with the bigger gun.

The 194mm turret was similar in conception and operation to the 164.7mm turret. Power for training was provided by a single electric motor with manual backup. There were two glycerine-filled recoil cylinders beneath the gun and two spring-loaded run-out cylinders atop the gun. Two binocular sights were provided, the gun was elevated manually, and firing was mechanical.

The electric bucket hoists held two shells and six third-charges (ie two complete rounds). On arrival in the working chamber the shells were off-loaded onto a horizontal ring-shaped carrier and the charges into lockers.

The shells were lifted into the gunhouse outside the guns by means of a small duplex hoist worked by hand from the firing chamber, and the gun was loaded via a rotating tray with the gun depressed to –5°; the bagged charges were passed by hand through two circular hatches in the turret floor. Each turret had ready-use stowage for 12 complete rounds (12 shells + 8 charges in the gunhouse, 28 charges in the working chamber).

The 194mm casemate guns were trained and elevated manually. Each of the casemates had a hoist similar to that of turrets, except that only one complete round was lifted and the shell and charges were in superimposed horizontal trays. There was ready-use stowage for twelve complete rounds around the rear wall of the casemate. A trolley transported the ammunition from the hoist or the

TABLE 4: AMMUNITION FOR THE MAIN AND SECONDARY GUNS

Type of projectile	Weight of projectile	Bursting charge	Propellant charge	Weight of broadside per minute:			
				No. of guns	Weight of projectile	Rounds per minute	Weight of broadside
305mm				*Patrie*			
APC	349.4kg	8.15kg Mélinite (2.3%)	129.0kg BM15 (÷3)	4 x 305mm	349kg	1rpm	1396kg
SAPC	348.4kg	18.57kg Mélinite (5.3%)	[as above]	9 x 164.7mm	55kg	3rpm	1485kg
164.7mm							2881kg
APC	54.9kg	0.97kg Mélinite (1.8%)	20.7kg BM10/11 (÷2)				
SAPC	52.3kg	3.10kg Mélinite (5.9%)	[as above]	*Démocratie*			
194mm				4 x 305mm	349kg	1rpm	1396kg
APC	86kg	1.40kg Mélinite (1.6%)	38.5kg BM13 (÷3)	5 x 194mm	86kg	2rpm	860kg
SAPC	88kg	4.3kg Mélinite (4.9%)	[as above]				2256kg

DÉMOCRATIE: ARMOUR PLATE THICKNESS MAIN BELT

Démocratie: Protection

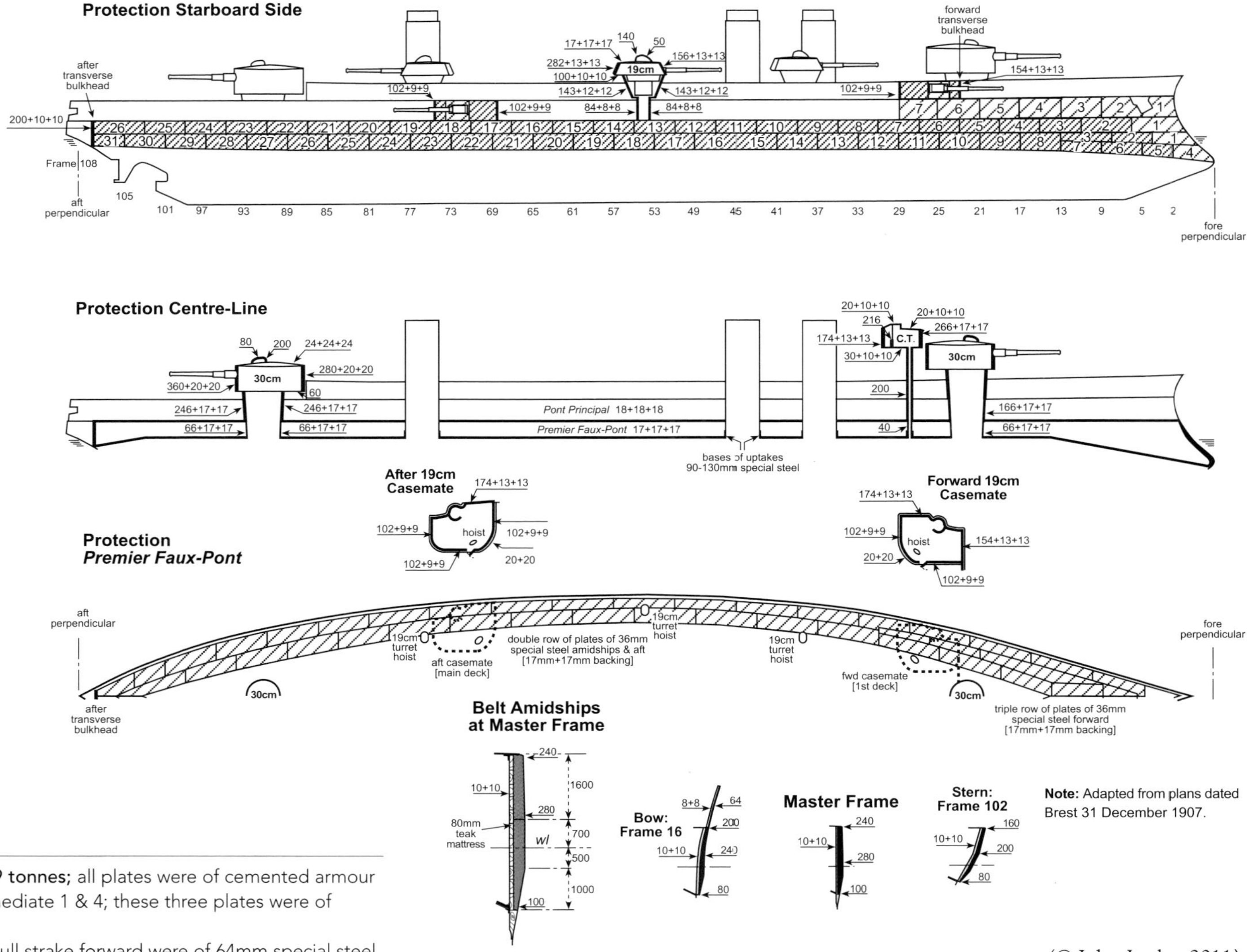

No.	Upper Strake upper/lower edge	Lower/Intermediate Strakes upper/lower edge
1	140/180	180/180
2	160/200	220/220
3	180/220	240/240
4	200/240	180/80
5	220/260	180/80
6	240/280	220/80
7	240/280	240/80
8	240/280	260/80
9	240/280	280/100
10	240/280	280/100
11	240/280	280/100
12	240/280	280/100
13	240/280	280/100
14	240/280	280/100
15	240/280	280/100
16	240/280	280/100
17	240/280	280/100
18	240/280	280/100
19	240/280	280/100
20	240/280	280/100
21	240/280	280/100
22	240/280	280/100
23	200/240	280/100
24	180/220	280/100
25	160/200	280/100
26	140/180	280/100
27	–	280/100
28	–	260/80
29	260/80	240/80
30	240/80	200/80
31	180/80	–

Protection Starboard Side

Protection Centre-Line

Protection Premier Faux-Pont

After 19cm Casemate

Forward 19cm Casemate

Belt Amidships at Master Frame

Master Frame

Bow: Frame 16

Stern: Frame 102

Note: Adapted from plans dated Brest 31 December 1907.

(© John Jordan 2011)

Total weight of armour belt: **1,837.49 tonnes**; all plates were of cemented armour except Upper Strake 1, Lower/Intermediate 1 & 4; these three plates were of special steel

The seven plates (1-7) of the upper hull strake forward were of 64mm special steel

Liberté: Midship Section at Fr.47

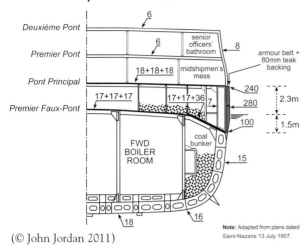

(© John Jordan 2011)

Note: Adapted from plans dated Saint-Nazaire 13 July 1907.

ready-use racks to the breech of the gun, which as with the turrets was loaded via a rotating tray with the gun depressed to –5°. There were sights on either side of the gun.

Protection for the 194mm guns was generally thicker than for the 164.7mm guns. The face and sides of the turrets were composed of five plates of 156mm cemented armour on a double layer of 13mm steel; the rear wall, which had to balance the turret, comprised a single plate of 282mm special steel. The truncated cone (*parapet tronconnique*) which provided the fixed protection for the working chamber and roller path was of 143mm special

steel on a double 12mm backing layer which protected the working chamber and roller path. The tubular ammunition trunk below was protected by 84mm plating above the main deck, reducing to 14mm behind the side belt.

The casemates had faces of 174mm cemented armour on a double layer of 13mm plating, with internal walls of 102mm special steel. The ammunition hoists were protected by 20mm steel on a double layer of 15mm plating down to the level of the lower protective deck. The thickness of the forward transverse bulkhead was increased from 120mm to 154mm (see proection plan).

Compared with the first two ships the *Démocratie* class had four additional magazines and shell rooms amidships. A total of 2000 194mm rounds (200rpg) were provided, of which 500 were AP and 1500 SAP. There were also 78 cast iron shells and 20 exercise shells. The elimination of the mid-ship casemate guns made possible an increase in the 65mm provision.

Manning requirements

Manning requirements for the main and secondary guns were 180 in the first two ships, 132 in the *Démocratie* class. Each 305mm turret was served by 18 men, the 164mm turrets by 15 men, the 194mm turrets by 10 men, and the casemate guns by 9 men.

Machinery

The machinery layout was identical in all six ships. The engine room, divided into three by partial longitudinal

Démocratie at La Pallice 6-9 September 1913, following fleet manoeuvres in the Atlantic. She was serving as 2nd ship in the 2nd Division of the Second Battle Squadron at this time, hence the two white bands on the second funnel. Note the 6ft Barr & Stroud rangefinders atop the bridge structure, and the distinctive hump low on the bow which was designed to ease the anchor into the hawsehole. (Philippe Caresse collection)

A fine view of Liberté at New York in late September 1909. From 25 September to 9 October there was an elaborate commemoration of the 300th anniversary of Henry Hudson's discovery of the Hudson River and the 100th anniversary of Robert Fulton's first successful commercial application of the paddle steamer. France was represented during the celebrations by a large naval contingent which included the three ships of the 2nd Division of the First (Mediterranean) Squadron: Justice (flagship of Rear-Admiral Le Pord), Liberté and Vérité. The organisers used the event not only to celebrate the achievements of Hudson and Fulton, but also the status of New York City as a world city. Ships and memorials were illuminated by electricity(!) over the course of the two-week celebration, and on the evening of 25 September there was an impressive firework display which was reflected in the Hudson River. (Library of Congress)

watertight bulkheads, was amidships, with the associated condensers immediately abaft their respective engines. There was a large boiler room forward, divided into three by two partial transverse bulkheads and surrounded by coal bunkers, and a smaller one aft. The dynamos and auxiliary machinery were on the Second Platform Deck, between the forward boiler room and the engine room (see GA plans).

Justice in 1913. Her bridge structure has been modified, and two of the 47mm ATB guns have been moved to the roof of the after 305mm turret. The two white bands on the first funnel mark her out as flagship of the 2nd Division of the Second Battle Squadron. (Marius Bar, courtesy of Philippe Caresse)

View from the foremast onto the upper deck of Vérité, *showing the after 194mm single turrets and the uncluttered upper deck amidships. Note the 47mm ATB guns on the flying decks which extended outboard from the after superstructure.* (Philippe Caresse collection)

Engines & Shafts

The three vertical triple expansion engines were housed in separate watertight compartments, and delivered a total of 17,500ihp for 18kts to the shafts. The engines for *Démocratie*, *Patrie*, *Justice* (built by FC Méditerranée) and for *Vérité* (AC Gironde) were three-cylinder models with HP, IP and LP cyclinders. Those for *République* and *Liberté* (built by AC Loire) were four-cylinder models with two LP cylinders.

The three shafts were fitted with bronze three-bladed propellers. The wing propellers had a diameter of 5m, the centre-line propeller 4.85m – *République* originally had propellers of 4.85m and 4.8m respectively. In July 1903 it was decided to fit the last ship, *Vérité*, with four-bladed propellers (5m/4.8m). There was a single balanced rudder with a surface area of 28.5m? directly abaft the centre shaft, powered by a steam-powered servo motor.

The quarterdeck of Liberté, *with an excellent view of the after 305mm turret. Note the standard collimator structure abaft the turret.* (Philippe Caresse collection)

Boilers

Patrie was to have received a Normand-type small-tube

TABLE 5: BUILDING DATA

Name	Builder	Laid down	Launched	Completed*
République	Arsenal de Brest	27 Dec 1901	4 Sep 1902	12 Jan 1907
Patrie	FC Méditerranée (La Seyne)	1st Apr 1902	17 Sep 1903	15 Jun 1907
Démocratie	Arsenal de Brest	1st May 1903	30 Apr 1904	13 Jan 1908
Justice	FC Méditerranée (La Seyne)	1st Apr 1903	27 Oct 1904	1st Mar 1908
Liberté	AC Loire (St. Nazaire)	1903	19 Apr 1905	16 Mar 1908
Vérité	AC Gironde (Bordeaux)	April 1903	28 May 1907	11 Sep 1908

* *Clôture d'Armement*

boiler similar to those of the armoured cruiser *Jeanne d'Arc*, but the plans were revised on 20 December 1902 in favour multitubular boilers with large water collectors. *République, Patrie, Justice* had 24 Niclausse boilers rated

TABLE 6: GENERAL CHARACTERISTICS

Displacement (legend): 14,870 tonnes (*Patrie*)
14,900 tonnes (*Démocratie*)

Dimensions:

Length pp	133.80m
Length wl	131.00m
Length oa	135.25m
Beam	24.25m wl
Draught	8.20m mean

Propulsion:

Boilers	24 Niclausse boilers, 18kg/cm² (R/P/J) or
	22 Belleville boilers, 21kg/cm² (D/L/V)
Engines	three-shaft 3-cylinder VTE (P/D/J/V) or
	three-shaft 4-cylinder VTE (R/L)
Horsepower	17,500ihp (P/R), 18,000ihp (D/J/L/V)
Speed	18 knots (designed)
Coal	900/1800 tonnes
Endurance	8,400nm at 10kts

Armament:

Main guns	4 - 305mm/40 Mle 1893/96M in twin mountings
Secondary guns	18 - 164.7mm/45 Mle 1893/96M in six twin mountings and six casemate mountings (R/P) or
	10 – 194mm/50 Mle 1902 in six single mountings and four casemate mountings (D/J/L/V)
ATB guns	13 - 65mm/50 Mle 1902 in single mountings
	8/10 – 47mm/50 Mle 1902 in single mountings
Torpedo tubes	2 submerged tubes for 450mm torpedoes (6 torpedoes Mle 1904).

Ammunition:

305mm	65rpg (260)
164.7mm	220rpg (3960) or
194.7mm	200rpg (2000)*
65mm	450rpg (5860)
47mm	550rpg (5500)

Protection:

Main belt	280mm max.
Decks	54mm PBS + 51/70mm PBI
305 turrets	360-280mm
194 turrets	156-282mm
164 turrets	138-256mm
Conning tower	266-174mm

Complement:

As flagship	44 officers + 765
As private ship	32 officers + 710 men

* stowage later increased to 2265 rounds

Notes:

PBS (*Pont Blindé Supérieur*)	Upper Armoured Deck
PBI (*Pont Blindé Inférieur*)	Lower Armoured Deck
ATB	Anti-Torpedo Boat

18kg/cm²; *Liberté, Vérité* and *Démocratie* received 22 Belleville boilers rated at 21kg/cm².

In the Niclausse ships there were sixteen boilers in four rows of four in the forward boiler room, and eight (two rows of four) in the after boiler room. The Belleville ships had sixteen boilers in the forward boiler room but only six in the after boiler room.

The boilers were placed back-to-back, with each group of eight/six exhausting through a single funnel. The boiler seatings of the after group were raised to accommodate the shafts. Each of the five *rues de chauffe* (*rue 2* in BR1 served two rows of boilers) had its own ventilation trunking.

The engine rooms required 114 personnel, the boiler rooms 112.

Endurance

Normally 900 tonnes of coal was embarked, with a maximum of 1800 tonnes at deep load. There were 16 bunkers with a capacity of 1000 tonnes beneath the lower protective deck, and 54 'reserve' bunkers capable of holding 800 tonnes in the *entrepont cellulaire*. Endurance was 8400nm at 10 knots – 40% greater than *Suffren*.

The *Patrie* class was to have had mixed firing, and in the original design oil tanks with a capacity of 52,000 litres were provided. The decision to abandon mixed firing was made on 1st December 1904, and the volume allocated to oil stowage was reallocated to coal bunkerage.

Conclusions

The *Patrie* class were good steamers; they were far more economical at cruising speed than their turbine-powered consorts of the *Danton* class, which meant less frequent coaling when they served in the central Mediterranean during the Great War. They were also excellent gunnery ships at the relatively short battle ranges for which they were designed.

However, the first of the six, *République*, was completed around the same time as HMS *Dreadnought* and the last, *Vérité*, almost two years later. The constant delays in their construction, due in part to the complexity of their design but principally to constant tinkering with the original plans, meant that not only were they more costly than had been anticipated, but they were already obsolescent when they entered service. The *Patrie* class had been designed for a 'decisive' battle range of 2000-3000m, the modified *Démocraties* for 3000-4000m. Yet by 1909, when these last four ships were little more than a year old, it was being assumed even by the French that battle ranges would be 6000-8000m. The Marine Nationale, obsessed with 'hail-of-fire' tactics which they felt had been vindicated by Tsushima, and unconvinced that effective fire control would be possible at the longer ranges now being contemplated, failed to fully comprehend the implications of the all-big-gun ship for future naval engagements and suffered as a consequence.

When war broke out in August 1914, the five surviving *Patries* – the sixth ship, *Liberté*, was lost to a magazine explosion at Toulon in 1912 – remained the core of the French *1ʳᵉ Armée Navale* in the Mediterranean, serving as the 2nd Battle Squadron (*2ᵉ escadre de ligne*) alongside

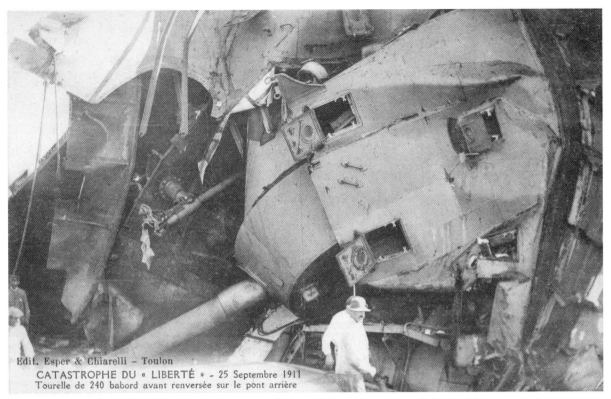

Edit. Esper & Chiarelli – Toulon
CATASTROPHE DU « LIBERTÉ » – 25 Septembre 1911
Tourelle de 240 babord avant renversée sur le pont arrière

At 05.31 on 25 September 1911 a fire broke out in one of the forward 194mm magazines of Liberté while she was anchored at Toulon. Twenty minutes later there was a massive explosion which completely destroyed the ship and damaged some of her consorts (see the photo of République). One of the upended 194mm turrets is seen here. Following her loss there was a major enquiry similar to the one which followed the loss of Iéna only four years previously; it again concluded that the instability of the Poudre B propellant was responsible for the fire and subsequent catastrophic explosion. (Philippe Caresse collection)

the six 'semi-dreadnoughts' of the *Danton* class (*1ʳᵉ escadre de ligne*). France's first two dreadnoughts, *Courbet* and *Jean Bart*, had only recently been completed and were not yet fully worked up. Although history has not been kind to the *Patries*, they were first-line units in 1914 and remained so throughout the war.

Footnotes:

1. Bertin was appointed Director of the *Constructions Navales* (CN) section in 1896, and headed the newly-created *Section Technique* (STCN) from 1897.
2. Unusually, given the previous predilection of the Marine Nationale for the names of military heroes and famous

The after part of République *in the aftermath of the* Liberté *explosion, which was so severe it projected a 37-tonne plate of armour onto the quarterdeck of her half-sister, moored 350 metres away.* Démocratie *also suffered damage. (Philippe Caresse collection)*

A prewar view of Vérité. *The absence of funnel markings suggests that the photo was taken between 1908 and 1911.* (Marius Bar, courtesy of Philippe Caresse)

battles, the names of the new battleships reflected republican values: Motherland, Republic, Democracy, Liberty, Truth and Justice – Equality and Fraternity would have been inappropriate choices for a large, powerful warship! Their successors of the *Danton* class would be even less politically 'neutral', and would bear the names of prominent historical figures associated with the French Revolution (see *Warship 2013*).

3. Later replaced by two Barr & Stroud 6ft rangefinders.

4. Despite this, there was increasing concern on both sides of the Channel regarding the possibility of the upper protective deck being struck obliquely by shell when the ship was at the end of her roll, hence the move to boost the thickness of the upper protective deck at the expense of the lower one, which effectively became a 'splinter' deck.

5. There is significant variation in the published figures for the muzzle velocities of contemporary French shell, even where these relate to performance with a particular type of shell. The figure of 865m/s published in Norman Friedman, *Naval Weapons of World War One* (Seaforth Publishing, 2013), seems excessive for a 40-calibre gun, even though the data ws taken from official French Navy documentation; Prévoteaux (*op. cit.*) gives only 780m/sec.

6. Increased to 71rpg in the later ships.

7. By 1904 the Royal Navy was conducting long-range gunnery practices between 4000yds and 6000yds.

The 1re Armée Navale in one of its eastern Mediterranean anchorages (probably Keratsimi, Kefalonia) during 1916-17. The battleships nearest the camera are Vérité *(flagship of the 1st Division, 3rd Battle Squadron – single white band on first funnel) and* Patrie *(flagship of the 2nd Division, 3rd BS – two white bands on first funnel). Beyond them are the* Danton-*class battleship* Voltaire *(flagship of the 2nd Division, 2nd BS – two white bands on first funnel) and two of her sisters. Between* Voltaire *and* Patrie *is the dreadnought* Jean Bart *(3rd ship, 2nd Division, 1st BS – two white bands on third funnel). The two destroyers in the foreground are 300-tonne boats of the* Claymore/Branlebas *series.* (Philippe Caresse collection)

THE INCREDIBLE HULKS:
The *Fisgard* Training Establishment and its Ships

Aidan Dodson describes the after-life of a series of Victorian big ships, as homes for the Royal Navy's Mechanical Training Establishments, in particular of the *Fisgard* boy artificers' training establishment in Portsmouth harbour.

Amongst the myriad results of the whirlwinds that were Admiral Sir John ('Jackie') Fisher's tenures as Second and First Sea Lords during the early years of the twentieth century was a major overhaul of the training of the Royal Navy's technicians – the key to the increasingly-technological navy of the new century. In particular, the training of such individuals amongst new-entrant boys was to be facilitated by new Mechanical Training Establishments (MTEs) at Portsmouth, Chatham and Devonport – the first two catering for artificers, the third mechanicians. HM Ships *Fisgard*, *Tenedos* and *Indus* duly commissioned on 1 January 1906 under the first Inspecting Captain of MTEs (Reginald Hall, later Director of Naval Intelligence during the First World War), who was double-hatted as the Commanding Officer of *Fisgard*. It was intended that those under instruction would also be undertaking useful repair work, especially on ships 'in commission in reserve'.

Each of these 'ships' was actually a constellation of old warships which had been reduced to stationary roles – colloquially 'hulks'. It had been a long-standing practice to employ old ships in such a way as, until well into the twentieth century, naval bases and dockyards had limited built infrastructure. Thus, a wide range of functions – for example headquarters, accommodation, training, and even coal-storage – was carried out afloat.[1] At Portsmouth, until 1903 many the personnel of the naval depot (HMS *Victory*) were housed aboard the former ships-of-the-line *Marlborough*, *Duke of Wellington*, *Hannibal* and *Asia*. Broadside-armed vessels had expansive gun-decks that could easily be adapted for a wide range of purposes, while properly-seasoned wooden hulls could, with proper maintenance, last for decades beyond the point at which a ship had become obsolete as a fighting unit. Thus, the naval harbours of the British Empire were all home to significant numbers of hulks.

The Home Destroyer Depot Ship Programme

By the last years of the nineteenth century, such wooden vessels were being joined by the first generations of broadside-armed metal-built warships, which shared their basic internal arrangements and whose wrought-iron structures were also particularly durable. Although obsolete by the end of the 1880s, most of the early ironclad battleships still lingered on the effective list, even the venerable *Warrior* still being carried as a 'Cruiser 1st Class' in 1900.

The former central battery ironclad Invincible, *second ship of a class of four medium-sized battleships which, together with their pair of Swiftsure-class half-sisters, spent much of their careers on foreign stations. Here, she is shown depot ship at Portland during the summer of 1904, having been re-named* Erebus *to free her name for new construction. She could be distinguished from her sisters by her retention of the full mainmast. (World Ship Society via Richard Osborne).*

Principal modifications to Audacious *and* Invincible. (Drawn by the author)

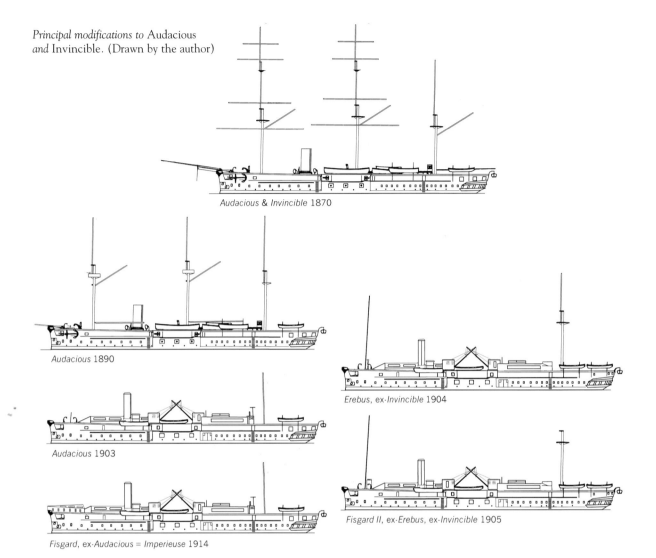

Audacious & Invincible 1870

Audacious 1890

Audacious 1903

Erebus, ex-Invincible 1904

Fisgard, ex-Audacious = Imperieuse 1914

Fisgard II, ex-Erebus, ex-Invincible 1905

On the other hand, most had not been to sea for years and were to a greater or lesser extent dismantled.

It was at the turn of the century when it was finally recognised that such vessels would not be used as fighting ships again, but that their sturdy hulls were highly suitable for subsidiary roles, to supplement and replace the surviving 'wooden walls'. A new requirement that had recently come into being was that for depot ships for what were still termed Torpedo Boat Destroyers (TBDs). The small size of such units meant that they were unable to support the volume of stores carried by larger vessels, while their habitability was at best marginal. Accordingly, in 1902 it was directed that five old broadside and central battery ironclads were to be rebuilt as stationary depot ships for TBDs based in home waters as follows:[2]

Chatham: *Audacious.*[3]
Portsmouth: *Warrior*[4] and *Invincible.*[5]
Devonport: *Triumph*[6] and *Valiant.*[7]

Of these ships, *Valiant* had been formally employed as a (non-commissioned) depot for TBDs at Devonport since 1897, with *Triumph* recommissioned there as a depot ship

on 24 June 1901, albeit essentially unaltered. The others had all been laid up at their prospective duty-ports for some time, although in 1900 a proposal had already been put forward to convert *Warrior* (by now dismasted) into a lay-apart store for TBDs (ie to hold material belonging to individual TBDs that could not be accommodated on the TBD herself). This had involved the conversion of the battery into a storage space, with further stowage provided on a roofed section of the upper deck, and a pair of derricks erected between the funnels.

It was intended that *Audacious* should be the lead-ship for the programme, funding being approved in advance of that for the other vessels. The drawings developed during her refit (at Chatham under the direction of Captain Charles G. Dicken, her interim commanding officer and also in command of all Home TBDs as of 26 February 1902) were to form the basis for that of the other ships, which were 'to be fitted as much alike as possible in the app[d] principles' (while three of the vessels were sister or half-sister central battery ships, *Warrior* and *Valiant* were broadside armed, with *Warrior* significantly larger than the rest). Key features of the ships as converted were to be: distilling equipment for the production of TBD boiler feed-water; workshops and associated artisan staff sufficient to deal with normal wear and tear and small accidental defects to TBDs; and bays for their lay-apart items. The depot ships would also provide bath, drying and recreation facilities for the occasional use of TBD crews, with the further ability to accommodate two spare TBD crews. The ships would be without their own motive power and be housed over: the view was that they would not be mobile bases as was later to be the case for depot ships, but normally be permanently moored at TBD baseports and towed should a change of location be required.

Audacious commissioned at Chatham on 16 July 1902 under Captain Henry Tottenham, and work began on stripping her, preparatory for the installation of new equipment: this included the removal of all her existing machinery and the armoured doors from her battery. Installation of the new workshop equipment was begun in October, with work completed in August 1903. The following month she was towed to Felixtowe via Harwich by the paddle tugs *Diligent* and *Advice*,[8] arriving on 17 September to take up duty as the parent of twenty-six TBDs.

As such, *Audacious* had a complement of fifteen officers, seventeen Petty Officers, twenty-nine seamen, eight boys, thirty-three marines and 119 engine room personnel. The latter were intended to service the attached flotilla, rather than *Audacious* herself, as her own machinery was restricted to three Belleville boilers (from the eighteen removed from the cruiser *Hermes* during her concurrent reboilering) at the fore-end of the boiler room, for running ship's services (including electric lighting) only. Her former engine room now housed a large engineers' workshop, equipped with lathes and drills and a shaping machine, while the midships bunkers and magazine housed the auxiliary machinery workshop, forward of which the after part of the boiler room housed a number of blacksmiths' and coppersmiths' forges and casting gear, plus evaporators for the production of the boiler feed-water for the TBDs.

The lower deck housed extensive washing facilities and the lay-apart store bays, together with officers' cabins and offices. More of the latter and messes for WOs, POs and seamen were to be found on the main deck, whose former battery held further lay-apart store space. The upper battery was used for torpedo storage, with the upper deck

containing heads, bathrooms and reading rooms, carpenters' and armourers' workshops and offices. Much of the upper deck was roofed-in, with galvanised iron roofs with skylights, while a pair of motor cranes were installed *en echelon* atop the upper battery, of 3-ton capacity on the port side and 5-ton on the starboard, 'for easy transhipment of stores and gear'.

Warrior also commissioned on 16 July 1902, under Captain J.M. de Robeck, with a small complement of ten, as TBD parent at Portsmouth. However, no funds had yet been approved for her reconstruction, although the earlier plans making her a lay-apart store were revived before being superseded by full depot ship conversion under the 1903/04 Naval Estimates. In August 1903 planning was well underway, with *Audacious*'s electrical circuits available to form the basis of those of *Warrior*. However, money was still lacking, any substantive work being slipped to the prospective 1904/05 Estimates, although there had been hope since August 1902 that the removal of machinery could be expedited in *Warrior* (and also *Invincible*) to speed the ultimate refit.

Nevertheless, in October 1903, *Warrior* was still untouched when it was proposed that *Valiant*'s sister, *Hector*, should take her place in the depot ship conversion programme. The latter had been earmarked to relieve the old wooden frigate *Ariadne* as the workshop and power plant for the Portsmouth torpedo school HMS *Vernon* when *Ariadne* was moved to the new torpedo school at Sheerness, but the year-long timeline for *Hector*'s conversion was not coherent with the required date of *Ariadne*'s move. However, it appeared that *Warrior* could be altered within six months, and she was thus withdrawn from the depot ship programme (to be replaced by *Hector*), paying off on 31 March 1904 and becoming *Vernon III* the next day.

Triumph was also languishing unfunded, although commissioned to provide TBD support services from 1 September 1903 onwards; however, by February 1904 she had had her machinery removed, while still providing accommodation, training and office space for her TBD flotilla, ultimately being completed on the lines laid down by *Audacious* during the second half of 1904, albeit with some additional workshop machinery, provided on the

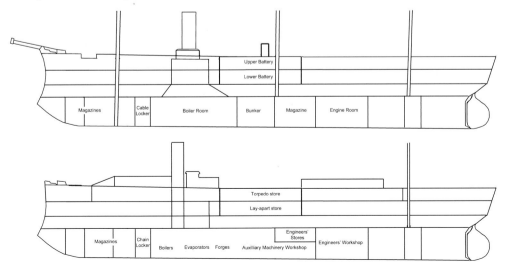

Longitudinal sections of Audacious, *showing the modifications made during her conversion from a battleship to an unpowered depot ship.* (Drawn by the author)

basis of lessons learned from the service of *Audacious* and *Invincible*.[9] By the time *Triumph* had been completed, she and many of the other old ships had been renamed, freeing up their historic appellations for new acquisitions; thus, on 21 March 1904, she became *Tenedos*. *Audacious* was briefly to be *Ariadne* before settling down as *Fisgard* on 31 March.[10] *Invincible* was renamed *Erebus*, being towed to Portland from Portsmouth to take up her TBD depot duties on 30 May 1904. However, the whole 'dumb' depot ship programme was halted in January 1905, to be replaced by a new generation of depot ships that could move without the need of tugs. As a result, *Hector*, still unconverted at Portsmouth, was sold for scrap on 11 July.

Tenedos paid off on 28 February, *Fisgard* on 14 March and *Erebus* on the 21st of the same month. *Erebus* was relieved at Portland by the 1883 armoured cruiser *Imperieuse*, under the new name *Sapphire II*, which arrived there on 8 February 1905, under the tow of the cruiser *Cumberland*. She lay alongside *Erebus* until the 14th transferring gear, after which *Erebus* was towed back to Portsmouth by *Cumberland*'s sister *Kent* to pay off. In contrast to the stripped *Audaciouses*, *Sapphire II* retained her propulsion machinery and most of her armament, only her secondary battery being removed on conversion; further replacement (mobile) depot ships were provided the following year.[11] On the other hand, *Valiant* for the time being continued in use at Devonport with a comple-

ment of seven, no concrete plans ever having been made for her reconstruction.[12]

The three fully-converted ships were, however, retained for further service. Their extensive workship facilities fitted them well for redeployment in the new MTEs: *Fisgard* and *Erebus* were moved to Portsmouth, while *Tenedos* was taken from Devonport to Chatham in preparation for their new duties.

The Mechanical Training Establishments

Fisgard

Plans issued in June envisaged that the Portsmouth establishment would comprise 350 trainees plus staff. The officers, instructional staff and maintenance crew (amounting to 174) were to be housed in *Fisgard*, together with classrooms and workshops; the whole of *Erebus* was to be given over to classrooms and workshops. The trainees were to be accommodated in the old 2nd rates *Asia* (1824, since 1862 flagship of the Portsmouth Admiral Superintendent and local living ship prior to the opening of the RN Barracks in 1903) and *Hindostan* (1841 – never commissioned). The latter had been since 1862 the accommodation ship for officer cadet training establishment *Britannia* at Dartmouth, currently housed in the former 1st rate *Prince of Wales* (1860), but was soon to be

View of Portsmouth Dockyard in late September or early October 1905, showing the components of the Portsmouth Mechanical Training Establishment as originally envisaged, grouped on the northern margin of the dockyard, split between Fountain Lake and No. 3 Basin. Erebus and Fisgard are to be seen in the centre-rear of the photograph: Erebus in the basin, with Fisgard on the other side of the jetty. Forward of her is Asia and forward of the latter, Hindostan. On the far left of the shot, outside the jetty, is the housed-over former armoured cruiser Nelson, while on the far right, in No. 4 Basin, may be seen the bows of the brand-new scout cruisers Forward and Foresight. Adjacent to them, laid up, are the battleships Thunderer (front) and Devastation; a number of unidentified vessels are moored between them and northern edge of the basin. Out in Fountain Lake is a cruiser of the Cressy, Diadem or Drake class, while in the foreground, in No. 9 Dock, is Boscowen (ex-Minotaur). A former broadside ironclad, she had been in stationary training service at Portland from 1895 to September 1905 and would soon be moved to Harwich for further such service (renamed Ganges in 1906). (National Museum of the Royal Navy)

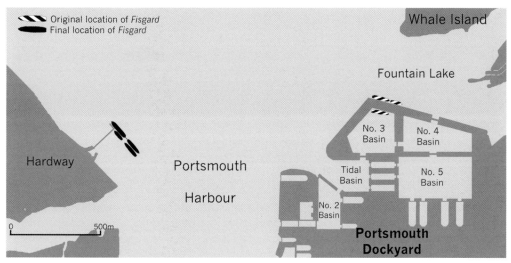

Original location of *Fisgard*
Final location of *Fisgard*

Whale Island

Fountain Lake

No. 3 Basin

No. 4 Basin

Tidal Basin

No. 5 Basin

No. 2 Basin

Portsmouth Dockyard

Hardway

Portsmouth

Harbour

0   500m

The locations of the Fisgard *establishment in Portsmouth Harbour.* (Drawn by the author)

Proposed arrangement in Dockyard

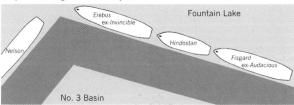

Fountain Lake

Erebus ex-*Invincible*

Hindostan

Fisgard ex-*Audacious*

Nelson

No. 3 Basin

Arrangement in Dockyard

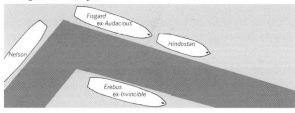

Fisgard ex-*Audacious*

Hindostan

Nelson

Erebus ex-*Invincible*

Arrangements off Hardway

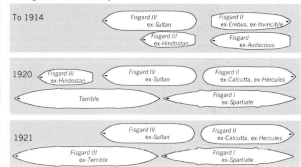

To 1914

Fisgard IV ex-*Sultan*

Fisgard II ex-*Erebus*, ex-*Invincible*

Fisgard III ex-*Hindostan*

Fisgard ex-*Audacious*

1920

Fisgard III ex-*Hindostan*

Fisgard IV ex-*Sultan*

Fisgard II ex-*Calcutta*, ex-*Hercules*

Terrible

Fisgard I ex-*Spartiate*

1921

Fisgard IV ex-*Sultan*

Fisgard II ex-*Calcutta*, ex-*Hercules*

Fisgard III ex-*Terrible*

Fisgard I ex-*Spartiate*

surplus with the opening of the on-shore college in September.[13] Following the removal of various *Britannia*-specific fittings and the filling-in of her orlop deck ports and the temporary filling of those on the lower deck to ensure seaworthiness, she was towed to Portsmouth on 16 August.

To fit them for their new roles, a number of modifications were made to the ships, work being carried out by supernumerary artisan ratings from the Portsmouth depot. *Fisgard* was further roofed-in fore and aft of her present roof, while skylights were added over the upper battery, which was being adapted to house classrooms, and a new wardroom fitted to replace the old one, which was to become a classroom. *Erebus* also received skylights in the upper battery to provide illumination for the boiler shop that was installed below, while her quarterdeck was roofed-in to serve as a gymnasium. Roofing work was nearly complete by 29 August 1905 and on 12 October *Erebus* and *Hindostan* were respectively renamed *Fisgard II* and *Fisgard III* (the ex-*Audacious* remained without an ordinal).

There was some discussion as to where the establishment should be placed, the initial plan being along the outside of Fountain Lake Jetty. It was then decided that the ex-*Erebus* should be placed inside, and finally that the ex-*Hindostan* would be adequate as living accommodation,

making *Asia* surplus. The latter was considered for reallocation to the Chatham MTE but, following rejection (see just below), she was sold for scrapping in April 1908. However, by 1906 the impending reconstruction of this part of the dockyard meant that the *Fisgards* were moved to moorings off Hardway, on the western side of Portsmouth Harbour.

By December, it had been decided to add a fourth vessel, the central battery ship, *Sultan*,[14] which became *Fisgard IV* when the establishment commissioned. Unlike the other two ironclads, which had been largely unaltered prior to being reduced to subsidiary duties, *Sultan* had undergone comprehensive reconstruction from October 1892 to March 1896, having been wrecked off Malta in 1889 and, although still carrying her old obsolete muzzle-loading main battery, had been equipped with modern boilers and triple expansion engines. Her addition allowed the trainees to gain experience with machinery of current design (which was also almost 'as new', *Sultan* having spent almost her entire career since 1896 laid up in reserve).

During late 1906 and January 1907 a number of alterations were made to the ex-*Sultan*, her foremast being removed and the forepart of the ship roofed-in. The erection of a workshop atop her upper battery was planned for funding under the 1908–09 estimates. Work was also undertaken on other ships of the constellation, the roof of the pattern-makers' shop in *Fisgard II* being extended forward in October 1908. By the following autumn, the head (lavatory) accommodation in *Fisgard I* was being found inadequate for the number of men using the ship.

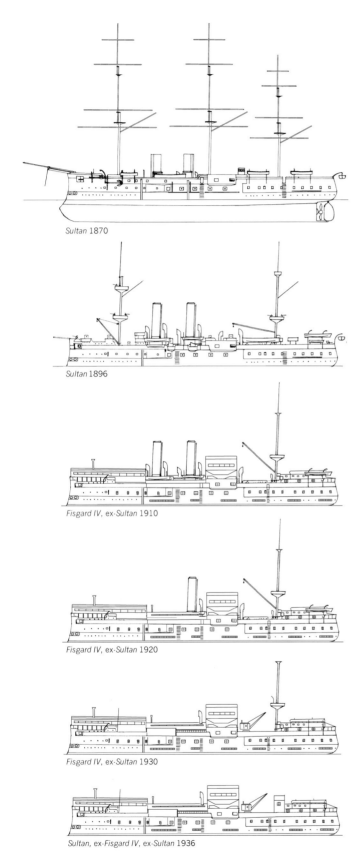

Sultan 1870

Sultan 1896

Fisgard IV, ex-Sultan 1910

Fisgard IV, ex-Sultan 1920

Fisgard IV, ex-Sultan 1930

Sultan, ex-Fisgard IV, ex-Sultan 1936

Principal modifications to Sultan. *(Drawn by the author)*

Wholly-new heads with forty seats plus two urinals were added on the forecastle, replacing the sixteen seats on the upper deck under the forecastle, the starboard ones being removed, with the port set left in place against emergencies.

Indus

At Devonport, the existing constellation of ships named *Indus*, previously providing local workshop facilities, was decommissioned on 31 December 1905, to recommission as a Commander's billet the following day as the base's MTE, although continuing to provide workshops for local supernumerary artificers. The establishment[15] comprised *Indus* (ex-*Defence*),[16] *Indus II* (ex-*Temeraire*)[17] and *Indus III* (ex-*Bellerophon*),[18] the latter two vessels having been converted for their roles by Palmer's at Jarrow, arriving respectively on 10 April and 1 April 1904 (towed respectively by the *Orlando*-class cruisers *Immortalité* and *Undaunted*).[19] *Indus II* was intended to provide electricity to the other two ships, losing her engines (but retaining her boilers) and gaining two 100-kilowatt dynamos. Her former engine room became a carpenters' shop, while she was also equipped to act as store-ship for the port's part of the Reserve Fleet. Work on *Indus III* included the removal of her after four boilers (leaving three) and the dismantling of much of her machinery (generally left in position, however), rearranging the interior for accommodation purposes and the erection of a large corrugated-iron workshop on the upper deck to house the principal instructional facilities, including machinery, a drawing office, a model room, and a gymnasium.

Tenedos

Meanwhile at Chatham, the *Tenedos* establishment also commissioned under a Commander, the former *Triumph* becoming *Tenedos I*, the existing station depot, *Pembroke* (ex-*Duncan*, 1st rate, 1859), becoming *Tenedos II* to accommodate both the trainees and the officers and ship's company (121 men). To provide the latter with electrically-lit facilities, it was proposed to move *Asia* from Portsmouth following her rejection from *Fisgard*. However, the previous September, the opening of the new Royal Naval Barracks at Shotley had released as surplus the 2nd rate *Ganges* (1821); she proved suitable and, as much closer to Chatham than *Asia*, became *Tenedos III* in June, allowing *Tenedos II* to become primarily an accommodation ship for trainees.

The life of *Tenedos* was short, as in 1910 it was decided that the ships were taking up so much space in the Chatham basin that the establishment should be moved to Devonport and merged organisationally with *Indus*. Thus, *Tenedos I* and *III* were towed round to Plymouth, where they became *Indus IV* and *Indus V* (*Indus* herself [ex-*Defence*] then being renamed *Indus I*). *Tenedos II* was left behind, the ship being sold for scrap in October.

War

The remaining two MTEs went about their business until the outbreak of war in August 1914. Then, the deployment of the Grand Fleet to Scapa Flow brought about a

Sultan *as Fisgard IV in 1912, showing her initial modifications, in particular the removal of her foremast and the erection of a number of large deckhouses.* (World Ship Society via Richard Osborne)

Above: The Fisgard *establishment in its first Hardway configuration, shown in 1912. On the right are* Fisgard *(front) and* Fisgard II *(rear), while on the left are* Fisgard III, *and behind her* Fisgard IV. (National Maritime Museum)

Left: Fisgard III *and* IV *in 1912.* (World Ship Society via Richard Osborne)

The Devonport counterpart of Fisgard *was HMS* Indus. *Here, in a view taken between 1910 and 1914, we see in the foreground* Indus V *(ex-*Tenedos III, *ex-*Ganges)*, with behind her* Indus II *(ex-*Temeraire)*,* Indus I *(ex-*Defence) *and* Indus IV *(ex-*Triumph)*. The mast behind* Indus II *is that of* Indus III *(ex-*Bellerophon)*.* (Abrahams, courtesy World Ship Society via Richard Osborne)

demand for workshop and accommodation facilities in that barren location. The *Audacious* type ex-depot ships, with their extensive workshops and accommodation, were judged ideal for providing such support. Accordingly, on 16 September, *Fisgard* and *Fisgard II* were towed from Portsmouth Harbour en route to the Orkneys. However, the following day the ships and their tugs ran into heavy weather five miles off Portland, and although *Fisgard* was safety brought to refuge in Plymouth, *Fisgard II* began to ship water through her hawse pipes. Although attempts were made to correct her trim by shifting machinery, and by her tugs, *Danube II* and *Southampton*, to tow her toward Portland, the ship capsized around 1620 at position 50.25N, 02.30W. Six ratings, eleven dockyard personnel and four (or six – sources differ) civilian contractors lost their lives out of the sixty-four men aboard for the voyage. Her wreck lies upside down in some 65 metres of water, and was Designated in 2009 under the Protection of Military Remains Act 1986.

Fisgard continued her interrupted voyage north, arriving at Scapa on 1 October; two weeks later, she was renamed *Imperieuse*. In the event, her workshops were little used; instead she acted primarily as headquarters ship for the naval base, accommodating various heads of function and, perhaps most importantly for the officers and men of the Grand Fleet, the local post-office.[20] The loss of *Fisgard II* resulted in her being significantly over-crowded, and a replacement for the former *Invincible* was fitted out at Liverpool as an accommodation ship during June/September 1915. Unfortunately this vessel, the former armed merchant cruiser *Caribbean* (ex-*Dunottar Castle*),[21] also foundered en route to the Orkneys, in heavy weather off Cape Wrath on 27 September 1915, with the loss of fifteen men.[22] In the event, however, the disarmed *Majestic*-class battleship *Victorious* arrived in March 1916, following a six-month refit at Palmer's, Jarrow that gave her workshop and accommodation facilities. *Victorious* was originally due to leave the Flow in September 1919, with the ex-*Audacious* (which had paid off in her own role in July) taking her name and duties

Photographs of the short-lived Tenedos *establishment at Chatham are rare. This shows* Tenedos II *(ex-*Duncan)*, with the bow of* Tenedos *(ex-*Triumph) *just visible on the left.* (Author's collection)

(possibly as *Victorious III*), but as the former pre-dreadnought did not actually depart until the following March, the change was cancelled. *Imperieuse* also remained at Scapa until the end of March 1920, when she was moved to Rosyth as a store hulk until sold for scrap to T.W. Ward on 15 March 1927; she was broken up only a few miles away at Inverkeithing.

The Devonport constellation also gave up ships for the wider war effort, *Indus IV* being transferred from Devonport to Invergordon under the name *Algiers* in October 1914 to serve as a store hulk. She was joined by *Akbar* (ex-*Indus II*) the following January, which had spent a few months as a reformatory ship at Liverpool after also being removed from Devonport the previous autumn. The former *Triumph* and *Temeraire* were sold for scrap in January and May 1921, respectively.

Fisgard *Renewed*

The Portsmouth establishment had now been reduced to the accommodation ship *Fisgard III* and the limited instructional facilities available on *Fisgard IV*. As continued artificer training was naturally vital for the war effort, replacements were brought forward for the 'missing' hulks during 1915. First, the central battery ironclad *Calcutta* (ex-*Hercules*, renamed in 1909, to free the name for the new dreadnought laid down that year)[23] was allocated to *Fisgard* in October 1914 and towed to Portsmouth from Shotley, where she had been in use as a boys' training ship since April 1914. She became the new *Fisgard II* in April 1915.

The elder half-sister of *Sultan*, *Hercules* had undergone a similar reconstruction in 1892/93 with new machinery, but had seen no sea service, spending her last commissioned year from 1904 to 1905 as a signal school and administrative flagship of Commander-in-Chief Portsmouth. When paid off in this role, she had been steamed to Gibraltar in 1906 to serve as a barracks for

Base, depot and repair ships at Long Hope in Scapa Flow in 1916/17. From the left: Victorious; *the repair ship* Assistance; Imperieuse *(ex-*Fisgard, *ex-*Audacious*). (C.W. Burrows, *Scapa and a Camera* [London, 1921])*

dockyard employees, moored on the inner side of the breakwater. Although externally apparently unchanged, she was disarmed and extensively refitted. The fore part of the lower deck had had eighteen cabins added, while on the main deck a recreation room and canteen had replaced the aftermost 9in gun, together with the captain's cabin and admiral's staff accommodation. Various additional openings were cut in the hull to provide windows for these cabins. Bathrooms and a large kitchen replaced the old marines' mess, the former central battery being divided into cabins, more of which occupied the seamen's messes between the battery and the bow. Finally, on the upper deck, the admiral's apartments made way for cabins, which also filled most of the available space on the deck itself as far forward as the bridge. The forecastle, formerly housing two 7in chase guns, was adapted as the new crew space. The ship had been towed back to Britain in 1914 by the cruiser *Sutlej*.

To fit out the former *Calcutta*, which formally became *Fisgard II* on 17 July 1915, consideration was given to obtaining the requisite machinery from the MTE at Chatham, but in view of the potential disruption in time of war, it was decided to order new equipment for installation; the work on this took a number of years, and was not fully complete in 1920. Structurally, as completed, she was housed over fore and aft, losing both masts and the fore-funnel[24] and gaining two Mirrlees diesel generators and a heavy crane on the port side amidships. As with the

*The ex-*Temeraire *was withdrawn from* Indus *in 1914, and was replaced by the* Astraea-*class protected cruiser* Flora; *the ex-*Triumph *was also withdrawn at the same time, without replacement. In this 1919-22 photograph we see, from the left:* Indus II *(ex-*Flora*)*, Indus I *(ex-*Defence*) and* Indus V *(ex-*Tenedos III, *ex-*Ganges*), with the mast of* Indus III *(ex-*Bellerophon*) behind. (Abrahams)*

The two vessels withdrawn from Indus both ended up as store hulks at Invergordon. They are shown here in 1918/19 moored outboard of the disarmed Majestic-class battleship Mars, which served as a depot ship there from September 1916. The inner ship is Akbar, the former Indus II (ex-Temeraire), the outer one Algiers (ex-Indus IV, ex-Triumph). Akbar still shows the barbette on her aft deck that made her unique amongst British central battery ironclads, while Algiers retains all the key external features of the unpowered TBD depot ship conversions, including the motor cranes atop the former upper battery. (Author's collection)

previous *Fisgard II*, she was primarily intended as a floating workshop, with few resident staff – ironically given her previous extensive refitting as a dedicated accommodation vessel!

Second, to replace the former *Audacious*, the protected cruiser *Spartiate*[25] was brought forward from her role as a Portsmouth stokers' training ship (which she had performed since 1913), and became *Fisgard I* (with ordinal) on the same day that *Calcutta* was renamed. Unlike the ex-*Audacious*, she was not equipped with workshops (which were from now on restricted to *Fisgard II* and *IV*), and was essentially an accommodation vessel, the principal early alteration being the addition of an oil-fired galley on the upper deck.

The old *Fisgard III* was now a decidedly-archaic means of housing the trainees, and in 1919 a much more modern facility was allocated in the form of the former large protected cruiser *Terrible*.[26] Together with her sister, *Powerful*, she had been earmarked for subsidiary duties before the war, with *Powerful* having been stripped of propelling machinery and housed over as a boys' training establishment at Devonport, and commissioned as such on 23 September 1913.

Terrible on the other hand had been under consideration for conversion to a coal hulk, the removal of her guns having been approved on 14 July 1914 while she lay in Reserve at Pembroke. It had been estimated that she could hold some 12,000 tons of coal, although not suited for the storage of oil. Plans and costings were being prepared on the basis of those for the broadside ironclad *Agincourt* (C109, launched 1865, converted 1908–10) and the troopship *Jumna* (C110, launched 1866,

converted 1905), and stability calculations being made on the basis of the removal of her armoured deck and other fittings. However, with the outbreak of war, was brought forward and used as a transport and troopship to the eastern Mediterranean with her main battery left intact but her secondary armament reduced to four guns. On her final voyage she left Mudros on 11 December 1915, calling at Malta from 14 December to 6 January 1916 and arriving at Portsmouth on the 16th, to pay off on the 26th.

It had now been decided that she should be converted into an accommodation hulk along the lines of her sister, and dismantling was begun soon afterwards.[27] Her 9.2in

A view of Gibraltar Dockyard, sometime between 1906 and 1914. Hercules is to be seen moored against the breakwater, serving as an accommodation ship, The ship in dry dock in the foreground is an armoured cruiser of the Devonshire class. (Author's collection)

guns were allocated for the re-arming of the monitors *Marshal Ney* and *Marshal Sault* (although only *Ney* was actually so modified), with her four remaining 6in also going to *Ney*.[28] In March she was first allocated as to replace the former 1st rate *Marlborough* (1855) as *Vernon II*, but in the event she recommissioned on 28 January 1918 as a tender to *Victory*, while work on converting her into a stationary accommodation vessel was still ongoing. As such she hosted training courses as well as victualling large numbers of ratings and officers – sometimes 1,500 a day; she also provided personnel for special tasks and to ships. The first work to complete was the commanding officer's accommodation, but extensive plumbing (mainly heating) and wiring work, including installing new generators, ran until November, punctuated by other structural work such as work in the boiler rooms and cutting deckheads to allow the installation of new ventilation trunks.

Terrible continued her duties into 1919, although the numbers of men being fed and managed dropped off rapidly, rarely exceeding 600 a day. Allocated to *Fisgard* in April 1919, *Terrible* continued in her role in the dockyard until 1 September, when she paid off into Care and Maintenance. She finally joined *Fisgard* in November, but did not formally become *Fisgard III* until August 1920. At this point, *Hindostan* reverted to her original name, preparatory for sale; she was sold on 10 May 1921 to J.B. Garnham, Charlton, the ship being broken up by Castle's at Long's Wharf, Woolwich.[29]

The Final Phase

By the time she joined the three other *Fisgards*, the former *Terrible*'s armament and upper deck casemate armour (but not that on the main deck) had been removed, as had her copper sheathing (but not its wood backing). The boat deck had been roofed over to provide a church and ten teaching rooms and a roofed structure had been added

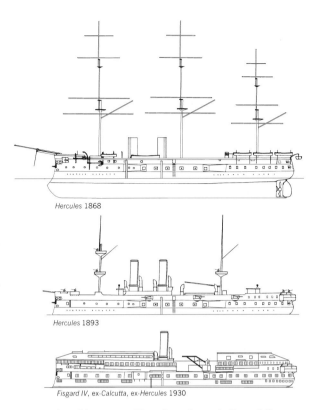

Hercules 1868

Hercules 1893

Fisgard IV, ex-Calcutta, ex-Hercules 1930

Principal modifications to Hercules, *ultimately* Fisgard II. (Drawn by the author)

over the forecastle, housing the heads; the ship also had a gymnasium. The main deck had been adapted as a sleeping and chest stowage flat. In her aft boiler room, all sixteen original boilers (Belleville water-tube units) had been removed, the rear group being replaced by cylindrical boilers to provide for domestic purposes, exhausting through a new funnel, the others by two 200kW steam dynamos and a further dynamo driven by a MAN diesel

Fisgard II (ex-Hercules) in 1920, showing her extensive housing-in, opening up of the hull to provide interior illumination and heavy crane amidships. Her diesel generator was the main source of power for the establishment. (Author's collection)

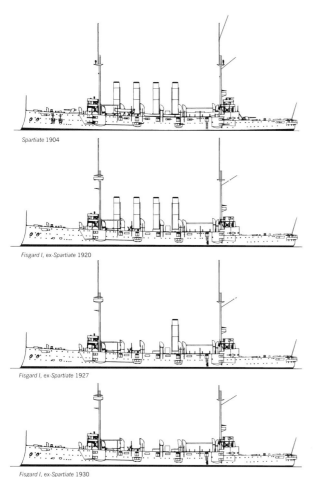

Spartiate 1904

Fisgard I, ex-Spartiate 1920

Fisgard I, ex-Spartiate 1927

Fisgard I, ex-Spartiate 1930

Principal modifications to Spartiate, *ultimately* Fisgard I.
(Drawn by the author)

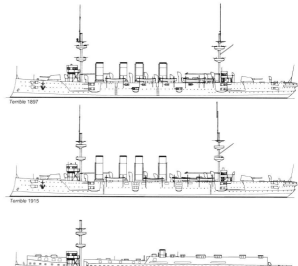

Terrible 1897

Terrible 1915

Fisgard III, ex-Terrible 1920

Principal modifications to Terrible, *ultimately* Fisgard III.
(Drawn by the author)

(presumably salvaged from a German submarine). Three further boilers had been taken out of the next-forward boiler room, leaving thirteen in place, partly dismantled and with the uptakes removed; the same was true of the forward two boiler rooms (eight Bellevilles each). The main and auxiliary machinery remained intact except for the main engine connecting rods, although tailshafts, propellers and rudders had all been removed. The only bunkers left in use were those abreast the after boiler room, the upper bunkers having been adapted as wash-places. As refitted, the former *Terrible* is reported as drawing 17ft 3in forward and 24ft aft.

Following the loss of the workshop spaces when the ex-*Audacious* and ex-*Invincible* were allocated to Scapa Flow, work had begun on making *Fisgard IV* into a workshop, particularly since her cylindrical boiler/triple expansion machinery was becoming increasingly irrelevant as a training aid in an era of watertube boilers and geared turbines. The last time that her main machinery was recorded as used for training was in December 1918, the engines being removed from the ship (together with the propeller) in the autumn of 1919, leaving behind just the engine room feed tank, bilge pump and donkey engine. The aft four boilers (and their funnel) were removed at the same time, the remaining boilers and funnel having been taken out by November 1924. As inclined in April

1920, she displaced 7,900 tons, with a draught of 21ft 6in forward and 24ft 6in aft (compared with 9,290 tons and 25ft 6in light / 28ft 9in in her heyday). A 5-ton electric crane was added around this time. *Fisgard I* was reduced to a single funnel by 1927, itself gone by 1930.

Although few boilers were thus left in use on the ships, and then only for local domestic purposes, they were old, second-hand or both, and in 1926 it was pointed out that all would be life-expired by 1930. To be able to continue to use the hulks, new boilers would have to be provided, but the cost-effectiveness of this was judged doubtful.[30] No space was available at Portsmouth to enable a move ashore, but the former Naval Detention Barracks at Chatham was identified as suitable as an alternative location, and it was consequently determined that the establishment would indeed move not only ashore but also to Kent. As a result, the post of Inspecting Captain, MTEs was to be abolished on 1 January 1932: *Fisgard* apprentices would leave Portsmouth on Christmas leave on 23 December 1931, to return to what was now Fisgard Block at Chatham on 6 January, where the new entry of boy artificers would have reported two days previously.

As part of the planning process, it was suggested that *Fisgard III* might be towed to Chatham to provide accommodation for 800 boys, but it was decided that towage and conversion costs made this non-viable. Then, it was then proposed that she remain at Portsmouth with *Fisgard II* to run residual courses in (amongst other things) turbines, internal combustion engines and oil fuel for engineer officers, and provide accommodation for supernumerary engine room artificer and artisan ratings.

However, in the event, only *Fisgard IV* would have a future role, reverting to her old name of *Sultan* and taking on the ongoing residual training roles, the three other ships being sold for scrap in July 1932. *Fisgard I* and *II* went to T.W. Ward, respectively at Pembroke and Morecambe (with *Fisgard II*'s final demolition at Preston) and *Fisgard III* to Cashmore at Newport. On the other hand *Sultan*

continued in service until 1946, as a minesweeping depot ship between 1940 and 1945. Paid off on 16 July 1946, there was brief consideration as to whether she might have yet a further role; however, she was handed over to the British Iron and Steel Corporation and allocated to Arnott Young for demolition on 13 August, arriving at Dalmuir on 8 October. *Sultan*'s name survives as that of the Defence School of Marine Engineering and the Royal Naval Air Engineering and Survival School at Gosport (commissioned in 1956), where one of her anchors is still preserved. The name *Fisgard* was also resurrected in 1946 when the artificer training school at Torpoint was commissioned with the name (artificer training had moved from Chatham in 1940); it paid off in 1983.

The *Indus* establishment had been paid off on 15 August 1922, by which time it comprised three survivors from the pre-war constellation, *Indus I, III* and *V*, plus *Indus II*, the former protected cruiser *Flora*, which had replaced the ex-*Temeraire* in 1915. The intent had been that the ex-*Flora* should be replaced post-war by *Victorious*, brought back down from Scapa, but although she arrived at Devonport in March to refit for the role and was given the name *Indus II*, this refit never took place, as it had now been decided to close the establishment. Given her workshop facilities it was then planned to refit *Victorious* as a harbour depot ship, but this work was never completed, the old battleship being broken up at Dover in 1923. *Indus I* (with her ordinal removed) lingered as a

By the time this photograph was taken around 1923, Fisgard I *and* IV *had each been reduced to a single funnel; the ship in the background is again* Courageous, *which was then serving as flagship of the Portsmouth Reserve, as well as a turret drill ship.* (National Museum of the Royal Navy)

floating workshop until sold for scrap in August 1935 – although she remained on the Navy List until 1946! – and *Indus V* became a boys' training ship under the name *Impregnable III* (her fourth) until sold for scrap in 1929; the other two ships were sold for scrap in December 1922.

Footnotes:

1. For a review of the 19th century use of hulks at British naval bases, see G.A. Ballard, 'Victorian Hulks under the White Ensign', *Mariner's Mirror* 31 (1945), pp.23-32.

2. This article has been pieced together from various primary sources held at The National Archives, Kew, and the National Maritime Museum's outstation at the Brass Foundry at Woolwich: I am particularly indebted to Andrew Choong Han Lin for all his help at the latter. Principal sources consulted have been Ships Cover 195 (Depot Ships), plus the Covers, 'As Fitted' drawings and logs of individual vessels, together with published Navy Lists. There are, however, large holes in the surviving documentation: some Ship's Covers are missing, and the Covers that survive rarely include documentation relating to the period following a ship's departure from front-line service. It should be noted that many published sources contain detail errors regarding the careers of the vessels covered here, including even the admirable B. Warlow, *Shore Establishments of the Royal Navy*, revised and enlarged edition (Liskeard: Maritime Books, 2000).

3. Central battery ironclad, by then classified as a 3rd class battle ship; launched 1869; 6,000 tons, armed with ten 9in and four 6in when in active service.

4. 1st class cruiser (broadside ironclad – 1860; 9,137 tons; four 8in, twenty-eight 7in).

5. Sister of *Audacious*.

6. 3rd class battle ship (1873; 6,640 tons; ten 9in, four 6in); she was a half-sister of *Audacious* and *Invincible*.

7. Screw iron ship (broadside ironclad – 1863; 6,710 tons; two 8in, sixteen 7in).

8. 1898 and 1899; 700 tons.

9. No records appear to survive of the core refitting dates of *Invincible* and *Triumph*; that they did actually receive the same full reconstruction as *Audacious* is made abundantly clear by photographic evidence.

10. Similarly, *Black Prince* was to be *Nankin* for ten days before becoming *Emerald*.

11. *Sapphire II* remained at Portland, the ex-torpedo boat carrier

TABLE 1: SHIPS COMPRISING THE MECHANICAL TRAINING ESTABLISHMENTS, 1906–1932

Name	1906–1914	1915–1920	1920–1932
Fisgard	ex-*Audacious*	–	–
Fisgard I	–	ex-*Spartiate*	ex-*Spartiate*
Fisgard II	ex-*Invincible*	ex-*Hercules*	ex-*Hercules*
Fisgard III	ex-*Hindostan*	ex-*Hindostan*	ex-*Terrible*
Fisgard IV	ex-*Sultan*	ex-*Sultan*	ex-*Sultan*
Name	**1906–1910**	**1910–1914**	**1915–1922**
Indus	ex-*Defence*	–	–
Indus I	–	ex-*Defence*	ex-*Defence*
Indus II	ex-*Temeraire*	ex-*Temeraire*	ex-*Flora*
Indus III	ex-*Bellerophon*	ex-*Bellerophon*	ex-*Bellerophon*
Indus IV	–	ex-*Triumph*	–
Indus V	–	ex-*Ganges*	ex-*Ganges*
Name	**1906–1910**		
Tenedos	ex-*Triumph*		
Tenedos II	ex *Duncan*		
Tenedos III	ex-*Ganges*		

Hecla (1878) served at Portsmouth, with the converted cruisers *Leander* (1882) at Chatham, *Blake* (1889) at Devonport and *Blenheim* (1890) servicing a special detached flotilla of eight 27-knotter TBDs.

12. Although it has often been stated in print that she was renamed *Indus IV* in 1904, the Navy List gives no indication of this; rather, she remained under her own name 'for duties in connection with Torpedo Boats and Torpedo Boat Destroyers' until she became *Valiant (Old)* before April 1914 (not 1916 as usually stated), when she is listed as a lay-apart store for the 7th Flotilla at Devonport. She became *Valiant III* in January 1918 and was converted to a floating oil tank in 1924; she was sold in December 1956 and was broken up in Belgium.

13. The former *Prince of Wales* was then hulked and eventually sold for scrap in 1914 (broken up 1916); afloat facilities for the college were provided successively by the sloop *Espiegle* (1900) and the cruiser *Pomone* (1897). Today, what is now the Britannia Royal Naval College has the former minehunter *Hindostan* (ex-*Cromer*, 1990).

14. 3rd class battle ship (central battery ironclad – 1870; 9,290

The Fisgard *establishment in the twilight of its existence, on 11 September 1930. Only* Fisgard II *and III retain any funnels.* (Author's collection)

TABLE 2: CHANGES OF NAME OF PRINCIPAL COMPONENTS OF THE MECHANICAL TRAINING ESTABLISHMENTS

	1890	1898	1904	1905/6	1910	1914	1915	1920	1922	1932	Fate
Audacious	>	>	*Fisgard*	>	>	*Imperieuse*	>	>	–	–	BU 1927
Bellerophon	>	>	*Indus III*	>	>	>	>	>	–	–	BU 1922
Defence	>	*Indus*	>	*Indus I*	>	>	>	>	*Indus*	>	BU 1935
Duncan	*Pembroke*	>	*Tenedos II*	>	–						BU 1910
Ganges	>	>	>	>	*Tenedos III*	*Indus V*	>	>	*Impregnable III*	–	BU 1929
Hercules	>	>	*Calcutta*	>	>	>	*Fisgard II*	>	>	>	BU 1932
Hindostan	>	>	>	*Fisgard III*	>	>	>	*Hindostan*	–	–	BU 1921
Invincible	>	>	*Erebus*	*Fisgard II*	>	–	–	–	–	–	Lost 1914
Spartiate	>	>	>	>	>	>	*Fisgard I*	>	>	–	BU 1932
Sultan	>	>	>	*Fisgard IV*	>	>	>	>	>	*Sultan*	BU 1946
Temeraire	>	>	*Indus II*	>	>	>	*Akbar*	>	–	–	BU 1921
Terrible	>	>	>	>	>	>	>	*Fisgard III*	>	–	BU 1932
Triumph	>	>	*Tenedos*	>	>	*Indus IV*	*Algiers*	>	–	–	BU 1921

tons; eight 10in; four 9in; four 4.7in).

15. Inscribed on the Navy List as a single entity, with the component ships not formally named.

16. Screw iron ship, armour-plated (broadside ironclad – 1861; 6,150 tons; two 8in, fourteen 7in).

17. 2nd class battle ship (central battery/barbette ironclad – 1876; 8,540 tons; four 11in, four 10in, six 4in). She had had a pair of Belleville boilers added for training purposes, separate from the one retained original boiler, when commissioned as depot ship for the Fleet Reserve at Devonport in July 1902.

18. 3rd class battle ship (central battery ironclad – 1865; 7,550 tons; ten 8in, four 6in, six 4in).

19. Information on their conversions (unfortunately unreferenced) is available at http://www.plymouthdata.info/Royal%20Navy%20Estabs-RN%20Artificers%20Training%20School-Indus.htm.

20. See C.W. Burrows, *Scapa and a Camera* (London: Country Life, 1921), 10-13.

21. Former Royal Mail Steam Packet (ex-*Union Castle*) passenger liner (1890; 5,625tons).

22. The Board of Enquiry blamed her loss on the unfamiliarity of the ship's carpenter with the vessel, in particular for failing to ensure that all scuttles were closed before going to sea.

23. 3rd class battle ship (central battery ironclad – 1868; 9,300 tons; ten 10in, two 9in, three 7in, two 6in, six 4.7in).

24. No documentation survives regarding the treatment of her machinery, although some boilers were retained and used for ship's services purposes. In parallel with other ships that were adapted for duty in *Fisgard* (see below), it is likely that the remaining boilers and main engines were dismantled to a greater or lesser degree, and possibly removed.

25. *Diadem*-class protected cruiser (1898; 11,000 tons; sixteen 6in, fourteen 12pdr).

26. *Powerful*-class protected cruiser (1895; 14,200 tons; two 9.2in, twelve 6in, sixteen 12pdr).

27. *Terrible* may be seen with her guns, funnels and mainmast removed in the background to the lower photograph on p.50 of J.J. Tall and P. Kemp, *HM Submarines in Camera 1901–1996* (Stroud: Sutton Publishing, 1996), showing the submarine *J1* soon after commissioning (which occurred on 15 March 1916).

28. This rearming was the result of the failure of *Ney's* diesel engines, the intent being to transfer the monitors' 15in guns

to new ships; in the event, *Soult's* engines proved satisfactory and she retained her original guns. When *Ney* was re-armed again in 1916/17, the 9.2in was removed and sent to join the other ex-*Terrible* piece ashore in France (I.M. Buxton, *Big Gun Monitors: Design, Construction and Operations 1914–1945* [Barnsley: Seaforth Publishing, 2008], 88).

29. Some of her teak timbers were used in the construction of Liberty's department store in London, as was oak from the 1st rate *Bulwark* (ex-*Impregnable*, ex-*Bulwark*, ex-*Howe* – 1860; 4,236 tons), formerly part of the *Impregnable* boys' training establishment at Devonport (R. and L. Tait, *History of Castles shipbreaking*, http://www.castleshipbreaking.co.uk/ebook/ebook.htm, [88], [103]).

30. ADM 116/2528 – FISGARD – Transfer of Mechanical Training Establishment to Chatham.

The stripped hulk of Fisgard II (ex-*Calcutta*, ex-*Hercules*) *soon after arriving at T.W. Ward's scrapyard at Preston in December 1932, following stripping at Morecambe.* (World Ship Society via Richard Osborne)

THE BONFIGLIETTI PROJECT:

An Aircraft Carrier for the Regia Marina

The plans of Lieutenant-General Filippo Bonfiglietti for an aircraft carrier, which date from 1929, have only recently come to light. **Michele Cosentino** looks at the most highly developed Italian carrier project to emerge during the interwar period.

By the end of the First World War, the Royal Italian Navy (*Regia Marina*) had gained useful experience in naval aviation operations. Its airships, seaplanes and aircraft had carried out a significant number of war missions, mostly along the eastern coast of the Adriatic, and by November 1918 the Italian Fleet Air Arm totalled 640 seaplanes and aircraft, 15 airships, 42 naval air stations, and 3,750 personnel. The one area of weakness was the lack of suitable naval vessels capable of taking aircraft to sea. Only one seaplane carrier, *Europa*, was in service; she operated mostly from Valona Bay, in Albania, and was decommissioned in 1920.[1]

The initial postwar thinking on carrier aviation emerged in articles published from 1919 onwards in the Italian Navy's official magazine, *Rivista Marittima*. These articles discussed a future Italian carrier able to embark and operate both seaplanes and wheeled aircraft. In 1919-20, Ansaldo produced a preliminary design to convert the former battleship *Francesco Caracciolo* into an aircraft carrier. *Francesco Caracciolo* had been designed during the First World War and was being completed in an Italian shipyard; however, changing priorities within the *Regia Marina* prevented her completion and ended with her scrapping. An Ansaldo preliminary design for an aircraft carrier, possibly a private venture, was not taken further.

Discussions within the Italian Navy concerning aircraft carrier requirements began c.1923, but conflicting views meant that proposals were not developed into a proper design. Meanwhile, in March 1923, the Italian government established an independent Air Force (*Regia Aeronautica*) which took over responsibility for all current and future aircraft. This resulted in the Italian Fleet Air Arm being officially disbanded and most of its assets, including aircraft, bases, and personnel being grouped into an auxiliary air arm for maritime operations. The planned force structure for the latter, however, was never fully implemented because funding was scarce and the newly established *Regia Aeronautica* had its own agenda and priorities.

In February 1922, the Washington Treaty allocated to Italy a total standard tonnage of 60,000 tons for the construction of aircraft carriers. Individual ships could not displace more than 27,000 tons,[2] so in theory the *Regia Marina* could plan and build two 27,000-ton carriers or

any combination of smaller units within the total limit of 60,000 tons. Taking these constraints into account, senior Italian admirals convened in August 1925 to discuss two things: whether the *Regia Marina* required an aircraft carrier and, should such a need emerge, what kind of aircraft carrier should be built. The view of all but one of the admirals was that the *Regia Marina* did not have a requirement for an aircraft carrier. A preliminary design for a hybrid cruiser-carrier which had resulted from a previous (albeit vague) requirement was also discussed, but the committee flatly rejected it.

The net result of these decisions was a modernisation plan for the *Regia Marina* based solely on conventional surface combatants and submarines. The only concession to embarked aviation was in the form of another conversion involving a former ferry, *Città di Messina*. She had been designed and constructed in the La Spezia Naval Dockyard in 1921, purchased by the *Regia Marina* and eventually transformed into the seaplane tender *Giuseppe Miraglia*. This time the conversion involved the installation of two hangars, separated by a central deckhouse. Each hangar could house five or six assembled seaplanes and its upper part was equipped with a fixed pneumatic catapult. A further six aircraft were stowed broken down in dedicated spaces, thus bringing the total number of embarked aircraft to almost eighteen. However, because of her modest performance – maximum speed was no greater than 18.5 knots – *Giuseppe Miraglia* could operate only as a seaplane tender for aircraft that were to be embarked upon Italian battleships and cruisers.[3]

An Unprecedented Opportunity

In 1927 Vice-Admiral Romeo Bernotti[4] became the Vice Chief of the Naval Staff, a position that ranked him fourth in a hierarchy that included the Minister, the Undersecretary, and the Chief of the Naval Staff. Bernotti was a brilliant and educated naval strategist and a strong supporter of naval aviation, and it was this rather than his position that gave the *Regia Marina* its opportunity to build a new aircraft carrier. In 1928 Bernotti drafted a five-year shipbuilding plan that included an 'experimental' aircraft carrier. Her construction was, however, framed in

The seaplane carrier Giuseppe Miraglia *was a converted ferry. She was equipped with two fixed catapults (fore and aft) and could carry 16-18 seaplanes. (Italian Navy, Historical Office)*

the more general context of cooperation with the *Regia Aeronautica*, as Bernotti also proposed the establishment of a fully-fledged naval aviation arm which would include a shore-based component and an embarked component.

While the political authorities assessed the shipbuilding plan, in May 1928 the Naval Staff analysed and consolidated directives that called for a 15,000-tonne aircraft carrier. Four units of this displacement could be built in accordance with the Washington Treaty. Staff requirements stipulated the same endurance as for major surface combatants, an armament based on eight 152mm (6in) in twin turrets for protection against destroyers, and sixteen 100mm (3.9in) anti-aircraft guns in eight twin mountings. Protection would be similar to that of the *Condottieri* class cruisers currently being built. Special provisions were required for underwater protection, including the aviation fuel tanks. The Naval Staff required an embarked air wing of at least 28 aircraft: it was to comprise fighters, bombers and reconnaissance planes; the composition of the air wing could vary according to mission, but the models were as yet unspecified.

In June 1928, the design requirements were sent to the Naval Ship Design Committee, the department of the *Regia Marina* responsible for designing new warships. Lieutenant-General Filippo Bonfiglietti, Naval Engineering Corps of the Italian Navy,[5] was the Deputy Chief of the Committee (see biography p.60). He began work on a preliminary design which would meet the requirements set by the Naval Staff.

Meanwhile, the shipbuilding programme faced opposition from within the Italian cabinet, especially the Ministry of the *Regia Aeronautica*, the final decision being to fund the construction of new major surface warships, and to procure new classes of destroyers and submarines in order to push for the long-term goal of achieving naval parity with France. However, the *Regia Marina* decided to

continue work on the aircraft carrier project because Benito Mussolini, as Prime Minister and Minister of the Navy, had authorised the design of an experimental carrier so that the Italian government could perform a more exhaustive analysis of this type of warship. It was then decided that some aircraft were to be assigned to the auxiliary aviation arm for the Navy. This led the *Regia Marina* to understand that the *Regia Aeronautica* would not oppose the construction of an aircraft carrier – an assumption which proved to be seriously in error.

Bernotti then updated the requirements for the aircraft carrier and included them in a new planning document, entitled 'Our Maritime Policy'.[6] The major change was the composition of the embarked air wing, which now included 42 aircraft, equally divided among fighters, bombers and reconnaissance planes.

The Bonfiglietti Project: Operational and Technical Characteristics

While political discussions were underway, Bonfiglietti was already developing the design of the aircraft carrier and carefully examining all the relevant aspects.[7] He described his activities in a summary report which is the main source of this article. Bonfiglietti began his work by examining the features of other aircraft carriers then in service or being built by other nations. In particular, Bonfiglietti examined *Hermes*, *Eagle*, *Argus* and *Courageous* from the Royal Navy; *Langley*, the *Lexington* class, and another unit (probably *Ranger*) from the US Navy; *Hosho* and *Akagi* from the Imperial Japanese Navy; *Albatros* from the Australian Navy; and *Béarn* and *Commandant Teste* from the French Navy. Features in the list of aircraft carriers compiled by Bonfiglietti included dimensions, armament, number of embarked aircraft, and

Two of the designs which influenced Bonfiglietti: HMS Hermes (left), commissioned in July 1923, and the US Navy carrier Ranger, seen here at her launch on 25 February 1933 at Newport News, Virginia. Hermes was the world's first carrier to be designed from the keel up, while Ranger was often taken as a yardstick by the Italian designers during the interwar period. Like the Bonfiglietti carrier of 1929, both were purpose-built, whereas the other major carriers completed during the 1920s were conversions of capital ships.
(World Naval Ships Forum / US Navy Heritage Command)

machinery. The information about the Japanese ships seems to have been based on educated guesses, while that on *Albatros* and *Commandant Teste* was peripheral as they were seaplane carriers. However, the content of this list shows that the *Regia Marina* was well informed about contemporary air-capable ships.

After examining all available technical documentation, Bonfiglietti and his assistants calculated that the minimum requirements for an aircraft carrier able to perform her mission efficiently were a flight deck with a

length of 183 metres, a standard displacement of 10,000 long tons and a maximum speed of 29 knots. Bonfiglietti also investigated the possibility of increasing the length of the flight deck, and with it the displacement, in order to augment the number of sorties, but decided not to go beyond certain limits for two reasons. Firstly, the Washington Treaty limits had to be strictly adhered to; secondly, a greater operational flexibility was imperative for the *Regia Marina*. He thus reasoned that two 15,000-ton carriers with 84 aircraft would be more effective oper-

A photograph of the model, showing the hull shape and the length of the island. (AFB – Bonfiglietti Family Archive)

A view from the starboard bow, showing the forward part of the flight deck. (AFB)

A starboard quarter view, showing the prominent 'round-down' at the after end of the flight deck. (AFB)

ationally than a larger ship with fewer than 84 aircraft. It was estimated that a 15,000-ton carrier would cost c300m lire, roughly equivalent to a *Zara*-class cruiser.

Bonfiglietti opted for a standard displacement of 15,000 tons.[8] There were two main points to consider. The first was to design a hull-form which could accommodate the required length of the flight deck and the desired hangar dimensions, and which would also ensure appropriate underwater protection. The second was the choice of propulsion machinery, which was to deliver 29 knots.

In analysing propulsion requirements, Bonfiglietti compared several types of hull form and calculated that a two-shaft arrangement delivering 70,000shp would achieve the desired maximum speed of 29 knots. Bonfiglietti initially considered an all-diesel configuration, using the same engines the German Navy had chosen for the *Panzerschiffe* of the *Deutschland* class. According to Bonfiglietti, an all-diesel configuration would allow placement of the exhaust ducts on the hull sides or astern, thus freeing up more surface area on the flight deck. However, the *Regia Marina* had no experience with diesel engines on surface warships, so Bonfiglietti eventually opted for a steam propulsion plant similar to that fitted in the *Trento* class cruisers, but with two shafts instead of four. Moreover, Bonfiglietti decided to install a single large vertical funnel so that smoke would not inhibit flight deck operations.[9]

The result of these preliminary decisions was an aircraft carrier with a flight deck which extended the full length of the hull, and an island located on the starboard side. The latter housed the bridge and other upperworks, the funnel, as well as the medium-calibre guns. To overcome stability problems, Bonfiglietti decided to install a Pugliese-type underwater protection system and this, as explained later, was configured to counterbalance the weight of the island. As far as protection was concerned, engagements with battleships and cruisers were to be

CHARACTERISTICS OF THE 1929 PROJECT

Displacement:	15,240 tonnes standard
	17,540 tonnes full load
Dimensions:	
Length:	210m pp, 220m oa
Beam:	30m max., 22.82m wl
Moulded depth:	17.97m (flight deck)
	11.17m (hangar deck)
Draught:	5.55m (std); 6.12m (fl)
Propulsion:	Two-shaft geared steam turbines,
	70,000shp = 29 knots
Endurance:	1,800nm at 29 knots
	4,200nm at 20 knots
Aircraft:	12 Fiat BR1 bombers
	12 IMAM Ro.1 recce
	18 Fiat CR20 fighters
Armament:	8 – 152mm (4 x II)
	16 – 100mm (8 x II)
	8 – 37mm (4 x II)
Protection:	Belt 60mm
	Decks 35mm/40mm/60mm
	CT 100-40mm
Complement:	1,112 officers & men

avoided. This allowed vertical protection to be limited to the ship's vitals, thereby ensuring a sufficient degree of horizontal protection against air attacks.

Bonfiglietti was in favour of fitting only anti-aircraft guns. However, there is evidence that traditionalists in the *Regia Marina* were concerned about attacks from fast destroyers and cruisers, and lobbied successfully for the installation of 152mm guns to provide protection against surface attack.

By this point, Bonfiglietti had two design constraints:

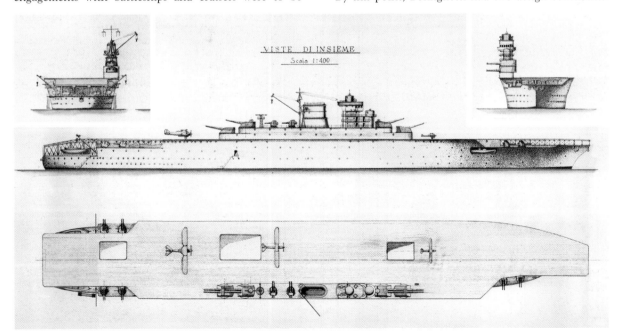

Outboard profile and plan of the Bonfiglietti carrier of 1929, with bow and stern views. (AFB)

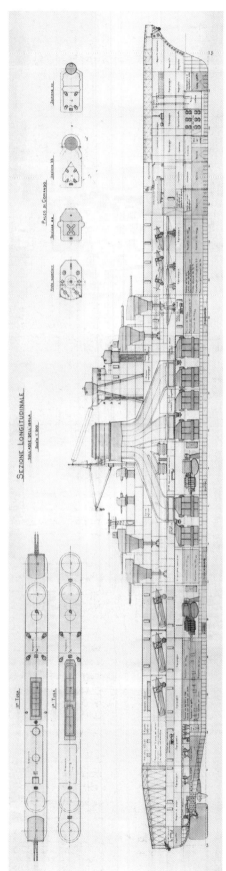

Inboard profile of the carrier, showing the internal spaces of the hull. At top left, the first and second levels of the island; at top right, the upper bridge decks.

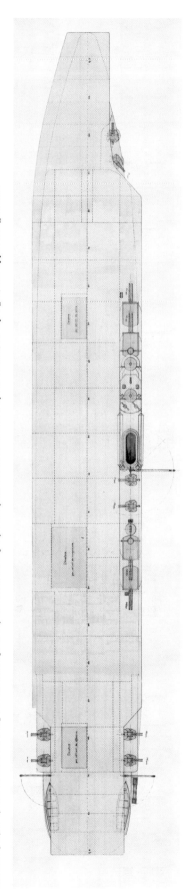

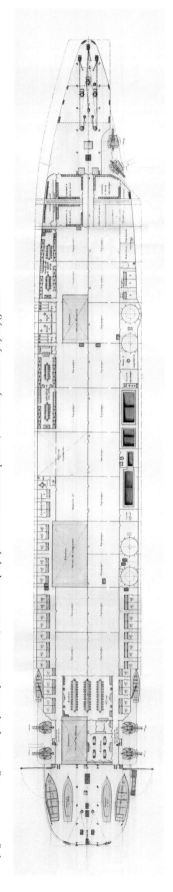

The flight deck: the larger aircraft lift was for bombers, the mid-ship lift for reconnaissance planes, and the forward lift for fighters.

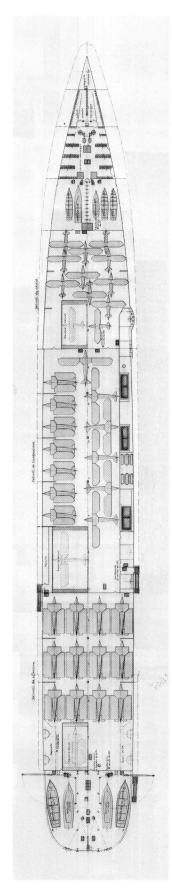

Above: The continuous gallery deck directly beneath the flight deck (Deck 1) was termed the 'forecastle deck' and housed the accommodation for the enlisted personnel and the petty officers (forward, port side), the officers' wardrooms (aft, centre), and the officer cabins for the aviation personnel (aft, to the sides).

The hangar deck (Deck 4): as in other contemporary carrier designs, this was the weather deck. The plan shows how the parked aircraft were to be accommodated. The bombers and half the complement of reconnaissance aircraft are shown with folded wings.

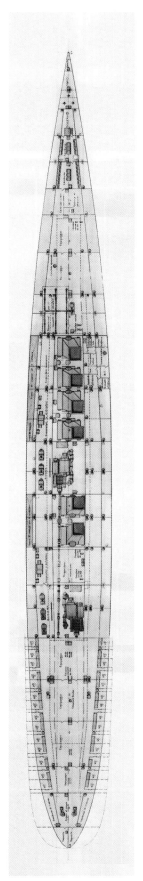

Deck 5 (platform deck), one level below the hangar deck. The fore and after sections housed crew quarters and officer cabins, while the central section formed the upper part of the machinery spaces. Note the turbo-generators to port of the boiler and engine rooms.

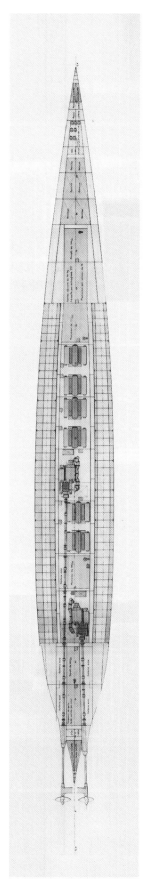

Deck 7 (hold), which housed three boilers rooms and two engine rooms on the centre-line. The drawing also shows the two shafts and the compartmentation of the Pugliese underwater protection system. (All plans AFB)

The layout of the main guns of the Bonfiglietti design was clearly influenced by the US Navy's Lexington (seen here at anchor in April 1938) and her sister Saratoga. The 8in (203mm) twin turrets of the two American ships were replaced by additional HA guns in 1941-42. (US Navy Heritage Command)

standard displacement and the number of embarked aircraft. He therefore carefully considered aspects related to flight operations, notably: the length of flight deck required for take-off and landing, the capacity of the hangar, platform stability (especially in bad weather), and the number of aircraft lifts needed to handle aircraft movement between the hangar and the flight deck. Another potential constraint was how to make a safe transit through the Taranto canal, which allowed access to the naval dockyard where the aircraft carrier would be maintained and refitted. The dimensions adopted by Bonfiglietti for the initial project are detailed in the accompanying table (p.47).

The design met the qualitative limitations of the Washington Treaty and the requirement for operations with the battle fleet. Full load displacement was calculated as 17,540 tonnes. The difference between this and the standard displacement was about 2,300 tonnes, a figure which included feed water for the boilers (150 tonnes), fresh water for crew services (120 tonnes),

potable water (45 tonnes), and fuel (1,950 tonnes). The fuel tanks were located within the underwater protection system. Fuel oil was to be replaced by seawater as it was consumed in order to preserve the integrity of the protection system, so that the full load displacement remained unchanged even after steaming for long periods.

Analysis of the Bonfiglietti plans has helped to understand the layout of the ship. The hull was virtually symmetrical from the keel to the flight deck. There was a 165m-long hangar structure amidships, and the outer ends of the flight deck were supported by pillars and lattice structures seated on the weather deck. The flight deck extended the full length of the hull and was unobstructed for roughly 140 metres. The after part was cut away on both sides to accommodate the anti-aircraft guns, while

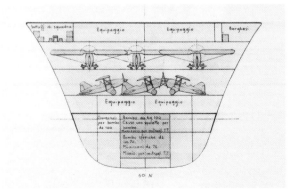

Transverse section at Frame 60, showing the two-level hangar for fighters, with the magazines for air weapons beneath. (AFB)

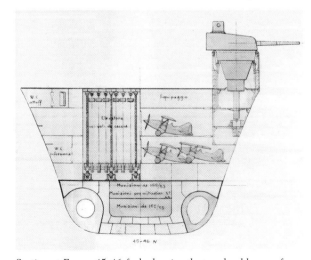

Section at Frame 45-46 fwd, showing the two-level hangar for the fighter aircraft and the forward aircraft lift, with the magazines for the forward 152mm guns beneath. (AFB)

the forward section was cut away on the starboard side only. At the forward edge of the flight deck to starboard, and one deck level below, there were two 100mm HA gun mounts. At the after edge of the flight deck, also one level below, were two pairs of 100mm gun mounts and some of the service boats. The flight deck had a maximum width of 30m, and the after section had a 10° incline (or 'round-down') 10 metres long.

Bonfiglietti did not consider installing catapults because they were seen as a source of complexity and might have caused technical problems. Although it would have been possible to install models already tested on *Miraglia* and other Italian cruisers, Bonfiglietti seems to have thought catapults unnecessary because he considered that the length of flight deck, the relatively low weight of the embarked aircraft, and the head wind generated when the ship reached full speed were sufficient for aircraft take-off.[10]

The dimensions chosen for the hull provided a length/beam ratio of 9.2, not dissimilar to that of the British *Courageous* and *Furious*, both conversions of battlecruisers. As for draught, the principal criterion was to distribute the maximum propulsive power between two shafts and two efficient, large-diameter propellers that worked within a 6-metre water column. The island was placed almost amidships to starboard, and was some 80 metres long and approximately 6 metres wide. The main body of the island was two decks high. The forward part accommodated two 152mm gun turrets, the bridge, the conning tower, and other operational spaces. The central part was occupied by the funnel and a pole mainmast with a handling derrick, while the after part accommodated two 100mm HA mounts, a short lattice structure for the after rangefinder, and a second pair of 152mm gun turrets.

For the hangar Bonfiglietti adopted British practice, in which the hangar itself contributed to the longitudinal strength of the hull. The latter was seven decks high, with much of its volume being occupied by the 145m-long hangar. One of the distinctive features of the design was the continuous gallery deck directly beneath the flight deck, which allowed better protection for the hangar and a superior arrangement of crew spaces.[11]

The hangar was specifically sized to accommodate particular types of embarked aircraft (see plans of Hangar Deck and section views). The after section was designed to house twelve bombers with folded wings; it was 48 metres long and 4 metres high. The central section was 65 metres long and housed up to thirteen reconnaissance planes, seven of them with folded wings. The forward hangar section was split into two levels, each of them 3.7m high. The upper level housed eleven fighters, and the lower level seven; all the fighters had unfolded wings. The hangar was divided into three sections by transverse bulkheads. The bulkheads had a structural function and ensured some degree of protection against fire. In defining the hangar dimensions Bonfiglietti incorporated a small margin to take into account a possible change in the composition of the embarked air wing.

As in contemporary British carriers, all aircraft were stowed in the hangar when not involved in operations. Additionally, the aircraft stowage was conceived so that the heavier aircraft, when lifted to the flight deck and readied for take-off, had a longer run than the lighter aircraft. Three 5-tonne aircraft lifts linked the flight deck to the hangar. They were offset to port of the centreline and each of them served a single hangar section. According to the design report drafted by Bonfiglietti, the after and mid-ship lifts could only handle aircraft with folded wings, while the forward lift allowed the handling of aircraft that were stowed in the two levels of the forward hangar section.

Protection and Hull Strength

Passive defence directives formulated by the *Regia Marina* for the Bonfiglietti project were based on information, albeit scarce, about the experience gained with British and US carriers. As already noted, in principle the carrier was not to be directly engaged in a naval battle; protection against large/medium-calibre guns, which would take

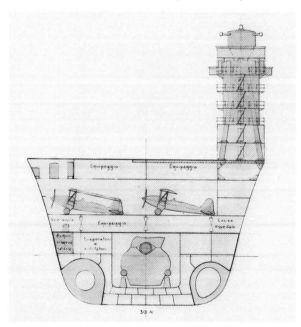

Section at Frame 30 fwd, showing the hangar for the reconnaissance aircraft above, Boiler Room no.2 and the island/conning tower. (AFB)

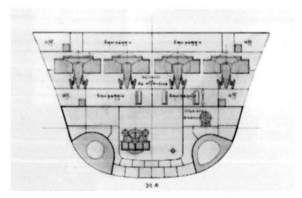

Section at Frame 30 aft, showing the hangar for the torpedo bombers with the forward engine room beneath. The turbo-generator to starboard appears to be an error: the deck plan view (p.49) shows it to port (AFB)

a significant portion of displacement, was therefore not required. However, some light vertical protection was incorporated capable of withstanding a lucky shot from small-calibre guns.

Bonfiglietti adopted a 60mm belt amidships over a length of approximately 90 metres. The belt extended 1.65m below the waterline and 2.85m above, to protect the machinery spaces and some of the fore and after magazines. The avgas tanks were protected by 50mm vertical plates, while the hangar sides were 20mm. The hangar deck was also the weather deck and had a thickness of 40mm. The 60mm main armoured deck was one level below the hangar deck and formed the upper part of the citadel. The horizontal protection scheme also featured a 35mm flight deck and the 15mm gallery deck. The conning tower had protection which varied from 100mm to 40mm, while 30mm plates protected other vital spaces such as the steering gear and the magazines for small-calibre guns which were located outside the citadel. The nickel-chromium steel plates that formed the vertical and horizontal protection were secured directly to the structural elements of the frames and decks.

The underwater protection was based on the Pugliese system.[12] To withstand the effects of an underwater explosion, the hull bottom was reconfigured so that most of the energy pressure generated would be absorbed by a structure filled with water or fuel that included a watertight cylinder. The cylinder was placed below the waterline, at the level of the bilges, and extended for most of the length of the hull. For the carrier design, Bonfiglietti opted for both a Pugliese system and a triple bottom, and this system extended throughout the length of the machinery spaces and magazines. However, the diameter was varied in order to counterbalance the weight and position of the island. On the port side the cylinder had a diameter of 240mm and a thickness of 30mm, while the whole structure had a 510mm diameter. On the starboard side, the inner (watertight) cylinder was larger in cross-section, so the weight of heavy oil was reduced. The fuel contained in the outer structure was to be gradually replaced by seawater, which would increase the displacement due to the different densities. This increase was calculated as 300 tonnes and would be compensated by the ongoing consumption of fresh water for boilers and crew usage.

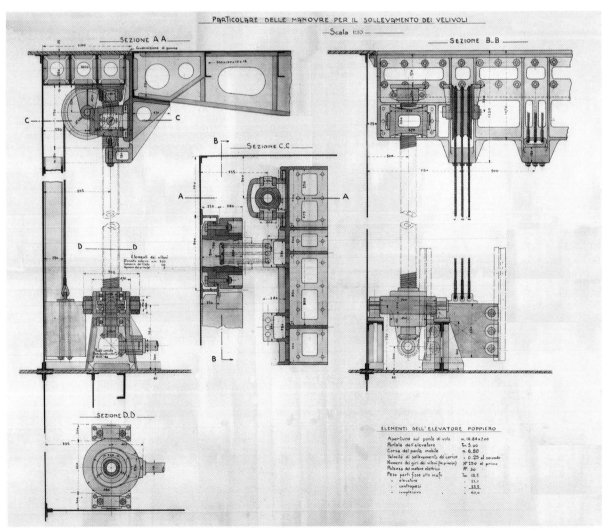

Drawings showing the mechanisms of one of the aircraft lifts. The high level of detail demonstrates just how advanced this project was. (AFB)

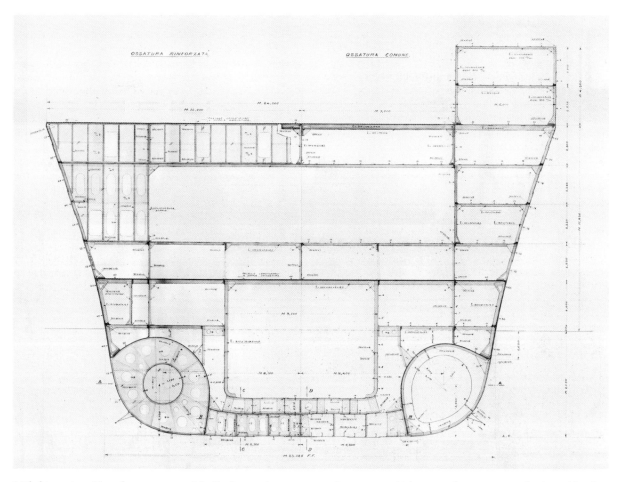

Mid-ship section. Note the asymmetry of the Pugliese underwater protection system, which was used to compensate for the weight of the island to starboard. (AFB)

Thus, the full displacement would remain almost unchanged during a carrier mission.

As for the strength of the hull, Bonfiglietti split the ship vertically into two parts divided by the hangar/weather deck. The lower part included the triple bottom and the Pugliese system; its structural elements were mostly longitudinal with several longitudinal bulkheads. The upper part had a structure which was predominantly transversal, including several sided reinforcing struts running from the hangar deck to the flight deck.

Bonfiglietti intended to test the strength of the whole structure, especially the Pugliese system, by using several scale models, and was confident of obtaining encouraging results. As for stability, Bonfiglietti addressed various situations by carrying out calculations and predicting the various curves of righting levers. For full load displacement conditions, Bonfiglietti obtained a metacentric height of 1.49m; he estimated this would be sufficient even with a wind gusting to 120 km/h. In these conditions Bonfiglietti calculated that the carrier would achieve a maximum heel of 7°, which was acceptable given the high carrier freeboard and the high reserve stability.

Aircraft & Armament

Unlike other surface combatants, the payload of the aircraft carriers needed to include a combination of embarked air wing and naval guns, together with their ammunition stowage.

The *Regia Marina* had selected three types of aircraft for embarkation in the carrier: the Fiat BR1 bomber, the Fiat CR20 fighter, and the IMAM Ro.1 reconnaissance aircraft. All were land-based biplanes and it is unclear whether, at the time the carrier was designed, navalised or folded-wing variants were under development.

The Fiat BR1 was a two-seat bomber in service with the *Regia Aeronautica* during the 1920s. It had a 10.47m-long fuselage and two seats in tandem; the forward seat was for the pilot, while the rear was for the observer/bomb aimer and sported a swivelling machine gun. Wing area was 77.20m^2, while the empty weight totalled about 3,530kg. The BR1 was powered by a 700hp Fiat A.14 engine, attached to a two-bladed, fixed-pitch wooden propeller. Top speed was 240km/h, and the payload included 1,000kg of bombs. The BR1 had a fixed landing gear, featuring two large forward wheels connected to the lower part of the fuselage and the lower wings by a tubular structure; a landing skid was located in the rear part of the fuselage.

The IMAM Ro.1 was a single-engine, two-seat aircraft in service with the *Regia Aeronautica*; it was produced in Italy during the 1920s under licence from the Dutch company Fokker. The Ro.1 was 9.46m long, had a wing area of about 40m^2, and a take-off weight of 2,175kg. The forward cockpit was solely for the pilot, while the observer/gunner occupied the rear cockpit. The fuselage had a structure made of welded steel tubes with a canvas skin, while the landing gear included a pair of forward wheels and a rear-landing skid. An Alfa Romeo Jupiter IV 420hp radial engine gave a top speed of 255km/h, while range was 1,200km.

The Fiat CR20 was a single-engine, single-seat fighter with a length of a 6.71m and had a wing area of 25.50 m². The fuselage had a mixed skin, with metal plates on the forward section and canvas over the rear section. The maximum take-off weight was 1,390kg, while the Fiat A20 410hp engine allowed a top speed of 270km/h and a range of about 850km. The armament included two 7.7mm machine guns. The CR20 had been in service since 1927, and had participated in operations in Libya and in Ethiopia.

Taking into account staff requirements and aircraft dimensions, Bonfiglietti calculated the space needed for each plane. He was, however, unduly optimistic in his belief that space for the embarked air wing could be increased should Italian industry develop a 'true' naval aircraft. Bonfiglietti assigned each type of aircraft its own hangar section. Bombs, torpedoes and ammunition were stowed in fore and after magazines adjacent to the magazines for the 100mm guns. There were also 24 ready-use torpedoes for the BR1 which were stowed in the after hangar section.

The medium-calibre gun selected by Bonfiglietti was the Ansaldo Mod.1926 152mm. This gun had recently

The Fiat BR1 was a two-seat biplane bomber in service with the Regia Aeronautica *during the 1920s. The aircraft shown in this photo is fitted with a torpedo.* (Archive Giorgio Apostolo)

The Fiat CR20 was a single-engine, single-seat fighter in service from 1927. (Archive Giorgio Apostolo)

The IMAM Ro.1 was a single-engine, two-seat aircraft in service with the Regia Aeronautica *for reconnaissance roles and produced in Italy under licence from the Dutch company Fokker.* (Archive Giorgio Apostolo)

been installed on board four light cruisers of the 'Condottieri' type and had a firing cycle of six rounds per minute. The twin turret weighed 83.7 tonnes and the guns could fire AP or HE shells. At the gun's maximum elevation of 45°, the maximum range for AP shell was 22,600m, while the range when firing HE rounds was 24,600m.

The 100mm guns which provided anti-aircraft defence were installed in shielded twin mountings and were employed as the standard secondary battery on all Italian cruisers built during the 1920s. The guns were a 1924 redesign by OTO Melara of a Czech cannon that had

been fitted in Austro-Hungarian torpedo boats during the First World War. Each mount weighed about 4.8 tonnes and had a firing cycle of about ten rounds per minute. Elevation for the guns was between –5° and +85°, and the HE shell had a maximum rage of 15,000m at 45°. Four 37mm twin mounts, located on the island, provided close-range air defence.

Machinery and Personnel

Bonfiglietti approached the analysis of power requirements by adopting a hull shape with a block coefficient of

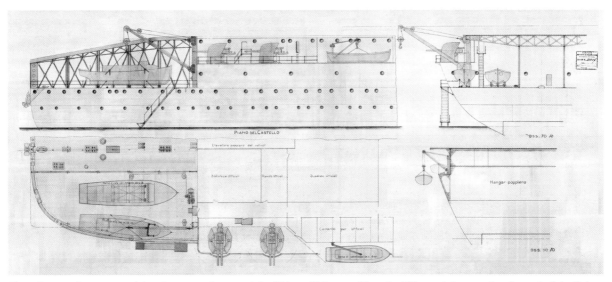

Plans showing the position of the after service boats and the 100mm HA guns. Note the 10° round-down at the after end of the flight deck. (AFB)

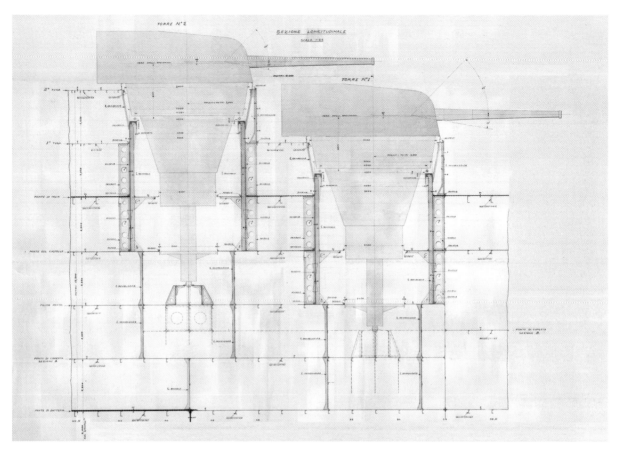

Above: *Inboard profile of the two forward turrets. The drawing shows the ring bulkheads, the handing rooms, and the overall structure.* (AFB)

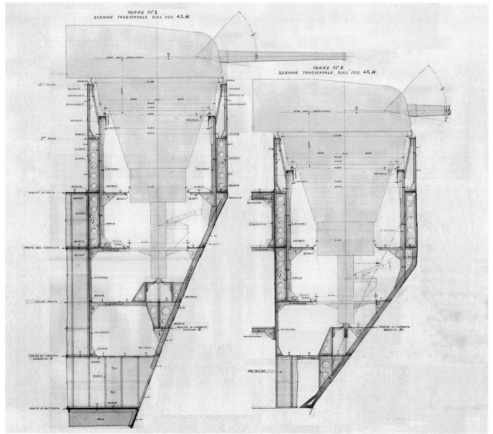

Left: *Section views of the forward turrets.* (AFB)

0.57, and by using model tank tests and the results of trials with the cruiser *Trento*. He opted for a total installed power of 70,000shp on two shafts, with endurance ranging from 1,800nm at 29 knots to 4,200nm at 20 knots. The triple bottom was used to provide additional fuel tanks in order to increase endurance.

The steam turbine plant comprised six water-tube boilers and two sets of single-reduction geared turbines. The boilers, which were smaller than those fitted in the *Trento* and '*Condottieri*' class cruisers, were located in pairs in three centre-line boiler rooms to allow sufficient space outboard for the Pugliese underwater protection system. The forward turbines drove the port shaft, the after turbines the starboard shaft (see plan of Hold, p.49). Each propeller had a diameter of 4.4m and turned at a maximum 260rpm.

The layout of the machinery met safety, buoyancy, and navigational requirements, and the ship was designed to survive with three adjacent compartments flooded. Each of the boiler and engine rooms was 14 metres long, and the after boiler room was separated from the after engine room by the after 152mm magazines. Locating the boiler rooms in the central section in the hull allowed all the exhaust ducts to be grouped together into a single large funnel. This avoided a separation which would have implied a two-funnel configuration and a consequent lengthening of the island. Bonfiglietti also took measures to avoid the hangar becoming overheated when the ship was steaming at high speed: the hangar floor was covered with insulating material and equipment installed to facilitate air exchange.

To generate the required electrical power, Bonfiglietti opted for six 180kW turbo-alternators located in two separated spaces outboard of the engine rooms (see plan of Platform Deck, p.49), to port. They fed a power distribution system similar to that installed in the *Zara* class cruisers. The turbo-alternators were driven by steam from the main boilers when the ship was underway, and by auxiliary boilers when in port; the auxiliary boilers also powered the heating system for the crew spaces when underway. There was a single 40m^2 semi-balanced rudder, and Bonfiglietti did not rule out installation of an auxiliary forward rudder to improve manoeuvrability, especially in confined waters.[13]

The Naval Staff decided that the aircraft carrier should have a complement of 1,112 officers and men, divided between Navy and Air Force personnel. This would include 78 officers (25 Navy and 53 Air Force), 137 non-commissioned officers (95 Navy and 62 Air Force), 1,192 seamen, and six civilians. Priority was given to Air Force personnel (pilots and technicians), an indication that at the time of the project the *Regia Marina* foresaw an operational 'coexistence' with the Air Force. Most of the crew accommodation was located on the gallery deck below the flight deck, while officers' quarters were located as tradition demanded in the after section of the hull (see plans of Gallery and Platform Decks, p.49).

The Variants

As already discussed, the preliminary design carried out by Lt.-Gen. Bonfiglietti stemmed from general requirements formulated by the Naval Staff in late 1928. So when Bonfiglietti sent his preliminary report to the Chief of the Design Committee in December 1929, he hoped that the design might fulfil their requirements and be '…useful as a basis for executing further studies that would lead to a possible construction programme'. The content of this preliminary report is, therefore, important in understanding Italian aircraft carrier design and construction. Some idiosyncratic elements, developed by Bonfiglietti after the work was concluded, are also of interest.

In the summer of 1930, the Italian Naval Staff and the Naval Attaché in London exchanged letters regarding the construction of smaller carriers that might house an air wing of sufficient size and capability to meet operational requirements. In consequence, Bonfiglietti developed three variants of his basic design named 'A', 'B', and 'C'. He then sent this new study to the senior constructor, but nothing resulted.

The 'A' and 'B' variants had a standard displacement of 14,000 tons and dimensions apparently inspired by the US Navy's *Ranger*, while for the 'C' variant Bonfiglietti proposed a carrier of only 10,000 tons. The first two variants were smaller than the original design so the flight deck was shorter; they were also slower with reduced protection, and less well armed. The general layout, the number of aircraft, and the underwater protection system, however, remained unchanged. Bonfiglietti also proposed a different layout of the main guns for the 'B' variant and a shorter island in order to create sufficient space for aircraft landings.

The 'C' variant was even less capable in terms of speed, protection, armament, and the number of embarked aircraft. The flight deck was also shorter, and the Pugliese system was replaced by a tighter subdivision into compartments in the lower part of the hull. Bonfiglietti did, however, highlight that all these solutions were alternative proposals that needed a careful in-depth analysis before acceptance. He was also probably not overly concerned about how these designs would be received, as he was confident that his original design, which was more detailed and better thought out, would be accepted as part of a new shipbuilding programme. Furthermore, Bonfiglietti stated that he would consider adopting a diesel propulsion system, as that solution would greatly reduce the size of the island, and consequently increase the area of the flight deck.

When Lt.-Gen. Filippo Bonfiglietti retired,[14] Italian naval policy and fleet modernisation and development were still based on 'Our Maritime Policy' by Bernotti. It was within this framework that Italy defined its position at the Naval Conference which took place in London from January to April 1930. That conference ended with an agreement between the United States, Britain and Japan that extended to all categories of warship. The London Treaty upheld the quantitative and qualitative limitations for capital ships and aircraft carriers between the major naval powers agreed at Washington in 1922. Meanwhile, the 1929 economic crisis was heavily affecting armaments procurement, thus paving the way for more stable political relationships among European nations. The British government played a key role in March 1931 by supporting a potential naval agreement between Italy and France. This was based on various

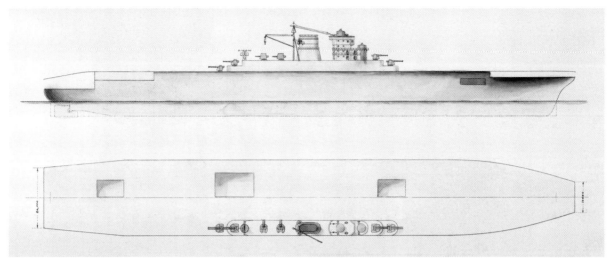

External profile and plan of Variant 'A'. Displacement was reduced to 14,000 tons standard, but the air wing still comprised 42 aircraft. (AFB)

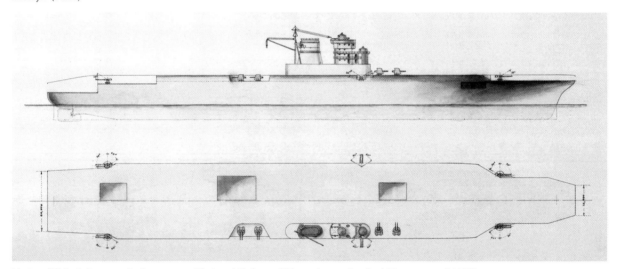

Variant 'B' had the same displacement as Variant 'A', but a different layout for the 100mm guns. (AFB)

issues, including naval parity and new warship construction procedures. Under the impression that Rome and Paris had signed a formal, binding agreement Bonfiglietti, who had recently retired, developed in April 1931 a fourth variant ('D'), which he sent to the Chief of the Design Committee.

The basic assumption made by Bonfiglietti for this new variant was an agreement between the *Regia Marina* and the *Marine Nationale* that would allocate to each navy a total of 34,500 tons for aircraft carriers.[15] Bonfiglietti quickly rejected the idea of building a single large carrier with the maximum displacement of 27,000 tons. He also rejected the idea of building two or three 10,000-ton ships because of the unacceptable constraints this limited displacement would impose on flight deck length. Instead, he proposed two other options: building two carriers each displacing 17,270 tons, or three ships of 11,515 tons. Both options would meet the tonnage requirements of a hypothetical Italian-French agreement.

The first option implied ships of greater size than Bonfiglietti's original design. This would make for a

better balance between speed, protection, armament, hangar layout, and embarked aircraft. However, the international trend towards smaller carriers with modest performance had the advantage of making any future Italian carrier more affordable. Thus, Bonfiglietti's definitive 'D' variant had a standard displacement of 11,500 tons. The flight deck was 200 metres long and 28 metres wide. There was also a dramatic reduction in the size of the island, which would allow a large flight deck area for aircraft operations. The propulsion plant, comprising four boilers and two sets of turbines, would give a top speed of 26 knots. The layout of the machinery would meet safety requirements with a four-compartment standard. A significant aspect of the new design was the placement of the exhaust ducts along the carrier's side, thus eliminating the funnel and decreasing the size of the island. The adoption of diesel engines and diesel generators would have facilitated this choice.

Bonfiglietti proposed an armament comprising four Ansaldo-type 120mm twin shielded LA gun mounts and four 100mm twin HA mounts. All these mountings were

Variant 'C' was smaller than the two previous variants and had fewer embarked aircraft. (AFB)

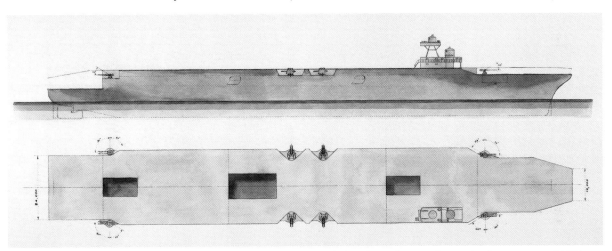

Variant 'D' had a standard displacement of 11,500 tons. Bonfiglietti worked on this preliminary design after his retirement. (AFB)

to be located one level below the flight deck. The gun layout facilitated flight operations but limited the arcs of fire, in particular for the 120mm guns but also for the HA guns if air attacks were carried out along the ship's axis.

The smaller island and its new forward position would leave a 140m-long area available for landing on, making it possible to incorporate a 10° incline at the after end of the flight deck. The island would house some of the operational and fire control spaces. The three aircraft lifts were on the center-line, which served to strengthen the upper hull. The relatively small size of the hull would not allow the Pugliese system to be installed, but Bonfiglietti was still confident that careful, tight subdivision of the lower hull would meet safety requirements. Reducing the standard displacement to 11,500 tons inevitably led to a smaller air wing composed of 30 aircraft: 12 fighters, 8 bombers, and 10 reconnaissance planes. However, Bonfiglietti was confident that, with the adoption of aircraft with folding wings, hangar volume was sufficient to embark 42, divided in a similar fashion as in his original design.

Bonfiglietti highlighted that this 'D' variant proposal was preliminary and would require much more detailed analysis in the event of a positive decision. However, since the proposal was based on his previous design experience, Bonfiglietti declared that it could serve as the basis for detailed design work, which would hopefully be followed by a firm order.

As with the original design, the *Regia Marina* declined to make any decisions about the construction of an aircraft carrier on the basis of the variants proposed by Bonfiglietti. Indeed, there were few lines on the subject in the minutes of a meeting of the staff of the Italian armed forces held in November 1931, and no further discussion of the proposals took place.

Conclusions

Because the *Regia Marina* never proceeded with the carrier design developed by Filippo Bonfiglietti and there was no operational experience to inform analysis, the merits of the design can be assessed only through a theoretical comparison with contemporary foreign construction.

An analysis of Bonfiglietti's summary report shows that the objective pursued by Bonfiglietti and the *Regia Marina* was three-fold. Firstly, the Italian Navy was keen to exploit the residual Washington tonnage allocation (45,000 tons) for future and similar carrier construction. The second aim was to obtain the best ship possible, based on contemporary Italian knowledge of the complex issues related to aircraft carrier design. Finally, the *Regia Marina* wanted to construct an aircraft carrier in order to build up experience in naval air operations. A subsidiary, but important issue was the search for naval parity with France. The aircraft carrier *Béarn* was already in service and was perceived, both in Rome and Paris, as the first unit of an aircraft carrier squadron that could change the power balance in the Mediterranean.

Taking into account the comparatively small size of the Bonfiglietti carrier and the contemporary foreign vessels then in service or projected, this comparison takes into account the British *Hermes*, the French *Béarn*, and the US Navy's *Ranger*. With reference to the general layout, the Bonfiglietti carrier was in many respects similar to the other three vessels. The French and US carriers also had the outer ends of their flight decks supported by open structures.[16] However, one negative aspect of the Italian design was that the island was too long when compared with the length of the flight deck, due to the need to accommodate the main guns and their fire control directors.

In terms of performance, a top speed of 29 knots was adequate for both aircraft take-off requirements and fleet operations. The adoption of the Pugliese system and the balance pursued by Bonfiglietti between vertical and horizontal armour were two important features that provided the ship with adequate protection. The size of the embarked wing (42 aircraft) was similar to that of *Béarn* (40 aircraft); the Italian carrier embarked fewer aircraft than *Ranger* but more than *Hermes*. However, a big question mark remains over the performance of the aircraft chosen for the Italian carrier, and for her ability to carry out multiple launches.

It should be noted that the Regia Marina chose the aircraft for the Bonfiglietti carrier only on the basis of their size (weight and dimensions) and missions; their performance would have been validated by a thorough campaign of tests and trials on board the carrier, possibly preceded by a full involvement of the *Regia Aeronautica* in the aviation aspects of the project. Unfortunately, at that time the relationship between the *Regia Marina* and the *Regia Aeronautica* precluded the close cooperation between the two services which would have resulted in well-conceived accommodation and handling arrangements for the ship's aircraft.

To conclude, the aircraft carrier conceived by Filippo Bonfiglietti was a balanced design, and technically significant when put in the context of contemporary Italian knowledge. It is regrettable that it was not pursued, especially if one considers the highly detailed documentation prepared by Bonfiglietti. The next step would have been to define the technical specifications and to sign a contract with a shipbuilding company, which would have

been entrusted with the detailed design and the subsequent construction of the ship. With this in mind, it should be noted that the size of the ship presented a problem in relation to the domestic shipbuilding capacity during that period. The only suitable building ways in Italy that could accommodate such a ship were in Trieste and Genoa, and these shipyards were engaged in the construction of the cruiser *Fiume* and the ocean liner *Rex* respectively. Construction of the aircraft carrier could theoretically have taken place in 1930, even though by 1928 the construction of both *Fiume* and *Rex* had suffered delays. A further difficulty was that following the completion of *Fiume*, the Trieste shipyard would begin the construction of the liner *Conte di Savoia*, while the cruiser *Bolzano* would occupy the slipway vacated by *Rex*. Only a political decision would have resolved this situation and ensured that the *Regia Marina* could build and operate its first aircraft carrier.

Filippo Bonfiglietti: a Biography

Filippo Bonfiglietti was born in Tivoli, Rome, on 8 January 1868. After completing high school, he undertook a year of national service as a soldier in a cavalry regiment. He was discharged in 1887 as sergeant. In 1892 Bonfiglietti graduated as a civil engineer from the University of Rome and later joined the Naval Engineering Corps of the Royal Italian Navy. As a second class naval engineer, Bonfiglietti attended the Higher Naval School of Genoa and in 1894 graduated with a degree in Naval Engineering. In 1896 Bonfiglietti became responsible for supervising the construction of *Regina Elena*, an armoured cruiser being built at the La Spezia naval shipyard. Then in 1904, after the reorganisation of the ranks of the Naval Engineering Corps, Bonfiglietti became a Captain. At the same time he was posted to the Ministry of the Navy, in Rome. He was promoted to Major in 1908 and Lieutenant Colonel in 1913, and assigned to the Navy's Technical offices in Genoa, then La Spezia and finally Castellammare di Stabia, nearby Naples. In 1917 Bonfiglietti became qualified to teach Naval Construction at the faculty of Engineering at the University of Genoa and was promoted to Colonel in 1918. Later, he became head of the Naval Shipyard at Castellammare di Stabia where he spent three years. In 1924 Bonfiglietti was posted to the Directorate of Naval Construction for the Ministry of the Navy in Rome, and was subsequently promoted to General of the Naval Engineering Corps. Afterwards he headed the Information and Studies office within the Italian Navy Design Committee and was later promoted to Lieutenant General. Bonfiglietti retained that position until January 1931 when he retired due to age limits. Despite his retirement he was later connected to several technical and scientific activities, including the design of a seaport in Loano, a small Italian town where he died on 17 December, 1939.

During his career Bonfiglietti designed several types of warship and auxiliary as well as managing the construction of several warships for the *Regia Marina*. In 1918 he designed a class of auxiliaries which were built in a private

Lieutenant-General (Naval Engineering Corps) Filippo Bonfiglietti in his winter ceremonial dress. He headed the Studies Office of the Italian Navy's Design Committee for several years. (AFB)

shipyard and saw service in the Second World War. Bonfiglietti also played a part in the final design phase of the two *Trento* class heavy cruisers – the first major surface combatants built by the *Regia Marina* after the conclusion of the Washington Treaty. He designed the *Zara* class cruisers, which were widely considered a significant improvement on the *Trentos*, and the cruiser *Bolzano*. Then, before working on the design of the aircraft carrier described in this article, he designed a torpedo boat of 770 tonnes with a speed of 34 knots. He also had a role in the design of the first series of light cruisers later commissioned by the *Regia Marina*.

Footnotes:

1. *Europa* was a converted freighter built in 1895 in Glasgow. The conversion took place at La Spezia Naval Dockyard. *Europa* had a full load displacement of 8,800 tonnes and could carry and operate 16 seaplanes, eight of which had to be assembled. Her charateristics were broadly similar to contemporary seaplane carriers then in service in the Royal Navy and other European naval forces.

2. The maximum gun calibre permitted for an aircraft carrier was 203mm (8in), but no limit was set on the number of embarked aircraft.

3. Several seaplane models that were to be embarked in the *Regia Marina*'s major surface combatants were tested on *Giuseppe Miraglia*. She then participated in the Abyssinian war in 1935, carrying disassembled planes from Italy to Eritrea. In 1939 she took part in the Albanian campaign, carrying small tanks. During the Second World War, *Giuseppe Miraglia* was based at Taranto and supported the seaplanes embarked in battleships and cruisers. She was decommissioned in 1950.

4. Romeo Bernotti was born in 1877 and joined the Italian Navy in 1899. He fought in the First World War and in 1922 established the Italian Naval War College. He was the author of many important articles and books on naval matters. His revolutionary attitude was, however, an obstacle for him and meant he could not reach the highest ranks in the *Regia Marina*. In 1938, Bernotti was promoted to Vice-Admiral but given a low-level position. He died in 1974.

5. The Naval Engineering Corps of the Italian Navy was equivalent to the Corps of Naval Constructors in the Royal Navy, but included only commissioned officers. Ranks were as in the Italian Army.

6. 'Our Maritime Policy' was a wide-ranging and exhaustive document that included doctrinal, organisational and technical precepts for the coherent development of the Navy. It carefully defined Navy structure and options within the framework of Italian military policy and available resources.

7. The entire set of drawings, plans and reports prepared by Lt. Gen. Filippo Bonfiglietti resurfaced in 2008 and were used to write an article for the Italian magazine *Storia Militare*. These documents are direct evidence of Italian technical knowledge in the field of aircraft carriers. The grandson of Filippo Bonfiglietti, bearing the same name as his grandfather, has kindly provided the illustrative material for this arfticle.

8. Equivalent to 15,240 metric tonnes, the unit of measurement for displacement used by the Regia Marina and other continental European navies.

9. From a design point of view, this configuration was very similar to that adopted for British and US aircraft carriers.

10. Bonfiglietti also decided not to install arresting gear because of conflicting information from abroad. The *Regia Marina* assumed that the British carriers were not going to be fitted with arresting gear, although their installation seemed to be confirmed on US carriers.

11. At the time this continuous gallery deck was not a feature of foreign aircraft carriers; however, it would be widely adopted for postwar carriers designed and built during the 1950s and 1960s.

12. The then-Lieutenant-Colonel Umberto Pugliese, Naval Engineering Corps of the Italian Navy, developed the system shortly after the First World War. He later became renowned for the design of the *Littorio*-class battleships.

13. A forward rudder had been installed on the armoured cruiser *Regina Elena*, whose construction had been managed by the then-Major Filippo Bonfiglietti.

14. Bonfiglietti reached the age of retirement on January 1931.

15. This figure was significantly less than 60,000 tons allocated to Italy and France by the 1922 Washington Treaty and confirmed in London in 1930.

16. *Hermes* had an open structure at the stern, but in the final design the bow was plated up.

NIGHT ACTION, MALAYA 1942

In his second article for *Warship*, **Peter Cannon** looks at the Royal Navy's first surface engagement of the Pacific War, when the veteran destroyers HMAS *Vampire* and HMS *Thanet* attempted to evade a screen of no fewer than 21 Japanese warships and auxiliaries to attack two amphibious transports off the Malayan town of Endau during the early hours of 27 January 1942.

The loss of Force Z, HM Ships *Prince of Wales* and *Repulse*, off Malaya on 10 December 1941 effectively ended the overcommitted Royal Navy's strategy of defending Britain's Far Eastern interests, including the dominions of Australia and New Zealand, from the newly-developed naval base in Singapore. Thereafter the time-consuming concentration of a major Eastern Fleet was undertaken in the safer waters of Ceylon, leaving poorly-equipped ground and air forces to hold Singapore. The light naval forces remaining in theatre were primarily concerned with the safe arrival of additional troops and logistics, and made no attempt to contest Japanese sea control.

By 26 January 1942, British Empire ground forces defending Malaya had been comprehensively defeated. In their retirement towards Singapore Island along the only major road and rail communications servicing the length of the peninsula, the hard-pressed formations were dangerously susceptible to a seaborne outflanking movement. When a Japanese amphibious task force was detected approaching the eastern coastal town of Endau in the

southernmost state of Johore early on the 26th, British fears appeared to have been realised. A major east-west lateral road began at Endau and two Australian battalions successfully holding back an enemy overland advance in the area were at risk of being overwhelmed by a fresh landing. If the Japanese subsequently either cut the main trunk road or drove south for the Singapore causeway, the entire Empire force risked envelopment and destruction.

Japanese campaign planning included an amphibious assault on Johore to complement the southerly thrust down the western side of the peninsula. However, rapid progress as well as concerns over effective British naval and air intervention saw a four-infantry-battalion assault downgraded to a logistics operation on 19 January. Still enjoying the original heavy naval escort, two assault transports would land airfield construction stores, ordnance and personnel to secure airfields for the support of future operations. With the survival of the retreating forces seemingly in the balance, the impending landings prompted the Royal Air Force to commit its slender remaining aerial striking forces to contest them. These aerial attacks were supported by two of the navy's oldest destroyers in the RN's only post-Force Z offensive operation of the campaign.

The Landing at Endau

The Imperial Japanese Navy's (IJN) Malaya Seizure Force, allocated to support the conquest of Malaya, was assigned almost in its entirety to support the Endau operation. Two Japanese army transports, the 6,477-ton *Canberra Maru* and 8,614-ton *Kansai Maru*, carried the Japanese Army's 96th Airfield Battalion and were escorted by the First Escort Unit, built around Rear-Admiral Hashimoto Shintarō's 3rd Torpedo Squadron.[1] The squadron nominally consisted of 16 destroyers of the *Fubuki* class in four divisions led by the 18-year-old light cruiser *Sendai*, commanded by Hashimoto's Flag Captain Shimazaki Toshio. However, for this operation, only Destroyer Division 11's *Hatsuyuki*, *Fubuki*, and *Shirayuki* and Destroyer Division 20's *Yugiri*, *Amagiri* and *Asagiri* were present. They were reinforced by Commander Fujita Tomozō's 1st Minesweeper Division, comprising *W1*, *W2*, *W3*, *W4* and *W5* as well the converted auxiliaries *Otowa*

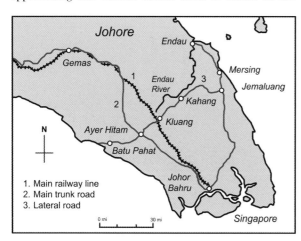

Main road and rail communications in Johore, 1942. An amphibious assault against the Endau-Mersing area of Johore would potentially allow an enemy force to advance along the lateral Kahang-Kluang-Batu Pahat road and cut off the entire British army retreating down the main north-south road and railway towards Singapore. (Drawn by the author)

HMAS Vampire *as she appeared at Endau. Armament visible from left to right is: 'X' 4-inch gun, 3-inch HA gun in place of the original after triple torpedo tubes, HA platform with two single 2-pdr HA guns mounted en echelon, forward triple torpedo tubes, second HA platform mounting quadruple 0.5-inch Vickers machine guns, twin Lewis .303 MG on the starboard bridge wing along with 'B' and 'A' guns. The 9-foot FQ2 rangefinder and Light Type Director may also be discerned atop the Upper Bridge. The photo was taken from HMAS* Manoora, *Indian Ocean, 4 March 1942. (Training Ship Vampire Collection)*

Canberra Maru *in Melbourne's Port Phillip Bay, 28 June 1936. (Allan C. Green Collection, State Library of Victoria)*

Maru and *Rumoi Maru*, together with Commander Hayashi Toshinari's 11th Submarine Chaser Division of *CH-7*, *CH-8* and *CH-9* and four unidentified converted patrol boats.[2]

Sendai was an obsolete design, with seven 5.5in guns in single open mountings and four twin 24in torpedo tubes, but had been upgraded with modern fire control systems and retained a good turn of speed of 32-33 knots. Rated at 34 knots, the large destroyers of the *Fubuki* class were some of the most powerful ships of their kind in the world at that time. They were armed with six 5in guns in three twin enclosed mountings, one forward and two aft, as well as nine 24in torpedo tubes in three triple mountings. Built as all-out attack vessels, modern Japanese destroyers were more specialised than their jack-of-all trades British counterparts, and were ideally suited to the aggressive close-in night combat doctrine pursued by the IJN.

Rear-Admiral Kurita Takeo provided distant cover for the operation, and was responsible for the interception of British warships attempting to contest either the Endau operation or the concurrent invasion of the nearby Anambas Islands. The 26th saw Kurita cruising to the north-east of Endau with the heavy cruisers *Kumano* and *Suzuya*, light cruiser *Yura* and the destroyers *Ayanami*, *Isonami* and *Shikinami*.[3]

The assault force did not complete its concentration until the morning of 26 January, shortly before being sighted 10 miles north of its objective by Royal Australian Air Force Hudson bombers at 0745. Led in by the minesweepers the force anchored at 0915, approximately five to six miles off the eastern point of the Endau estuary, where they immediately began landing troops. The

Kansai Maru *pre-war*. (US National Archives and Records Administration)

escorts were defensively deployed in a semi-circle out to an approximate eight-mile radius, primarily against a perceived threat of British submarines. Following completion of the first landing phase at 1130, the transports moved to a position two to three miles offshore at 1200, and it was in this second anchorage they would spend the night.

The British Response

The series of British and Australian bombing attacks on the Endau landing force between 1505 and 1830 on 26 January 1942, employing obsolete aircraft such as the Vickers Vildebeest biplane, were pressed home against Japanese Army fighters with the utmost gallantry. Fifteen aircraft were lost, 35 aircrew killed, at least nine wounded and four captured, two of whom were executed. Despite enthusiastic claims of 11 bomb hits on the two transports and another on a cruiser, both transports continued unloading having suffered nothing more than splinter damage from the considerable number of near misses along with eight killed and 18 wounded. *Sendai* remained unscathed.

As the RAF attempted to disrupt the landing, the only remotely suitable warships available in Singapore that day were the 23-year old British Admiralty 'S' class destroyer HMS *Thanet*, and the 25-year old Australian 'V' class destroyer HMAS *Vampire*. *Thanet*, under the command of Commander Bernard Davies RN (Retd), remained virtually in her as-built configuration, whilst *Vampire*, under Commander William Moran RAN, was newly recommissioned with a raw crew.

Singapore's local naval commander, Rear-Admiral Ernest Spooner, ordered the destroyers to arrive off Endau in the middle of the night. Whilst *Thanet* retained both twin sets of 21in torpedo tubes to augment her three 4in guns, *Vampire*, armed with four 4in guns, carried a next-to-useless 3in HA gun in place of her original after triple

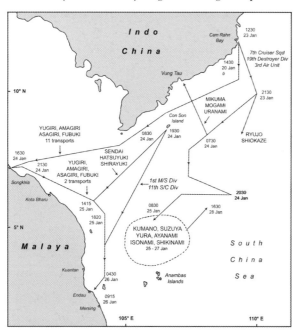

Japanese 1st Escort Unit and covering forces track chart, 20-28 January 1942. The two transports were detached from a Singora (Thailand)-bound convoy on 24 January; their close escort of four destroyers were augmented by Sendai *and two destroyers the following day, and the minesweeper and submarine chaser divisions the morning of the assault.* (Drawn by the author)

TABLE 1: **IMPERIAL JAPANESE NAVY 1ST ESCORT UNIT COMMAND ARRANGEMENTS 26 JANUARY 1942**

3rd Torpedo Squadron		Rear Admiral Hashimoto Shintarō (Etajima Academy Class 41, 1913)
	Sendai	Captain Shimazaki Toshio (Class 44, 1916)
11th Destroyer Division	Divisional Commander	Captain Shōji Kiichirō (Class 45, 1917)
	Hatsuyuki	Lieutenant Commander Kamiura Junya (Class 53, 1925)
	Fubuki	Commander Yamashita Shizuo (Class 50, 1922)
	Shirayuki	Lieutenant Commander Sugahara Rokurō (Class 51, 1923)
20th Destroyer Division	Divisional Commander	Captain Yamada Yūji (Class 46, 1918)
	Yugiri	Commander Motokura Masayoshi (Class 51, 1923)
	Amagiri	Commander Ashida Motoichi/Motokazu (Class 50, 1922)
	Asagiri	Lieutenant Commander Arai Yasuo (Class 53, 1925)
1st Minesweeper Division	Divisional Commander (*W-1*)	Commander Fujita Tomozō/Yūzō (Class 46, 1918)
11th Submarine Chaser Division	Divisional Commander (*CH-8*)	Commander Hayashi Toshinari/Risaku (Class 50, 1922)

Note: Alternative personal names reflect the fact that the original Kanji characters have multiple possible pronunciations reflecting the private nature of Japanese personal names. Etajima Class years are years of graduation.

Source: Sakamoto, Seiki & Fukukawa, Hideki, *Nihon Kaigun Hensei Jiten* (*Japanese Navy Organization Dictionary*), Fuyō Shobō Shuppan Tokyo, 2003.

TABLE 2: **ROYAL NAVY ENDAU STRIKE UNIT, 26 JANUARY 1942**

HMAS *Vampire* (Senior Officer)	Commander William Moran RAN (Cadet Midshipman 1917)
HMS *Thanet*	Commander Bernard Davies RN (Retd.) (Special Entry Cadet 1917)

21in mounting, leaving her with only the forward set of tubes. In *Thanet* and *Vampire* one would have been hard pressed to find two older, more obsolete destroyers still in the front-line role for which they had been designed in any of His Majesty's navies. And now, with Moran as senior officer, the small force sailed at 1630 to run the gauntlet of the Malaya Seizure Force with only seven torpedoes between them.

Having assumed the first degree of readiness at 1919, *Vampire* and *Thanet* approached the Endau area at 25 knots. Their close inshore transit between the Malay Peninsula and the islands to the east inadvertently avoided the threat of Kurita's covering forces. However, Hashimoto's close escort was fully alerted to the possibility of a surface attack during the night based upon erroneous reports of two British light cruisers at sea, the reports having been received prior to Moran's undetected departure from Singapore. Furthermore, poor Allied intelligence gained from returning aircrew revised the number of reported enemy destroyers down from twelve to two, information radioed to Moran and Davies at 2255, setting the scene for a first-rate disaster.

The Anglo-Australian and Japanese forces were about to engage in the most difficult and confusing of all naval actions, night fighting. It is well known that the IJN had trained long and hard to attain a tactical edge over its potential adversaries, but what is less well appreciated is that the RN had built upon its practical First World War night fighting experience and trained its personnel accordingly. Aggressive, close-in night action in all weather conditions was an integral part of British doctrine, with exercises and instructions heavily emphasising initiative. By 1942, the British and Australians had established their dominance in night surface actions over the Italians in the Mediterranean. Therefore, on paper at least, the IJN and RN were the world's two most profi-

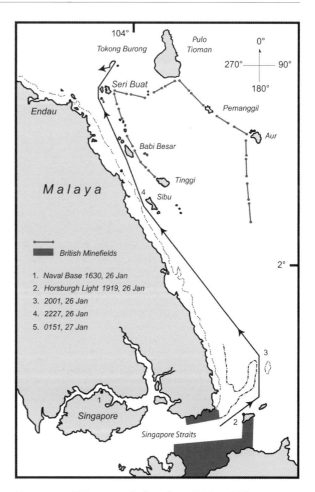

Vampire and Thanet *track chart from 1900 on 26 January to 0151 on 27 January.* (Drawn by the author)

TABLE 3: ALLIED SHIPS

HMAS *Vampire*

Builder:	J. Samuel White & Co. Ltd., East Cowes
Ordered:	April 1916 (Emergency War Programme)
Building dates:	Laid down 10 Oct 1916;
	Launched 21 May 1917;
	Completed 22 Sep 1917
Transferred to RAN:	11 October 1933
Pennant number:	I68

General Characteristics (1941)

Displacement:	1,090 tons standard; 1,457 tons full load
Dimensions:	312ft x 29ft 6in x 18ft 3in

Complement:

Designed:	128: 13 officers, 115 men
1942:	141: 9 officers, 132 men

Propulsion:

Boilers:	3 x White-Foster; load on safety valves 250lb/in^2
Engines:	2-shaft Brown Curtis single reduction geared turbines (each set HP ahead, LP ahead & astern) 27,000shp, 350rpm; 2 x 3-bladed propellers, 9ft 6in
Speed (designed):	34kts trial, 32kts full load

Full Power Trials

Date	RPM	Speed	Place	Sea	Period since Docking & State of Ship's Bottom
15.09.1917:	348	Not Taken	English Channel		
23.01.1920:	314	31.8kts	North Sea	Calm	3 months, fairly clean
02.04.1930:	307	30.6kts (Land fix)	Alicante Bay, Spain	Slight swell, 90ftm	2 months, fairly clean
31.05.1938:	313	27.7kts (Land fix)	Bass Strait	Rough, 40ftm	9 months, dirty
19.05.1939:	307	28.7kts (Land fix)	Bass Strait	Moderate	4 days, clean

High Speed Steaming Jan-Mar 1941

RPM	Speed
286	27kts
280	26.5kts
275	26kts
254	24.5kts
250	24kts
240	23kts
230	22.5kts
212	21kts

Note: During these three months of high-speed war steaming 286rpm is the highest figure recorded.

Fuel and Fresh Water

Oil fuel (total, 95% capacity):	368 tons
Oil fuel (war tanks, 95% capacity):	321 tons
Fresh water (tanks):	7.3 tons
Fresh water (feed):	5.1 tons
Fresh water (RFW):	24.2 tons

Recorded Performance (1941)
Fuel Consumption

Speed	Endurance	Consumption
28.0kts	720nm	305 tons
20.0kts	1,575nm	97.3 tons
15.0kts	2,220nm	52.0 tons
12.0kts	2,440nm	37.7 tons
11.0kts	2,500nm	34.0 tons
		(most economical speed)

Water Consumption (Harbour) per 24 hrs

1 hr notice for full speed:	5.0 tons
In harbour (distilling):	5.4 tons
In harbour (non distilling):	2.5 tons

Water Consumption (Sea) per 24hrs

Boilers at full power:	24 tons
At sea (other services):	2.5 tons
Output of evaporators:	36 tons

Armament (January 1942)

4 x 4-inch QF Mk V guns on 4 x CPII mountings (30° elevation); 140rpg (+ 50 star shell)

1 x 12pdr 12cwt (3-inch/40) gun on HA/LA Mk IX mounting

2 x 2pdr QF Mk II pom-poms

4 x 0.5-inch Vickers Mk III machine guns on 1 x Mk II quad mounting

4 x .303-inch Lewis machine guns on 2 x twin mountings

3 x 21-inch Mk IV torpedoes (515lb warhead) in 1 x triple TR Mk I mounting

4 x depth charge throwers

2 x depth charge rails

Type 123 ASDIC

Fire Control

Nine-foot FQ-2 rangefinder on MQ 1 mounting

Light Type Director with Henderson Gun Director Firing Gear Mark II

2 x Dumaresq Mk VIII rate and deflection instruments, 1 x Vickers Range Clock

4 x Torpedo Control Disks Mk II**, 3 x Torpedo Deflection Sights Mk II

HMS *Thanet*

Builder:	Hawthorn Leslie & Co. Ltd., Hebburn
Ordered:	June 1917 (Emergency War Programme)
Building dates:	LD 13 Dec 1917; L 5 Nov 1918; C 30 Aug 1919
Pennant number:	H28

General Characteristics (1941)

Displacement:	905 tons standard; 1,220 tons full load
Length:	276ft x 26ft 8in x 16ft 3in

Complement:

1921:	97: 5 officers, 92 men
1942:	109: 7 officers, 102 men

Performance

Speed	Endurance	Consumption
28kts	980nm	204tons
20kts	1,940nm	74 tons
15kts	2,740nm	39 tons
13kts	2,950nm	32 tons
11.5kts	2,990nm	27tons

Propulsion

Boilers:	3 x Yarrow water tube; load on safety valves 250lb/in^2
Engines:	2-shaft Brown Curtis single reduction geared turbines (each set HP ahead, LP ahead & astern) 27,000shp, 360rpm; 2 x 3-bladed propellers
Speed (designed):	36kts trial, 32.5kts full load
Speed (builder's trials):	33.35kts (26,303shp)

Fuel and Fresh Water

Oil fuel	301 tons
Fresh water (tanks)	4.5 tons
Fresh water (feed)	5.0 tons
Fresh water (RFW)	15.0 tons

Note: Performance, fuel and fresh water data for *Thanet* is unavailable. Data from RAN records for Admiralty 'S' Class vessels, 1929.

Armament (January 1942)

3 x 4-inch QF Mk IV guns, on 3 x CPIII mountings
(30° elevation); 160rpg
1 x 2pdr QF pom-pom
4 x 21-inch Mk IV torpedoes, (515lb warhead) in
2 x twin DR Mk IV mountings
2 x depth charge rails
Type 133 ASDIC

Fire Control

Sextant Rangefinder
Light Type Director with Henderson Gun Director Firing Gear Mark II
2 x Dumaresq Mk VIII rate and deflection instruments,
1 x Vickers Range Clock
4 x Torpedo Control Disks Mk II**,
4 x Torpedo Deflection Sights Mk II

HMS Thanet, *Portsmouth 1935.* (The Wright and Logan Collection, Royal Navy Museum)

TABLE 4: JAPANESE SHIPS

Sendai

Completed:	19 April 1924
Displacement (1940):	7,982 tonnes full load
Dimensions:	532ft x 46ft 6in x 29ft

Propulsion

Boilers:	12 x Kanpon RO GŌ type, 260lb/in²
Engines:	4-shaft geared turbines, 90,000shp
Speed (1942):	32-33kts
Radius of Action:	6,000nm at 14kts

Armament (January 1942)

7 x 5.5-inch Type 3 LA guns (7 x I); 30° elevation
Type 94 Mod. 3 FC Director + 4m rangefinder tower
4 x 25mm guns (2 x II Type 96 mountings)
4 x 13.2mm machine guns (1 x IV Type 93 mounting)
8 x TT (4 x II) for 24in Type 8 torpedo (761lb warhead)

Armour

Belt 2½in HT, deck 1⅛in HT

Fubuki class destroyers (Types I & II)

Completed:	Type I: Fubuki/Shirayuki 1928, Hatsuyuki 1929
	Type II: Asagiri/Yugiri/Amagiri 1930.
Displacement:	2,660 tonnes full load (Hatsuyuki)
Dimensions:	389ft x 34ft x 10ft 6in
Complement:	13 officers, 194 men

Propulsion

Boilers:	4 x Kanpon RO GŌ type, 290lb/in²
Engines:	2-shaft geared turbines, 50,700shp
Speed (1942):	33-34kts
Radius of action:	5,000nm at 14kts

Armament (January 1942)

6 x 5in Type 3 guns (3 x II); 120rpg
Type I: Model 'A', 40° elevation; light director gunsight
Type II: Model 'B', 75° elevation; Type 94 Mod. 3 FC Director
Type I: 2 x 13.2mm Type 93 MG (1 x II)
Type II: 4 x 13.2mm Type 93 MG (2 x II)
9 x TT (3 x III) for 24in Type 90 torpedo (827lb warhead)

Canberra Maru

Diesel engine motor ship / general cargo vessel

Registered:	Osaka Syosen KK, Osaka, Japan.
Builder:	Mitsubishi Zosen Kaisha, Japan.
Completed:	1936
Tonnage:	6,477 tons (gross)
Length:	446.0ft
Speed:	17.5kts

Kansai Maru

Diesel engine, twin-screw motor ship / general cargo vessel

Registered:	Harada Kisen KK, Osaka, Japan.
Builder:	Yokohama Dock Co. Ltd, Yokohama, Japan.
Completed:	1930
Tonnage:	8,614 tons (gross)
Length:	461.7ft
Speed:	17.5kts

cient exponents of night fighting, although the RN at least remained hitherto unaware of its opponent's level of expertise.

Penetrating the Screen

Upon arrival in the area, brilliant moonlight prompted Moran to avoid any inshore patrols and search to the north, towards Tokong Burong Island, before approaching Endau. Nothing was sighted, but the moon's disappearance behind dark clouds at 0151 saw the two destroyers alter course south-west to sweep the target area at 15 knots. Visibility was estimated at two miles, and the force kept the large island of Palau Tioman astern to reduce the likelihood of their silhouettes standing out against the horizon. At 0237 *Vampire* identified an enemy destroyer 30 degrees off her starboard bow, speed 15 knots. The ship's gunnery team swung into action, the main armament tracking the target in harmony with the director, awaiting the order to shoot. Whilst not established at the time, evidence indicates that Commander Ashida's *Amagiri* failed to sight the intruders and steamed away into the darkness as *Vampire*, with *Thanet* two cables astern, withheld fire and continued into the anchorage having penetrated the outer screen.

Vampire's lookouts sighted a second ship, identified as an old destroyer of the *Akikaze* class, less than a mile closer inshore at 0240. There was little hope of avoiding

an encounter, as the target lay almost directly ahead at point blank range. Both Allied commanding officers had fully expected to at least have to fight their way out, and Moran decided to attack with torpedoes. With *Vampire* steering 258°, the enemy slowly came abeam to starboard on a virtually reciprocal course. An enemy report was made by wireless telegraphy (W/T) to Singapore as the Torpedo Control Officer (TCO) ordered the torpedo armament into action from the bridge. The tubes crew were ordered to 'Stand by' and train their hand-worked weapons to 90 degrees on the starboard beam.

The order was relayed from the bridge by electrical order transmitter and voicepipe direct to the mounting and acknowledged by reply transmitter when carried out; moving the tubes off the centreline also illuminated the bridge's starboard 'Tube Ready' lamp. Firing directly abeam was standard procedure in these ships to avoid the bridge deflection sights being on a different bearing to the tubes. The torpedoes would be aimed by swinging the ship herself, the TCO warning the Captain when the sight was 10-15° off the point of aim with the helm then being eased to allow a slight time interval between firings. This ensured a small angle of spread between the torpedoes to reduce the risk of their colliding with one another.

The two First World War-pattern Mk IV torpedoes in tubes 'A' and 'C' were now set for their maximum speed setting of 8,000 yards at 35 knots, with running depths of six and eight feet respectively. The target initially appeared to be stationary and the TCO intended to fire

W-4, 1st Minesweeping Division, mistaken for a small destroyer in the dark. (Kure Maritime Museum, Japan)

Sendai, Flagship of the 3rd Torpedo Squadron, as she appeared in 1934. (Kure Maritime Museum, Japan)

directly along his line of sight, but just before the starboard sights came on it was realised that she was under way at approximately 12 knots. Four knots right deflection, calculated on the torpedo control disk to compensate for the target's motion left to right, was hurriedly applied to the sight at the last second and relayed to the tubes by electrical deflection transmitter.[4] At 0242, two minutes after sighting the second Japanese ship, the TCO's remote firing pistol sounded the tubes' firing buzzer before launching both weapons on a bearing of 350° at a range of only 600 yards. No spread was used while Moran slowly altered the ship's course to port at a rate of one degree every two seconds, the point of aim being the target's forward gun position.

The two opposing forces had actually sighted one another simultaneously. The 820-tonne *W-1* class minesweeper *W-4*, with a silhouette easily mistaken for a small destroyer in the dark, was patrolling the central area to the east of the anchorage at 12 knots, approximately

two miles north-west of Aceh Island.[5] Sighting two unidentified warships, *W-4* was attempting to identify them when the leading vessel suddenly engaged her with torpedoes. As *Vampire* immediately increased to full speed and swung away to the south-east, her bridge staff observed one torpedo to miss barely 15-20 yards ahead whilst the second passed directly beneath *W-4*. This weapon was most likely yet to settle to its running depth, despite the range being within the Mk IV's performance envelope against a shallow-draft vessel.[6]

Thereafter followed an inexplicable delay in the passing of an 'enemy' alarm to the flagship, as *W-4* took more than 20 minutes to alert one of her consorts, Commander Yamashita's *Fubuki*, by flashing light. The situation was compounded by the position being erroneously reported as north-west of Sembilang Island, six miles east of *W-4*'s actual location. Japanese records also state that *W-4* fired two rounds of 4.7in at close range at her assailants, but both Allied COs reported no visible reaction aboard the

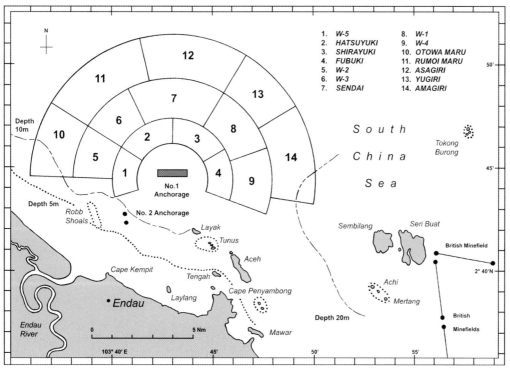

1. W-5
2. HATSUYUKI
3. SHIRAYUKI
4. FUBUKI
5. W-2
6. W-3
7. SENDAI
8. W-1
9. W-4
10. OTOWA MARU
11. RUMOI MARU
12. ASAGIRI
13. YUGIRI
14. AMAGIRI

Japanese patrol screen positions as depicted in the War Diary of the 3rd Torpedo Squadron, 27 January 1942. (Drawn by the author)

Australian 'V&W' class destroyer launching a practice torpedo from 'B' tube, 1930s. (Wilson P. Evans Collection, State Library of Victoria)

Japanese ship. The alarm was finally broadcast to all ships by *Fubuki* at 0305, with *W-4* addressing a clarification signal by W/T ten minutes later to *Sendai* to inform command that she had been fired upon.

Observing no reaction from *W-4*, Moran believed his force remained undetected and altered course again to the south-west as he confirmed *Thanet* retained her full outfit of torpedoes. Judging by the positions of the patrolling ships encountered so far, Moran was now confident that the transports must lie closer inshore, and the Allied ships again reduced speed to 15 knots in order to make their wakes less conspicuous. However, 30 minutes of careful steaming inshore saw the two ships approaching shoal water with no further contact. Moran reluctantly concluded that the transports were not in the immediate vicinity and decided to end the operation.

From analysis of the available track charts and narratives, it appears that Moran's force was unlucky in sighting neither the transports at anchor discharging cargo nor their light screen, some two to three miles off Cape Kempit. However, differing track chart scales and levels of detail make it difficult to assess just how close the Allied destroyers came to their targets. Moran's force wheeled around to starboard and increased speed with

the intention of gaining some sea room before heading out of the anchorage. The Japanese never knew how close they came to an embarrassing incident. If the two destroyers had got amongst the transports there were only three small submarine chasers and four converted patrol boats, armed only with light anti-aircraft weapons, to stop them.

Nevertheless, *Vampire* and *Thanet*, effectively surrounded by shoal water and Japanese warships, were still a long way from safety. Two vessels, one on the port bow, the other astern, both thought to be destroyers, were sighted at 0318 as the ships worked to the north away from the shallows. Moran, still looking for a fight, prepared to attack. With no chance of keeping gun 'A' arcs open on their run from the anchorage, he immediately signalled Davies by flashing light to alter away to starboard onto the retirement course of 110° and engage with torpedoes.

At 0315, 10 minutes after *Fubuki*'s 'enemy' alarm, Lt.-Commander Sugahara's *Shirayuki* was steering a reciprocal course to the two Allied ships at 12 knots as *Vampire*'s last remaining torpedo was set to its high speed setting and trained to port at 270 degrees. As Moran slowly turned to starboard at one degree per second, 'B' tube was fired with a deflection of 11 knots left. At a range of 1,500 yards, the apparently unsuspecting destroyer was just inside the range at which a small ship was considered to be a good torpedo target. As soon as the Australian ship had fired, Davies turned *Thanet* to starboard outside of *Vampire's* wake and launched his entire outfit of four torpedoes as the port sights came on.

Sighting unidentified ships, *Shirayuki* altered course to port to come in behind the intruders just as the torpedoes were hitting the water, causing all five to miss ahead, *Vampire's* by 50 yards. The reaction on the Australian bridge can only be imagined. Moran was an experienced torpedo specialist but it only took a slight miscalculation to miss with a straight running torpedo, even at close range, and the enemy's movements suggested they had observed 'B' tube's discharge. *Shirayuki* later reported that she positively identified the ships as enemy at 0315 '…as a result of their hostile action' but her actions in accelerating after the Allied ships and attempting to communicate with them by flashing light indicate a definite concern for friendly fire.

In the meantime, *Vampire* and *Thanet*, their primary weapons expended, raced south-east at full power. The Japanese, both during and following the war, believed the enemy had approached their anchorage from the shallow inshore waters to the south-east in the vicinity of Aceh and Layak Islands, after the moon had set and using the shadow of the mainland and islands as cover.[7] They never suspected that the destroyers had actually penetrated their screen from the north-east and that they had the run of the heavily defended anchorage for almost an hour.

Running Action

Night actions, when even commanding officers on their own bridges had a limited grasp of what was occurring around them, are generally the most difficult surface engagements of the period to reconstruct. Up to this point, the accounts recorded by both sides largely match. However, from the moment the first gunnery salvos were fired, perceptions diverge significantly and the narrative will now deal with both sides in turn. On the Allied side, neither Moran nor Davies cite any definite timings for

events following the 0318 sighting of *Shirayuki*, and time lapses in their reports can be interpreted in different ways.

Notwithstanding his later assertions of decisive action, Sugahara's *Shirayuki* took 16 minutes, a full 26 minutes after the initial report of enemy ships in the anchorage, to finally engage. Receiving no replies to her challenges, despite intentionally un-shading her signal lamp, *Shirayuki* eventually lit up *Thanet* with her powerful searchlight. This illumination, aided by the light of another vessel farther away to port, revealed both destroyers steaming hard on their line of retirement making considerable quantities of smoke in an effort to conceal their retreat. Davies, now trailing five cables astern of *Vampire*, immediately commenced a tight zigzag in a vain attempt to throw off the illumination as the first 5in salvo sailed over *Vampire* to hit the water off her starboard bow. The time was 0331, and very soon both ships were manoeuvring desperately under increasing fire.

Moran gave the order to open fire as the first enemy salvo was landing. Having intended to engage thin-skinned transports laden with troops and military stores, *Vampire's* gunners had ensured plentiful supplies of High Explosive (HE) shell at the guns. Instead of switching to the lower capacity Semi-Armour Piercing (SAP) rounds preferred for warship targets, the Australians engaged with what was to hand. Moran's appreciation was that alterations made by his force and the Japanese now placed both enemy ships to port, the nearer of the two firing at *Thanet* with the other locked in a duel with *Vampire*. The Australians mistakenly identified all the destroyers they sighted in the darkness as belonging to the old *Akikaze* or similar classes; although these would have been formidable opponents, the position was worse than Moran realised. With *Shirayuki* and her sisters rated at 34 knots in combat condition (at least on paper), there was no way the two old destroyers could outrun them and they certainly could not outgun them. The British and Australians were now fighting for survival.

On the bridge, *Vampire's* Gunnery Control Officer (GCO) had the director laid on a target at a range of 4,000 yards with no deflection set, the point of aim being the enemy's searchlight for the duration of the action. None of the combatants was fitted with radar, and the

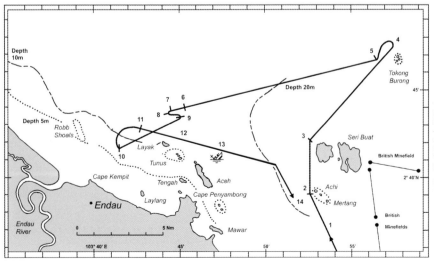

Vampire and Thanet track chart 0001-0400, 27 January 1942. (Drawn by the author)

1. *VAMPIRE & THANET* course 335°, 12kts
2. 0110: Course 360°, 12kts
3. Altered towards Tokong Burong
4. Sweep to the north of Tokong Burong
5. 0151: Altered course towards Endau, 15kts
6. 0237: Japanese destroyer bearing Green 30
7. 0240: 2nd Japanese destroyer ahead 600yds
8. 0242: *VAMPIRE* fires 2 torpedoes, increase to 25kts
9. Altered course SW, 15kts
10. 0313: Altered to 110°, 25kts
11. 0318: 3rd Japanese Destroyer off port bow
    VAMPIRE fires 1 torpedo, range 1,500yds
    THANET fires 4 torpedoes
12. Gun action with Japanese surface forces, 28kts
13. *THANET* lost in position 02° 41N 103° 47E
14. 0400: *VAMPIRE* to Singapore, 28kts

engagement would be fought by both sides using optical fire control equipment relying on illumination. Davies recorded that the enemy was obviously present in greater numbers than indicated by earlier intelligence from Singapore as they '…did not use star shells but [were] confident in the use of several searchlights.' With enemy searchlights providing perfect aiming points for the Allied gunners and escape into the darkness the only option, Vampire and Thanet's 24in searchlights remained shuttered in line with RN night fighting doctrine.

All four of Vampire's 4in guns fired in unison by director control, both forward guns on an extreme after bearing as the target was still well astern. Splashes from the first salvo were observed to fall well short and to the left of the target. A deflection correction of 'right four knots' and a standard night-spotting range adjustment of 'up 800 yards' were ordered to bring the next salvo closer to the target.[8] However, making a stable gunnery platform of his ship was not Moran's top priority; one enemy hit in a vital area could doom either of the Allied ships. Loss of fire control efficiency was accepted as Vampire was kept continuously under wheel to throw off the enemy's spotting corrections. Moran called violent course alterations by voicepipe to the coxswain on the helm a deck below in the wheelhouse throughout the gunnery engagement. As the action continued, the forward 'A' and 'B' guns found themselves masked for the ensuing four salvos while 'X' and 'Y's

second salvo threw up plumes of water in line, but still short of the target. Further 'up' corrections were applied, but shells continued to fall short and subsequently began to drift to the right of the target.

Thanet Crippled

The British gunners opened fire at a target fine on the port quarter with 'B' gun amidships and 'X' gun aft as shells began falling around their ship. Some minutes had elapsed between the Japanese opening fire and Thanet's guns getting into action, enough time for the Australians to fire three salvos and apply spotting corrections. As Thanet steamed amidst the towers of water engulfing her, Davies manoeuvred to cover Vampire before attempting to get behind his own smokescreen. But after firing only three salvos, a shell hit Thanet on the port side which penetrated the engine room and severed both the main and auxiliary machinery steam lines.

Neither Thanet nor Vampire was built with unitised machinery spaces to allow them to continue steaming on one shaft following the loss of a boiler or engine room. The machinery arrangements in both ships made them especially vulnerable to even a single hit due to the expendable nature of the small, mass-produced destroyer designs of their era. Two boiler rooms in series fed main

'X' Gun in action, HMAS Vampire, 1938. (Argus Newspaper Collection of Photographs, State Library of Victoria)

Thanet's *sister ship Admiralty 'S' class HMS Stronghold. Similar in appearance, she also served in the Far East; her Light Type Director and lack of an optical coincidence rangefinder is apparent from this photo taken from HMS Kanimbla, South of Sunda Strait, 28 January 1942.* (Lt-Cdr Donald Dykes, RANR(S) (Retd))

steam to two turbines and auxiliary steam to two turbo generators in the same engine room.

A 50.7lb 5in shell bursting in the forward end of the 108ft-long engine room, crammed with main and auxiliary machinery, could stop the ship, whereas a hit in the after part would certainly do so. With no emergency diesel generator, this one hit thus brought both shafts to a stop and caused power and lighting to fail throughout the ship. The old destroyer was felt to give a violent lurch while swinging to starboard and losing speed. She was soon dead in the water, her fate sealed. With *Thanet* fine on the port quarter, the Australians looked on as a large column of sparks shot skywards from the vicinity of the after torpedo tubes, followed by great clouds of steam from her uptakes lit by the enemy searchlights as boiler room personnel lifted their safety valves.

There was nothing at all that Davies or his men could now do to save *Thanet*. Only 'X' gun would bear on the enemy, its crew remaining in action until knocked out by shellfire. The whole after part of the ship was enveloped in escaping steam, rendering the area 'practically untenable'. It is not clear how many casualties were sustained in either the engine room or at 'X' gun, but the effects of the exploding Japanese shell in the confined machinery space and the resulting escape of high-pressure steam were potentially catastrophic. It was obvious to the Australians that *Thanet* was in a bad way. She was last sighted with a pronounced list to starboard as *Vampire* continued to race to the south-east, trading broadsides with her own assailant.

Vampire's *Escape*

Aboard *Vampire*, it appeared from the volume of fire being directed at her that she was being targeted by at least two ships, one possibly a cruiser. With Moran occupied manoeuvring the ship and making tactical decisions, the task of hitting the enemy from a very unsteady platform fell upon the GCO and his gunnery team. *Vampire's* fire control equipment had been state-of-the-art for destroyers in 1917 but was rudimentary by 1942 standards, its efficacy further degraded by the conditions under which the action was fought. The upper bridge mounted a nine-foot rangefinder and pedestal-mounted 'Light Type' director gun sight with fitted Henderson gyro firing gear on the centreline. Dumaresq rate and deflection instruments were also mounted on either side of the bridge. The central gunnery control position was the Transmitting Station (TS) on the forecastle deck below the wheelhouse.

In a daylight action, a Rate Officer on the bridge estimated enemy course and speed to be set on the Dumaresq. The TS received ranges electrically transmitted from the range taker. The rate at which the range was changing and estimated deflection from the Dumaresq operator, as well as range and deflection spotting corrections from the GCO, were received by voice-pipe. However, due to visual target estimation difficulties, the Rate Officer was usually dispensed with at night as was the Dumaresq due to its lack of a night sight. As the ship manoeuvred, the GCO would have found himself alone estimating deflection as well as the constantly and rapidly changing range rate, and factoring these variables into the spotting corrections passed to the TS.

In the TS, range and range rate were manually set on a Vickers Clock to determine gun range. Estimated deflection was passed by voicepipe from the TS back up to the director sight setter to be applied at the director; the director providing a training bearing directly to 'follow the pointer' receivers at the guns. Range and deflection were transmitted electrically, as well as by voicepipe, to the sight setters at each gun. If employing the director's Henderson gear with its separate telescope, the director layer kept the crosshairs of his night sight upon the enemy's searchlight and depressed his firing key. The electric firing circuits of all loaded guns would only be energised when the ship's roll corresponded with the firing angle, normally parallel to the horizontal plane, set on the director. Alternatively, the layer could employ the director's standard sights, and wait until his cross-wires rolled on before depressing the key to fire the guns instantaneously.

Gunnery conditions were good. The enemy ships kept up a high rate of fire using director systems supported by 'very good' searchlights. *Sendai* was fitted with three powerful 110cm (43.3in) lights and the destroyers a single, manually operated 90cm (35.4in) light. *Vampire*'s director and gun crews, all of them standing, had to battle against the ship's roll, yaw and constant alterations of course. Furthermore, everyone fighting the ship on the upper decks worked in the constant glare of enemy searchlights.

Viewing darkened targets through *Vampire*'s director telescope was difficult, and ranges would have had to be estimated. But with the enemy searchlights burning, neither the director nor the rangefinder had any trouble fixing upon points of light. The GCO would also have found spotting the fall of shot at the ranges indicated relatively straightforward, with HE shells exploding in calm water being shown up by background-attenuated light from the searchlights. However, dazzling muzzle flash, produced when incompletely burned gases momentarily ignited upon contact with air as they exited the barrel, could impair the night vision of control personnel. British cordite of the period produced a notoriously bright flash, and gunnery details within Moran's report appear to indicate that the Japanese were not using flashless cordite.[9]

Vampire was straddled several times but not hit, the nearest shell falling 25-30 yards to starboard of the engine room hatch, just aft of amidships. The destroyer that *Vampire* was exchanging fire with was now on her port beam and apparently overhauling her. Moran reported that *Vampire* attained a speed of 28 knots in comparatively shallow water during the action which was '...a most creditable performance for this ship.' It is not known how her *Fubuki* class opponents performed off Endau at full power but they should have easily had the edge on the Australians by a few knots. It should also be noted that *Vampire* lost speed every time she put her helm over to dodge the arrival of the next salvo.

With the large volume of incoming fire, Moran knew it would only take one hit in a machinery space, as with *Thanet*, to cripple his ship. To make matters worse, one of six 12.5in electric fans providing forced draught air, critical to the performance of the open-faced boilers, was giving trouble. Its failure would reduce available power

and result in the ship's speed falling to 25 knots, a potentially critical, if not fatal situation given present circumstances. Furthermore, the frequent alterations of course, combined with the gunfire smoke and flashes, searchlight beams, as well as the smoke screen made land fixes impossible and navigating the shallow confined waters exceedingly dangerous.

With no fitted hoists, ammunition supply parties manhandled ordnance from the forward and aft magazines and shell rooms to the upper decks. As the guns, firing in semi-automatic mode, recoiled and ejected spent cartridge cases onto the deck, the next shell and separate brass cartridge case combination had already been placed on the loading tray to the left of the breech by the two loading numbers. The tray worker pushed the tray in line with the open sliding breech, rammed the ammunition home with a clenched fist which automatically closed the breech, before pulling the tray clear for reloading and firing.

Vampire's target remained on the port beam, the Japanese evidently having opened out as the action developed. The sight setters received a range of 8,000 yards for the nineteenth salvo and raised the gun layer's gun sight on the left hand side of the mounting for the new range. The layer then used his elevation hand wheel to increase gun elevation and bring his telescope cross wires back onto the target. On the right hand side of the mounting, the trainer used his training hand wheel to line up his training receiver's black pointers to correspond with the director's red pointers.

With fire having drifted off to the right of the target, the GCO passed a deflection of two knots left. Corrections were applied and transmitted before the director layer depressed his trigger. This time, two 31lb 4in shells were seen to hit the target; orange flames were observed on either side of the searchlight, extinguishing it. Moran quickly checked fire, an electric 'push' on the bridge ringing bells at each gun, as the enemy disappeared in the darkness. The Australians believed these hits to have been sufficient to knock the Japanese ship out of the fight as she never re-engaged.

The GCO shifted target to another destroyer fine on the port quarter, the TS receiving the order 'Shoot!' Corrections were applied and the fire gong rang as the TS passed the order 'Fire!' to the director layer, who engaged with 'X' and 'Y' guns when his sights were on. But with the shell splashes invisible in the darkness, fire was again checked.

Moran now ordered a chemical smoke float cast overboard, not only to bolster his own smoke screen but to confuse the Japanese and possibly assist *Thanet*.[10] The British ship was still visible astern to the north-east illuminated by an enemy destroyer and taking fire. As well as gaining a lead on his pursuers, he also hoped to draw them over British minefields to the east of the engagement area. Despite his awareness of their positions, the tactic was still fraught with danger and took no account of the unknown field laid by the IJN in the area to seaward of Endau in the days leading up to the war. For the first time since the beginning of the gun action, *Vampire* was not illuminated or being fired upon as the float went over the side to add to the heavy funnel smoke streaming astern on her starboard quarter.

As the float bobbed in the ship's wake emitting thick white smoke, it suddenly lit up with flame and a shower of sparks. A ship on *Vampire*'s port quarter, presumably the cruiser with two widely spaced searchlights, engaged it. The Australians were momentarily illuminated again but not fired on, possibly because the searchlight was beyond its own effective range or because the beams aimed at the smoke float across *Vampire*'s wake obscured the ship from other ships within range. Moran saw his chance to completely shake off the enemy in their apparent confusion, and for just over half an hour the Australians, having successfully negotiated the narrow shallow channel to safety in a singular feat of navigation under fire, were merely spectators as they watched the searchlights and continuous gunfire astern. They formed the impression that enemy ships were actually engaging one another after mistaking the smoke float for *Vampire*, including a destroyer not showing a searchlight who was presumed to be their former pursuer.

While *Vampire*'s luck was holding on her run from the anchorage, *Thanet* settled deeper in the water soon after being immobilised. Under heavy but not particularly accurate fire, Davies gave the order 'Prepare to abandon ship'. When the enemy destroyers closed and their shooting improved, Davies gave the order to abandon *Thanet* before walking through his doomed ship to ensure everyone had escaped. While making his way forward from the engine room hatch past 'B' gun, a salvo struck somewhere on the port side and pitched him into the water, there to join the remainder of his crew weathering shell bursts and flying splinters.[11] Battered into a wreck by gun fire, but abandoned in good order, HMS *Thanet* rolled over to starboard and sank soon afterwards off Aceh Island, her large white battle ensign still seen to be flying from her foremast head.

The Japanese Picture

Unlike the Allied account, the Japanese report compiled by Rear-Admiral Hashimoto and his staff offers a clear timeline, but its authors are silent as to exactly why *Shirayuki* was taken by surprise and then took so long to engage the intruders. This may be explained by confusion created by *W-4*'s incorrect report. Furthermore, despite recording *Fubuki*'s 0305 'enemy' alarm and *W-4*'s 0315 signal confirming she had been attacked, the report also states that it was only after '...*Shirayuki* started to attack the enemy ship, [that] the rest of the fleet finally realised the enemy attack', suggesting a good degree of uncertainty within the Japanese force.

When fire was opened under searchlight illumination at 0331, *Shirayuki*'s target was the leading enemy destroyer, later identified as *Vampire*, at a range of 4,500 metres (4,900 yards). Few references regarding speeds for Japanese units were recorded, but accounts and Japanese machinery operating procedures indicate it may have taken some time for *Shirayuki* to accelerate and overhaul the intruders.[12] She reported several hits from her opening salvos, resulting in fires in the first destroyer, at which point the damaged enemy ship began laying down a smoke screen. However, at approximately 0333, *Shirayuki* suffered a complete loss of electrical power.

With the target fine on her starboard bow, the aft 5in mountings (Nos. 2 & 3) engaged on their forwardmost bearings of approximately 30 degrees. The muzzles of mounting No. 2 were firing directly above the main generator switchboard in the engine room and the blast tripped the main breaker to one of the ship's two 33kW steam-driven turbo generators. As both generators were running in parallel there was an immediate overload in the second unit, tripping its breaker as well. Power failed

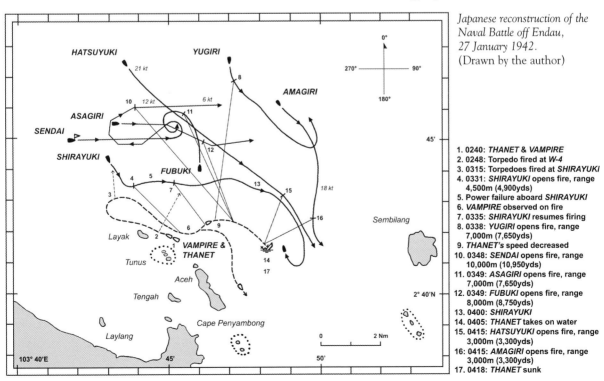

Japanese reconstruction of the
Naval Battle off Endau,
27 January 1942.
(Drawn by the author)

1. 0240: **THANET & VAMPIRE**
2. 0248: Torpedo fired at **W-4**
3. 0315: Torpedoes fired at **SHIRAYUKI**
4. 0331: **SHIRAYUKI** opens fire, range 4,500m (4,900yds)
5. Power failure aboard **SHIRAYUKI**
6. **VAMPIRE** observed on fire
7. 0335: **SHIRAYUKI** resumes firing
8. 0338: **YUGIRI** opens fire, range 7,000m (7,650yds)
9. **THANET**'s speed decreased
10. 0348: **SENDAI** opens fire, range 10,000m (10,950yds)
11. 0349: **ASAGIRI** opens fire, range 7,000m (7,650yds)
12. 0349: **FUBUKI** opens fire, range 8,000m (8,750yds)
13. 0400: **SHIRAYUKI**
14. 0405: **THANET** takes on water
15. 0415: **HATSUYUKI** opens fire, range 3,000m (3,300yds)
16: 0415: **AMAGIRI** opens fire, range 3,000m (3,300yds)
17. 0418: **THANET** sunk

Shirayuki, *Type I Fubuki Class, 11th Destroyer Division, as completed.* (Kure Maritime Museum, Japan)

throughout the ship, including supply to the gun mountings and searchlight, forcing *Shirayuki* to cease fire. It took engineering staff two minutes to get both generators back online, but a series of electrical problems plagued the ship for the ensuing 15 minutes.

The simultaneous restoration of power to the after gun mountings and the searchlight caused another overload that disabled the power training and elevation in both mountings. When their crews resumed firing, using torches to operate the manual training and elevation gear, the blast of all four guns firing simultaneously shorted fuses in mounting No. 2, knocking out power to the gun chamber as well as lighting. While the fuses were being changed, both mountings ceased firing for a minute before power was finally fully restored.

After *Shirayuki* restored electrical power at 0335 and struggled to overcome the ensuing blast-related difficulties aft, her gunnery team found only one ship visible, just outside of the enemy smoke screen and 2,800 metres (3,050 yards) distant. This ship, *Thanet*, was mistaken for the original target and taken under fire. It was not until 0338, seven minutes after *Shirayuki* commenced the gun action, that a second Japanese warship engaged. *Yugiri*, Captain Yamada's divisional leader, was steaming southeast from her patrol sector and opened fire at what was thought to be *Thanet*, 7,000 metres (7,650 yards) away on her starboard bow.

Seven minutes later, the Japanese observed that concentrated fire had slowed their target considerably, but

at least *Yugiri* had spotted *Vampire* as she signalled the squadron by Radio Telephone (R/T) at 0345 that 'The enemy is two destroyers.' Immediately upon receiving this information, Rear-Admiral Hashimoto issued his first order of the action by W/T, to 'Advance towards the enemy', to both *Yugiri* and Lt.-Commander Arai in *Asagiri*, the latter destroyer being just to the north-east of *Sendai*. At the same time Commander Fujita's *W-1*, somewhere to the north, engaged *Thanet* with her two 4.7in guns. However, Fujita soon decided that he might be interfering with other units chasing the fleeing enemy, and ceased fire after 12 rounds.

Sendai remained in her patrol sector manoeuvring at 12 knots. At 0348, she settled on an easterly course and Captain Shimazaki opened fire with six-gun broadsides on the same target being bombarded by the destroyers 10,000 metres (10,950 yards) to the south-east. One minute later, *Asagiri* and *Fubuki* (the latter being fine on *Sendai*'s port bow) opened fire at 7,000 meters (7,650 yards) and 8,000 metres (8,750 yards) respectively.

Upon opening fire, the flagship signalled the whole squadron by R/T (all further Japanese communications utilised this method unless otherwise noted) to 'Fire with searchlight illumination at the enemy destroyers'. At this point *Sendai* and four destroyers were illuminating and engaging the same target and it was soon apparent that their victim had been immobilised. *Yugiri* signalled at 0354 that a fire had broken out in one of the enemy destroyers. At about the same time, Sugahara in *Shirayuki* became concerned that congestion in the battle area was putting their own ships at risk of friendly fire and signalled Hashimoto recommending an order to check fire.

Hashimoto was not in a position to issue detailed instructions to his destroyers at this point. The enemy's position in relation to each of the Japanese ships was open to debate, and *Vampire*'s smokescreen wasn't making things any clearer. Hashimoto was also concerned that many of his ships were manoeuvring in close proximity to their targets upon receipt of *Shirayuki*'s report, and at 0355 advised them to 'Be careful [not to fire] at ships on our side'. This was amplified three minutes later to Destroyer Division 20's *Yugiri*, *Asagiri* and *Amagiri*, the last still steaming south from her patrol position, with the order

TABLE 5: 1st ESCORT UNIT: INITIAL OPENING OF FIRE AND RANGES, 27 JANUARY 1942

	Time	Range
Shirayuki	0331	4,500m (4,900yds)
Yugiri	0338	7,000m (7,650yds)
W-1	0345	Unknown
Sendai	0348	10,000m (10,950yds)
Asagiri	0349	7,000m (7,650yds)
Fubuki	0349	8,000m (8,750yds)
Amagiri	0415	3,000m (3,300yds)
Hatsuyuki	0415	3,000m (3,300yds)

Source: JACAR: Battle Report 3, Part 4, p.18, Artillery Battle Situation in the Night Battle at the Endau Mooring Area before the Dawn of January 27th; JDA, *Senshi Sosho Volume 24*, p.595 – Diagram of the Naval Battle of Endau.

TABLE 6: 1st ESCORT UNIT AMMUNITION EXPENDITURE AGAINST SURFACE ATTACK, 27 JANUARY 1942.

		Target – *Vampire*	Target – *Thanet*
W-4	4.7-inch	2	
Shirayuki	5-inch	18	82
Yugiri	5-inch		66
W-1	4.7-inch		12
Sendai	5.5-inch		72
Asagiri	5-inch		61
Fubuki	5-inch		102
Amagiri	5-inch		6
Hatsuyuki	5-inch		50

Source: JACAR: Battle Report 3, Part 4, p.18, Artillery Battle Situation in the Night Battle at the Endau Mooring Area before the Dawn of January 27th.

to 'Hold fire' in an attempt to clarify the situation.

Twelve minutes after the composition of the enemy force was confirmed, the Admiral endeavoured to take more resolute control of his six powerful destroyers and ensure the destruction of both intruders. He ordered *Yugiri* to attack the other ship at 0357, before three minutes later dividing his destroyer force in two in an attempt to regain control of the situation. Captain Shōji's Destroyer Division 11, *Hatsuyuki* (Divisional leader), *Shirayuki* and *Fubuki*, were ordered to concentrate on the enemy ship that *Sendai* was illuminating and sink it, while Captain Yamada's Destroyer Division 20 was to attack the other enemy ship. However, it was now too late to do any more than despatch the cornered *Thanet*, which at 0355 was observed to be stationary.

Vampire was last sighted by *Yugiri* at 0355 between Aceh and Sembilang Islands, disappearing into her own smoke-screen at high speed on a course of 120°. Her escape was not appreciated aboard *Sendai* for some time, as both divisional commanders in *Yugiri* and *Hatsuyuki* were asked whether the other enemy ship was visible. *Yugiri* confirmed at 0405 that only one ship, *Thanet*, was in sight. When she was again ordered to pursue the other ship, she clarified three minutes later that the she had lost sight of her in the smoke. At 0410 Hashimoto signalled 'If your ship is navigating in close range with the fleeing enemy, inform the name of your ship', but none of his ships remained in contact with the Australian destroyer and his order went unanswered.

Meanwhile, *Thanet* remained illuminated and under heavy fire. At 0400 *Shirayuki* reported her shells hitting the target, and five minutes later watched the British ship begin to settle by the stern. *Fubuki* was also firing fast and observed five or six hits at 0410. For Hashimoto, the scene was made somewhat clearer by his 0415 order for all ships using searchlight illumination to turn on their individual identification lights. At the same time, it was clear that the enemy ship caught by his forces was sinking, and he did not welcome *Hatsuyuki* and *Amagiri* opening fire on her at this point.

Hatsuyuki had steamed from the northernmost point of the anchorage patrol screen at a reported 21 knots, while *Amagiri* evidently approached from the north-east at a leisurely 18 knots. Both ships now engaged the stationary hulk visible to starboard at 3,000 metres (3,300 yards) but *Amagiri* ceased fire after only six rounds as a Japanese ship, most likely *Shirayuki*, fouled her range. *Hatsuyuki*, on the other hand, commenced with rapid broadsides and only checked fire after expending 50 rounds in a couple of minutes, despite Hashimoto directing *Shirayuki* (by flashing light) to order both newcomers to stop shooting. At the same time, he radioed Destroyer Division 11 to cease fire.

At 0418 *Shirayuki* reported 'The enemy ship has sunk', as *Thanet* finally succumbed to the combined firepower of eight Japanese warships. She was seen to go down 4,300 metres (4,700 yards) and 025° off Aceh Island.[13] Hashimoto now ordered Destroyer Division 11 to 'Leave one ship against the fleeing enemy destroyer' while the remainder resumed formation. Despite this somewhat ambiguous signal *Shirayuki*, in close proximity to where the British ship had sunk, signalled that she would '…now

go to capture the enemy cutters'. Her intentions were confirmed by Hashimoto at 0430 as the remaining ships of his force were directed to return to their original patrol positions, still on high alert. The flagship had not attempted to give chase at any point during the action and remained in her sector, even reducing speed to 6 knots while firing on *Thanet*. The Japanese official history attributed the decision to return the escorts to their patrol positions to the danger of British mines thought to have been laid to the south; however, this does not take into account the order to send a ship after *Vampire*.

Aftermath

Commander Davies, four officers and 61 ratings of *Thanet*'s crew are known to have evaded the Japanese in the days after the action and returned to Singapore, while one officer and 11 ratings were either killed in action or perished in the water. A further officer and 31 ratings were rescued by *Shirayuki*. The Lieutenant was held for interrogation by the IJN and survived the war, but the 30 men landed at Endau were never seen again.[14] They are presumed executed and disposed of in unmarked graves, a common enough occurrence during the Malayan campaign. Thus, a total of 42 British officers and men either lost their lives in the waters off Aceh Island or ashore at the hands of the Imperial Japanese Army.

Vampire found herself well clear of the battle area by 0400, 18 minutes before *Thanet* went down. The defective boiler room fan finally failed on the run home, but the Australian destroyer arrived alone at Sembawang naval base at 1000 having suffered no damage or casualties. Her gunners had fired 74 rounds with no misfires or failures. Moran congratulated his gunnery team on an impressive performance in light of the fact that the new ship's company had not conducted a full calibre firing; for the GCO, 20-year-old Temporary-Acting Sub-Lieutenant Percy Thomson, it was his first-ever shoot!

Kansai Maru completed unloading and sailed under escort in the early hours of 28 January, while *Canberra Maru* followed around noon with the remainder of the force. The First Escort Unit arrived back in Cam Ranh Bay on 30 January to be joined by Admiral Kurita's covering force the same day.

Despite the loss of *Thanet*, Commander Moran believed that he and his ship's company had outwitted and outfought a vastly superior Japanese force in the early hours of 27 January. In many ways, he was right. However, notwithstanding the fact that his force engaged the enemy only after they had searched the anchorage and failed to find the transports, the outcome of the battle, if somewhat fortuitously, remains a victory for Rear-Admiral Hashimoto. He not only sank one of the enemy warships sent against him, but the landing operation that was his responsibility remained unhindered.

Analysing the Action

The naval action off Endau was the second surface engagement of the Pacific War, and despite Japanese propaganda claims of a resounding victory, the less-than-satisfactory results against a weak adversary prompted disquiet within the IJN. The outcome added to a Japanese tactical error three days earlier in which the escorting 4th Torpedo Squadron left an amphibious landing at Balikpapan, Borneo, exposed to chase a submarine contact, just as four United States Navy destroyers penetrated the anchorage and destroyed four out of twelve transports.

As at Balikpapan, the well-documented IJN pre-war training did not prevent the unsatisfactory result at Endau. The small coordinated Allied force of ships, vessels designed for agility and low visibility at night, initially enjoyed a decided tactical advantage against the defensively dispersed Japanese before concentration of numbers and firepower was able to seize the initiative.

Despite intelligence predicting a surface attack by the Royal Navy, a number of Japanese failings and delays added to the inevitable difficulties contemporary navies faced in gaining situational awareness in the dark. Poor lookout performance, *W-4*'s delayed and incorrect enemy report, *Shirayuki*'s failure to report her initial actions to the flagship, together with valid friendly-fire concerns appear to have resulted in a significant degree of confusion within the escort force. It took until *Yugiri*'s 0345 confirmation of two enemy destroyers for command to coordinate a response. Effective control was established only after the battle was for all intents and purposes over.

Rear-Admiral Hashimoto's force had actioned an existing battle plan, not found within surviving documents, to deal with an incursion, and his subsequent report was candid in his appreciation of Japanese failings, including his own. Overall, command and control of the 1st Escort Unit was not well integrated and had failed to respond quickly enough. Not only did the force suffer from a lack of co-ordination between the 3rd Torpedo Squadron and the 1st Minesweeper Division, but integration problems (not explained) were also acknowledged between the 11th and 20th destroyer divisions: 'The battle off Endau did not have a well co-ordinated command because the battle had ships from the 11th and 20th Destroyer units as well as the 1st Minesweeper unit.'

This should not come as a surprise. Vice-Admiral Kondō Nobutake, commander of all IJN forces assigned to the southern area of operations, of which the Malaya Seizure Force was a component, described the formation as a makeshift unit without experience of training together to fight at night.[15] This was cited as a contributory factor in his decision not to concentrate his available strength and force a surface action with *Prince of Wales* and *Repulse* the night before they were destroyed by naval aircraft.

Hashimoto identified failures in not detecting the enemy until it was almost too late, not alerting the remainder of the force to the enemy's presence early enough, and the lack of a swift counter-attack. While admitting that the enemy had been difficult to see after the moon had set, especially against the shadow of Aceh Island, Hashimoto considered the failure of *W-4* and *Shirayuki* to realise they were under attack until they were at the point of being sunk by torpedoes unacceptable. *W-4*'s ensuing failure to report the incursion by radio also critically delayed other ships getting into the fight. When

it materialised, the Japanese response was far too slow, lacked aggression and concentrated needlessly on the crippled *Thanet*. *Shirayuki*'s shifting of fire to *Thanet* saw the other Japanese ships concentrate upon her and lose track of *Vampire*.

However, Hashimoto did not attribute all the blame to his subordinates. He observed that command in *Sendai* was located too far away from the scene of the action, and that he had '…failed to issue a timely or appropriate order for the pursuit.' Furthermore, the fear of steaming into an area sown with British mines hampered the chase and eventually led to its cancellation. 'Regretfully, we let the enemy get away'.

In Singapore, Rear-Admiral Spooner believed that despite the loss of *Thanet*, the way in which the action was fought would have a positive effect on the RN in the Far East, in that they would now feel more than a match for the Japanese when on equal terms. Wildly optimistic reports from airmen, coupled with erroneous observations from *Thanet* survivors the following morning, also led to a belief that the two transports had indeed sunk and that an enemy destroyer had been destroyed by her own forces in the dark. Whilst friendly fire, based on Australian observations as well as Japanese concerns, is entirely possible, no actual damage was done.[16] Commander-in-Chief Eastern Fleet, Vice-Admiral Sir Geoffrey Layton in Colombo, believed that Moran had '…handled his force well, and fought an admirable action'.

The Allied destroyers were somewhat unlucky not to hit either *W-4* or *Shirayuki* after surprising both ships, but all navies of the period found hitting small targets with torpedoes statistically unlikely. Japanese destroyer doctrine, at least as promulgated in October 1943, held that enemy 'Destroyers will be put out of action by gunfire. Torpedoes will be used only when absolutely necessary.' *Vampire* running and manoeuvring wildly was never a good target, whilst the stationary *Thanet* would have been a waste of a torpedo. Once engaged, the Australians fought an intelligent action but one which they were fortunate to survive. Under attack by qualitatively superior destroyers, Moran not only manoeuvred aggressively to throw off his opponent's aim, but refrained from using his searchlight in accordance with British doctrine. The First World War had taught the RN that searchlights were generally more of a danger to the illuminating ship, a lesson the Japanese and Americans would learn for themselves later that year.[17]

Firmly on the defensive, Moran had no alternative but to continue steaming for safety when *Thanet* was immobilised. Engaged by numerous Japanese vessels, reversing course to support the British destroyer would have only guaranteed *Vampire*'s destruction. He did not know the extent of *Thanet*'s damage and evidently held out some hope of her escaping in the confusion. That he did make good his escape from ships which, on paper, should have caught and sunk him, is a perfect example of circumstances on the day rendering theoretical comparisons of competing ship designs irrelevant. While the *Fubuki* class destroyers should have enjoyed a tangible speed advantage over the elderly Australian ship, the irresolute tactical employment of the 3rd Torpedo Squadron off Endau allowed *Vampire* to slip away.

Moran commented on the apparent inability of the enemy to operate effectively at night, expressing his amazement that two enemy ships had allowed *Vampire* and *Thanet* to pass them at point-blank torpedo range without apparent reaction. To him it indicated either very poor lookout-keeping or night blindness. 'In fact the ability at night fighting of these destroyers and the cruiser was very poor and very lucky for us'.

Not surprisingly for a confused battle fought in complete darkness, establishing exactly who was firing at whom is far from straightforward. British, Australian and Japanese reports, all with their own strengths and weaknesses, differ significantly. These accounts point towards a *Shirayuki* versus *Vampire* gunnery duel beginning at 0331. However, *Shirayuki* concludes this action barely two minutes later with her loss of power having fired 18 rounds (three broadsides), while *Vampire* fired 70 to 72 rounds under heavy return fire against the same, clearly observed target.

Although Japanese war diaries from this period are considered quite reliable, the fact that they document only 20 shells, including the two discredited rounds from *W-4* being fired at *Vampire*, and no fewer than 456 at *Thanet*, suggests something seriously amiss in their reconstruction of events. The Japanese record the gun action lasting 47 minutes: from 0331 to 0418. If *Sendai*'s opening salvo at 0348 coincides with Moran's appreciation of a cruiser firing on his smoke float approximately 30 minutes before gunfire ceased, it fits neatly within the timeline and indicates *Vampire* being in action for around 15 minutes.

Despite their weapons having a theoretical firing interval of three to four seconds, Australian gunners in 'V' & 'W' class destroyers were trained to fire every 7.5 seconds (or eight rounds per minute) with the ship yawing and periodically changing course. However, maximum firing rate was only sustained once the range was established and rapid salvos ordered, which did not occur at Endau. Firing 70 to 72 rounds at her initial target (approximately 20 broadsides and salvos) in the assumed 15-minute time frame equates to a firing interval of 45 seconds – a realistic estimate taking into account the need to spot and apply corrections with the ship constantly under wheel. *Vampire*'s action was over by approximately 0346.

Lt.-Commander Sugahara's account also fails to explain why, if he did engage *Thanet* from 0335 at only 2,800 metres, it took *Shirayuki* 43 minutes to close and expend 83 rounds sinking a target disabled soon after the commencement of the action. Nor does it account for the 'considerable number of near misses' she experienced from return fire, as they certainly did not come from *Thanet*. The confused nature of the battle makes it impossible to account for these critical discrepancies, but it appears that *Shirayuki* was indeed *Vampire*'s opponent.

With only *Shirayuki* and, from 0338, *Yugiri* in action before the Australians disengaged, it is possible that *Yugiri*'s fire on two ships laying smoke beyond the effective range of her searchlight may have been responsible for both the fatal hit on *Thanet*, as well as additional fire the Australians believed was being directed against them. Whether *Sendai* initially opened fire at the smoke float or

not, she was certainly illuminating *Thanet* 12 minutes later. Thus, *Asagiri* and *Fubuki* also concentrated their opening fire on the crippled destroyer. The one certainty is that in engaging so late *Hatsuyuki* and *Amagiri* only fired at the British ship.

The other major anomaly within accounts of the action is that of damage. Only minor blast damage was reported in *Asagiri*, caused by the after guns firing on their forward-most bearings – damage easily repaired by ship's company. *Shirayuki* maintained that she was not hit during the encounter, only reporting a single serious casualty from a shell splinter. Conversely, she was also adamant that she had set *Vampire* on fire.

Conclusion

In the wider context of the Malayan Campaign, Endau was a minor, largely inconclusive skirmish quickly consigned to the footnotes of history. The importance of the action lies in the impression of Japanese night fighting incompetence it created amongst their adversaries. Following receipt of the Endau action reports, Vice-Admiral Layton signalled Allied commands on 13 February that the Japanese Navy had considerable difficulty fighting at night.[18] He stated that the Japanese '…do not usually succeed in seeing before being seen and are very liable to confusion, rash use of searchlight illumination and opening fire on their own side… It seems therefore that we should exploit this feature … to the utmost and our policy should be to seek night actions by every means.'[19] With little to no information on the subsequent night actions off Java available to the Allies, the mistaken impression thus formed influenced Allied thinking until the Battle of Savo Island on 8 August 1942, when the Japanese achieved a stunning victory over a combined Australian and American force.

In contrast to the prevailing myth of the IJN as masters of night fighting, the battles of early 1942 indicate that the IJN's performance often fell short of what was expected of it. Endau is one of those examples.[20] The Australian and British navies, on the other hand, were well trained, confident and experienced in fighting at night, having demoralised the Italian Navy in nocturnal actions in the Mediterranean. When the Americans, with a combination of hard-won experience, superior materiel and the mastery of radar turned the tables on the Japanese, such myths were demolished.

Acknowledgments:
A two-part version of this article was published in the Naval Historical Society of Australia's *Journal of Australian Naval History*, Volume 8, No. 2, September 2011 and Volume 9, No. 1, March 2012. The author would like to particularly thank Captain Ian Pfennigwerth RAN (Retd.), former editor of the *Journal* and one of Australia's most prominent naval historians, for his wide-ranging support over the last decade as well as the Australian War Memorial's Haruki Yoshida and Colonel Tim Gellel, Australian Army, for their excellent Japanese translations. Technical advice offered by John Brooks, Vincent P. O'Hara, John Roberts and Commander John Smith RAN (Retd.) is also greatly appreciated.

Principle Sources:

National Archives of Australia (NAA), MP1185/8, Item 1932/2/3, HMAS 'Vampire' Report of Operation off Endau, Operation off Endau 26th / 27th January, 1942.

Japan Centre for Asian Historical Records (JACAR), The National Institute for Defence Studies, Ministry of Defence, Tokyo, Japan: Detailed engagement report and wartime log book from January 1 to 30, 1942, 3rd Torpedo Squadron.

Bôeichô Bôei Kenshûjo Senshishitsu (Military History Department, National Institute of Defence Studies, the Defence Agency) ed. *Hitô, Marê hômen kaigunshinkô sakusen* (*The Philippine Islands and Malaya Areas: Naval Advance Operations*). Senshi Sôsho Volume 24, Tokyo: Asagumo Shinbunsha, 1969.

Footnotes:

1   Japanese names are presented as family name followed by given name.

2   The patrol boats are not identified in available primary and secondary Japanese sources.

3   Kurita had detached the heavy cruisers *Mogami* and *Mikuma* and destroyer *Uranami* to patrol off Indochina, as well as the aircraft carrier *Ryūjō* and destroyer *Shiokaze* to directly support the invasion of the Anambas Islands. *Ryujo*'s aircraft played no part in the Endau operation.

4   *Vampire*'s bridge torpedo control equipment comprised a portable torpedo control disk to calculate the director angle for maximum target speeds of 35 knots. The angle was set on separate pedestal-mounted torpedo deflection sights either side of the bridge which were graduated for the speed settings of the ship's torpedoes. This process took some time, especially if additional adjustments were required. Modern British ships combined these functions in the Torpedo Sight Type B. Type H firing pistols were located adjacent to the sights together with voicepipes to the tubes. A central control position mounted separate Graham's electrical order and deflection transmitters to the mounting and a 'Tube Ready' lamp box. The TR (Triple Revolving) Mk I mountings were fitted with an identical deflection sight (and control disk) for local control, voicepipe, order receiver, reply transmitter, deflection receiver and firing buzzer. *Thanet*'s arrangement was similar except for push box firing pistols, Chadburn's mechanical telegraph system in lieu of *Vampire*'s electrical system, firing buzzers and rattlers on fore and after DR (Double Revolving) Mk IV mountings respectively operated by pushes on the bridge. With no reply transmitter, acknowledgment of telegraph orders was via bridge gongs energised by pushes at the tubes.

5   American destroyers also mistook 711-tonne Japanese minesweepers for destroyers at the Battle of Balikpapan.

6   It is possible that the last-second fire control solution resulted in a snap shot. An operator could estimate deflection on the torpedo sight itself if, as often happened at night, there was insufficient time to employ the control disk.

7   Admiral Mikawa achieved a similar advantage against HMAS *Canberra* and USS *Chicago* on his initial approach during the Battle of Savo Island on 9 August 1942, allowing him to engage before his targets could react. The side which first achieved a fire control solution at night invariably held the advantage during both world wars.

8   British gunnery and torpedo control measured lateral movement across the line of sight in knots – an angular, as opposed to speed value.

9   Flashless cordite charges, better described as reduced flash, were defined by the RN as '…unlikely to attract the attention of the naked eye under normal atmospheric conditions at ranges of 3,000 to 4,000 yards' at night. Aside from star shell, such charges for guns up to 5.25in were only just making their way to the fleet by June 1942 and would not have been carried by *Vampire* at Endau. Despite reliable English-language sources stating the IJN employed such charges, Moran observed enemy gun flashes from considerable distances during the battle.

10 The white chemical smoke reflected light, making it impenetrable to searchlight beams at night.

11 Claims made many years later of the Japanese machine gunning survivors in the water are not supported by contemporary reports.

12 The Japanese destroyers were reportedly steaming at 12 knots, known as 'Standard Speed'. To develop the revolutions required to accelerate from 'Standard' to a nominal destroyer 'Battle Speed 4' or 30 knots theoretically took 15 minutes 30 seconds with a further four minutes and 30 seconds to the highest standardised speed of 32 knots known as 'Battle Speed 5'. A *Fubuki* cruising at 12 knots, but at immediate notice for speeds over 21 knots, powered her two shafts via cruising turbines coupled to intermediate stage induction turbines referred to in the IJN as 'simple turbines'. Upon the order to accelerate, speed would be slowly increased using the simple turbines before disconnecting cruising turbines between 198rpm (20 knots) and 208rpm (21 knots). Connection of the shafts' high- and low-pressure turbines, and disconnecting of the simple turbines, could not be undertaken until the latter's pressure fell to a nominal pressure in the first stage whilst accelerating.

13 *Thanet*'s wreck lies in 18 metres of water in position 02°41.79N, 103°47.44E, but has been heavily salvaged to the point of destruction.

14 British and Japanese archival research conducted during the late 1990s by RN veteran Geoff Drummond failed to uncover any trace of the men, and their fate remains a mystery.

15 Kondō used the word *ugōnoshū*, 'rabble', in describing the improvised nature of the unit.

16 Friendly fire incidents at night were not uncommon in the Pacific during 1942.

17 Japanese doctrine laid heavy emphasis on fighting with searchlight illumination, with star shell available to be employed by cruiser flagships to clarify the situation over a wide area or if searchlights were considered ineffectual. Cruisers and destroyers would open fire at 9,000 and 6,000m respectively with corresponding optimum battle ranges of 5,000 and 3,000m.

18 C-in-C Eastern Fleet signal to Australian and New Zealand Naval Boards, American, British, Dutch, Australian Naval Command (ABDAFLOAT), Admiralty and Admiralty delegation Washington, 1227Z 13/2/42.

19 A 24 January report from the Dutch submarine *K16* of a Japanese destroyer being sunk by gunfire in an area devoid of Allied warships was also cited, as well as fragmentary reports of the Battle of Balikpapan.

20 In addition to Balikpapan, the Battle of the Java Sea was beset by numerous Japanese tactical errors while the Battle of Sunda Strait actually commenced with HMAS *Perth* and USS *Houston* between the widely dispersed escort and their dependent transports.

THE SUBMARINE *MARIOTTE,*
Known as 'The Toothbrush'

Nicknamed 'the toothbrush', the submarine *Mariotte* was one of the most distinctive early submarine designs. For many years she held the record for underwater speed. In this article **Philippe Caresse** looks at how she came to be built, and at her subsequent career, which ended with her loss while attempting to penetrate the Dardanelles.

Edme Mariotte was a French priest and physicist; he was born in Dijon c.1620 and died in Paris on 12 May 1684. A member of the first Academy of Sciences from 1668, he was responsible for the law which states that the volume of a gas varies inversely as the pressure. He gave his name to one of the earliest submarines to serve in the French Navy, a boat with an unusual silhouette and remarkable performance characteristics.

The *Mariotte* emerged from a competition initiated by the Navy Ministry on 6 February 1906 for a submersible of 530 tonnes, which was to have sufficient surfaced speed to accompany a squadron of battleships and an endurance of 100nm in the dived condition.

Ingénieur de 1ère classe Charles Radiguer proposed a design with moderate buoyancy and high freeboard which would have good sea-keeping qualities. The hull-form had an unusually high length/beam ratio to secure high speed, and the silhouette was unusual in that it featured an exceptionally high casing forward which served as a breakwater when the submarine was running on the surface. This particular feature was responsible for the submarine's nickname 'brosse à dents' (Eng: toothbrush).

Radiguer submitted his project to the Navy Minister Gaston Thomson, who accepted it in December 1906.

Characteristics

The hull was divided into nine compartments, with five internal trim tanks, an internal central ballast tank and three external ballast tanks, with a total volume of 70.3m³. The hull was fitted with six pairs of lifting rings of cast steel, which were faired into the casing. To ensure the continuity of the hull they were filled with tallow and covered by sheets of lead. Two lead safety weights were housed in the keel and could be released by a single lever located in the control room.

The keel of the submarine was painted in Schweinfurth green and the upper works were dark green on red lead.

The conning tower, which was of non-magnetic steel, was 1.68 metres above the waterline, and was fitted with scuttles for the helmsman and the lookouts. The raised

CHARACTERISTICS

Displacement (light):	544.50 tonnes light, 633.64 tonnes dived
Length:	64.75m pp, 61.53m wl
Beam (max.):	4.30m max., 3.31m wl
Draught (max.):	3.82m
Freeboard (fwd):	2.47m fwd, 0.57m aft
Depth (keel to CT):	7.25m
Armament:	four bow torpedo tubes two Drzewiecki drop collars eight 450mm torpedoes
Propulsion:	two Sautter & Harlé 6-cylinder, 4-stroke diesels, 2 x 700CV two Breguet electric motors, 2 x 500CV
Speed (max.):	14.20 knots surfaced, 11.70 knots dived
Diesel fuel:	16.58 tonnes
Radius (surfaced):	1658nm at 10kts, 1200nm at 12kts, 829nm at 14kts
Radius (dived):	143nm at 5kts, 57nm at 8kts, 30nm at 11kts
Maximum diving depth:	35 metres
Complement:	3 officers, 6 petty officers, 23 men

forward casing, which was in the form of a breakwater, housed the Drzewiecki drop collars for the torpedoes, the windlass, a dinghy, the compass for course/bearing, the telephone buoy and the surface galley.

A 640kg grapnel was fitted in a well located between the torpedo tubes; the 26cm cable was 120m long. Unusually, the *Mariotte* was equipped with rudders fore and aft; there were also two pairs of diving planes, one forward, the other aft.

The submarine was fitted with an 89mm steel towing hawser, but a ministerial instruction of 27 May 1911 stipulated that the *Mariotte* should not be used for towing.

There was a Type C day periscope and a Type F periscope for use at night. There were three compasses:

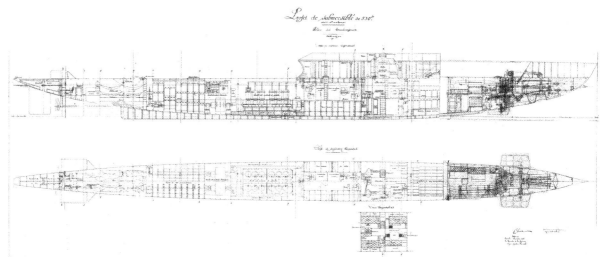

General arrangement plans for Mariotte, *dated Paris December 1906. (CAA)*

the Mle 1905 magnetic compass for course was mounted at the forward end of the conning tower; a second was housed in the forward section and could be raised 1.2m above the casing; and the third was an Anschütz gyro compass in the control room.

The electric motors were powered by two groups of 124-cell batteries. Each was divided into two half-batteries of 62 cells which could be coupled together in series or in parallel. Lighting on board was normally from a 115V circuit, while the emergency circuit was 12V. The two diesel engines were started by the electric motors, which drove two shafts fitted with bronze propellers 1.72m in diameter each weighing 445kg. The fuel tanks had a volume of 20.42m³.

The accommodation for the crew was as follows. The non-commissioned personnel were housed in the after compartment, which was fitted with twelve bunks and seven hammocks, together with two pull-down tables and lockers. The petty officers had three bunks and three hammocks in the forward compartment, immediately abaft the torpedo tubes; the compartment was fitted with two washbasins and a table. The officer accommodation was directly beneath the control room, to which it was connected by a vertical ladder. In this relatively confined space was the captain's sleeping cabin, to starboard, equipped with a bunk, a washbasin and various storage units. To port was the captain's dining room, with a sofa, table and shelving. Abaft the captain's accommodation were the two sub-lieutenants' cabins, each with a sofa, a table and a washbasin. Opposite the access ladder was a bottle-type WC. There were further bottles in the battery

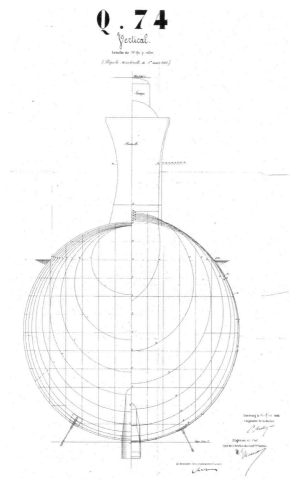

Body plan dated Cherbourg 1st March 1908. (CAA)

One of the two 4-stroke, 6-cylinder diesel engines, which were built by Sautter & Harlé. (DR)

The Mariotte *on trials at Cherbourg. The doors for the Drzewiecki torpedo drop collars are open in the raised casing forward.* (F.C. collection)

Diving trials of the Mariotte *in the Cherbourg roads in August 1911.* (Private collection)

This image of the Mariotte *during her speed trials is of poor quality, but is unusual in showing a jury-rigged compass platform on the forward casing and officers seated forward of the conning tower.* (DR)

compartment, and one for use on the surface in the raised forward section. For the preparation of meals, there was an electric galley in the lower torpedo tube compartment and an oil-fuelled stove in the raised section. There was sufficient stowage for twelve days' provisions.

Service History

The order for the *Mariotte* was placed on 31 December 1906. The submarine was laid down at Cherbourg on 30 March 1908 and launched on 2 February 1911. Only the starboard electric motor was in place, as the port-side unit was already under repair. The hull was immediately docked, and the trial to ensure watertightness of the hull took place on the 9th.

The captain of the *Mariotte*, appointed from 1st January 1911, was *lieutenant de vaisseau* (LV) André Matha (1873-1915).[1] Matha had taken part in the first expedition to the Antarctic led by Jean-Baptiste Charcot. He would later be appointed, together with *capitaine de vaisseau* (CV) Du Merle, to the inquest into the near-sinking of the submarine *Rubis* on 4 August due to defective ballast pipework.

From 3 May to 21 June the port-side electric motor was re-installed following repairs, and trials of the *Mariotte* followed for five days. From the end of June to mid-July the submarine was docked for a refit and repairs to her port-side motor. Various failures in the propulsion machinery immobilised her during this period, the incidents continuing through 1911 into 1912. The official diving trials took place between 8 and 22 August, and tests on the torpedo-launching apparatus ensued until 22 September.

In early September, following the embarkation of the batteries and adjustments to the starboard electric motor, *Mariotte* underwent speed trials in the dived condition; she achieved 11 knots, easily surpassing the record currently held by the submarine *Archimède* – a record she would hold for 35 years. On 21 November she successfully attempted a 25-metre dive. However, on 27 December 1911 the air heater of a Type 1909 R torpedo in the port-side upper tube exploded, resulting in some minor damage.

On 25 March the journal *Le Yacht* reported the first trials of the diesel engines. These were delivered three years later than specified in the contract because factory

The Mariotte, *winner of the 1906 submarine design competition, at sea.* (SHM)

trials had been protracted. When finally embarked, the engines were judged satisfactory once the sump oil and the compressors had been changed.

The diesel engines were installed from 1st March to 28 July 1912. Following numerous breakdowns, the official trials took place from 23 October to 11 December. On 14 December it was declared that the submarine had successfully run full-power trials for six hours along the outer harbour wall at Cherbourg. She then undertook a 10-metre dive, which took only 25 seconds, and the trials were pronounced satisfactory. Successful torpedo firings following at the end of January.

After a complete overhaul of her propulsion machinery, the *Mariotte* was commissioned (*armement définitif*) on

Left and below: *Two early views of the* Mariotte, *whose distinctive configuration earned her the nickname 'the toothbrush'.* (DR/Private collection)

Members of Mariotte's crew relaxing on deck as she returns from a sortie in the Cherbourg roads. (Private collection)

5 February 1913. A ministerial despatch dated 16 January had already assigned her to the 2nd *escadrille* of the 2nd Light Squadron of submarines based at Calais. She would join her new grouping on 11 February and would conduct several training sorties in the Channel.

On 20 February the *Mariotte* visited Brest and moored in the first basin of the commercial port. In the early afternoon, Rear-Admiral Favereau inspected the boat. Towards the end of his visit, two seamen attempted to light the oil-fuelled galley stove at the end of the raised forward section, which was used when the ship was on the surface. The stove promptly exploded, setting fire to the uniforms of the seamen, who had no choice but to jump into the water. Initially treated in the offices of the port, they were subsequently sent to hospital; however, their injuries were not serious. The submarine left Brest on 28 February to continue her navigation training. She called in at Cherbourg on 9 April, having conducted exercises with the destroyer *Escopette* and the submarines *Volta*, *Brumaire* and *Pluviôse*, with visits to Boulogne and Le Havre.

The *Mariotte* returned to Cherbourg around 20 April for repairs to one of her diving planes which had been damaged by a wave. Following these repairs she would visit Rouen with the *Escopette* and the submarine *Frimaire*. On 9 May the destroyer and the *Mariotte* visited Brest, then Quiberon. After conducting torpedo firings, the 2nd Light Squadron called in at Lorient, Brest and Cherbourg, returning to Calais for the visit of the King of Denmark. There followed a period of routine activity for the next few months then, on 22 September, the *Mariotte* and the *Nivôse* arrived in Brest for a series of exercises. On 1st October LV Auguste Joseph Pierre

Fabre took over command of the submarine.[2]

In 1914 the Trials Commission reported:

> The *Mariotte* is sensitive to the helm both on the surface and when dived, but when surfaced her handling is affected by the wind. The boat behaves well with a head sea or with the sea on the beam; however, with a following sea the boat only rises when the swell reaches the breakwater forward; the casing fills rapidly but drains slowly, causing the boat to wallow. The buoyancy of the submarine (15.5%) is clearly insufficient: the forward section does not rise sufficiently with the swell, and the after section not at all.
>
> The armament of the submarine comprises four internal torpedo tubes. That gives her an advantage over other boats: it means that with her two [internally stowed] reserve torpedoes she has six torpedoes which can be readily accessed at sea, which are protected from the waves and also from the effects of pressure when diving to extreme depths.
>
> In conclusion, the *Mariotte* is an exceptional type of submarine which has met all the targets set for her except in respect of her speed and radius on the surface at the designed 10 knots. She dives well, and the well-designed hull form has made possible an impressive speed of 11.5 knots underwater. The four internal bow tubes and the two lockers for reserve torpedoes allow her to maintain six torpedoes in a good state of maintenance in all conditions. Our only reservation is that improvements in buoyancy and stability would have ensured better sea-keeping when running on the surface.

Unfortunately the submarine's log went down with the boat, so it is difficult to be precise regarding her activity

The Mariotte *moored in the Carnot basin of the port of Calais. Behind her: the submarines* Brumaire, Volta *and* Nivôse. *(DR)*

The Mariotte *at the moorings of the submarines of the 2nd* escadrille *of the 2nd Light Squadron based at Calais.* (Private collection)

The destroyer Escopette, *which accompanied Louis Blériot during his aerial crossing of the Channel, with the* Mariotte *on the right of the picture.* (Private collection)

during the first months of the Great War, notably her transfer to Toulon and her sorties off the coasts of Provence.

However, with the opening of operations in the Dardanelles, several French submarines were despatched to the area. Their objective was to penetrate the straits, infested with mines and anti-submarine nets, with a strong current descending from the Sea of Marmara into the Aegean, and to attack enemy shipping with torpedoes. In November 1914, the submarines *Faraday* and *Le Verrier* were tasked with surveillance of the zone, as their limited radius of action and the inadequacies of their machinery did not permit them undertake such an aggressive mission. At 03.20 on 15 January 1915 the *Saphir* penetrated the straits and foundered four hours later, having made it as far

as Koum Kaleh. Having freed herself, she again ran aground around midday on a beach at Nagara. With her engines full astern, *Saphir* suddenly freed herself but sank in 70 metres of water. Having released her safety weights, the submarine broke the surface only to be met by artillery fire. The only choice open to her captain, LV Fournier, was to scuttle his submarine.

On 1st May 1915 it was the turn of the *Joule* to be lost; she sank with all her crew after striking a mine.

As the *Mariotte* possessed both the speed and radius to pass through the straits, it was no surprise to find the boat assigned to the French Dardanelles squadron. She left Toulon in early July 1915, and making a number of stops on the way for maintenance and replenishment, arrived at Lemnos having apparently suffered no major problems.

The Mariotte *moored at Lemnos in July 1915.* (SHM)

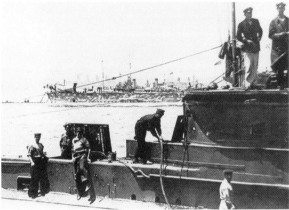

The British submarine E 14 *getting underway at Moudros in July 1915. The* Mariotte *can be seen in the background.* (DR)

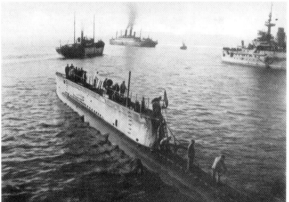

Mariotte *leaving the moorings of the* Gaulois *on the evening of 25 July 1915. On the right, the battleship* Charlemagne. (Moreau collection)

While awaiting her turn to join the action, the *Mariotte* was moored with the battleship *Gaulois*. On 25 July, she received her orders and departed Moudros with a view to entering the Dardanelles the following night. Captain Fabre had made a reconnaissance flight over the straits and had studies the routes taken by the British submarines. The report he made following the loss of the *Mariotte* is reprinted here.

The report of LV Farbre:

Left the anchorage at Moudros at 1800 on 25 July 1915. Made a test dive in the outer anchorage to check all equipment functioning correctly. Remained submerged for approximately 15 minutes. Dive successful. Set course for Sedd-el-Bahr under the escort of a destroyer, arriving around 2330. Moored to the stern of the destroyer *Poignard* and spent two hours recharging the batteries using the submarine's own engines. There was a full moon and the sea was flat calm. At 0312 on 26 July let go moorings and set course for the straits, rounding Sedd-el-Bahr Head (Cape Helles) at a visual distance of 400 metres. The course we were due to follow, part surfaced and part

dived, had been carefully located on the map following the indications in the reports of the British submarine captains who had successfully passed the straits. At first we headed N 48 E on one engine, having flooded the central ballast tank to reduce the silhouette of the submarine. We then followed the coast on the European side of the straits at a distance of 200-300 metres. Having crossed the Souan-Dere trench, at 0408 we dived to 8 metres in order not to be picked out by a searchlight projector which had just been switched on, but which had not yet found us. Seeing that the current was taking us too close to the coast, I altered course 2° to starboard. According to the markings on our map and taking into account our speed, which had been carefully calculated, we were due to exit the minefield at 0530. At 04.45 we dived to 25 metres as we entered the minefield. There were no incidents during the 25-metre dive; the submarine was handling well with angles of 10° forward and aft. At 0530 I decided to prolong the dive for five minutes to be sure that we had cleared the minefield. At 0534 there was a jolt forward as if we had grounded on the soft bottom; I came to 10 metres to get bearings and to determine the cause of the

This rare photo of Mariotte *is alleged to have been taken in the Dardanelles in July 1915; however, the camouflage she wore when lost is not visible in this image, which begs the question as to when she received it. (Private collection)*

incident. As soon as we attempted to come up, the starboard motor failed – the circuit-breaker had jumped – and the port motor increased its revolutions to compensate. The boat had a positive angle of 15° and a list to starboard of 13-14°; the immersion of the centre of the boat was 13 metres and stable. The positive angle and the list progres-

sively declined to 8° and 3-4° respectively and then settled. I attempted to restart the starboard motor but again the circuit-breakers activated. I attempted to turn to port 180° to return to Sedd-el-Bahr to try to free the starboard propeller, but the boat would only turn 15-20°. I attempted the same manoeuvre to starboard, with the

The destroyer Poignard, *last witness to the sailing of the* Mariotte. *(DR)*

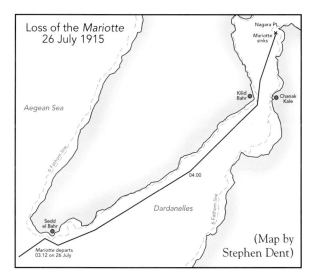

Loss of the *Mariotte*
26 July 1915

Nagara Pt.

Mariotte
sinks

Aegean Sea

Kilid
Bahr

Chanak
Kale

04.00

Dardanelles

Sedd
el Bahr

Mariotte departs
03.12 on 26 July

(Map by
Stephen Dent)

same result. It became clear that both the bow and the stern of the boat were entangled in some obstruction, and that it would be impossible to return to Sedd-el-Bahr. I decided to blow out the tanks aft to see what the nature of this obstruction was. This expedient also had the advantage of clearing the water which had accumulated on the floor of the motor room while the boat had been stalled at a positive angle and which was a legacy of our 25-metre dive. Blowing out the after ballast tank initially had little effect, then the boat was suddenly released; the conning tower broke the surface and was instantly fired on by a Turkish battery located close to Chanak-Kale at a distance of only 200 metres. Through the periscope I could see that there was a mine on the starboard bow brushing against the hull. I immediately gave the order to dive again.

The dive was very slow because of our lack of speed, and the conning tower was penetrated by enemy shells; the upper section of the air intake was destroyed. Deciding that the submarine was lost I halted the dive and ordered the crew to don lifebelts. I destroyed all confidential and secret documents while the crew disabled the electric motors by setting fire to them, the batteries by causing them to short-circuit, and the diesels by smashing all the vulnerable parts. I opened the conning tower while we blew out all tanks. As the battery at Chanak-Kale continued to fire on us during these operations, I sent sub-lieutenant (EV) Masson on deck to signal to the enemy guns to cease fire; the Turks immediately complied. I ordered 'abandon ship'; this was conducted with perfect discipline and in total silence. CPO Goulin and EV Bossy remained on board with me to check that all the sea-cocks had been opened.

The conduct of the crew was uniformly praiseworthy. Once the abandonment of the vessel had been decided, all equipment in every compartment was disabled under the supervision of the officers and petty officers. Order reigned right to the end, there was no panic and no scramble to get off the boat. On the contrary, the crew showed great presence of mind and courage. The Turks sent a boat to pick up the survivors and the crew was assembled on deck ready to disembark. When I arrived on deck I had the immense satisfaction to be greeted by cries of *Vive la France!* and *Vive le commandant!*

Signed: A Fabre

On 3 April 1919, *capitaine de corvette* Fabre appeared before the Naval War Council at Cherbourg to explain the loss of his vessel. He was defended by *lieutenant de vaisseau* Charcot, well know for his polar explorations. The council, which was presided over by Rear-Admiral Villette, acquitted Fabre unanimously.

The commission of enquiry concluded that the loss of the *Mariotte* was due to a mine cable wrapping itself around the starboard propeller.

A last echo of this incident, albeit one fired by imagination rather than the facts, can be found in the 2 March 1927 edition of the newspaper *Ouest France*, which announced under the headline 'Turkish government to refloat the submarine *Mariotte*, sunk in the Dardanelles in 1915':

> Yesterday we announced in our maritime column that the submarine *Mariotte* would be refloated by the Turkish government. The [French] Naval Ministry has received no official word on this subject. In any case, an intervention to recover the wreck could be made only by the Foreign Office.

It goes without saying that this project would not be pursued, and this would be the last time that *Mariotte* was mentioned by the media; she would henceforth be completely forgotten. It is in fact now possible to see the wreck of the submarine, which is lying in 5 metres of water off Cape Nara. However, in order to do this it is necessary to obtain permission from the Turkish Navy, as these waters belong to a naval base with restricted access.

Postscript

Three of the survivors of the sinking died in captivity during 1915-16; the others were repatriated after the war.

Many were subsequently honoured by the French. LV André Bossy, the executive officer of the *Mariotte*, and LV Louis Masson were awarded the Croix de Guerre, and both these officers and *Premier maître électricien* Georges Goulin the Légion d'Honneur. *Second-maître* (*timonerie* – signals) René Goasduff was awarded the Military Medal and Croix de Guerre. The captain and 27 other members of the crew were mentioned in despatches (*ordre de l'Armée de Mer*) for their calm performance under fire and for ensuring that their submarine did not fall into the hands of the enemy.

Acknowledgements:
This article was translated from the original French by John Jordan.

Footnotes:
1. André Matha would be listed as 'disappeared' on 26 May 1915 following a land battle involving the landing company of the armoured cruiser *Dupleix*.
2. Auguste Joseph Pierre Fabre was born on 7 August 1874 and joined the Navy in 1892. A *Chevalier de la Légion d'Honneur*, promoted *capitaine de corvette* (CV) on 1st July 1917 and *capitaine de frégate* (CF), he was appointed commander of the submarines in Bizerte in 1920. Fabre died suddenly at Lorient in 1924 while serving on the staff of Vice-Admiral Jehenne.

THE AIRCRAFT CARRIERS OF THE *SHÔKAKU* CLASS

The IJN carriers of the *Shôkaku* class were highly rated even by their opponents, and were arguably the best of the prewar carrier designs. **Hans Lengerer** looks at the conceptual aspects of their development and the technical advances they incorporated.

With the end of the treaty period approaching, and an end to the qualitative and quantitative restrictions which were agreed at Washington 1922 and London 1930 in prospect, the principles for the defence of the Empire and the necessary force structures were revised for the third time in June 1936. The future number of aircraft carriers was to be ten, of which four (*Hôshô, Akagi, Kaga* and *Ryûjô*) were already in commission and two (*Sôryû* and *Hiryû*) were under construction, while the conversion of the submarine support ships *Tsurugisaki* and *Takasaki* (future *Shoho* and *Zuiho*) was planned.

The displacement of the medium-sized carriers *Sôryû* and *Hiryû* had been restricted by the treaties. In order to ensure qualitative superiority over their foreign counterparts the IJN determined that the new ships would be larger than their immediate predecessors. The construction of two such ships, temporarily designated 'warships no.3 and no.4', was included in the Third Naval Replenishment Programme of 1937 alongside two battleships of the *Yamato* class and other lesser warship types. They would be the first Japanese carriers to be designed and built outside treaty limits and under the new, relaxed budgetary restrictions; in consequence the Navy General Staff (NGS) requirements were ambitious.

The air group was to comprise:

– 18 (+2 reserve) fighters Type 0 ('Zero')
– 27 (+5) dive bombers Type 99 ('Val')
– 27 (+5) torpedo bombers Type 97 ('Kate')
– Total: 72 (+12) aircraft = 84[1]

The reserve planes were to be stowed in the hangar and were to be easily assembled (ie not completely broken down); this had implications for the size of the hangar, as considerable space was needed for the reserve aircraft. Air weapons were to comprise 90 x 800kg bombs, 306 x 250kg bombs and 540 x 60kg bombs, and there was to be stowage for 496 tonnes of aviation fuel.

Maximum speed was to be 34.5 knots, and endurance 10,000nm at 18kts. The armament was to be exclusively against aircraft, and was to comprise 16 Type 89 40-cal 12.7cm HA guns in eight twin mounts, and 36 Type 96 25mm MG in twelve triple mounts. The magazines were to be protected against 800kg bombs released from horizontal bombers at an altitude of 3,000m, and against 8in (20.3cm) shells fired at ranges between 12,000m and

20,000m. The machinery spaces were to have protection against 250kg bombs released from dive bombers and against 5in (12.7cm) shell.

These requirements make it clear that the NGS wished to incorporate all the experience gained in the design, construction and operation of the earlier carriers. The number of aircraft (for the original requirement, see footnote 1) corresponded to the capacity of *Akagi* and *Kaga* (91 and 90 respectively) after conversion, speed was the same as *Sôryû* and *Hiryû*, while endurance was superior to in any of these four carriers. The anti-aircraft armament was similar to *Kaga* as rebuilt, and protection against bombs, shells and torpedoes was significantly improved compared to *Sôryû* and *Hiryû*. With their large aircraft capacity, high speed, good endurance, heavy AA armament and strong protection the new carriers were, in theory, an advance in every operational respect on their predecessors. It remained only for the design engineers of the Basic Design Section of the Navy Technical Department (NTD) to be able to realise the staff requirements.

The aircraft carrier design team, headed by Lt.-Cdr. (later Rear-Ad.) Yagasaki Masayuki, created an enlarged and generally improved version of *Hiryû*. The most noteworthy point was the position of the island/bridge to port, at approximately half the length. However, when both ships were already under construction, the design was revised to the arrangement adopted for *Kaga* and *Sôryû*. The redesign was begun at the end of 1938 and approved by the NTD Technical Conference on 13 February 1939 after details were discussed in no.3 committee on the 7th; the report was submitted to the Navy Minister on 27 March and the revision authorised. Rear-Admiral Fukuda Keiji, then chief of the Basic Design Section, made a lengthy statement about the reasons for the change. The arguments which follow are drawn from the minutes of the conference.

Rationale for the Positioning of the Island

The reason for placing the bridge amidships in *Akagi* and *Hiryû* was to meet the request of the Navy Air Technical Department (NATD) to increase the length of deck available for take-off. The NATD explained that the after half of the flight deck was sufficiently long for landing on, but for take-off the bridge became an obstruction when

A particularly clear starboard broadside view of Shôkaku *moored in Yokosuka naval port two weeks after her commissioning ceremony on 8 August 1941. Note the prominent shields on the HA and MG mountings abaft the funnels to protect the guncrews from smoke and gases. In contrast, the mounts located forward of the funnels are of the standard type – although in this photo they are covered by canvas. The ship remained at the builder's for an unusually long time after her completion, presumably for final adjustments, as her completion date had been advanced by three months to enable her to prepare for the anticipated hostilities (despite delays in the delivery of the main turbines and boilers). Note the Type 94 fire control director atop of bridge; two more are mounted at flight deck level forward and aft of the island structure. Note also the removable covers on the funnels. (Fukui Shizuo collection)*

located approximately one third of the flight deck's length from the bow, where the planes had not yet gained sufficient speed, and turbulence around the bridge affected their steering. If the bridge was located amidships it facilitated the preparation of the aircraft for take-off, and was also preferable if aircraft were landed over the bow. However, positioning the bridge amidships brought it too close to the exhaust uptakes on the starboard side; it therefore needed to be relocated to port. From a stability point of view the port-side position was advantageous because the weight of the bridge and the uptakes cancelled one another out. This design was discussed in the NTD Technical Conference with the agreement of the NATD, and experiments were then conducted to determine the effect on air flow over the flight deck and the streaming of smoke.

Before the fitting-out of *Akagi*, a wooden mock-up of the bridge was placed in the intended position, and the carrier sailed from Yokosuka to Sasebo to measure the air flow over the deck, and to test the impact on the take-off and landing of aircraft and the steering of the ship. The conclusions drawn from the experiments give the impression that the decision to locate the island amidships and to port on *Akagi* and *Hiryû* was made on the basis of inconclusive results in testing. It was stated that 'the influence on air flow over the deck could not be investigated sufficiently(!), but the position of the bridge did not pose a problem for landings'; it was further stated that 'from the viewpoint of steering of the ship it is preferable to have the bridge in the fore part of the ship... and it is

proposed to compensate for the poor visibility forward by an auxiliary bridge'.

However, after construction of the new carriers had already begun, negative opinions regarding the arrangement of the bridge of *Akagi* and *Hiryû* were expressed; the view was advanced that air flow over the flight deck on these two ships had a negative effect on take-off and landing operations compared to *Kaga*. There was also concern about the shorter landing area, which could become a serious problem as future aircraft increased in size and had higher landing speeds.

In the autumn of 1938 the NATD and NTD addressed the issue of whether the construction of the *Shôkaku* class should proceed in accordance with the original design, or whether the position of the bridge should be changed to starboard. In October and November 1938, 451 test landings and take-offs were made from the flight deck of *Akagi*.[2] The landings were filmed to provide a basis for discussion, and the air flow over the deck was made visible by the generation of steam at the bow. The conclusions took into account day and night landings with the wind from various directions, and resulted in a decision to change the position of the bridge on the *Shôkaku* class to that of *Kaga* and *Sôryû*, the sole proviso being that this revision should 'not ... have a significant influence upon the completion dates'.

The redesign had to be undertaken in a hurry because of this proviso, and required a degree of improvisation and compromise. Because of the advanced state of the construction of *Shôkaku*, the relocation of the supporting

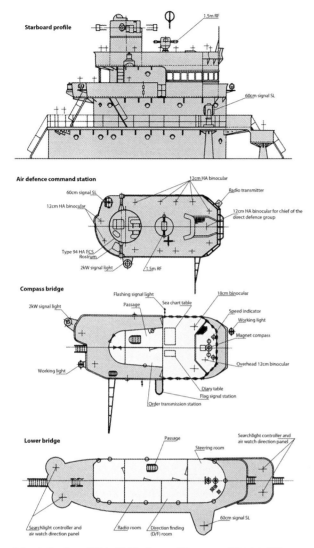

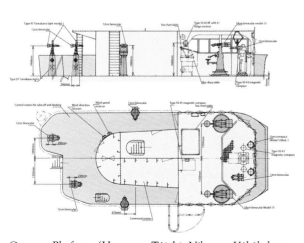

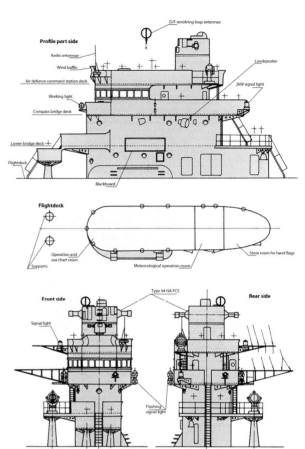

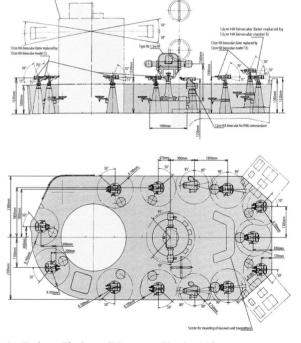

Island: Starboard Side & Platforms. (Hasegawa Tôichi, *Nihon no Kôkûbokan*, adapted by Waldemar Trojca)

Island: Port Side & Fore/Aft Views. (Hasegawa Tôichi, *Nihon no Kôkûbokan*, adapted by Waldemar Trojca)

Compass Platform. (Hasegawa Tôichi, *Nihon no Kôkûbokan*, adapted by Waldemar Trojca)

Air Defence Platform. (Hasegawa Tôichi, *Nihon no Kôkûbokan*, adapted by Waldemar Trojca)

TABLE 1: BUILDING DATA & FATE

	Builder	Laid down	Launched	Completed	Fate
Shôkaku (No.3)	Kure N.Y.	12 Dec 1937	1 Jun 1939	8 Aug 1941	Torpedoed 19 Jun 1944 US *Cavalla* (SS 244), 11°50N/ 37°57E (140nm N of Yap Is.). Stricken 31 Aug 1945.
Zuikaku (No.4)	Kawasaki, Kobe	28 May 1938	27 Nov 1939	25 Sep 1941	Sunk 25 Oct 1944 US carrier-based aircraft, 19°20N/125°20E (220nm ENE of Cape Engaño). Stricken 31 Aug 1945.

structure for the bridge inside the hangars and most of the ventilation ducts from port to starboard would have caused construction delays, so they were left as originally designed. The result was a reduction in the hangar area for the forward section of the upper hangar, which was made narrower to accommodate the supporting structure for the new island (the number of aircraft which could be stowed in the hangar decreased by one); however, it was expected that this loss of hangar area could be compensated by a change in the way the aircraft were stowed.[3] The flight deck was extended 1m on the port side and the width outboard of the island to starboard reduced to 0.5m in order to re-balance weights, and the change also involved the fitting of 100 tonnes of ballast on the port side, which increased trial displacement to 29,800 tonnes. It was also calculated that maximum speed would be reduced from 34.2 knots to 34.0 knots – this fear proved to be groundless – and radius from 10,000nm to 9,700 miles at 18knots. Other consequences were the shortening of the take-off deck to 72 m (accepted by the NATD) and a marked improvement in visibility forward from the compass platform (reduction of the 'dead' zone from 200m to 170m).The items most discussed at the NTD Technical Conference were the reduction in the firing arcs of some HA guns and MGs and their fire control systems because of the new bridge arrangement, but little could be done beyond relocating some of the searchlights and their controls.

Construction

The most significant events were the work in connection to the redesign – there was close cooperation between the main personnel responsible in the NTD, the Kure N.Y. and the Kawasaki Shipyard – and the acceleration of the construction of *Zuikaku* because of the probable outbreak of the war; her scheduled building period was some four months shorter than that of sister *Shôkaku*. In the event, the completion dates had to be put back for both ships early in 1941 due to the late delivery of key items of the propulsion plant (boilers, main engines and most of the auxiliary machinery). However, once these materials were delivered, the completion date was advanced in preparation for war and no delay was permitted. Table 1 gives the key dates of construction, and the principal dimensions of the ships are in Table 2.

Flight Deck

The flight deck was 242.20m long and 29m wide, decreasing to 18m at the bow and to 26m aft; the flight deck area was roughly comparable to *Akagi* after conversion. The flight deck was fitted with wood planking except for forward of the first aircraft lift and abaft the after lift. The after part of the steel deck had a non-skid paint which had the appearance of rough emery paper, and the fore part was covered with thin strips of steel 200mm long and 16mm wide, welded to the deck at various angles.

Like the British Royal Navy the IJN favoured enclosed hangars, in contrast to the open hangars of the later US

TABLE 2: PRINCIPAL DIMENSIONS

Length:	238.00m pp, 250.00m wl, 257.50m oa
Beam:	29.00m wl
Depth:	23.00m
Flight deck:	
Length	242.20m
Width	29.00m amid, 18.00m fwd, 26.00m aft
Height above wl:	
Trial condition	14.13m
Full load	13.68m
Hangars:	
Upper	200m x 24m max.
Lower	180m x 20m max.
Displacement:	
Trial	29,800 tonnes
Full load	32,105 tonnes
Light load	24,170 tonnes
Suppl. light load	24,770 tonnes
Draught:	8.87m (mean) trials, 9.32m full load
Freeboard:	
Forward	10.00m (anchor deck)
Amidships	8.80m (upper hangar deck)
Aft	6.60m (boat deck)

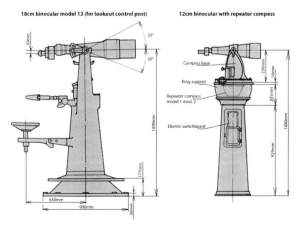

18cm & 12cm Binoculars. (Hasegawa Tôichi, *Nihon no Kôkûbokan*, adapted by Waldemar Trojca)

Navy carriers. The upper hangar deck was generally the strength deck – the sole exceptions being *Taihô* and *Shinano* – and the flight deck was made as light as possible structurally. The criterion for flight deck strength was a landing load twice the weight of the heaviest type of aircraft in current service. This was achieved by placing transverse beams as supports at every frame and making every other beam a heavy one of about 460mm depth. Longitudinals, criss-crossing the beams, provided additional strength for the transverse structure, but had a relatively wide spacing. This light structure was an essential element in the conception of the sides of the upper hangar as 'blow-out walls' (see below).

The flight deck extended nearly the full length of the hull, and in order to withstand the hogging and sagging forces to which it was subjected when the ship rolled and pitched, it was divided into nine sections by fitting eight expansion joints from close to the bow to just abaft the after lift. [4]

It was accepted that the higher the flight deck above the waterline, the better for the operation of aircraft. On the other hand, the greater the 'sail' area when the ship was subjected to cross-winds, the greater the angle of heel.[5] It was decided that the height of the flight deck above the waterline should be at least 12m, and preferably 13m. In the final design the height in trial condition was 14.13m, reducing to 13.68m in the full load condition due to the increased draught.[6]

The anchor deck (the forward part of the upper hangar deck which extended below the flight deck to the bow) was kept clear of fittings which might obstruct take-off; a theoretical line with an angle of 13° was drawn from the forward edge of the flight deck to the top of the bow, and no fitting was allowed to project above the line. This requirement originated from experience with *Akagi* in her original three-level flight deck configuration; when planes took off from the upper flight deck they occasionally struck the foremost part of the lower flight deck on take-off. However, the arrangement of the flight deck of *Shôkaku* class was radically different, and there was only a very short distance between the forward edge of the flight deck and the bow, so the comparatively small angle of 13° was sufficient.

It was intended to fit two catapults, and the necessary preparatory work (recesses, covers, guides, etc.) was carried out. The IJN began studies of the so-called 'Warship Take-off Forward Equipment' (*Kanpatsu sokushin sôchi*) when *Kaga* was built, but failed to develop an operational catapult until the end of the war. The difficulty of installing catapults over the expansion joints is often given as a reason, but this may be only part of the truth.

Hangars & Lifts

As in earlier IJN fleet carriers there were two superimposed hangars, served by three aircraft lifts. The forward lift measured 13m (L) x 16m (W), and the centre and after lifts 13m(L) x 12m (W). The forward lift was larger so that aircraft landing on could be struck down quickly with their wings still deployed. The lifts were operated by electric motors and speed was controlled by a Ward-Leonard system. The platform was counter-weighted, and the two hoisting wires at each corner of the platform were connected to winches mounted on the same shaft and driven by a motor located in the lift pit. With a maximum speed of 50m/sec the lift took 15 seconds to be raised from the lower hangar deck to the flight deck. The lift platforms were secured to the flight deck by large brackets which were mounted on hinges and swung under the platform manually. Because of the rolling and pitching of the ship, rollers were used in the guide paths and buffers were also mounted to compensate for these movements. However, the lifts could still jam if exposed to major shocks, as evidenced by the bomb damage sustained by *Shôkaku* in 1942.

The upper hangar was 4.85m high, the lower 4.7m. Each was divided into three compartments by the forward and centre lifts. The upper hangar was about 200m long from the after elevator to the anchor deck and the width varied between 18.5m (above the boiler rooms) and 24m. The plans of *Shôkaku* show the decrease in width resulting from the redesign of the island. The lower hangar was shorter, the length of the forward section being reduced by about 20m to serve as crew quarters. The width of this hangar varied between 17.5m and 20m. The total hangar floor area of 5,545m² permitted the stowage of the required 72 (+12 reserve) aircraft provided that the planned types were embarked.

The IJN recognised the heavy damage a bomb hit would cause to the flight and hangar decks and also to the hangar walls. The protection of areas as large as the hangar walls was impossible because of topweight considerations, so a means of releasing the expanding detonation gases was considered the only effective countermeasure. The basic idea was to make the supports for the flight deck (pillars) as strong as necessary and the plates between them very thin so that they would be blown out in the event of an internal explosion, thus providing expansion openings for the gas pressure and minimising damage. Prior to the completion of the *Shôkaku* class, Kure N.Y. carried out experiments in August 1940 using large-scale models. The results may be summarised as follows:[7]

1) The expansion of the detonation gases within the entire volume of the hangar means that a lower maximum pressure is attained. Many expansion openings should therefore be distributed over the whole area. The amount of pressure reduction cannot be accurately measured because no comparative experiments are undertaken under the same conditions, and a new experiment has to be carried out at each time. However, due to the rapid transformation of the explosive from solid into gas condition (within 1/10,000sec) a marked reduction in the intensity of the pressure wave cannot be expected unless the openings are very large

2) The proposal to reduce the extent of the damage by expansion openings is effective provided the pressure can escape not only horizontally but also vertically.

3) The larger the expansion openings per 100m³ volume, the better. However, it is estimated that 1.2m² per 100m³ should be sufficient. The cover plates should therefore measure approximately 1.3m x 0.8m.

4) During the experiments, the covers were blown out at

0.75kg/cm² pressure. Pressures below this figure will not be generated by an explosion; the normal pressure will be about 3kg/cm².

Based upon these conclusions, the upper hangar walls of *Shôkaku* class (and also *Taihô*) had so-called expansion openings. However, *Shôkaku's* bomb damage at the Battle of the Coral Sea and the later Battle of Santa Cruz demonstrated that even though the 'blow-out wall' idea worked, in both cases the flight deck was destroyed, mainly because the assumption that a bomb would pierce the lightly structured flight deck and detonate only when it struck the upper hangar (strength) deck was in error. Moreover points 1 & 2 in the above conclusions suggest that IJN did not expect too much from the blow-out plate system.

Island Bridge

According to Fukuda's statement in the aforementioned Technical Conference, 'the structure of the bridge is the same as *Hiryû* in the final study, which involved a full-scale sized model'. For a ship the size of the *Shôkaku* class the floor area of the four decks was barely adequate, and the briefing of the air crews, which should have taken place in the air operations room on the second deck, had to be moved to the flight deck prior to major strikes.

The after end of the island was 166m from the after edge of the flight deck, and the island projected 2.7m onto the flight deck, so the distance between the island and the centre-line was only 11.3m, and the overall width of the flight deck was reduced to 26.2m at this point. (These figures provide further evidence that the island had to be relocated 1m inboard because of the redesign.)

Hangar & Flight Deck Equipment

Lighting
Pilot landings were assisted by sets of guide lights. The

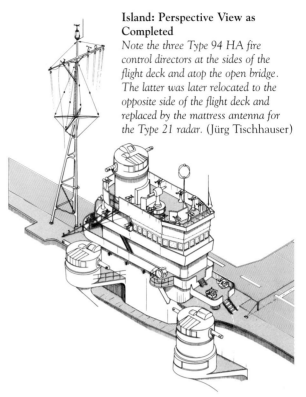

Island: Perspective View as Completed
Note the three Type 94 HA fire control directors at the sides of the flight deck and atop the open bridge. The latter was later relocated to the opposite side of the flight deck and replaced by the mattress antenna for the Type 21 radar. (Jürg Tischhauser)

equipment was used by day and at night, the intensity of the light being regulated according to the conditions. It comprised a pair of red lamps (*shômontô* = 'stationary shining door') and a group of four blue lamps (*shôseitô* = vertical moveable shining star); the former moved in the horizontal plane while the latter was fixed. The lights were mounted on outriggers on both sides of the flight deck aft. The pilot aligned his aircraft with the landing path using the parallel light of these arrays; the general angle of landing was between 4° and 6°.

For night landings, the round-down at the after end of the flight deck was marked by red lights (*kambi*), and

Zuikaku at Kobe on 25 September 1941. The open anchor deck forward of the hangar and the thick support posts for the flight deck some 10 metres abaft the bow were characteristic features of Japanese carrier design. (Fukui Shizuo collection)

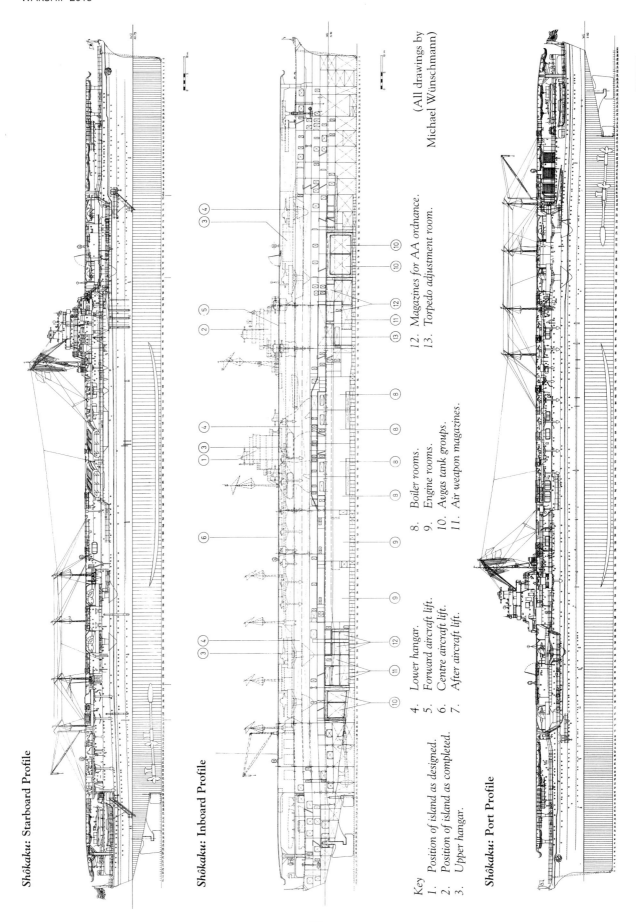

Shōkaku: Starboard Profile

Shōkaku: Inboard Profile

Shōkaku: Port Profile

(All drawings by Michael Wünschmann)

Key
1. Position of island as designed.
2. Position of island as completed.
3. Upper hangar.
4. Lower hangar.
5. Forward aircraft lift.
6. Centre aircraft lift.
7. After aircraft lift.
8. Boiler rooms.
9. Engine rooms.
10. Avgas tank groups.
11. Air weapon magazines.
12. Magazines for AA ordnance.
13. Torpedo adjustment room.

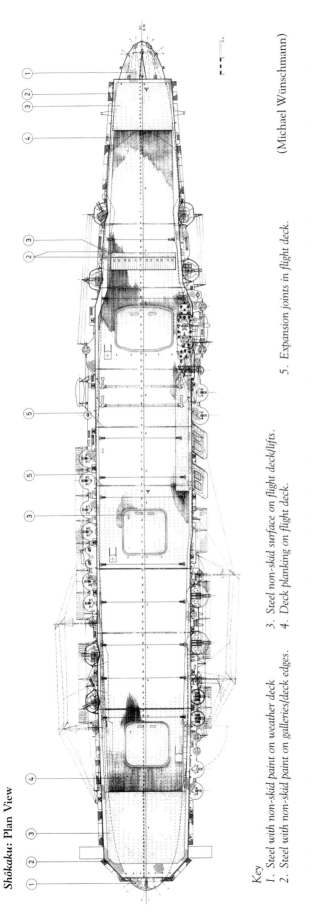

Shôkaku: Plan View

(Michael Wünschmann)

Key
1. *Steel with non-skid paint on weather deck*
2. *Steel with non-skid paint on galleries/deck edges.*
3. *Steel non-skid surface on flight deck/lifts.*
4. *Deck planking on flight deck.*
5. *Expansion joints in flight deck.*

white deck lights were arranged along the centre-line and at the sides of the flight deck; the latter were fluorescent tubes some 20cm long with reflectors. The pilot was informed about wind speed via a separate signal lamp. In addition, searchlights could also be used to guide aircraft in; however, these were used sparingly, as they increased the danger that the carrier would be discovered by enemy aircraft or submarines.

Arresting gear and crash barriers

Arrester gear (*chakkan seido sôchi*) was developed in order to slow an aircraft on landing. The flight decks of *Shôkaku* and *Zuikaku* were fitted with ten arrester wires connected to brake machinery of the Kure Type 4 Mod.2 (*Kure shiki yon gata kai*). This gear was developed by the Electric Research Division (*Denki jikkenbu*) of Kure N.Y. from July 1933 onwards. It was a modified version of the Kure-type Model 1 and was fitted from 1938 onwards. The Kure Type Model 5 arrester gear was also trialled but was not used operationally, so Model 4 (and its modifications) was the last type of arrester gear to see service with the IJN.

During landing operations the wires were suspended at a minimum height of 160mm by raising bars at the outer edges of the flight deck. Each wire was led down over guide pulleys to an arresting gear compartment below the lower hangar deck where the two ends were led to the sides of a winding drum inside which was a squirrel-cage rotor made of high resistance bronze. The drum and squirrel cage rotated around a six-pole stator energised with 120A at 120V at the maximum setting – the specific setting was selected according to the weight of the aircraft. (All Kure-type arresting gear used the same principle.)

When the tailhook of a landing plane caught the horizontal wire the drum made 1.5 turns and actuated the electric brake. The aircraft ran against the resistance of the brakes until its kinetic energy was exhausted, whereupon it came to a halt. The maximum distance for stopping an aircraft was 40m; retardation power was 2g. Maximum brake/retardation speed was 30m/s, maximum aircraft weight 4,000kg. It took twelve seconds to return the wire to its original position.

If a plane failed to catch any of the arrester wires with its arresting hook it was stopped by a crash barrier (*kassho seishi sôchi*). Three fixed barriers of the Naval Air Technical Arsenal (*Kôkûgijutsusho*) Type Model 3 Mod.1 (*kusho shiki san gata kai ichi*) were mounted as shown in the plan view. According to Fukui two mobile barriers were on board, but these are not listed in the official ship's book. The equipment used a system of hydraulic brakes. Each fixed barrier had three wires (lower, centre and upper) which were stretched between two posts mounted at the sides of the flight deck. These posts were raised to the correct height and lowered pneumatically. The wires were attached to a separate pneumatic-hydraulic arresting unit installed at the port side of the upper hangar deck. If an aircraft engaged the wires a system of pulleys caused a ram to be pushed into a hydraulic cylinder, thus forcing oil through a series of constrictions into an air-loaded accumulator. The shape of the constrictions and the increasing pressure of the air resulted in rapid retardation with much less movement in comparison to the arresting gear. The

Shôkaku was heavily damaged by four bomb hits in the Battle of the Santa Cruz Islands on 26 October 1942. Following temporary repairs at Truk she left for Yokosuka, entering the naval port on 6 November. Repairs at Yokosuka NY then took until early March 1943. This photo was taken on 18 March 1943 in Tokyo Bay during the subsequent aviation trials and shows a Type 97 torpedo bomber whose hook has just caught an arrester wire and brought the aircraft to a halt just short of the centre lift; deck handling personal can be seen running from the sides towards the aircraft. Note the two crash barriers in the lowered position in the foreground; the wires were raised on bars on both sides of the flight deck. The thick strip at the lower edge of the photo appears to be a steel plate covering an expansion joint. The wireless masts have been lowered for landing operations, and there is a destroyer on plane guard duty astern. (Fukui Shizuo collection)

maximum braking distance was 7m, and the maximum brake force was 4g (ie twice that of the arrester gear) so damage to the aircraft was unavoidable. Maximum brake speed was 15m/s, maximum aircraft weight 4000kg, and the barrier could be raised or lowered in 2.5 seconds.

Wind break
Forward of the first aircraft lift there was a wind break. This was raised when aircraft were on the flight deck, and lowered into a recess flush with the deck during flight operations. Holes were drilled into some 30% of the surface area of the shield, and it could be kept in the raised position with wind speeds up to of 50m/s (180km/h). When this value was exceeded it was lowered into the recess; it could be raised again in 30 seconds against wind speeds up to 35m/s (126km/h).

Avgas refuelling stations
There were a number of avgas refuelling points on the flight deck. They were supplied by two main gasoline lines, one for A type high-octane fuel (for starting up and high bursts of speed), the other for B type lower-octane fuel (for cruising). Sufficient fixed A-type refuelling stations were provided to ensure that any position could

be reached with a 25m flexible hose. For B-type fuel twice as many filling stations were provided. Hoses were fitted with pistol-type filling valves.

Fire-fighting equipment
Fire was a particular hazard on board an aircraft carrier. Carriers had large amounts of aviation fuel stored not only in tanks (see Protection) but sometimes even in drums in the hangar, so safety was a critical factor. Precautions taken ranged from the adoption of special casings for motors (to avoid sparks which could ignite avgas fumes) to the separation of the hangars into several fire-fighting zones by fire curtains, the use of two different agents for fire fighting (CO_2 and foam), and protection of avgas pipes and hoses.[8]

Boat Stowage

Boat stowage was a particular problem for a carrier. Because of the characteristic shape of the hull, twelve boats were stowed on the stern. These were as follows:

– three 12-metre motor boats (*Naikatei*)
– three 12-metre motor launches (*Naikaranchi*)

A starboard broadside view of the newly-completed Zuikaku, taken either in October or November of 1941. Note the downward curve of the flight deck overhang aft, painted with red and white longitudinal strips, and the boat deck beneath. Zuikaku's scheduled completion date had to be put back due to the late delivery of the main turbines/boilers and part of the auxiliary machinery. (Fukui Shizuo collection)

This photo was taken in November 1941 from the bridge of Zuikaku, looking forward, with the carriers Kaga (nearest camera) and Akagi in the background. Note the wind break in its recess in the flight deck in the foreground, the steel strip along the side of the flight deck, the expansion joint, the white centreline marking of the flight deck and the wind direction markings extending from its forward end at fixed angles. In the centre of the photo in the foreground there is a DF antenna, and to the right of it, in the starboard gallery, a bench for the aircraft handling personnel. The muzzles of the barrels of the two twin 12.7cm HA guns are protected by caps. (Fukui Shizuo collection)

– one 8-metre motor launch
– one 6-metre service boat (*Tsusen*)
– two 9-metre whalers
– two 13-metre special transport boats (*Tokusen unkatei*)

The boats were handled by 4-tonne cranes of the folding type and four boat hoists; there were also two 2.5-tonne motor winches and a single 1-tonne motor winch.

Protection

In terms of their horizontal and vertical protection and their underwater protection *Shôkaku* and *Zuikaku* were comparable to their foreign counterparts, and were markedly superior to earlier IJN carriers. The horizontal protection extended from the fore to the after avgas tank groups, and also took in the machinery spaces and the magazines for the air weapons and guns. New Vickers non-cemented (NVNC) and copper-alloy non-cemented (CNC) armour was secured to 25mm Ducol steel (DS) plating and was on two levels: at lower deck level above the machinery spaces as far as the forward aircraft lift, and at the level of the platform deck fore and aft, above the magazines. The thickness of the NVNC armour varied from 105mm (above the avgas tanks) to 132mm (above the magazines), while above the machinery spaces CNC armour of 65mm thickness, tapered towards the sides, was used. A belt of 46mm CNC armour formed the outer hull plating over the area covered by the armoured deck; the belt was 4.1 metres high of which 2 metres were below the waterline; the lower strake of the belt was secured to 50mm DS. The magazines outside this area were protected by 165mm thick NVNC armour with an inclination up to 25° and tapered to 75mm-55mm. The side armour extended from the armour deck to the 8mm flat which separated the watertight compartments from the heavy oil tanks below the waterline.

The layered underwater protection, which was in the form of a liquid-loaded 'sandwich', was the first such application in a Japanese warship and deserves special attention. Inboard of the outer hull plating there were four longitudinal bulkheads: inner bottom, wing passage bulkhead, torpedo bulkhead and splinter bulkhead (see schematic drawing p.107). According to Report S-01-9 'Underwater Protection' of the USNTMtJ, p.74, the torpedo bulkhead comprised two plates riveted together, the outer 18mm and the inner 12mm thick. This corresponds to the 30mm DS stated in various Japanese sources; however, the authoritative *Shôwa Zôsenshi* Vol.1, p.537, gives the thickness as 30-42mm, suggesting that the thickness of the outer plate may have been increased to 30mm fore and aft, where the depth of the torpedo protection was reduced by the tapering of the hull, for a combined thickness of 42mm.[9] The torpedo bulkhead extended from the armour deck to the outer plating of the ship's bottom. The inner bottom, wing passage and splinter bulkheads were of 8mm steel. The spaces between the outer and inner bottom and between the torpedo bulkhead and splinter bulkhead were divided into water-

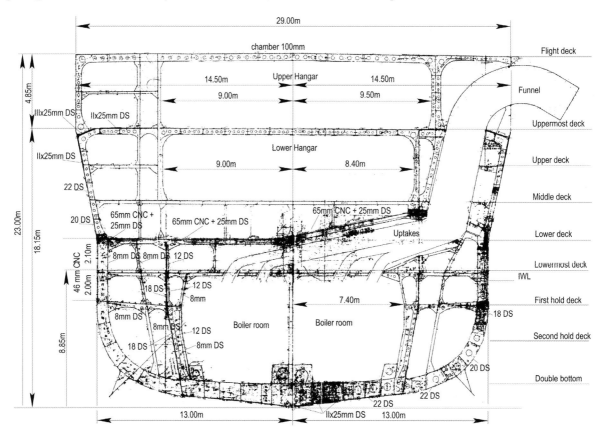

Shôkaku: Midship Section (Adapted by Waldemar Trojca from official plans)

tight void compartments; the spaces between the inner bottom, wing passage and the torpedo bulkhead were partitioned by transverse bulkheads and used as oil fuel tanks. The depth of the wing passage, which served as an expansion space for the detonation gases, was about 2.2m. It was normally filled with oil fuel, but was emptied in battle condition. The protective strength of this arrangement along the machinery spaces was calculated to have a joint efficiency of 53% against 450kg of explosive.[10] The weight of water which would flood these compartments in the event of a single torpedo hit was expected to be about 900 tonnes (the shaded area). Damage to the torpedo bulkhead was expected, but flooding of the machinery spaces should have been prevented by the splinter bulkhead. This assumption was based on the results of model experiments,[11] but was of doubtful validity; later experiments demonstrated that 'the objective could not be attained completely' (*Shōwa Zōsenshi*).

Following the loss of *Taihô* and *Shôkaku* in the Battle for of the Philippine Sea, unusual measures were taken to enhance the protection of the avgas tank groups fore and aft in *Zuikaku*. According to Fukui, bulges of 600mm-800mm depth were fitted below the waterline in the area of the tanks and filled with concrete. Hull resistance was significantly increased, and the bulges also caused a strange wave formation around the hull. However, high speed was no longer a key factor; survivability was the only factor which counted. Despite these measures, *Zuikaku* sank two months later having sustained multiple torpedo and bomb hits.

Damage Control System

Shôkaku and *Zuikaku* were the first carriers to have special compartments as part of the damage control system. The IJN began the installation of a damage control system from *Sôryû* onwards – it was limited to the

Taken on board Zuikaku at the end of 1942 or early in 1943, this photo shows the huge mattress antenna of the Type 21 radar atop the bridge; it replaced the Type 94 HA fire control director, which was relocated to the side of the flight deck. A second radar antenna was mounted in a recess in the flight deck formerly occupied by a Type 96 110cm searchlight projector, and like the latter was elevated prior to operation. The assembled crew are in formal dress, and the large 'sunburst' ensign at the tripod mast indicates a ceremonial day. The wind break has been elevated to the left of the commanding officer, who is giving his address. ((Fukui Shizuo collection)

use of oil fuel tanks – but when the studies for the battleships of the *Yamato* class were undertaken the system was greatly expanded. As with *Yamato*, the number and capacity of the heavy oil feed pumps was increased with a view to moving oil between the tanks for trim control, and the pipe systems were improved to permit this operation. Separate compartments were used for the control of list. However, as shown in the drawing of the underwater protection system, the heavy oil tanks outboard of

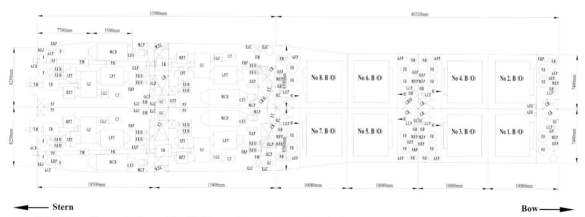

← Stern   Bow →

Layout of Machinery Spaces (Adapted by Waldemar Trojca from official plans)

Key:
C.T.	*cruise turbine*
C.G.C.	*cruise reduction gearing & coupling*
G.C.	*main gearing & coupling*
H.P.T.	*high pressure turbine*
I.P.T.	*intermediate pressure turbine*
L.P.T.	*low pressure turbine*
M.C.D.	*main condenser*
M.C.P.	*main condensate pump*

Note: all other abbreviations refer to the auxiliary machinery described in the text.

Area of Engine Rooms (ER)	581m²
Area of Boiler Rooms (BR)	608m²
HP per m² ER	275.4
HP per m² ER	263.2

TABLE 3: PROPULSION MACHINERY DATA

Power Rating and Propeller RPM

	Power rating	Total output	Propeller rpm
Ahead continuous rate	40,000shp	160,000shp	300
Cruise full rate	4,000shp	16,000shp	139
Cruise overload	5,500shp	22,000shp	155
Cruise allowable full power	12,500shp	50,000shp	204
Astern full	10,000shp	40,000shp	190

Planned Steam Pressure, Vacuum and Steam Consumption

	Steam pressure	Steam temp.	Condenser (top)	Steam consumption
Ahead full	26 kg/cm^2	335°C	700mmHg	3.7 kg/hr/shp
Cruise full	26 kg/cm^2	335°C	725mmHg	4.5 kg/hr/shp
Astern full	21 kg/cm^2	330°C	645mmHg	9.0 kg/hr/shp

Turbine Specifications

	HP	IP	LP	Astern	Cruise
Type	Kampon, impulse, single flow	[as HP]	Kampon, impulse, compound flow	[as HP]	[as HP]
Turbine rpm	2821	2821	2774	1567	7900
Propeller rpm	300	300	300	190	204
No. of stages	1 bucket wheel with double row; 2 bucket wheels with single row.	4 bucket wheels with single row.	[as MP]	1 bucket wheel with three rows.	1 bucket wheel with double row; 4 bucket wheels with single row.
Max. pitch circle diameter	1,100mm	1,270mm	1,420mm	1,250mm	550mm
Distance between centres of bearings	1,460mm	1,410mm	2,885mm	2,885mm	1,030mm
Pressure of steam chamber	27.00kg/cm^2	6.60kg/cm^2	1.26kg/cm^2	22.00kg/cm^2	27.00kg/cm^2
Pressure at 1st stage	11.50kg/cm^2	4.45kg/cm^2	0.74kg/cm^2	–	9.00kg/cm^2
Exhaust pressure	6.85kg/cm^2	1.34kg/cm^2	0.10kg/cm^2	0.18kg/cm^2	1.97kg/cm^2

Notes:

1. The rotation of the cruising turbines corresponds to the cruising allowable full power and the steam pressure to the cruising overload power.
2. The turbine blades were made of non-corrosive B steel[(otsu).

Specifications for Reduction Gearing

	Main Reduction Gearing		Cruise Reduction Gearing		
	Main Gear wheel	HP + IP Pinion	LP Pinion	Main gear wheel	Pinion
RPM	300	2,821	2,474	1,456	6,000
Pitch circle diameter of teeth	114.83in	12.21in	13.93in	23.76in	5.77in
No. of teeth	536	57	65	144	35
Length of teeth	1,240mm	640mm			
Diametrical pitch (DP)	5.39	7.00			
Helical angle	29°58'51"	30°0'21.8"			
Reduction rate	1.00	9.40	8.25	4.11	

Note:

Because the IJN lagged behind in the manufacture of reduction gearing, Kure N.Y. purchased two large and two small gear cutting machines (for wheels and pinions respectively) from the German Reineker Co. to manufacture the gearing for the Shôkaku and Yamato classes. Precision testers for checking the teeth after cutting (hence diameter above in inches) were purchased from the British David Brown & Co. in 1937. According to Japanese reports the gears cut by the new machines were excellent and required little adjustment (in contrast to the gears cut using older machinery). At the same time, the modules of the Japan Standard Specification were revised: diametrical pitch was now set at 5.39 M5 (obliquity angle 14.5°) and M 3.5 (obliquity angle 20°) instead of 7.00. There are indications that these new specifications were applied during the manufacture of the gearing for Shôkaku.]

Shaft Dimensions

	Outer diameter	Inner diameter	Length inboard shaft	Length outboard shaft
Thrust Shaft	490mm	370mm	6.90m	9.90m
No.1 intermediate shaft	490mm	370mm	6.60m	5.90m

No.2 intermediate shaft	490mm	370mm	9.50m	7.80m
No.3 intermediate shaft	490mm	370mm	–	9.50m
Stern Shaft	510mm	390mm	13.60m	12.70m
Propeller Shaft	540mm	410mm	18.39m	18.39m

Kampon Type Model B Boiler

Steam pressure	30kg/cm^2	Volume, combustion space	43.4^3
Steam temperature	350°C	Planned rate of combustion	7.8kg/m^2
Temperature of preheated air	135°C	Atomisers	8 Kampon Type 20 burners Model 3
Heating surface:			2 Kampon Type 20 burners Model 5
Evaporator tubes	903m^2	Cones	10 Kampon Type 110 Model 5
Superheater tubes	182m^2	Smoke screen ejector	1 x 2,000kg/hr
Air preheater tubes	454m^2		

Auxiliary Machinery (Engine Rooms)

	Type	Number
Circulating pump	Vertical, axial flow, turbo-reduction gear	4
Condensate pump	Horizontal, centrifugal, turbo-reduction gear drive	8
Lubrication oil pump	Vertical, gear type, turbo-reduction gear drive	8
Cooling water pump	Vertical, axial flow, turbo-reduction gear drive	4
Air ejector	Dual stage, triplex, injection type	8
Supply ventilation	Horizontal, axial flow, turbo-reduction gear drive	4
Supply ventilation	Horizontal, axial flow, electric drive	4
Exhaust ventilation	Horizontal, axial flow, turbo-reduction gear drive	4
Exhaust ventilation	Horizontal, axial flow, electric drive	4
Control room ventilation	Horizontal, electric drive 'Sirocco' type	5
Fire and bilge pump	Vertical, electric drive, centrifugal	4
Portable heavy oil pump	Horizontal, gear, electric drive	1
Evaporator	Centrifugal, tube with thermo compressor	4
Distiller	Vertical, direct (surface) heating	2
Distiller pump	Horizontal, axial flow, turbo-reduction gear drive	4
Feed water heater	Vertical, direct (surface) heating	4
Oil cooler	Vertical, internal oil, external water	4
Oil purifier	Vertical, electric drive, centrifugal	2
Auxiliary condenser	*Shokkyoku*(?) type	2
Auxiliary water circulating pump	Vertical, electric drive, centrifugal	2

Auxiliary Machinery (Boiler Rooms)

Main feed pump	Horizontal, axial flow, turbo-reduction gear	8
Auxiliary feed pump	Weir HD 8	8
Blower	Inverted, axial flow, turbo-reduction gear	6
Fuel oil service pump	Vertical, turbo-reduction gear	8
Fire and bilge pump	Vertical, electric drive	2
Auxiliary fuel oil service pump	Horizontal, electric drive, gear type	2
Auxiliary blower	Horizontal, electric drive, 'Sirocco' type	2
Lubrication oil cooling pump	Horizontal, turbo-reduction gear combined pump; oil gear, water centrifugal	8
Oil cooler	Vertical, internal water, external oil	8
Feed water heater	Vertical, direct (surface) heating	8
Fuel oil heater	Vertical *Kukkyokukan*(?) type	8
Blower for control room	Horizontal, electric drive, 'Sirocco' type	8

Auxiliary Machinery outside the Machinery Spaces

Smoke cooling pump	Horizontal, electric drive, centrifugal	2
Smoke ejector pump	Horizontal, electric drive, Elmo type	2
Fuel oil distributing pump	Horizontal, electric drive	3 (2 fwd, 1 aft)
Supply vent. for machine shop	Horizontal, axial flow, electric drive	1
Exhaust vent. for machine shop	Horizontal, axial flow, electric drive	1
Fore anchor windlass	Electric drive with gearing	1
Aft anchor windlass	Electric drive with gearing	1
Main steering gear	Electric drive, hydraulic	1
Auxiliary steering gear	Electric drive, hydraulic	1

TABLE 4: AIRCRAFT, ARMAMENT & OTHER EQUIPMENT

Aircraft & Aviation Equipment

Type 0 fighter (Zero)	18 (+2)
Type 99 dive bomber (Val)	27 (+5)
Type 97 torpedo bomber (Kate)	27 (+5)
Arrester wire Type Kure Model 4 Mod.2	10
Crash barrier Type Kusho Model 3 Mod.1	3
Aircraft lifts	3
Bomb lifts	2
No.80 (800kg) bomb	90
No.25 (250kg) bomb	306
No.6 (60kg) bomb	540
Catapult (planned)	1 set
[aerial torpedoes: see below]	

Armament & Associated Equipment

Type 89 12.7cm/40 HA guns (250rpg)	
in twin mounting	16 (8 x II)
Type 96 25mm MG (2,600rpg)	
in triple mounting	36 (12 x III)
12.7cm ammunition hoist (vertical)	16
MG ammunition hoist (vertical)	16
MG ammunition hoist (horizontal)	1
Type 94 HA FC director system	4
Type 95 MG FC director system	6

Underwater Weapons & Equipment

Kampon-type air compressor pump Model 3 Mod.1	5
Type 94 oxygen generator (planned)	1
Type 94 oxygen compressor (planned)	1
Compressed air flasks Type 2	8
Special oxygen flasks Type 2 Mod.1	5
Small-type paravane Mod.1	2
Minesweeping gear Mod.1	2
Model 2 bomb disposal chain Mod.1	13
Medium-sized M/S gear Model 1 Mod.1	2
Type 95 DC Mod.1	6
Aerial torpedo 45cm Type 91	45
Sonar Type 91 No.4	1

Optical Equipment

Type 14 6-metre duplex RF	2
Type 94 4.5m RF (part of the HA FCS)	4
Type 96 1.5m RF (part of the MG fire director)	3
18cm Type 13 binocular with direction indicator	2
12cm HA Type 13 binocular with	
direction transmitter and future setting	3
12cm HA binocular (fixed support)	2
Type 13 Mod.1 direction observation (bearing) plate	4
Direction observation (bearing) plate for HA	4

Navigation Equipment

Type 93 No.3 magnetic compass	1
Type 90 magnetic compass No.3 Mod.1	1
Type Armstrong No.3 gyro compass (double type)	1
Type 90 No.3 magnetic compass	1
Type 90 Model 2 Mod.1 depth meter	1
Type 92 No.2 Mod.1 pitometer log	1
Type 96 Model 1 dead reckoning tracer	1
Type 91 Mod.1 wind speed meter	1
Type 92 Mod.1 wind direction meter	3
Type 97 Mod.1 balloon	1

Electrical Equipment
Main Power Supply (AC)

AC turbo generator (600kW, 225V)	3
AC diesel generator (350kW, 225V)	2

Secondary Power Supply (DC)

Generator: 1kW x 2, 50KVA x 2, 20KVA x2, VA x 1, 6KW x 1	
Battery Type 3 Mod.1 (114 banks)	1
Battery Type 3 Mod.1 (112 banks)	4
Type 96 110cm searchlight Model 1	4
Type 96 searchlight director (controller)	4
60cm signalling searchlight	2
2kW signalling lamp Mod.2	2

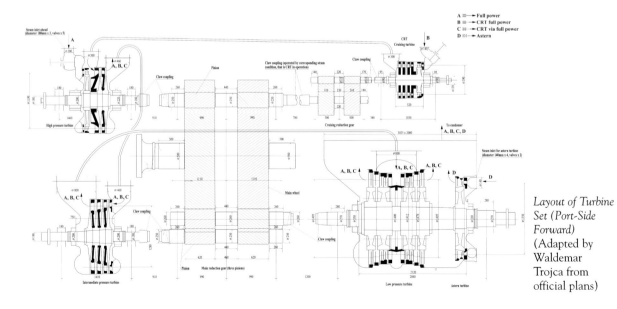

Layout of Turbine Set (Port-Side Forward) (Adapted by Waldemar Trojca from official plans)

Radio Equipment

Transmitters:		Ultra short wave 2kW	2
Long wave 500W	2	Ultra short wave 1kW	1
Short/long wave 500W	1	Radio direction finder, long/short waves	4
Short wave 500W	4	Detection:	
Medium wave 250W	2	Long wave D/F	1
Receivers:		Short wave D/F	2
Long wave	3	Long wave meter	4
Short/long wave	22	Medium wave meter	2
Short wave	2	Short wave meter	3
Voice radio (wireless telephone):		Ultra short wave meter	3
Medium wave	2	Wireless controller	4
Short wave	1	Typewriter for decoding	4
Ultra short wave 5kW	1	Hydrophone (planned)	1

Notes:

1. The list of weapons and equipment is as designed. There were numerous differences on completion. In particular, there were changes in the number and type of binoculars, and the oxygen compressors were suppressed (no oxygen-powered aerial torpedoes were embarked). The standard outfit of bombs was 60 x No.80, 60 x No.60, 312 x No.25, 528 x No.6, and 48 x No.3; they were raised from the magazines to the hangar decks via one large and one small weapons lift. It is reported that nine torpedoes could be readied for operation simultaneously.

2. After the Battle for Midway the number of fighters was increased from 18 (+2) to 27 (+5), while the number of dive bombers embarked was reduced correspondingly. The original aircraft types were to have been replaced by newer models, but it was 1944 before new aircraft were embarked.

3. Each time *Shôkaku* was repaired following bomb damage the number of 25mm MG was increased. In May 1942 two triple mounts were added at the bow, two at the stern and two fore and aft of the island, and in October an additional triple MG was mounted on the centre-line between the two located at the bow and stern, making for a total of 20 triple mounts. Ten 25mm single MG were added prior to the Battle of the Philippine Sea in June 1944. Following the loss of *Shôkaku* in the battle, *Zuikaku's* close-range AA armament was again reinforced. She now had eight 12.7cm twin HA mountings, twenty triple 25mm mountings, twenty-six fixed single 25mm and ten transportable single 25mm (total: 96 MG).

4. *Shôkaku* was the first IJN carrier to be equipped with radar. The antenna of the Type 21 (air search), which had recently been accepted into service, was mounted atop of the bridge between the end of August and early October 1942, and a second radar of the same type was added after October, the antenna taking the position of the former No.3 110cm retractable searchlight (mounted in a flight deck recess). When the first radar was mounted, the type 94 HA FCS mounted atop the bridge was relocated to a newly-constructed sponson to port, almost opposite the bridge. Prior to the Battle of the Philippine Sea (*A Gô Sakusen*) in June 1944, Type 13 air search radar was also installed with the antenna fixed to the light tripod mast abaft the island.

5. In August 1944 Kure N.Y. mounted eight 28-tube rocket launchers on two newly-built platforms similar to (but larger than) the MG sponsons. The launchers to starboard were located immediately forward of the forward HA guns. A fire control director was installed, and four rocket launchers were mounted in line. The length of the sponson was 12 m. The platform to port was located abaft the after HA gun group; the FC director and launchers were mounted in the same way as the starboard group. On forward and after arcs the launchers could fire within 30° of the ship's axis. The 12cm multiple rocket launcher and its projectile are described in *Warship* No.34 (April 1985), pp.125-133.

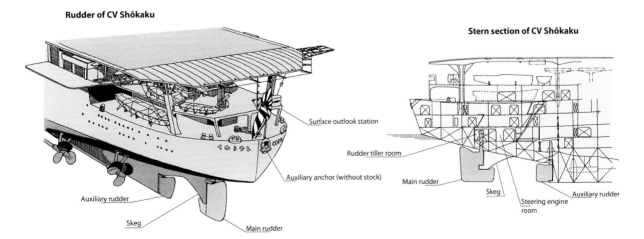

Rudder of CV Shôkaku

Surface outlook station

Auxiliary anchor (without stock)

Auxiliary rudder

Skeg

Main rudder

Stern section of CV Shôkaku

Rudder tiller room

Main rudder

Skeg

Steering engine room

Auxiliary rudder

Shôkaku: *Stern* (Hasegawa Tôichi, *Nihon no Kôkûbokan*, adapted by Waldemar Trojca)

the machinery spaces were emptied under battle conditions, and in the event of a torpedo hit, undamaged tanks could be flooded correspondingly as a supporting measure.

Machinery

In order to attain the required speed of 34.5 knots, the turbines were designed to develop 160,000shp[12] on four shafts. This was the highest output of any existing Japanese warship; it exceeded that of the *Yamato* class by 10,000shp and of the *Mogami* class cruisers by 8,000shp. A striking feature of the propulsion plant was that the cruise turbines were designed for a speed of 26 knots.[13] An abbreviated account of the official 'Engine Planning and Specifications for No.3 Warship' (19 pages including drawings) is given below. (Paragraphs 1 [General Hull Specifications] and 11 [Acceptance Run] are omitted.) For the data see the accompanying tables.

Engine Layout

When steaming full ahead, 160,000shp in total to be generated by four turbines and eight oil burning boilers; boiler steam pressure to be 30kg/cm² at 350°C. Length of the machinery spaces to be 74.22m (engine rooms 33.90m; boiler rooms 40.32m – see drawing for details).

Main Engines

Main engines to have a four-shaft arrangement with Kampon high pressure (HP), intermediate pressure (IP) and low pressure (LP) turbines driving each shaft via reduction gearing. One set of turbines to be installed in each of the four engine rooms: the turbines driving the inner shafts to be installed in the after engine rooms and those driving the wing shafts in the forward engine rooms. Each propeller shaft to be driven by three-pinion single-reduction gearing transmitting a total of 40,000shp at 300 rpm. (The HP and cruise turbines were outboard of the IP and LP turbines, with the cruise and LP turbines abaft the gearing and the HP and IP turbines forward; the cruise turbines had separate two-pinion reduction gearing). The astern turbines to be housed within the casings for the LP turbines. An electric and a manual turning unit to be fitted at one end of the pinion shaft of each LP turbine.

Main Condensers

Each set of turbines to be equipped with a condenser with the following characteristics:

Cooling area:	1,387m²
Length of outer casing:	4.45m
Outer diameter of tubes:	16mm
Thickness of tubes:	1.2mm
Number of tubes:	6,200

Shafts and Propellers

For the dimensions of the shafts see the accompanying table. The propeller shaft thrust bearing to be of the Mitchell type; thrust not to exceed 20kg/cm² on the white alloy pad. The claw brake to be installed at the junction of the intermediate shaft and the stern shaft; to hold the shaft at three quarters of the specified full power torque.

Propellers to have the following characteristics:

Diameter:	4.20m
Pitch:	4.40m (approx.)
Developed area:	11.77m² (approx.)[14]

Boilers

Eight boilers to be located in eight boiler rooms; the latter to be of the open type. For the specifications for the Kampon Type Model B oil-burning boilers see the accompanying table.

Uptakes and Funnels

Two funnels: the forward one to serve the forward group of four boilers and the after one the after group. The funnels to be angled downwards on the hull side. The specifications for the uptake and funnel areas for one boiler to be as follows:

Boiler top	4.33m²
Uptake area above middle deck	3.46m²
Funnel	3.03m²

Auxiliary Machinery

For the types and number of units see the accompanying table.

Repair Facilities

The repair shop to be of battleship standard.

Weight of Machinery

Estimated weight of machinery is as follows:

Main engines	675t
Shafting and propellers	360t
Auxiliary machinery	290t
Boilers and accessory equipment	545t
Uptake and funnel installations	120t
Pipes, cocks, valves, etc.	360t
Miscellaneous	185t
Total (without feed water)	2535t
Feed water (trial condition)	250t
Total (with water/trial condition)	2785t

On trials which took place in June 1941, *Shôkaku* attained 34.37 knots with 161,290shp and 307 shaft rpm at a displacement of 30,003 tonnes. EHP was calculated as 76,000 with a propulsion coefficient of 0.475, slightly in excess of the average value for carriers and identical to that of *Sôryû*. *Shôkaku*'s sister *Zuikaku* was slightly faster: 34.58 knots with 168,100shp. Steam generation per boiler was 103 tonnes/hour, which almost matched that in the *Suzuya* and *Sôryû* classes and *Kaga* following her conversion.

With the cruise turbines running at 'allowable maximum power' (50,000shp), speed was 26 knots, sufficient to obtain the speed of 13m/s wind over deck necessary for aircraft take-off in calm conditions. Note the huge increase in output between maximum cruise speed and maximum speed: more than 110,000shp was required to increase speed from 26 knots to 34.5 knots. A total of 5000 tonnes of heavy oil was required to attain the required endurance of 9700nm at 18 knots.

The bulbous bow and the stern configuration, with its twin rudders, were adopted following experiments conducted in the course of the design of the 'super-battle-ships' of the *Yamato* class. The semi-balanced main rudder had an area of 34.367m² and was placed abaft the propellers. Forward of it was a balanced auxiliary rudder with a surface area of 11.995m². This arrangement had been adopted for fast ships belonging to other navies, notably the battlecruisers of the Imperial German Navy and the French treaty cruisers of the *Duquesne* class.

Armament

The anti-aircraft armament of the *Shôkaku* class comprised eight Type 89 40-cal 12.7cm twin HA gun mountings. The guns could be elevated to 90° and depressed to -8°; mountings firing across the flight deck could engage targets on the opposite side only down to +12°. The mountings to starboard were numbered using odd numbers (1-7) from fore to aft, while those on the port side had even numbers (2-8).The two after mount-

Shôkaku: Underwater protection at Frame 172 (from aft)

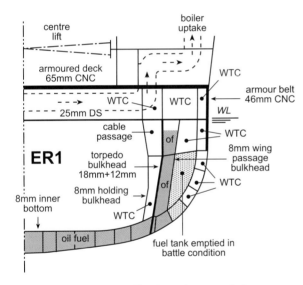

Flooding after torpedo hit

c.900 tonnes of water floods underwater protection system but held by 8mm inner bulkhead

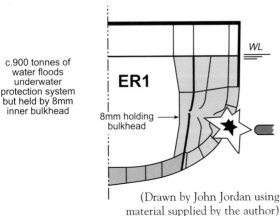

(Drawn by John Jordan using material supplied by the author)

ings to starboard (Nos.5 & 7) had shields to protect the crews against smoke and gases from the funnels. Ammunition provision was 250 rounds per gun plus 12 training rounds (*nendo jô*).

For the purpose of fire control the 12.7cm mounts were divided into four groups, and each group had its own designated Type 94 HA director: two were fitted to starboard fore and aft of the bridge, one atop the island, and the fourth to port abreast the bridge.

For close-range AA defence there were twelve Type 96 25mm triple MG: six to port, and six to starboard. Each pair of MG mountings had its own Type 95 fire control director. As with the 12.7cm mountings, the two mount-ings to starboard abaft the funnels had shields. The mountings to starboard were numbered using odd numbers (1-11) from fore to aft, while those on the port side had even numbers (2-12). Ammunition provision was 2600 rounds for each 25mm mounting, plus 100 training rounds.

The anti-aircraft armament was stronger than that of *Akagi* and *Kaga*, and fire control provision was markedly superior. During the war radar was fitted, the number of MG mountings increased (see table notes), and new types of aircraft were embarked. Despite this, the IJN failed to keep pace with the rapid technical developments on the Allied side.[15]

Complement

The planned complement was 75 commissioned officers, 56 special duty officers, 71 warrant officers and 1458 petty officers and ratings, for a total of 1660 officers and men. This figure was undoubtedly increased during wartime with the fitting of additional AA guns, radar and rocket launchers, but reliable data is lacking.

Appendix: Underwater Protection Arrangement of the Shôkaku *Class*

To prevent the destruction of the torpedo bulkhead by multiple splinters generated by the break-up of the structure in the immediate vicinity of the detonation point and the direct impact of the detonation gases, systematic model experiments were carried out from 1935. Because the speed of splinters is substantially unaffected by the width of the air space, and because within the usual width of the air space (ca.3m) the force of the detonation has considerable destructive power, it was of the utmost importance to find protective methods to reduce the effect of the splinters before they struck the torpedo bulk-head. In addition, damage might be increased by the inrush of water through the hole caused by the detona-tion, thereby underlining the importance of an undam-aged bulkhead.

In the end the IJN arrived at the following conclusions:

– A water layer is more effective than either an air layer or a bulge filled with watertight steel tubes.
– The depth of the water layer should be 600mm, and the compartment should be filled to no more than 90

For the Battle of Leyte Gulf, October 1944, Zuikaku was assigned to V-Ad. Ozawa Jisaburô's First Mobile Fleet, which was tasked with acting as a diversionary force to enable the main IJN battle force to penetrate the gulf and disrupt the Allied landings. This photo, taken on 25 October 1944, shows Zuikaku in the centre, the light carrier Zuihô in the background and the anti-aircraft destroyer Wakatsuki in the foreground; the ships are manoeuvring off Cape Engaño. Zuihô appears to be down by stern and Zuikaku gives also the impression of being damaged. However, much of the smoke visible is from the firing of the HA guns and also the 12cm rocket launchers. Leyte Gulf was to be the last great battle of the Pacific War; Ozawa lost all four of his carriers to air attack or gunfire. (Fukui Shizuo collection)

An aerial view of the damaged Zuikaku taken by an American aircraft at 1230 on 25 October 1944; speed is estimated to be 15 to 18 knots. Note the camouflaged flight deck and the damage to the forward elevator. Despite the huge clouds of black smoke emitted by the two funnels the downward-angled configuration of the latter means that the hot gases are kept clear of the flight deck. The US Navy photo caption states that the ship had already sustained major damage, but that the fires appear to have been contained because of the countermeasures adopted by the IJN during the war (foam fire fighting system and use of fire-resistant paint – see the author's article on the carrier Katsuragi in Warship 2010). Multiple torpedo hits were claimed by the US planes, with the subsequent flooding of many compartments; Zuikaku would sink two hours after this photo was taken. (Fukui Shizuo collection)

percent of the capacity. (Experiments with deeper layers and capacity filling brought about inferior results; also, the deeper the water layer the narrower the air space, which was important for the expansion of the detonation gases and, hence, the dispersion of their force.)

– The water layer should be against the face of the protective bulkhead with the void outboard of it. In this way the water layer distributes the force of concussion over the entire surface of the protective bulkhead, thus greatly reducing the pressure per unit. In addition, the speed of splinters is reduced, and much of the heat of the gases consumed. The larger the width of the outer air space, the greater the expansion of the detonation gases.

– A straight bulkhead is superior to the curved type.

– It is very difficult for the torpedo bulkhead to resist the detonation pressure and maintain watertightness at the same time. To guarantee watertightness an additional watertight holding bulkhead ('back plate', or *seita*) should be fitted inboard of the torpedo bulkhead.

– From the point of view of weight, it would be uneconomical to carry water in the 'water layer', so heavy oil is used instead. As the fuel oil is consumed, it must be replaced by water in order to maintain the same level of protection – experiments had shown no combustion of fuel near the point of detonation.

It was concluded that the thickness of the torpedo bulkhead could be reduced by 50% if a liquid, as opposed to an air layer, was used. It was also calculated that flooding would be reduced by about 30%.

Note: If the conclusions in the study above, which was undertaken in 1941, are compared with the system devised for the *Shôkaku* class, it is evident that the arrangement adopted for the carriers was broadly in line with the findings, but that the width of the air space was insufficient, while the depth of the water/oil layer was excessive. By reducing the depth of the liquid layer to 600mm the air space (ie the emptied oil tanks) could have been increased to 2.8-3.2m, and by increasing the thickness of the protective bulkhead to from 30mm to 42mm the designed resistance (against 450kg explosive) would have been attained in accordance with the formula developed from the model experiments.

Footnotes:

1. The initial requirement had been 96 aircraft: 12 Type 96 fighters ('Claude'), 24 Type 96 bombers ('Susie'), 24 Type 97 attack planes (C3N - construction halted), 12 Type 97 reconnaissance aircraft and 24 reserve aircraft of various types. The total of 96 reflected the air complements of *Akagi* and *Kaga* after conversion. An air group on a par with the latter carriers had been perhaps the most important requirement of the NGS. However, the capacity of the *Shôkakus* was limited to a total of 84 by the appearance of new and larger aircraft types.

2. Two aircraft touched the bridge with their wings after landing and one plane went overboard.

3. In contrast to *Shôkaku's ad hoc* arrangements in the upper part of the hull, Kawasaki Kobe was able to devise a more complete solution because *Zuikaku's* construction was not so far advanced at the time of the decision.

4. According to Report S-01-3 of the US Naval Technical Mission to Japan (USNTMtJ), 'Surface Warship Hull Design', p.44, there existed no definitive criteria for roll, pitch, wind and snow loads as the basis for the design of the flight deck supporting structure; experience and judgement were the determining factors.

5. In *Maru Special* No.6 an example of *Zuikaku* is given according to which the maximum angle of heel was 40° when sailing in a typhoon with a wind speed of 50m/s. The ratio between the lateral areas above (wind pressure) and below the waterline (wetted) was 1.69.

6. The height of freeboard at the bow was greater than in *Hiryû*. After the experiences with *Ryûjô* and *Sôryû* the height was now sufficient, in combination with the marked flare of the hull sides, to ensure a dry anchor deck. Speed and reserve buoyancy were also factors in choice of the height of freeboard; height was the maximum possible taking into account stability, wind pressure area and air resistance. This is expressed by the depth/draft ratio, which was 2.59.

7. Data about riveting are omitted

8. For details see Lars Ahlberg & Hans Lengerer *Taihô* Vol.1, pp.63-76, AJ-Press 2004.

9. A similar arrangement was adopted for the contemporary French battleships of the *Dunkerque* and *Richelieu* classes (see John Jordan & Robert Dumas, *French Battleships 1922-1956*, Seaforth Publishing, 2009, p.48 & p.113).

10. The stated joint efficiency of 53% seems exceptionally low. Since the heavy oil tanks were adjacent to the protective bulkhead, oil-tight riveting would normally have been applied. A joint efficiency of 70-73% was regularly obtained by this method. The author therefore suspects that the figure '53' is a misprint for '73'. *Shôwa Zôsen-shi*, Vol. 1, p.657 appears to confirm this: when describing the liquid loading abeam the boiler rooms, it is stated that the bulkhead's ability to resist a 450kg torpedo warhead assumed a joint efficiency of 70% in respect of each protective plate.

11. According to data published by Fukuda Keiji, 9kg of explosive was detonated 1.52m below the water surface against models with and without a water layer of various widths and at distances 600mm-1,400mm from the hull. The conclusion was that with a water layer depth of 202mm the thickness of the torpedo bulkhead could be reduced by about 50%. The NTRI tested water layers in 1922, and conducted tests using the multi-layer underwater protection system of the US battleship *Colorado* in 1923.

12. The only other IJN warship with the same engine power was the carrier *Taihô*. (The author is indebted to the late Dr. Itani Jirô, who obtained a copy of the relevant documentation from the Historical Branch of the JMSDF at his request.)

13. Note that in the table showing rated power and propeller rpm, no fewer than three types of cruise operation are defined.

14. Actual values were diameter 4.20m, pitch 4.12m, pitch ratio 0.98, boss ratio 0.23, ratio of developed blade area 0.77, projected area 0.70. The propellers were of the 3-bladed ogival type and were of manganese bronze (*Kaigun Zôsen Gijutsu Gaiyô*, Vol.7, p.1678; *Shôwa Zôsenshi*, Vol.1, p.686).

15. For more data see 'Anti-Aircraft Gunnery in the Imperial Japanese Navy', *Warship* 1991.

RUSSIA'S CIRCULAR IRONCLADS: THE *POPOVKAS*

The circular ironclads *Novgorod* and *Vitse-admiral Popov* are probably the Russian ships best known to westerners, and have often been used to illustrate the foolishness – or outright incompetence – of Russian naval authorities. In this article **Stephen McLaughlin** takes a fresh look at these peculiar vessels.

Under the terms of the Treaty of Paris which ended the Crimean War (1854-56), Russia was allowed to have only six 800-ton corvettes in the Black Sea.[1] The General-Admiral of the Navy, the Grand Duke Konstantin Nikolaevich, an energetic and forward-looking leader, was naturally unhappy about this limitation, and in 1862 some attempts were made to design a vessel with 4.5in (114mm) armour on this tonnage, but it was soon realised that it would be impossible to combine thick armour, heavy guns and good sea-going qualities in a ship of such small size.

The next approach to the problem came in 1863, when the war minister, General D.A. Miliutin, wrote a 'very secret' memo to the director of the Naval Ministry, Admiral N.K. Krabbe, in which it was proposed that armoured self-propelled batteries be built to defend the Kerch Strait.[2] This narrow channel was the entrance to the Sea of Azov, where British naval raiding forces had wreaked a good deal of havoc during the Crimean War. Miliutin believed that by building strictly defensive craft, lacking any sea-going potential, Russia could avoid accusations of violating the Treaty of Paris. In August Krabbe had the Shipbuilding Technical Committee (*Korablestroitel'nyi tekhnicheskii komitet*, or KTK) investigate such batteries. The resulting design was apparently the work of naval constructor S.I. Cherniavskii. It showed a simple wooden-hulled ironclad with a shallow draught and a very low freeboard (10in/254mm); dimensions were 160ft x 42ft x 8ft 10in full load (48.8m x 12.8m x 2.7m).[3] It was armed with four guns (possibly 60pdr smoothbores or 8in rifles) housed in a rectangular casemate, which would also have rifle loop-holes. Armour over the hull and casemate was to be 4.5in (114mm), and the twin-shaft machinery would provide a speed of 5 knots. Although Emperor Aleksandr II approved the further development of this proposal in September, it seems to have been something of a dead-end.

By early 1864 attention had switched to building monitors of the *Uragan* class.[4] Because there was virtually no industrial base in southern Russia, it was assumed that the materials for the vessels would have to be manufactured at some distant place and transported to a shipyard where they would be assembled. This presented difficulties insofar as the railway network in south Russia was still undeveloped; however, Russia's vast inland waterways offered an alternative means of moving bulky materials. Captain-Lieutenant A.I. Fëdorov was sent to scout out potential building sites; having previously supervised the prefabrication of the monitors *Koldun* and *Veshchun* in Belgium, he was well acquainted with the sort of process that would be needed to build similar ironclads for the Black Sea. After travelling extensively throughout south Russia, he presented his report in November 1864. His conclusion was that by using the existing industrial and transportation network it would be possible to have the Votkinskii Iron Works (today the city of Votkinsk) fabricate the parts for monitors, then transport the materials down the river system for assembly at an existing boatyard at Kalach-na-Donu; the completed monitors could then travel down the Don River to the Sea of Azov. If the vessels were ordered in January 1865, Fëdorov believed that the first would be ready for launching in summer of 1866, and the second by the autumn of 1866 or the spring of 1867.

The commander of the Port of Nikolaev, Vice-Admiral B.A. Glazenap, now chimed in, arguing that ironclads were needed not only to defend the Kerch Strait, but the Dnepr-Bug estuary as well, and that no fewer than twenty-one *Uragan*-class monitors were therefore required. Better still in his opinion would be the construction of casemate batteries, since he believed that such vessels would be smaller and better protected than the monitors, as well as healthier for their crews in the warm climate of southern Russia; five would be needed for the Kerch Strait and three for the Dnepr-Bug estuary. Such purely defensive vessels, he argued, would not cause protests based on the Treaty of Paris; moreover, if they stayed within the Sea of Azov and the river system without actually entering the Black Sea, they might not be regarded as subject to the restrictions of the Paris treaty at all. As a result of Glazenap's proposal, in March 1865 the KTK worked out a design for an iron-hulled battery with the following characteristics:

Displacement:	2,037 tons
Dimensions:	210ft x 48ft 3in x 9ft 10in
	(64m x 14.7m x 3m)
Armament:	6 x 9in (229mm)
Protection:	5.5in (140mm) casemate,
	4.5in (114mm) belt
Machinery:	Twin screws

The guns could be shifted from one side to the other, so that all six could fire on either broadside.

In the end, both Glazenap's and Fëdorov's plans were rejected, and in November 1865 it was decided to establish an entirely new shipyard near the Kerch Strait for building both *Uragan* and *Smerch*-type turret ships. Preparatory work was started at the site in January 1866, and everything seemed set for the construction of the first Black Sea ironclads. However, later that year the empire was confronted by a tremendous financial crisis, as a result of which the Naval Ministry's budget was cut by 28%. Konstantin Nikolaevich, determined to continue the construction of the Baltic ironclads he considered essential for the defence of St. Petersburg, was forced to make deep cuts elsewhere in the budget. In October 1866 the Black Sea flotilla was abolished, and in 1867 the existing Lazarevskoe Admiralty (shipyard) at Sevastopol was turned over to the private ROPiT shipping line. Russia's nascent naval presence in the Black Sea was liquidated, and with it her plans for a fleet of defensive ironclads there.

The Popovkas: *Design*

General Miliutin, however, was not about to let the matter lapse. In the latter part of 1869, alarmed by Turkish ironclad construction and Austrian plans for building monitors on the Danube, he again called attention to the need for ironclads to defend the Black Sea coast, his concerns as before focused on the Dnepr-Bug estuary and Kerch Strait.[5] As a result a special conference was called to study the question of naval defences in the Black Sea. In addition to conventional turret ships the conference considered a proposal by Rear-Admiral A.A. Popov for circular ships, an idea that the respected Scottish shipbuilder John Elder had also recently put forward at the Royal United Service Institution.[6]

Popov later explained his rationale for choosing a circular form: he noted that Edward Reed, the former Chief Constructor of the Royal Navy,

> …said many years ago that by shortening the ship we diminish the extent of the surface which must be protected by armour, and by broadening the ship we increase the displacement or power to carry the armour. He said also that very moderate increase of steam power was needed to give to the short ship the same speed as to the long one…
>
> When my Government found it necessary to build ironclads for shallow water and special purposes, and as inexpensive as possible, I began to think about this question from the point of view of Mr. Reed. As a consequence, I shortened the ships and increased their breadth, and after investigation carried the principle to its extreme limit, making the breadth equal to the length.[7]

Popov's circular ship was to mount the most powerful guns then available to the Russian Navy, either 11in rifles or 20in smoothbores, in a 'fixed turret' – that is, an open-topped barbette. He originally thought that two propellers would be sufficient to drive the ship.

Whether conventional or circular ironclads were selected for construction there would be many problems to overcome – for example, the major port of Sevastopol still lacked railway connections with the rest of the empire.[8] Therefore a second special conference on Black Sea defences, chaired by the general-admiral, was convened in the latter half of December 1869. The result of the conference was a decision to build four small ironclads at the old Nikolaev Admiralty, at a total cost of four million rubles. The conference narrowed the choices to a vessel similar to the Baltic ironclads of the *Rusalka* class (1,882 tons, draught 11ft, four 9in rifles), or Popov's circular type. However, the characteristics specified by the army engineers for the ships – draught of about 11ft, main battery of 11-in guns, armour 'greater than on the largest foreign armourclads' – prejudiced the choice, for they ruled out a conventional ship like *Rusalka*.

Meanwhile, a circular test boat, with a diameter of 11ft, was built at St. Petersburg and ran her trials in April 1870 (a channel had to be hacked through the ice of the still-frozen Baltic for the purpose). The odd craft moved well, and was considered a success. When this was reported to the emperor, he ordered that the circular ironclads should be called *popovkas* – a diminutive form of their originator's name.[9]

Popov and his assistants were soon busy working out a variety of circular ironclad designs. Different combinations of hull diameter and armament were explored, including designs with barbettes or rotating turrets for 11in rifles or 20in smoothbores; the task of the designers was eased somewhat when the Naval Technical Committee (*Morskoi tekhnicheskii komitet*, MTK, which replaced the KTK in 1867) increased the permissible draught to 14ft.[10] On 26 May/7 June 1870 the results were presented to the general-admiral, who selected the 'maximum' popovka: 6,054 tons, 151ft in diameter, 12ft 6in draught, armed with four 20in smoothbores and protected by 21.7in armour. The MTK subsequently altered the armament to 11in rifles. An experienced naval constructor, Colonel A.V. Mordvinov, was chosen to oversee the detail design work, and the naval attaché in Britain, Rear-Admiral I.F. Likhachev, was soon buying the machinery and tools needed to equip the long-dormant construction workshops in Nikolaev.

However, apparently Admiral Krabbe soon had second thoughts about building a single huge vessel of a new and unproven type; estimates indicated the vessel would cost 4.14 million rubles, more than had been specified earlier for the construction of the four coast defence ironclads originally proposed. On 23 July/4 August 1870 he ordered the commander-in-chief of the Port of Petersburg to work out a programme for ten smaller circular ironclads, to be fabricated at St. Petersburg and Kronshtadt and assembled at Nikolaev. The port's constructors started with a much smaller hull, 80ft in diameter, and a displacement of 1,200 tons; each ship would be armed with two 9in rifles in a barbette, while the armour would be 6-8in. In order to

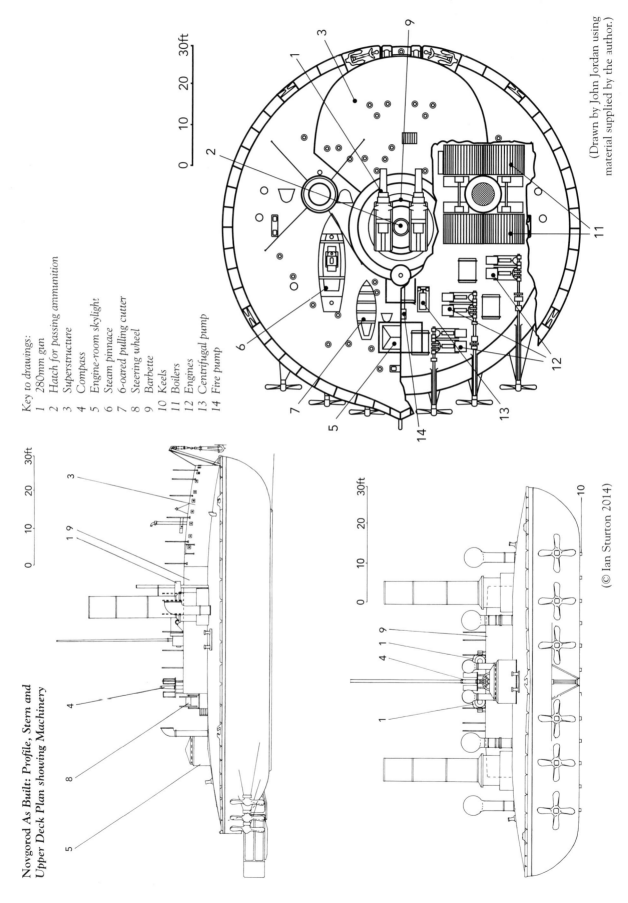

Novgorod As Built: Profile, Stern and Upper Deck Plan showing Machinery

Key to drawings:
1 280mm gun
2 Hatch for passing ammunition
3 Superstructure
4 Compass
5 Engine-room skylight
6 Steam pinnace
7 6-oared pulling cutter
8 Steering wheel
9 Barbette
10 Keels
11 Boilers
12 Engines
13 Centrifugal pump
14 Fire pump

(Drawn by John Jordan using material supplied by the author.)

(© Ian Sturton 2014)

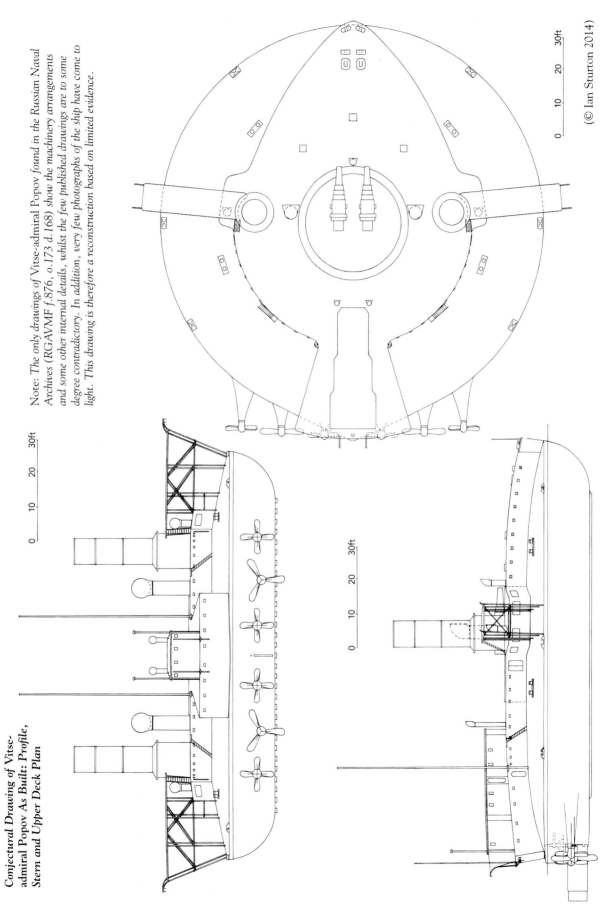

Note: The only drawings of Vitse-admiral Popov found in the Russian Naval Archives (RGAVMF f.876, o.173 d.168) show the machinery arrangements and some other internal details, whilst the few published drawings are to some degree contradictory. In addition, very few photographs of the ship have come to light. This drawing is therefore a reconstruction based on limited evidence.

(© Ian Sturton 2014)

Conjectural Drawing of Vitse-admiral Popov As Built: Profile, Stern and Upper Deck Plan

save money these craft would be propelled by four 70nhp engines taken from existing gunboats – 32 such engines were available, so only eight new ones would have to be built. The entire program would cost 9.5 million rubles and take 15 months to complete.

Faced with this competition, Popov was compelled to reduce the size and cost of his brain-child. He and his team worked out six new variants, and on 12/24 October 1870 the emperor approved the construction of a 96ft diameter vessel. The ship would be armed with two 11in guns, protected by 12in armour and propelled by four (later increased to six) engines. The cost of construction, shipment to Nikolaev and reassembly would be 1.94 million rubles per ship; the total cost, including improvements to the shipyards, was estimated at 8.5 million rubles.

While design work was underway on the popovkas, events were unfolding in Europe that could have changed the plans for naval defences in the south. On 19/31 October 1870 Russia's foreign minister, A.M. Gorchakov, announced the emperor's decision to renounce the Black Sea neutrality clauses of the Treaty of Paris. The moment was well chosen; Russia was supported by the Prussians, who at that moment were besieging Paris, leaving France powerless to interfere. Austria-Hungary, with Russian troops massing on her border – Russia's *quid pro quo* to Berlin, intended to prevent Vienna from seeking revenge for her recent defeat by Prussia – was also in no condition to object. Britain was thus diplomatically isolated. Despite protests, the Russian move had to be accepted, and was confirmed in March 1871 by an international conference held in London. Russia was free to rebuild her Black Sea Fleet, although it had to remain in that sea; no warships except those of the Ottoman Empire were allowed to pass through the Turkish Straits.

Despite this new freedom, however, the navy did not start planning the construction of a sea-going Black Sea fleet. Russia's economy could barely support the construction of a naval force in the Baltic, so, as Konstantin

himself wrote: 'An armourclad fleet for the Black Sea must have, for the time being, an exclusively defensive character'.[11] Therefore work on the defensively-oriented popovkas continued.

In January 1871 a temporary slipway was hacked out of the frozen ground at the New Admiralty yard in St. Petersburg. Construction of the first popovka actually began on 1/13 April 1871, the work going on in two shifts to speed things along. Meanwhile, a second small circular craft had been constructed. She was appropriately named *Kambala* (flatfish or flounder), and had a diameter of 24ft. She was powered by two 8nhp engines, and her trials in the summer of 1871 were considered a success.

Construction

The construction of the ironclad's hull went quickly, and was completed by the date of the official keel-laying ceremony, 17/29 December 1871. Within two weeks the hull, bolted together rather than riveted, had been disassembled and the parts were ready for shipment. The first batch arrived at Nikolaev on 21 March/2 April 1872 and re-assembly began eight days later on a specially prepared slipway. Because there was as yet no direct railway link to Nikolaev, the shipments were sent first to Odessa, then delivered to Nikolaev by river barges and steamers. The boilers, too large for railway shipment, had to be sent around Europe by ship to Odessa and then carried to Nikolaev by river craft.

Problems with the delivery of parts from St. Petersburg caused numerous delays in construction. Nikolaev lacked everything, including tools and even timber – it proved to be cheaper to buy Russian timber in England and have it sent to Nikolaev than to have domestic firms deliver it directly. In addition, the workers in Nikolaev were inexperienced. Complicating matters for the constructors was the fact that Konstantin Nikolaevich was determined to

Novgorod under construction at the New Admiralty shipyard in St. Petersburg. The sections of the hull were bolted together so that it could be disassembled and sent to Nikolaev by rail. (Courtesy of Sergei Vinogradov)

Novgorod at Nikolaev a few days before her launch. Her six propellers can be seen, as well as her rudder, angled over to starboard. This picture, and the next, make clear how primitive conditions were at the shipyard. (Courtesy of Sergei Vinogradov)

Another view of Novgorod *shortly before her launch, this time from the port side. The steering wheel can be seen abaft her barbette, which apparently still lacks its armour plating. The forward superstructure also appears to be incomplete. (Courtesy of Sergei Vinogradov)*

TABLE 1: CONSTRUCTION DATES

	Novgorod	Vitse-admiral Popov
Contracted:	—	—
Added to List:	13/25 Nov 1871	13/25 Nov 1871
Construction begun:	1/13 Apr 1871 (St. Petersburg)	Jan 1872; halted mid-1872; resumed to a new design in the spring of 1873
Laid down:	17/29 Dec 1871 (St. Petersburg)	27 Aug/8 Sep 1874
Reassembly begun:	29 Mar/10 Apr 1872 (Nikolaev)	—
Launched:	21 May/2 Jun 1873	25 Sep/7 Oct 1875
Entered service:	1874	1876
Builder:	New Admiralty Yard, St. Petersburg; reassembled at Nikolaev Admiralty	Nikolaev Admiralty
Constructor:	N.K. Glazyrin	?
Cost (hull and machinery):	2,830,000 rubles	3,260,000 rubles

Notes:

Added to List: The date a ship was officially added to the list of the fleet and given a name.

Construction begun: The date when the first iron was laid on the slipway.

Laid down: The date of the ceremonial keel-laying, not necessarily corresponding to an important stage in the ship's construction.

Vitse-admiral Popov under construction at Nikolaev, taken from off her starboard bow. The forward superstructure looks virtually complete, and most of the wood and copper sheathing is in place. (Courtesy of Dmitry Lemachko)

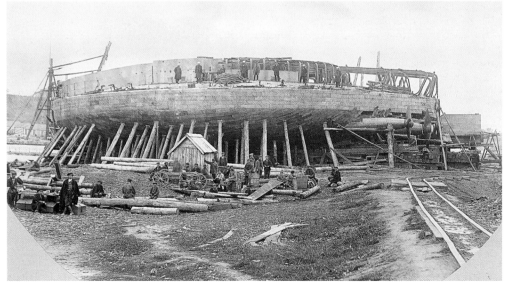

Another photograph of Popov under construction, this time from the port quarter. The framing for the after superstructure from the barbette to the stern is in place, as are the rudder and screws. Note the larger size and deeper placement of the inboard propeller. (Courtesy of Dmitry Lemachko)

attend the launch, which meant that the event had to dovetail with his crowded schedule. By early 1873 work was proceeding at a frantic pace, with 2,000 workmen bustling around the ship night and day. Even so, the launch date had to be postponed, and the ship finally took to the water on 21 May/2 June 1873. Christened *Novgorod* after one of the ancient cities of Russia, she was the first large Russian ship launched with her machinery and armour already mounted.

There had been changes to the design during construction, the most substantial being the addition of wood and copper sheathing, which increased the diameter of the hull by 5ft. This, combined with other changes (bronze propellers in place of cast iron ones, an increase in the number of false keels from seven to twelve, and so forth), led to a 400-ton increase in displacement, increasing draught by 1ft. The guns were finally mounted in September 1873; by this time the ship had already run her official machinery trials. She entered service in the following year.

The construction of the second circular ironclad, originally to be named *Kiev*, was begun at Nikolaev to the same drawings as *Novgorod*. But Admiral Popov, having introduced many alterations during the construction of the first ship, made even more substantial changes in the design of the second. The first of these modifications was the substitution of vertical compound engines for horizontal engines, for which Popov obtained approval in March 1872. Popov was given another opportunity to tinker with the design when work on *Kiev* was suspended in mid-1872 so that all available workers could be shifted to *Novgorod*. Moreover, he foresaw 'the necessity of improving the popovka, to make some changes in its construction indicated by experience' once *Novgorod* was completed.[12]

In July 1873 Popov reported on the preliminary trials of *Novgorod*, then went on to point out that, in order to counter powerful new ironclads like Britain's *Devastation*, the size of the *Kiev* had to be increased, so that she could carry thicker armour and heavier guns. On 3/15 August 1873 Popov presented what amounted to a new design to the MTK: the diameter of the hull would be increased by 19ft (the maximum that could fit in the available facilities at Sevastopol), the 11in guns would be replaced by 12in, and the thickness of the vertical armour would be increased to 18in. On 13/25 August the emperor granted his consent for the construction of the second popovka to these new drawings, and on 9/21 October an imperial *prikaz* (order) changed her name to *Vitse-admiral Popov*, in honour of her inventor.

With the approval of the new design it was necessary to dismantle some of the work already completed; this was done in the autumn of 1873.[13] The order to re-start work came on 15/27 October, but actual construction did not begin until the spring of 1874, with the launch planned for the autumn of 1875, and trials to follow in May 1876.

Facilities at Nikolaev were still far from satisfactory – for example, there was no floating crane of sufficient capacity to hoist the boilers aboard the ship, so one had to brought up (apparently from Sevastopol) – but as it was winter time the Ingul River was frozen, and a channel had to be cut through the ice to get the crane to the building

yard, causing a month's delay. A factory in south Russia, at Iuzovka, was contracted to supply some of the iron for the ship, but its products proved to be of such inferior quality that it was necessary to transfer the order to the Raivolovskii Works in Finland. Despite these and other problems, *Vitse-admiral Popov* was ready for trials in June 1876, only a month behind schedule.

A 'Utopia' of Circular Ironclads?

In several respects *Vitse-admiral Popov* was more than just a scaled-up version of *Novgorod*; Popov introduced a number of important changes in the design which, taken together, give the impression that its author was either forgetting the popovkas' original coast-defence rationale, or (more likely) was trying to prove that circular ironclads could be competent sea-going ships. Thus, during construction the superstructures were greatly expanded, to the point where they completely enveloped the barbette; this was done in order to improve the ship's seaworthiness – surely a minor concern for a vessel designed to operate in river estuaries. More telling were the changes in the propulsion plant; although the new design had six shafts, like *Novgorod*, the middle shaft on both sides was powered by two engines and had a larger screw that was set deeper in the water. This was intended to improve propulsive efficiency, but it also increased the draught by more than four feet, a considerable handicap for a ship intended to operate in shallow waters. Popov proposed two minor 'fixes' for this: first, since the larger propellers were three-bladed, by stopping them at the right position their immersion could be decreased somewhat; second, the stern could be raised by selectively flooding the between-bottom spaces in the bow. But these 'solutions' were obviously afterthoughts. Some effort was even devoted to equipping the popovkas with a sailing rig, and three small circular boats were built to test their handling under sail, but nothing came of this somewhat hare-brained scheme.

The impulse to scale the circular ironclad up into a full-fledged, ocean-going battleship was due not only to Popov's ambitions; it was also backed by Konstantin Nikolaevich, who was always seeking ways to improve Russia's naval position, especially if it could be done cheaply using new technologies. The circular ironclad seemed to offer just such a possibility; with its great carrying capacity and relatively small surface area, a ship with a round hull could carry the same heavy guns and armour as a much larger ironclad with a conventional hull. Spurred on by this prospect, in 1875 the Russian Naval Ministry requested, and the British Admiralty granted, permission for William Froude to carry out tests with models of several circular ships at Torquay, then the only towing tank in the world. In addition to the hull forms of *Novgorod* and *Vitse-admiral Popov*, Froude was asked to test a 'proposed' circular ship of 6,740 tons (160ft diameter, 13.7ft draught) with a speed of 14 knots, obviously intended to serve as the basis for a sea-going ship.[14] A young naval constructor and close associate of Popov, E.E. Guliaev, was sent to participate in the tests; having been educated at the School of Naval Architecture in South

Kensington, he was an apt choice.[15] In experimenting with the larger model, Froude found that it required five times the horse-power of conventional ships to achieve the desired speed of 14 knots. As a result, he suggested that an elliptical hull form would be more suitable, and Popov almost immediately took this idea to heart; he designed the imperial yacht *Livadiia* (4,420 tons, 260ft oa x 153ft x 7ft) as a prototype for a battleship of similar form. *Livadiia*, built by Elder's Clydeside shipyard, was an indifferent success; although she was very steady even in rough seas, her shallow draught and flat bottom subjected her to severe slamming during a storm in the Bay of Biscay on her voyage from Britain to Sevastopol. By the time she had arrived at her destination on 27 May/8 June 1881, her intended patron, Emperor Aleksandr II, was dead, killed by an assassin's bomb in March; his son and heir Aleksandr III harboured a deep dislike of his uncle, Konstantin Nikolaevich, and so he dismissed him from the post of general-admiral. The new emperor's younger brother, the Grand Duke Aleksei Aleksandrovich, became general-admiral. The new regime soon showed itself hostile to both the popovkas and their inventor; the new emperor himself sarcastically commented on Popov's 'rounding of our naval architecture', while the recently-appointed professional head of the Naval Ministry, Admiral I.A. Shestakov, referred to Popov's plans for an 11,250-ton elliptical-hulled battleship armed with eight 12-inch guns as Popov's 'utopia of circular-hulled armourclads'.[16] And so Popov's influence on ship design was abruptly terminated, bringing Russia's experiments with circular and elliptical ironclads to an end.

General Characteristics

After John Elder's death in 1869, some of his supporters claimed that Admiral Popov was presuming too much in his claims for the originality of his circular ironclad.

However, while Popov was certainly familiar with Elder and his work, it is clear that the Russian ships were substantially different to the proposals Elder had publicly described, which called for vessels with a convex hull form and waterjet propulsion, whereas the popovkas were flat-bottomed craft with conventional propellers. (Elder had apparently also considered the possibility of flat-bottomed circular armourclads, but never published this idea.) Ultimately, the controversy seems to have been resolved to the satisfaction of all, since toward the end of the 1870s Popov specifically recommended the Elder yard for both the construction of the imperial yacht *Livadiia* and the re-engining of the ironclad *Pëtr Velikii*.

Popov's choice of a flat-bottomed circular hull was deliberate, even though he knew that it was less hydrodynamically efficient than Elder's convex-bottomed ships (which minimised frictional resistance), because it allowed a greater displacement on a shallower draught. The popovkas had no keel, the hulls instead being built on a series of radial frames tied together with circular stringers. Structurally, *Vitse-admiral Popov* was a scaled-up version of *Novgorod*, with its flat bottom having a diameter of 96ft, as opposed to 76ft in the smaller ship. In both ships the sides curved upwards in the quadrant of a circle, while the double bottom was carried up around the turn of the bilge, creating a side-protection system of modest depth. *Novgorod* had twelve false keels, 8in deep, on the bottom of the hull, to distribute the weight of the ship evenly when she was docked; *Popov* had similar false keels, but details are lacking.

Freeboard at the sides was minimal – 18in in both ships – and the hull was topped by a convex deck with the barbette in the exact centre. An unarmoured superstructure extended forward from the barbette to the bow in both ships; it housed the captain's cabin, the wardroom and a portion of the crew's quarters; the rest of the crew was accommodated on the deck directly below the superstructure. As completed, *Novgorod* had no after super-

TABLE 2: CHARACTERISTICS AS DESIGNED AND COMPLETED

	Novgorod	Vitse-admiral Popov
Displacement:	2,491 tons normal 2,706 tons full load	3,600 tons full load
Dimensions:	101ft x 101ft x 13ft 6in max *30.78m x 30.78m x 4.11m max*	designed: 120ft (*36.57m*) diameter; actual: 126ft 10in x 117ft 8in x 14ft 9in draught (hull), 19ft (including propellers) *38.66m x 35.86m beam x 4.49m/5.79m*
Armament:	2 x 11in/20 (280mm) rifles spar torpedoes	2 x 12in/20 (305mm) rifles 4 x 8/mm spar torpedoes
Protection:	wrought iron armour *sides*: 9in (229mm) + 2in (51mm), tapering to 7in (178mm) below water *barbette*: 9in (229mm) + 2in (51mm) *deck*: 2.75in (70mm)	wrought iron armour *sides*: 9in (229mm) + 7in (178mm) *barbette*: 16in (406mm) *deck*: 2.75in (70mm)
Machinery:	six horizontal compound engines, six shafts, eight cylindrical boilers, 3,360ihp	eight vertical compound engines, six shafts, twelve cylindrical boilers, 4,480ihp
Speed:	6.5 knots	8.5 knots
Endurance:	200 tons coal, 480nm at full speed	250 tons coal, 540nm at full speed
Complement:	15 officers, 136 enlisted (14/123 in 1876)	19 officers, 187 enlisted

structure, but one was added later, and *Popov* had an extensive after superstructure from the beginning; she also had accommodations for an admiral.[17]. Aft of the barbette was an unprotected steering wheel, used for normal steaming, while in battle the ships were to be controlled from a wheel located below the armoured deck.

The drainage system followed the pattern of earlier ironclads, with a single master pipe running above the inner bottom; it was connected to the various compartments by branch pipes. In theory this allowed the entire pumping capacity to be brought to bear on flooding in any compartment. Total pumping capacity in *Novgorod* was about 15.75 tons/minute.

Initially, there were concerns about the sea-keeping abilities of these unique ships; on *Novgorod's* first voyages, the commander of the Black Sea Fleet, Vice-Admiral N.A. Arkas, ordered that she always be escorted by another vessel. Such precautions proved excessive; trials showed that she had an easy roll even in rough weather, rarely exceeding 7-8° – none of the available sources provide her metacentric height, but it must have been enormous. On the other hand, the ships lost headway very quickly in heavy weather, a phenomenon also discovered to a lesser extent on Reed's short, bluff British ironclads. On one occasion in the spring of 1877, *Novgorod* was unable to make any headway in Force 8 weather. The shallow draught also made for problems in some sea conditions, since the ships sometimes pitched their propellers out of the water, greatly reducing speed.

The blunt hulls also made for a very poor flow of water to the single rudder, reducing its effectiveness; it took 40-45 min for the ships to steer a complete circle by rudder alone, and in heavy wind and waves the ships were almost ungovernable. After weathering a Force 7 storm, *Vitse-admiral Popov's* captain reported that

> the vessel took on a lot of water through the hatches in front of the ventilators.... The steering wheel was torn out of [one's] hands, and the vessel did not answer the helm; it was necessary to steer by means of the engines, and to make fast the rudder.[18]

In fact, steering by the engines became the normal mode of operation for the ships, although this entailed a loss of speed.

Armament

Novgorod's armament consisted of two 11in/20 Krupp-pattern 28-ton guns mounted in a central barbette; these guns could penetrate 11in armour at 800 yards, and at an elevation of 14.5° had a range of 4,600 yards. The barbette had an outside diameter of 30ft, and ammunition was supplied from below through a central hatch.[19]

The mountings were designed by Major General F.B. Pestich. Edward Reed described the operation of the guns and their mountings in these terms:

> These guns stand in an open-topped fixed turret, and are each worked by seven men only. The loading arrangements, the running out and in, the elevation and depression, and the training of these guns, are all of the simplest character, and insure [sic] great rapidity of action. I observed one quality which these guns possessed, which our guns in revolving turrets do not possess. While capa-

TABLE 3: GUNS OF THE *POPOVKAS*

	11in Pattern 1867 (a)	12in Pattern 1867 (b)	4pdr/3.4in (c)	Hotchkiss (d) 5-barreled
Calibre:	11in/279.4mm	12in/304.8mm	3.4in/86.87mm	37mm
Dates:	1873	1875 (official trials)	1867?	1879
Weight:	25,979-28,698kg	35,682-39,038kg	460kg	209kg
Barrel length:	5,588mm/20 cal	6,096mm/20 cal	1,713mm/19.7 cal	740mm/20 cal
Bore/rifled length:	4,750mm/17 cal	5,169mm/17 cal	1,182mm/13.6 cal	616mm
Rate of fire:	6-8 minutes/round	c.14 minutes/round	?	32rpm
Projectiles and performance:				
Weight:	222kg	290kg	5.74kg	0.5kg
Charge:	36.4-37.5kg	53.2kg	0.615kg	0.08kg
MV:	392m/sec	447m/sec	306m/sec	442m/sec
Range:	3,704m @ 9.5°	2,963m @ 6°	3,294 @ 14.13°	2,778m @ 11°

(a) Based on a Krupp gun, four of which were delivered in August 1871. The Obukhovskii Works began manufacturing a domestic version of these guns in 1873.

(b) Based on a Krupp design, manufactured by the Obukhovskii Works. Only six guns were produced, of two slightly different patterns; all were mounted afloat (four in the Baltic Fleet battleship *Pëtr Velikii*, two in *Vitse-admiral Popov*).

(c) A standard field artillery calibre adopted for shipboard use. These short, low-velocity guns were used in cases where armour penetration was not the primary consideration. They were manufactured by the Obukhovskii Works and Krupp; the steel tube was not reinforced. The mounting was of the carriage type.

(d) It is not clear whether the popovkas carried the Hotchkiss 5-barrelled 37mm or the single-barrelled gun; on balance, the former seems more likely.

Sources: Shirokorad, *Entsiklopediia otechestvennoi artillerii*; Titushkin, 'Korabel'nye pushki epokhi paravogo i bronenosnogo flota'; Titushkin, 'Artilleriia russkogo flota v 1877-1904 gg'.

ble of being fired in parallel directions like our own guns, each has an independent action for training, so that, within certain limits, they can be directed at different objects.[20]

Each gun was indeed on an individual carriage, and these could be trained at different targets, although at some point their carriages would interfere with one another. They could also be locked so that they rotated together. The guns could be trained through 180º in 2-3 minutes, but despite the 'great rapidity of action' Reed observed, rate of fire was rather slow: one round per gun every ten minutes or so.

In *Vitse-admiral Popov* the main battery consisted of two 12in/20 41-ton Obukhovskii guns mounted in the central barbette with an external diameter of 34ft.[21] The mountings, of the Moncrieff 'disappearing' type, were designed by Lieutenant L.A. Rasskazov, and were ordered from Armstrong in England. But by the autumn of 1876 Anglo-Russian relations were strained due to disturbances in the Balkans, and there were fears that war might break out before their delivery. It was therefore decided to build mountings in Russia to a design based on *Novgorod's* gun carriages, but scaled up to take the 12in guns.

The guns received their first trials on 11/23 October and 15/27 November 1876; it was soon apparent that the substitute mountings were too weak – as were the nearby superstructures, which were damaged by blast. Both mountings and superstructures had to be strengthened; a circular bulkhead was added below the armoured deck, and the newly partitioned space between this bulkhead and the base of the barbette was used for six officers' cabins. Further gunnery trials in April 1877 were considered satisfactory, although there was still some blast damage. Nevertheless, the mountings were considered

insufficiently robust, and during the Russo-Turkish War (1877-78) Rear-Admiral N.M. Chikhachev, commander of Odessa's naval defences, reported that full charges could only be fired 'in case of extreme necessity'.

The British-built disappearing mountings finally arrived in Odessa in early 1878, but they were not installed until the autumn. The mountings were made from cast steel and training was done by two 40hp engines, which drove a large toothed ring, weighing 7 tons, on which the guns were mounted. Recoil and elevation were controlled by hydraulic mechanisms. When lowered, the guns were completely protected behind the barbette. Reloading took no less than 14 minutes. The ship conducted gunnery trials in November, during which it was noted that 'the mountings were lowered and raised smoothly'.

During the Russo-Turkish War *Novgorod* was fitted with two 4pdr (87mm) guns on the after superstructure as protection against torpedo boats. By 1892 two 37mm guns had been added. *Popov* entered service with four 4pdrs, mounted near the funnels below the navigating bridge wings. During the war two more 4pdrs were mounted on the bridge wings, and by 1892 two 37mm guns had been fitted.

During the winter of 1873/1874 *Novgorod* was fitted with a telescoping spar torpedo; *Vitse-admiral Popov* received similar gear at some point. During the design process, it was also suggested that *Popov* be equipped with side-mounted spar torpedoes, but this proposal was rejected.

Protection

Most of the armour plate was manufactured by the Izhorskii Works, the two popovkas requiring such a large amount that armour production for the Baltic battleship

Novgorod – section through side armour

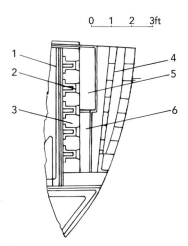

Key:
1 Side plating (38mm)
2 Channel iron (178mm)
3 Teak backing (229mm)
4 Wooden sheathing outside armour
5 Upper armour belt (229mm)
6 Lower armour belt (178mm)

Novgorod – section through barbette armour

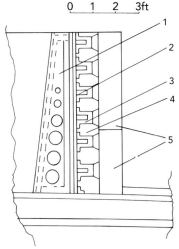

Key:
1 Iron support
2 Sheet iron (9.5mm)
3 Channel iron (178mm)
4 Teak backing (229mm)
5 Armour plates (229mm)

Vitse-admiral Popov – section through side armour

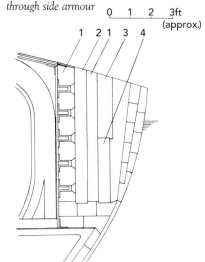

Key:
1 Teak backing
2 Inner armour belt (178mm)
3 Upper outer armour belt (229mm)
4 Lower outer armour belt (178mm)

(© Ian Sturton 2014)

Pëtr Velikii was delayed.[22] When a breakdown at the Izhorskii plant forced the Naval Ministry to order some 7in armour from Britain, a special authorisation was required because in 1866 the emperor had issued an order that all shipbuilding materials be Russian-made.

The vertical extent of the armour was exactly the same in both ships, extending from 18in above to 4ft 6in below the waterline, for a total of 6ft. *Novgorod's* side protection was made up of two strakes of armour, each 3ft high.[23] The upper strake was 9in thick and the lower 7in; the teak and channel iron of the backing were considered equivalent to another 2in of armour – hence the frequently seen figure of 11in for the side protection.

The heavier protection of *Vitse-admiral Popov* created difficulties, since the Izhorskii Works could not roll plate thicker than 9in, so a sandwich system of protection had to be used to achieve the desired thicknesses. The upper strake of the side armour was made up of an outer 9in layer and an inner 7in layer, with teak reinforced by channel iron between the plates. This was regarded as equivalent to 18in of solid armour. The lower strake of armour is nowhere described in detail, but it was held to be equivalent to 16in of solid armour; it was therefore probably made up of two 7in layers, again with teak and channel iron between.

Novgorod was the first Russian ironclad to mount her main battery *en barbette*; it was 7ft high and protected by 9in armour with teak backing, identical to the upper strake of belt armour. *Popov's* barbette was likewise identical to her belt, with a 9in outer plate and a 7in inner plate, with channel iron and teak in between.

Guliaev noted that the open-topped barbette was considered an adequate form of protection for the gun crew

> …because being intended for the defence of certain narrow straits and entrances they [the popovkas] can, when in action, occupy positions behind some defensive protection, such as submerged torpedoes [ie mines]; and, when attacked, can choose their own distance from the enemy, placing themselves always beyond the reach of rifle-fire.[24]

In *Novgorod* the lower portion of the funnels and the base of the engine room skylight were protected by 6in armour; details for these features on *Popov* are lacking. In both ships the rounded upper deck was protected by two layers of 1in iron plus a third layer of 0.75in, for a total thickness of 2.75in.

Machinery and Trials

The machinery for both popovkas was manufactured by the Berd (Baird) Works in St. Petersburg, once Russia's leading marine engineering firm. However, by the early 1870s there had been a serious falling-off in the quality of Berd's machinery; the engines and boilers of the Baltic Fleet's breastwork battleship *Pëtr Velikii*, also made by Berd, were plagued by so many problems that they eventually had to be replaced entirely.[25] *Novgorod* and *Vitse-admiral Popov* also suffered throughout their careers from problems caused by defects in workmanship and poor-quality materials.

The contract price for *Novgorod's* engines and boilers was 348,000 rubles, and the machinery was to be ready by 1/13 July 1872, but in the event was delayed by three months. There were six horizontal steam engines, each driving its own propeller. Steam was supplied by eight fire-tube boilers arranged in two boiler rooms located on either side of the barbette.

The control of so many engines was an interesting problem. Guliaev described the arrangements:

> There is one engineer for each side of the engine room, and both of them are stationed on a common platform upon which the starting and reversing gear, &c., for all the engines are fitted. Voice-pipes from above are led to this platform to transmit the captain's orders. The engines are supplied with Hearson's strophometers, so as to show at any moment the number of revolutions which each engine is making, and to regulate the uniformity of the speed accordingly.[26]

On 24 May/5 June 1873 – three days after her launch – steam was raised and *Novgorod*, still without guns, moved under her own power. Official trials were held in August; at 104rpm the ship made a bare 7 knots. The trials were conducted in something of a hurry, as the ship had to be prepared for a visit by the emperor; the acceptance commission did not even measure the indicated horse-power of the engines before accepting them as satisfactory. Fuel consumption was, as might be expected, prodigious; depending on the quality of the coal, it ranged from 1.6 to 2 tons per hour at full speed.

Throughout October 1873 Popov tinkered with the propeller pitch, trying to find the right combination to maximise speed. The final result was a 10ft pitch on the innermost propellers, 11ft on the next pair, and 12ft on the outermost pair. In the summer of 1874 *Novgorod* managed 7.5 knots. That was the highest speed she ever made; soon afterwards the speed dropped as the Berd engines began to show their defects.

The contract for *Vitse-admiral Popov's* machinery was signed in 1872 and was based on the construction of a ship similar to *Novgorod*; it therefore called for six vertical (instead of horizontal) compound engines and eight fire-tube boilers; when the ship grew larger it was necessary to add another two engines and four boilers to the contract.

As in *Novgorod* there were six propeller shafts, but in *Popov* the middle shaft on either side was driven by two engines. These shafts had three-bladed propellers, 14ft in diameter, as opposed to the other screws, which were four-bladed and had a diameter of 10ft 6in.

Vitse-admiral Popov ran her first machinery trials in June/July 1876, reaching 8 knots without much difficulty. But the official trials that followed soon after were marred by repeated machinery break-downs; the ship was forced to return to Sevastopol for repairs. Trials resumed on 10/22 August, when the ship ran a nine-hour trial, average speed being 8.25 knots with a maximum boiler pressure of 4.2 atmospheres. However, no attempt was made to push the engines or boilers to their contractual limits, for fear of damaging them. The acceptance commission nevertheless rated the machinery as satisfactory. Fuel consumption at full speed amounted to 2.15 to

3.3 tons per hour, depending on the quality of the coal. By the time of the Russo-Turkish War, she was considered good for only 6-6.5 knots.

Trials conducted before the Russo-Turkish War showed that *Vitse-admiral Popov's* large middle propellers were far more effective than the smaller screws; without them, she could barely manage 4 knots. On the other hand, in both ships the outermost engines contributed little to the vessels' propulsion, and the steam production of the boilers was insufficient to supply all the engines, so in 1876-1877 these engines were removed from *Novgorod*.[27] This reduced the total power from 480nhp/3,360ihp to 320nhp/2,000ihp, and her maximum speed fell to about 6 knots; by the time of the Russo-Turkish War, she was capable of only about 5 knots, although this was due at least in part to the fact that her bottom had not been cleaned in three years. Plans were made to remove the outboard engines from *Popov* as well, but the outbreak of the war in April 1877 forced a postponement. The two engines were finally removed in 1878, and as a result, the ship's total power was reduced from 560nhp/4,480ihp to 480nhp/3,066ihp, and her maximum speed was reduced by about 1 knot.

In 1879, after repeated problems with the Berd machinery, the director of the Naval Ministry, Admiral S.S. Lesovskii, ordered that *Vitse-admiral Popov* run trials until the engines met the contract specifications. The results of these trials are not given in available sources, but apparently the machinery remained unsatisfactory throughout her career.

Boats

Novgorod carried two steam cutters, which could also serve as torpedo boats, plus a six-oared boat and a four-oared boat. The ship's low freeboard and the curve of the upper deck allowed them to be stowed on crutches on deck without the use of davits; rails were used to lower them to the water. However, in the winter of 1873/1874 davits were fitted, so that the boats could be raised sufficiently to protect them from damage when heavy seas washed over the low deck.[28]

Vitse-admiral Popov carried all her boats on davits from the start, although when firing on after bearings they could be lowered to the deck to get them out of the way of the blast.

Modifications

As built, *Novgorod* had no after superstructure, but following her initial voyages it was decided to add more extensive deckhouses aft. This work was carried out in the winter of 1873/1874 while the ship was at the ROPiT yard in Sevastopol. Small deckhouses were built abaft the barbette, connected by a hurricane deck, and the engine room skylight was raised. A light enclosed wheelhouse was added atop the new superstructure. In an effort to improve the ship's sea-keeping qualities, the forward superstructure was also altered at this time, receiving a sharper forward end that overhung the bow slightly. The anchors were

Novgorod *As Reconstructed: Profile and Upper Deck Plan showing Machinery*

0   10   20   30ft

Key to drawing:
1   Location of 87mm gun
2   Wheelhouse
3   6-oared pulling cutter
4   Propeller
5   Bridge wing
6   280mm gun
7   Hatch for passing ammunition
8   Forward superstructure
9   Donkey engine
10 Boiler
11 Horizontal steam engine
12 Centrifugal pump
13 Fire pump
14 After superstructure

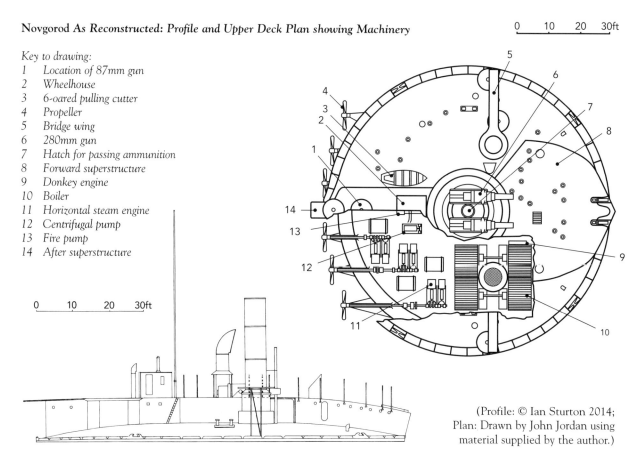

0   10   20   30ft

(Profile: © Ian Sturton 2014;
Plan: Drawn by John Jordan using
material supplied by the author.)

Novgorod in 1874. The photo can be dated by the location of the bridge wing that can be seen forward of the nearside funnel; this was added over the winter of 1873/1874; the following winter its inboard end was shifted to the base of the funnel. Other modifications made in 1873/1874 include the extension of the forward superstructure – difficult to see in this view – and the addition of a superstructure abaft the barbette, topped by the wheelhouse (with the compass on the roof). Note also the awning over the barbette. (P.A. Vicary collection)

shifted from the deck edge to hawse-holes on top of the superstructure, and bridge wings extending to the hull sides from the superstructure were also added at about this time. In the winter of 1874/1875 the inboard ends of the bridge wings were shifted from the superstructure to the funnels.

From the outset ventilation posed a difficult problem. As built, *Novgorod* had two small cowls near each funnel for the boiler rooms; there were two even smaller cowls at the forward end of the engine room skylight, while the main source of fresh air below decks was the central hatch in the barbette. Ventilation engines were fitted to circulate air within the ship. These arrangements proved inadequate, and eventually a large ventilation cowl was fitted over the central hatch of the barbette and the ventilation engines were removed. At the same time the mast had to be moved from inside the barbette to the forward side of the wheelhouse.

Sometime before the Russo-Turkish War *Novgorod* was fitted with improved sights for her 11in guns, as well as the Davydov system for automatically firing the guns electrically. During the war the wheelhouses were removed from both popovkas, as they blocked their arcs of fire on after bearings.

War experience led to other changes. The Turkish river monitor *Lüft-ü Celil* (often spelt *Lutfi Djelil*) had been destroyed by Russian artillery fire, reportedly due to a plunging shell that detonated her magazine. This led to concerns about the skylights and central hatches in the barbettes of the popovkas, so in both *Novgorod* and *Popov* these were provided with armoured covers with holes in them for ventilation. For reasons which are unclear, parts of *Novogorod*'s ventilation system were removed, which unsurprisingly led to severe heating in the boiler rooms; temperatures could reach 104-122ºF (40-50ºC), stokers were fainting and full speed could not be maintained. The ventilation engines removed in 1874/1875 had to be re-installed to improve air circulation. In *Popov* a ventilation engine removed from the Baltic Fleet battleship *Pëtr Velikii* was installed to improve the flow of air inside the ship.

In the early 1880s both ships were fitted with electric lighting, and in 1883 *Popov* was re-boilered; her old boilers were refurbished and transferred to *Novgorod*.

By 1893 the hulls and machinery of both ships were in poor condition, but with new battleships entering service with the Black Sea Fleet, the popvkas were regarded as having little military value, so no work was done.

Summing Up: Criticism and Reality

Soon after the popovkas entered service they became the target of a great deal of criticism in the Russian newspapers, which, under the liberal reign of Emperor Aleksandr II, experienced relatively mild censorship. As a result there was an extended debate over the merits of the circular vessels – so extended that two substantial collections of newspaper articles were published in book form.[29] This public controversy is the source of many of the criticisms that have been levelled against the popovkas over the years.

The central issue was the effect of the circular hulls on the steering of the ships. In a long article published in the newspaper *Golos* [The Voice] on 10/22 January 1875, it was claimed that

> ...during a trip along the Dnepr estuary, it [*Novgorod*] knocked over the buoys marking the channel, having all of a sudden been thrown several compass points off course while turning, and the helmsman had absolutely no confidence that he could steer her as he would have been able to do with other vessels.[30]

The other major charge levelled against the ships was their alleged tendency to spin (rather than simply wander off course). Ironically, this may owe its origin to Edward Reed, despite the fact that he was a staunch defender of these ships; in reporting his personal experiences of a trip aboard *Novgorod* in the great bay of Sevastopol, he described what happened when the ship was turned by reversing the engines on one side:

A well-known illustration of Novgorod (with Vitse-Admiral Popov in the right background) showing her in her final appearance, with a large ventilator cowl in the barbette, and the bridge wings anchored on the funnel bases rather than the forward superstructure. Note also what appears to be a 37mm Hotchkiss gun in the bridge wing. This illustration was one of a series of lithographs of Russian warships by Lieutenant V.V. Ignatius, published in La marine russe *(St. Petersburg, 1892). Ignatius rose to the rank of captain and was killed while commanding the battleship* Kniaz Suvorov *at Tsushima. (USNHHC, NH72525)*

The circular form is so extremely favourable to this kind of handiness that the *Novgorod* can easily be revolved on her centre at a speed which quickly makes one giddy. She can, nevertheless, be promptly brought to rest, and, if needed, have her rotary motion reversed.[31]

The two above items, if combined, may be the source of the widely reported tendency of the popovkas to spin uncontrollably in river currents. Fred T. Jane described it in these terms:

> On a trial cruise they [*Novgorod* and *Vitse-admiral Popov*] went up the Dnieper very nicely for some distance, till they turned to retire. Then the current caught them, and they were carried out to sea, whirled helplessly round and round, every soul on board hopelessly incapacitated by vertigo.[32]

It is easy to imagine how rumours of *Novgorod's* giddy spinning could have been combined with the ship wandering off course on the Dnepr to produce stories of their crews being rendered prostrate due to dizziness as the ships were swept uncontrollably downriver.

Other stories are more easily disproved; Jane claims that the popovkas were so unmanoeuvrable that 'no attempt to use them was made' during the Russo-Turkish War, but in fact the ships made several voyages in the Black Sea during and immediately after the war, twice traveling as far as the Danube; on one occasion, according to a recent Russian publication, 'the popovkas manoeuvred confidently on the river in strong currents'.[33]

Another version of spinning popovkas is that, if one gun was fired, the ships would rotate from the off-centre force of the recoil. This story seems to date from *Novgorod's* gunnery trials in November 1874, which revealed that the stops that held the gun platforms in place were weak, leading to the platforms themselves rotating when they fired.[34] Reinforcement of the stoppers put an end to this problem, but the stories remained.

There are also claims that any inequality in the thrust of the outermost engines, located so far from the centre-line, would drive the ships off course or cause them to rotate.[35] A specific origin for this story has not been

A rare photo of Vitse-admiral Popov from her port quarter. She had far more elaborate superstructures than Novgorod. Note the unusual mushroom-shaped structure with a framework on top – possibly a ventilator of some sort. (Courtesy of Sergei Vinogradov)

found, but it may owe something to Guliaev's description of the elaborate machinery control arrangements (quoted above under 'Machinery'), combined with the fact that the popovkas were often steered using their engines rather than their rudders.

Another fault attributed to the popovkas is that as their speed increased they tended to bury their bows into the sea. There was some truth in this, as William Froude discovered when testing circular hull forms at the request of the Russian Navy in 1876. But there was also an important qualification to this: it would only become dangerous if the forward superstructures were completely destroyed, and in that case the ship was unlikely to be in a condition to steam at high speeds. Moreover, Froude's experiments showed that, as the trim by the bow increased, the resistance of the hull's form *decreased* – a conclusion which has been less commonly recorded. Froude explained this phenomenon in the following terms:

> …eddies are usually formed behind, and not before, abrupt features of form; now a large proportion of the eddies so formed by these ships will undergo an increasing diminution, the nearer the abrupt turn of bilge aft is raised towards the surface of the water, by the depression of the bow; and the resistance due to them will be proportionately lessened in consequence.[36]

The combination of hull form and trim by the head led to a beneficial effect – but one unlikely to be of much use in practical terms!

In the final analysis, the popovkas seem to have been relatively effective coast-defence vessels; certainly their combination of armament and armour could only have been carried by a conventional ship of much greater draught. Their faults – and they certainly had faults – were exaggerated by critics, both in Russia and aboard, and have left as a legacy stories of uncontrollable ships designed by incompetent men.

Careers

Novgorod (an ancient city on the Volkhov River near Lake Ilmen, one of the great trading centres of mediaeval Russia): Trials began August 1873 and continued in 1874. Cruised to Taganrog on the Sea of Azov in 1875; October 1875 cruised the Crimean coast with Admiral Popov and Edward Reed, visiting Feodosiya and Yalta. Assigned to the defence of Odessa during the Russo-Turkish War of 1877-78, along with *Vitse-admiral Popov*. In the summer 1878 both popovkas cruised to Sulina, on the Danube. Stationed at Sevastopol throughout 1880s, with short summer cruises every year. 1/13 February 1892 reclassified as a 'coast defence armourclad'. By 1893 her hull and machinery were in poor condition. Handed over to the Port of Nikolaev for disposal on 19 April/1 May 1903; stricken 21 June/3 July 1903 and used as a storeship. Offered for sale to Bulgaria in 1908, but the offer was turned down.[37] Sold to private firm for scrapping in December 1911.

Vitse-Admiral Popov (left) and Novgorod (right) in Sevastopol's Southern Bay (Iuzhaia buchta) in the 1880s. Note the six small torpedo boats hauled up on shore; these appear to be several different types of first-generation boats, built at the time of the Russo-Turkish War of 1877-78; originally equipped with spar torpedoes, these craft were rearmed with tubes for Whitehead torpedoes in the 1880s. (Courtesy of Sergei Vinogradov)

Vitse-admiral Popov (Vice-Admiral Andrei Aleksandrovich Popov, 1821-1898, favourite of General-admiral Konstantin Nikolaevich and inventor of the Russian circular ironclad): Laid down as *Kiev*; renamed on 9/21 October 1873. Trials in 1876. Assigned (with *Novgorod*) to defence of Odessa during Russo-Turkish war (1877-1878). In company with *Novgorod* cruised to Sulina on the Danube in the summer of 1878. Gunnery trials continued after the war with new mountings. Throughout 1880s based at Sevastopol, making annual summer cruises. 1/13 February 1892 reclassified as a 'coast defence armour-clad'. By 1893 hull and machinery were in poor condition. 19 April/2 May 1903 turned over to Nikolaev port authorities for disposal, stricken 21 June/4 July 1903. Offered for sale to Bulgaria in 1908, but the proposal was rejected. Sold for scrap to a private firm in December 1911.

Acknowledgements:

I would like to express my gratitude to Sergei Vinogradov for providing materials used in writing this article. Sergei also contributed photographs, Dmitry Lemachko also very generously responded to my last-minute request for photos. I must also thank Yuri Apalkov and Ian Sturton for their fine drawings. My wife, Jan Torbet, improved the article greatly with her suggestions and (gentle) criticisms.

Sources:

The major source for these vessels is Andrienko, *Kruglye suda admirala Popova* (St. Petersburg: Gangut, 1994) and the same author's earlier article, 'Bronenostsy beregovoi oborony konstruktsii A.A. Popova' (*Sudostroenie*, no. 11, 1985, pp.58-61). Also useful are V.Iu. Gribovskii and I.I. Chernikov, *Bronenostsy beregovoi oborony tipa 'Admiral Seniavin'* (St. Petersburg: Leko, 2009, pp.40-45) and *Istoriia otechestvennogo sudostroeniia*, I.P. Spasskii, general editor (5 volumes; St. Petersburg: Sudostroenie, 1994-1996, vol. II, pp.84-93, 498-499).

Footnotes:

1. It may be noted in passing that it is not clear how the 800-ton size was to be measured, since there were several 'tonnage' formulae in use, and actual water displacement was not yet accepted as the standard measure for the size of warships.
2. The following paragraphs are based on *Istoriia otechestvennogo sudostroeniia*, 2:47-49; Gribovskii and Chernikov, *Bronenosets 'Admiral Ushakov'*, p.40; and Mel'nikov, 'Podgotovka k bronenosnomy sudostroeniiu na Chernom more', *Sudostoenie*, no. 1, 1978, pp.66-69.
3. V.D. Dotsenko, *Morskoi biograficheskii slovar'* (St. Petersburg: Logos, 1995), p.435; *Istoriia otechestvennogo sudostroenie*, 2:84.
4. For details of these vessels, see Stephen McLaughlin, 'Russia's "American" Monitors: The *Uragan* Class', *Warship 2012*, pp.98-112.
5. Jacob W. Kipp, 'Tsarist Politics and the Naval Ministry, 1876-81: Balanced Fleet or Cruiser Navy?' (*Canadian American Slavic Studies*, vol. 17, no. 2 [Summer 1983], pp.151-179), p.158.
6. For Elder's concept, see 'Circular Ships of War with Immersed Motive Power' (*Journal of the Royal United Service Institution*, vol. XII, no. LII (1868), pp.529-547; see also E.E. Guliaev (Goulaeff), 'On Circular Iron-clads' (*Transactions of the Institute of Naval Architects*, vol. XVII [1876], pp.29-61), pp.55-56, 60-61.
7. Quoted in Edward Reed, *Letters From Russia in 1875* (London: John Murray, 1876), p.16.
8. Kipp, 'Tsarist Politics and the Naval Ministry', p.158 n.22.
9. The Russian plural is *popovki*, but the anglicised version, 'popovkas', will be used here.
10. Kipp, 'Tsarist Politics and the Naval Ministry', p.159, mentions the 14ft limit, but does not say when it was adopted.
11. Andrienko, *Kruglye suda admirala Popova*, p.7.
12. Andrienko, *Kruglye suda admirala Popova*, p.14.
13. There is some confusion over just how much work had to be undone; Andrienko, *Kruglye suda admirala Popova*, p.14, says that the existing double bottom structure was dismantled. However, Goulaeff (Guliaev), 'On Circular Iron-clads', p.34, indicates that the existing double bottom structure of the second popovka was simply increased in diameter, without having to be dismantled.
14. The National Archives, Kew: ADM 226/1, William Froude, 'Report of Experiments with Models of Russian Circular Ironclads', 1 March 1876.
15. D.K. Brown, *A Century of Naval Construction: The History of the Royal Corps of Naval Constructors* (London: Conway Maritime Press, 1983), p.40; *Morskoi biograficheskii slovar'*, p.135.
16. Andrienko, *Kruglie suda admiral Popova*, p.37.
17. Goulaeff (Guliaev), 'On Circular Iron-clads', p.35.
18. Andrienko, *Kruglye suda admirala Popova*, p.23.
19. Goulaeff (Guliaev), 'On Circular Iron-clads', p.31.
20. Reed, *Letters From Russia in 1875*, p.17.
21. Goulaeff (Guliaev), 'On Circular Iron-clads', p.31.
22. V.V. Arbuzov, *Bronenosets 'Pëtr Velikii'* (St. Petersburg: Nauchno-Populiarnoe Izdanie, 1993), p.35.
23. Goulaeff (Guliaev), 'On Circular Iron-clads', p.31; *Conway's All the World's Fighting Ships, 1860-1905* (London: Conway Maritime Press Ltd., 1979), p.177. V.M. Tomitch, *Warships of the Imperial Russian Navy*, vol. 1: *Battleships* (San Francisco [?]: BT. Publishers, 1968), p.91, says the total height of the armour was 5ft 11in; this is probably a conversion error working back from a metric figure.
24. Goulaeff (Guliaev), 'On Circular Iron-clads', p.31.
25. V.V. Arbuzov, *Bronenosets 'Petr Velikii'*, pp.49-57.
26. Goulaeff (Guliaev), 'On Circular Iron-clads', p.32.
27. Andrienko, 'Bronenostsy beregovoi oborony konstruktsii A.A. Popova', p.61.
28. Goulaeff (Guliaev), 'On Circular Iron-clads', p.33.
29. *Popovka. Sbornik statei o kruglykh sudakh* (St. Petersburg: A.A. Kraevskii, 1875) and *Dopolnenie k sborniku Popovka. Eshche stat'i o kruglykh sudakh* (St. Petersburg: A.A. Kraevskii, 1875).
30. Reprinted in *Popovka. Sbornik statei o kruglykh sudakh*, p.168.
31. Reed, *Letters From Russia in 1875*, pp.45-46.
32. Fred T. Jane, *The Imperial Russian Navy* (originally published in 1904; reprint edition: London: Conway Maritime Press, 1983), p.175. Donald W. Mitchell, *A History of Russian and Soviet Sea Power* (New York: Macmillan Publishing Co., Inc., 1974), pp.178-179, repeats much the same story.
33. Andrienko, *Kruglye suda admirala Popova*, p.23.
34. Andrienko, *Kruglye suda admirala Popova*, p.12.
35. William Hovgaard, *Modern History of Warships* (reprint edition: London: Conway Maritime Press, 1978), p.40.
36. ADM 226/1, William Froude, 'Report of Experiments with Models of Russian Circular Ironclads', 1 March 1876.
37. *Conway's All the World's Fighting Ships 1906-1921* (London: Conway Maritime Press, 1980), p.411.

MODERN AIRCRAFT CARRIERS

In the latest of his series of feature articles on modern warship types,
Conrad Waters reviews the latest developments in carrier aviation.

In the seventy years since the end of the Second World War, the aircraft carrier has been a constant symbol of the hegemony exercised by the United States and its major allies amongst the 'western' powers. The ability of the US Navy, in particular, to project naval air power from forward-deployed carrier task groups has played a major part in conflicts ranging from the Korean War of 1950-53 to the most recent engagements in Afghanistan and Iraq. Throughout this time, a constant stream of technological developments has allowed naval aviation to keep pace with ongoing enhancements in the capability and sophistication of military aircraft. These have included the angled flight deck, mirror landing aid and steam catapults of the 1950s and, more recently, the ski-jump and Short Take Off and Vertical Landing (STOVL) operations popularly associated with the Harrier 'jump jet'.

The last-mentioned innovations, which facilitated fast jets being deployed on smaller ships, also opened up the possibility of aircraft carrier capabilities being acquired by a broader range of navies. In practice, however, fixed-wing aircraft carrier operation has remained very much a

rich man's club. The number of new units over the period has been largely balanced by those who have departed, unable to afford the continued cost of membership.[1] It is worth noting that this expense does not only involve the capital cost of the ship itself but also the aircraft, logistical support, extensive training and flotilla of escorts that are also prerequisites of effective aircraft carrier operation. Even the US Navy is struggling to maintain current aircraft carrier numbers against a backdrop of strict budget controls.[2]

Given this backdrop, it is not surprising that the number of ships intended for fixed-wing carrier operation currently under construction is relatively small. If unconfirmed reports of an indigenous Chinese design are ignored, these are limited to the *Gerald R. Ford* (CVN-78) and *America* (LHA-6) classes under order for the US Navy, the two *Queen Elizabeth* class carriers being assembled for Britain's Royal Navy and India's sole *Vikrant*. This chapter aims to examine the factors influencing these four designs and to assess what clues they hold to the likely future of aircraft carrier operations. Reference will also be

The US Navy Nimitz *class 'supercarrier'* George Washington *(CVN-73) pictured on operations in the Pacific in September 2014. Fixed-wing carrier operation is very much a rich man's club, and even the US Navy is struggling to maintain current numbers; at the time of writing it is uncertain whether funding will be available to pay for* George Washington's *mid-life refuelling and refit.* (US Navy)

TABLE 1: MODERN AIRCRAFT CARRIER DESIGNS

Class:	Gerald R. Ford (CVN-78)	America (LHA-6)	Queen Elizabeth	Vikrant
Builder:	HII – Newport News Shipbuilding Newport News, Virginia	HII – Ingalls Shipbuilding Pascagoula, Mississippi	Aircraft Carrier Alliance Rosyth, Scotland[1]	Cochin Shipyard Limited Kochi, Kerala
Country:	USA	USA	UK	India
Number:[2]	0+2+[1]	1+1+[1]	0+2+[0]	0+1+[0]
Keel Laid:[3]	14 November 2009	17 July 2009	7 July 2009 [4]	28 February 2009
Christened:[3]	9 November 2013	20 October 2012	4 July 2014	12 August 2013
Commissioned:[3]	[2016]	11 October 2014	[2017]	[2018 onwards]
Full Load Displacement:	100,000+ tonnes	45,000 tonnes	65,000 tonnes	40,000+ tonnes
Principal Dimensions:	317m (333m o.a.) x 41m x 12m Flight Deck: 333m x 78m	237m (257m o.a.) x 32m x 9m Flight Deck: 249m x 36m	263m x (284m o.a.) x 39m x 10m Flight Deck: 284m x 73m	262m o.a. x 62m f.d. x 8m Flight Deck: 262m x 62m
Propulsion:	Nuclear, 30+ knots Unlimited range.	Hybrid Electric Drive, 24 knots c.8,000 nautical mile range	IEP, 25+ knots c.10,000 nautical mile range	COGAG, 28 knots. c.8,000 nautical mile range
Aircraft Capability:	CATOBAR (4 EMALS) 3 aircraft lifts c.70 aircraft	STOVL 2 aircraft lifts 9 landing spots c.35 aircraft	STOVL (incl. ski-jump) 2 aircraft lifts 10 landing spots c.40 aircraft	STOBAR (incl. ski-jump) 2 aircraft lifts 6 landing spots c.30 aircraft
Armament:	Mk 29 octuple Sea Sparrow Mk 49 RAM Mk 15 Phalanx CIWS	2 x Mk 29 octuple Sea Sparrow 2 x Mk 49 RAM 2 x Mk 15 Phalanx CIWS	3 x Phalanx CIWS 4 x 30mm	Barak 8 SAM 4 x 76mm Oto Melara
Crew:	c.2,800 plus air group	c.1,100 plus troops	c.700 plus air group	c.1,500 incl. air group[5]

Notes:

1. The ships are being assembled at Aircraft Carrier Alliance member Babcock's Rosyth shipyard from blocks constructed at shipyards around the United Kingdom.
2. Refers to ships completed or under construction, with numbers in brackets those firmly planned.
3. Dates relate to the first of the class. Christening dates can vary significantly from actual float out or launch.
4. Date relates to formal commencement of work on the first major block.
5. Data is largely drawn from official press releases and other official sources. There is a degree of variation with respect to data in the public domain and the table should be regarded as being indicative only.

made to a number of helicopter carrier-type ships being brought into service capable of being adapted for STOVL fixed-wing operations.

USA: Gerald R. Ford (CVN-78) Class

The successor to the ten *Nimitz* (CVN-68) class nuclear-powered 'supercarriers' that first entered service in 1975, the *Gerald R. Ford* class ships are essentially an evolution of the previous type. The new class emerged from the CVX and CVN-21 development programmes, with advance fabrication work commencing in 2005 prior to award of a formal construction contract to Newport News Shipbuilding in September 2008. The keel of *Gerald R. Ford* was subsequently laid in November 2009 and she is expected to enter service in 2016. Key design characteristics are set out in Table 1. Affirming the US Navy's continued commitment to conventional Catapult Assisted Take-Off Barrier Arrested Recovery (CATOBAR) operations for its strike carriers, the CVN-78 design uses the basic *Nimitz* hull form but incorporates a number of significant innovations.[3] The overall intention behind the improvements is to increase the number

of aircraft sorties the new carriers can generate from their embarked air group whilst reducing the overall life-time cost of the ships' operation. A second unit of the class, *John F. Kennedy* (CVN-79), is currently under construction. At least one more, *Enterprise* (CVN-80), is planned.

The *Ford* class carriers will form the heart of the US Navy's carrier strike groups during the twenty-first century. All large US aircraft carriers have received a multi-mission (CV) designation since mid-1975, embarking a carrier air wing (CVW) comprised of squadrons equipped with a variety of aircraft types intended to carry out a wide range of complementary missions.[4] In practice, however, carrier air wings have become increasingly focused on the power projection, strike role since the end of the Cold War. This reflects the reduced threat posed by potential maritime opponents since the demise of the former Soviet Union, as well as the greater potency of alternative systems to carry out certain carrier air wing missions. For example, the US Navy has lacked a dedicated air-defence fighter since the F-14 Tomcat was retired in 2006. The increased air defence capability offered by the Aegis combat system, the associated AN/SPY-1 radar and the Standard series of surface-to-air missiles has allowed fast jet operation to be

The lead US Navy Ford *class carrier* Gerald R. Ford *(CVN-78) seen during flooding-out of her building dock at Newport News Shipbuilding during October 2013. She was subsequently christened on 9 November 2013 prior to a planned entry into service during 2016.* (US Navy)

concentrated on the F/A-18 Hornet family of multi-role strike fighters. These are currently largely used in the attack role.[5] Equally, however, the nature of likely strike missions is also evolving. In particular, the availability of large numbers of precision-guided land attack missiles means that the ability to conduct an all-out 'Alpha Strike' on a primary target with a full deck load of aircraft is of diminishing priority. A capability to provide ongoing, flexible support against a range of objectives is likely to be more important. The *Ford* class design reflects these trends, placing considerable emphasis on sustaining a high number of sorties over a considerable period of time.

The most obvious change from the previous *Nimitz* design in support of these evolving priorities is a radical re-design of the flight deck layout to provide increased deck space and enhance the flow of aircraft movements. Most significantly, a re-designed island with a smaller footprint has been located farther aft and the number of aircraft lifts reduced from four to three. These changes have facilitated a re-design of the arrangements for refuelling and rearming aircraft that have landed, which also involves the use of higher-capacity air weapons lifts and improved routing of ordnance from storage magazines to the refuelling and rearmament 'pit stops'. Reports also suggest that both storage capacity and replenishment capability have been enhanced to improve the *Ford* class's ability to sustain lengthy operations.

Less visible is the incorporation of a range of new technologies into the improved design, of which the most notable is the Electromagnetic Aircraft Launch System (EMALS). Replacing the traditional steam catapults that have been a feature of CATOBAR carrier operation from the 1950s, EMALS uses a linear induction motor to generate a moving magnetic field that propels an aircraft launch carriage down a track until take off speed is reached. The new system can be controlled with much greater precision than traditional steam catapults. This makes it easier to launch a broader range of aircraft with different take-off weights whilst producing less stress on their airframes. EMALS also recharges more quickly than steam technology and is claimed to be easier to maintain and operate, thereby facilitating both core aims of enhancing sortie generation and reducing overall costs. EMALS will be supplemented by new Advanced Arresting Gear (AAG), which also uses induction motor technology to replace the less precise hydraulic ram in the current Mk7 arresting system. AAG also reduces the amount of shock produced on airframes and is better-suited to handling lighter unmanned aerial vehicles (UAVs).

The improvements provided by the *Ford* class's enhanced flight deck design and the superior capabilities of EMALS are intended to sustain a sortie generation rate (SGR) of at least 160 sorties per day over an extended period, while permitting a surge to 270 sorties during a 24-hour fly day surge.[6] Whilst the previous *Nimitz* class carriers are capable of generating up to 240 sorties for a short period during a 24-hour fly day surge, their sustained SGR of 120 sorties per day is considerably fewer than for the new ships.

Whilst greater aircraft operating capacity is, perhaps, the greatest step forward provided by the *Ford* class, their combat capability benefits from other developments. In particular, shipboard surveillance capacity will be greatly enhanced by a new Dual Band Radar (DBR). This integrates two radars operating in different frequency bands through a common controller and single interface to the combat management system. An AN/SPY-3 multi-function radar produced by Raytheon and operating in the X Band (NATO I/J Bands) supports horizon search, low-altitude tracking and missile engagement functions. It is supplemented by a Lockheed Martin-built S Band (NATO E/F Bands) AN/SPY-4 radar that carries out volume search

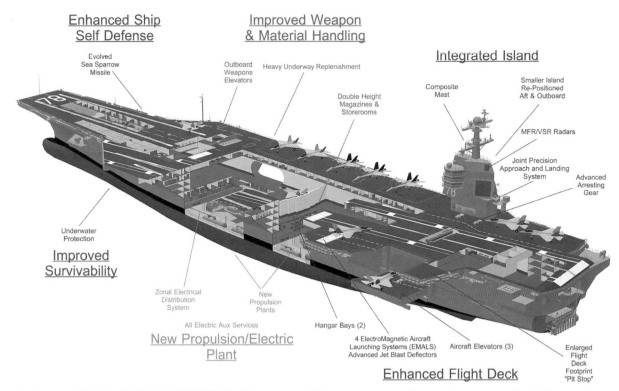

Enhanced Ship Self Defense

Evolved Sea Sparrow Missile

Improved Weapon & Material Handling

Outboard Weapons Elevators

Heavy Underway Replenishment

Double Height Magazines & Storerooms

Integrated Island

Composite Mast

Smaller Island Re-Positioned Aft & Outboard

MFR/VSR Radars

Joint Precision Approach and Landing System

Advanced Arresting Gear

Underwater Protection

Improved Survivability

Zonal Electrical Distribution System

New Propulsion Plants

All Electric Aux Services

New Propulsion/Electric Plant

Hangar Bays (2)

4 ElectroMagnetic Aircraft Launching Systems (EMALS) Advanced Jet Blast Deflectors

Aircraft Elevators (3)

Enlarged Flight Deck Footprint "Pit Stop"

Enhanced Flight Deck

A schematic of the Gerald R. Ford (CVN-78) highlighting some of the improvements in the new design compared with the previous Nimitz class. (US Navy)

and tracking duties.[7] Both systems are latest-generation active phased array radars, with each incorporating three non-rotating panels arranged flush with the island structure to provide 360-degree coverage. Replacing a number of conventional rotating radars, the DBR system assists overall air traffic control functions, whilst combining with shipboard electronic support measures (ESM) systems and airborne early warning aircraft to provide advanced warning of possible attack. It also supports engagements by the RIM-162 Evolved Sea Sparrow Missile (ESSM) surface-to-air missile which comprises the ship's principal surface-to-air defence system.

EMALS and the DBR are both power-hungry technologies. This has driven the adoption of a new, twin A1B nuclear reactor system produced by Bechtel Corporation that is able to support an electric generation plant that provides around two and a half times the generating capacity of the *Nimitz* class. A zonal electrical distribution system has been designed to circulate power to where it is needed. The greater capacity provided by the new generating plant has also been used to convert as much auxiliary equipment as possible, including galleys, laundries and heating systems, to electrical operation, as well as providing a significant margin for the introduction of future technologies such as lasers and dynamic armour. All these innovations serve further to reduce crew size, with manpower reduced by at least 500 compared with the core complement (ie excluding the air group) of a *Nimitz* class ship. Further money will be saved by a lengthier maintenance cycle, including a reduced number of docking periods. Altogether, the *Ford* class are expected to be c.US$4bn-US$5bn cheaper to operate than the

preceding design over a planned fifty-year service life.

The development of the *Ford* class design has not been without its problems. Estimated construction costs of the first-of-class vessel had grown by over twenty percent to US$12.9bn as of 2014, although it should be noted that around US$3.3bn of this total related to one-off class design and development expenses.[8] Delivery has also been delayed and there have been concerns over the reliability of many of the new systems incorporated into the ship, including EMALS, AAG and the DBR. The US Department of Defense's Director, Operational Test & Evaluation Office (DOT&E) FY2013 report on the CVN-78 programme highlighted these issues. It also suggested that the required SGRs would not be met in practice, largely because they were based on unrealistic assumptions. Nevertheless, the new carriers represent a pragmatic improvement of an existing, proven design through combining the lessons of forty years of operational experience with the adoption of intervening technological developments.

USA: America (LHA-6) Class

The US Navy remains firmly wedded to the concept of supercarrier operation. However, its fleet of large-deck, LHA/LHD-type amphibious assault ships are bigger than many aircraft carriers in other fleets and provide a secondary fixed-wing aviation capability based around embarked STOVL aircraft. As their name implies, the amphibious assault ships are primarily intended to support the transportation and deployment of amphibious forces

Sea-based trials of the experimental US Navy unmanned X-47B aircraft have been taking place since 2012; this image shows the aircraft being prepared for launch from Theodore Roosevelt *(CVN-71) in August 2014. Unmanned aerial vehicles tend to be lighter than conventional jets (cf. F/A-18 in background). The introduction of the EMALS catapult launch system in* Gerald R. Ford *(CVN-78) is more suitable than traditional steam catapults for launching these lighter aircraft and can also switch more quickly between manned and unmanned types. (US Navy)*

An image of Gerald R. Ford *(CVN-78) being towed along the James River in Virginia to her fitting-out berth at Newport News Shipbuilding on 17 November 2013. Prominent in this view is the re-designed island, which takes up less deck space than that used in the previous* Nimitz *class. The locations of some of the fixed arrays for the new DBR Dual Band Radar can also be seen. (Huntington Ingalls Industries)*

from the US Marine Corps, typically embarking a complement of helicopters and landing craft for this purpose. It would appear that the type's ability to carry out a wider aircraft carrier role has often been downplayed in spite of their extensive aviation facilities, probably due to fears that this would result in reduced investment in the core supercarrier force.[9] However, the existing eight *Wasp* (LHD-1) class ships commissioned from 1989 onwards were designed from the outset to carry out a potential 'sea control' role similar to that originally intended for the British *Invincible* class. A mixed force of AV-8B Harriers and SH-60/MH-60 anti-submarine helicopters would be embarked for this purpose. Amphibious assault ships have also been used to carry out strike operations on a number of occasions; for example *Kearsarge* (LHD-3) was deployed in this role during the intervention in Libya's Civil War in 2011. The future entry into service of the F-35B STOVL variant of the Lightning II Joint Strike Fighter (JSF) will further enhance the type's potential use for strike operations. As can be seen from Table 2, the new aircraft offers a combination of speed, payload and combat radius that is much closer to traditional CATOBAR naval aircraft than first generation jump jets.[10]

The latest iteration of the US navy's amphibious assault ship type, the *America* (LHA-6) class, reflects this potential. In particular, it places greater emphasis on aviation facilities than in previous ships to ensure the effective support of both the F-35B and the new MV-22B Osprey tilt-rotor transport aircraft. In similar fashion to the *Ford* class, *America* has evolved from an earlier design, in this case the *Makin Island* (LHD-8) variant of the *Wasp* class. *Makin Island* herself was something of a transitional ship. She incorporated a new hybrid electric drive system, combining gas turbine and electrical propulsion in lieu of her sister ship's steam turbines, in a *Wasp* class hull. The system essentially uses auxiliary electric motors powered from the ship's electrical grid for low speed operation up to speeds of c.12 knots, with gas turbine propulsion being clutched in when higher speed is necessary. *America* was ordered in June 2007 and laid down at the Pascagoula, Mississippi yard of Ingalls Shipbuilding in July 2009; she commissioned in October 2014.[11] The keel of a sister, *Tripoli* (LHA-7), was laid in June of the same year. The new class has the same hull form as the preceding amphibious assault ships and is reported to have approaching fifty percent commonality with *Makin Island*. Further design details are set out in Table 1.

The most significant – and controversial – innovation incorporated into *America* is the deletion of the well deck found in all previous US Navy amphibious assault ships so as to provide space for a larger aircraft hangar. Stowage for associated parts and aviation fuel is also substantially increased, whilst maintenance facilities have been improved and expanded.[12] The well deck in earlier ships facilitated the transfer of troops, vehicles and equipment to amphibious landing craft for transfer to the shore. However, recent operational experience has tended to place greater emphasis on the use of aviation assets for the transportation of troops and equipment in the initial stages of an amphibious assault. Vehicle stowage and hospital facilities have also been reduced compared with previous classes to accommodate increased aviation capa-

An overhead view of the flight deck of USS America *(LHA-6), showing the nine helicopter landing spots. Unlike other STOVL carriers, the design does not feature a ski-jump as this would impede helicopter operations. Note the size of the V-22 tilt rotors compared with the traditional helicopters embarked. (US Navy)*

bilities, but the troop-carrying capacity of c.1,900 Marines is unchanged. Press reports also suggest that magazine protection and other survivability features have been enhanced. A zonal electrical distribution system similar to that found on the *Ford* class is lighter and more survivable than the radial systems found on most previous US warship classes.

The new class's notional air group is officially reported as between six and nine F-35B jet aircraft, twelve MV-22B Osprey transports, four CH-53E Super Stallion heavy lift helicopters, between four and seven AH-1Z Viper attack helicopters and a pair of MH-60S utility helicopters. However, this load-out is flexible and it is understood that at least twenty F-35Bs could be supported in a mini-strike carrier role. It is planned to deploy the F-35B with effect from *America's* first operational deployment, but tests on *Wasp* suggest that adjustments will first need to be made to flight deck surfaces and equipment to prevent heat damage from the new jet's engine. As with previous US Navy amphibious assault ships, no ski-jump has been installed due to the impact this would have on the nine available helicopter operating spots. This confirms that the class's amphibious assault role remains paramount.

The *America* design is able to support and sustain significantly higher sortie generation rates than previous amphibious assault ships. Whilst no ship-specific figures have been publicised, a key performance parameter (KPP) of the F-35B variant is to be able to maintain a SGR of

TABLE 2: MODERN NAVAL FIGHTER COMPARISONS

Aircraft[1]	AV-8B+	F-35B	F-35C	F/A-18E/F	Rafale M (F3)	MiG-29K
Country	USA/UK	USA	USA	USA	France	Russia
Length	14.1m	15.6m	15.7m	18.5m	15.3m	17.3m
Wingspan	9.3m	10.7m	13.1m	13.7m	10.8m	12.0m
Wing area	22.6m^2	42.7m^2	62.1m^2	46.5m^2	45.7m^2	43.0m^2
Height	3.6m	4.4m	4.5m	4.9m	5.3m	4.4m
Max take-off weight	14,000kg	27,250kg	31,750kg	30,000kg	24,500kg	24,500kg
Engines	1 x F402-RR-408	1 x F135 + lift fan	1 x F135	2 x F414-GE-400	2 x M88-2E4	2 x RD-33MK
Thrust – max	10,500kgf (24,000lbs)	19,500kgf (43,000lbs)	19,500kgf (43,000lbs)	20,000kgf (44,000lbs)	15,500kgf (34,000lbs)	18,000 kgf (40,000lbs)
Speed – max[2]	1,100km/h	2,000km/h	2,000km/h	1,900km/h	2,400km/h	2,200 km/h
Service Ceiling	c.15,000m	c.18,000m	c.18,000m	15,200m	16,800m	17,500m
Combat Radius	550km	870km	1,140km	c.1,000km	c.1,000km	c.950km
Maximum G-load	8G	7G	7.5G	7.6G	+9G	8G
Weapons Stations	6	11	11	11	13	9
Radar	Raytheon AN/APG-65	NG AN/APG-81	NG AN/APG-81	Raytheon AN/APG-79	Thales RBE2	Phazotron Zhuk-ME
Carrier-Use:	*Wasp* Class (US) *America* Class (US) *Cavour* (Italy) *Juan Carlos I* (Spain)	*Wasp* Class (US) *America* Class (US) *Queen Elizabeth* Class (UK) *Cavour* (Italy)	*Nimitz* Class (US) *Ford* Class (US)	*Nimitz* Class (US) *Ford* Class (US)	*C de Gaulle* (France)	*Vikramaditya* India) *Vikrant* (India) *Kuznetsov* (Russia)

Notes:

1. Data has been compiled from manufacturers' documentation, supplemented by publicly available information as necessary. Due to considerable variations in published information, data should be regarded as indicative only.
2. Speed refers to maximum speed at altitude. Low level speed is considerably lower.

The new US Navy amphibious assault ship America (LHA-6) commenced sea trials in 2013 before commissioning in October 2014. She is optimised for fixed-wing operations, including the new F-35B Lighting II strike fighter and the MV-22 Osprey 'tilt rotor', and is capable of undertaking a secondary strike carrier role. (Huntington Ingalls Industries)

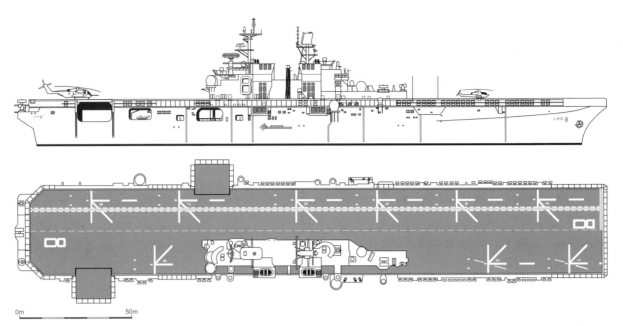

Plan and profile views of Makin Island *(LHD-8). The new* America *(LHA-6) design shares the previous ship's hull and propulsion system but has different internal arrangements better to support aviation operations. (© John Jordan 2011)*

three sorties per day and to increase this figure to four per day in a surge situation.[13] This would suggest the LHA-6 type ships should be able to sustain a SGR of 60 sorties per day over an extended period when configured as an aircraft carrier.

Some have been tempted to see construction of additional *America* class vessels as a cost-effective alternative to the strike carrier programme. Current unit cost is around US$3.5bn or only about a third of each *Ford* class. This would allow a greater number of vessels to be purchased and operated, countering fears that the current limited number of carrier strike groups is vulnerable to

targeting by precision weapons. However, this perspective ignores the two types' respective strengths. The carrier air wing embarked on the *Ford* class, encompassing a wide range of complementary types, provides a much broader aviation mission capability than that found on the smaller ships. The strike carriers also offer a number of less obvious benefits, for example a much greater capacity to stow aviation fuel for prolonged operations and the ability to use their nuclear propulsion to deploy swiftly at higher speeds. It should also be noted that amphibious assault ships are also sorely needed by a US Marine Corps that is short of specialised shipping, and which has had mixed

The new amphibious assault ship America *(LHA-6) seen in Guantanamo Bay, Cuba, in July 2014 during her delivery voyage from the Bay of Mexico to the Pacific. Unlike earlier US Navy amphibious assault ships, she has surrendered her well deck in favour of increased space for aviation operations. (US Navy)*

views on the *America* class's prioritisation of aviation capabilities. One reflection of these concerns is the US Navy's decision to re-instate the well deck in all further ships of the class from the planned LHA-8 onwards.

UK: Queen Elizabeth *Class*

An approach falling somewhat between the two US Navy carrier types is demonstrated by the British Royal Navy's *Queen Elizabeth* class CVF (future aircraft carrier) programme. Tracing its origins to studies to replace the much smaller *Invincible* class STOVL support carriers that commenced in the early 1990s, the project for a new strike carrier capability was formally confirmed in the 1998 Strategic Defence Review (SDR). The programme subsequently underwent a protracted gestation period as inter-related uncertainties relating to budget, industrial strategy, size and whether to adopt STOVL, CATOBAR or even Short Take-Off Barrier Arrested Recovery (STOBAR) aircraft were slowly resolved. A formal contract for two ships was finally placed in July 2008. The first of the pair, *Queen Elizabeth*, was floated out in July 2014 prior to expected delivery in 2017. Final assembly of her sister, *Prince of Wales*, commenced in the latter half of 2014. A noteworthy feature of the build process has been the fabrication of constituent blocks for the two ships at various yards across the United Kingdom prior to integration at Babcock International's facility at Rosyth, near Edinburgh. The programme is being overseen by an Aircraft Carrier Alliance comprising Babcock, BAE Systems, Thales UK and the UK Ministry of Defence (MoD).[14] Table 1 provides principal design characteristics.

The 1998 SDR placed carrier strike at the heart of a new expeditionary, power projection capability that reflected the changed strategic environment in the aftermath of the Cold War. The emphasis was therefore on embarking – and sustaining – a larger outfit of fast jets than had been possible with the *Invincible* class. These three ships had originally been focused on providing command and control facilities for helicopter-based anti-submarine warfare; however, their ability to operate STOVL Harriers of different types had steadily assumed more importance over time.

The required air group fluctuated as the *Queen Elizabeth* design evolved. However, the ultimate baseline settled on a complement of 36 fast jets and four airborne surveillance and control aircraft. By late 2000 it had been determined that the jets were to be the new US Joint Strike Fighter, for which Lockheed Martin's X-35 design was selected for development as the F-35 in 2001. An air group of the size contemplated demanded a large ship, which, in turn, engendered a debate as to whether the adoption of CATOBAR operation and the conventional F-35C variant of the JSF would be appropriate for the new vessels. Operating conventional carrier aircraft would have provided potential benefits in terms of aircraft acquisition cost, range and inter-operability with allied strike carriers. In the event, however, the Royal Navy's recent successful history of STOVL operations determined that

A view of the new British Royal Navy aircraft carrier Queen Elizabeth *in her building dock at Rosyth, near Edinburgh. She has been assembled from blocks fabricated at shipyards across the United Kingdom. (Aircraft Carrier Alliance)*

this was the chosen option, although the new carrier design was described as being adaptable to a CATOBAR configuration. The subsequent 2010 Strategic Defence and Security Review (SDSR) looked to reverse the STOVL decision by carrying out the adaptation on the second ship. However, the complexity and, hence, cost of the conversion was much greater than first envisaged. It was therefore determined in 2012 that both carriers would, after all, be completed in STOVL configuration and operate the F-35B.

As for the US Navy's larger *Ford* class, the ability to achieve a high SGR was a key consideration in the *Queen Elizabeth* class design. Original plans suggested a requirement to achieve a SGR of up to 150 sorties per day. However, this had reportedly reduced to a 24-hour surge rate of 108 fast jet sorties (ie three per aircraft), falling to 72 sorties per day (two per aircraft) thereafter, on the basis of the baseline strike-focused air group by the time the design was finalised. Interestingly, these figures are somewhat lower than the US Department of Defense KPP established for F-35B sorties.

Attaining the targeted SGR has required careful attention to ship design and it is notable that many of the factors influencing *Gerald R. Ford* are also reflected in *Queen Elizabeth*. The most obvious innovation, the adoption of two separate islands, was driven by the desire to

maximise flight deck area. This arrangement also allows the positioning of ship navigation (forward island) and flight control (aft island) functions in optimal positions, while providing a degree of redundancy for survivability purposes. The 'pit stop' servicing concept used by the US Navy has also been adopted, with Arming and Refuelling Points (ARPs) positioned on the edge of the flight deck to speed aircraft turnaround and keep the flying areas clear of personnel. Transportation of munitions and other stores is facilitated by an automated cargo handling system which adapts the latest land-based warehousing techniques to a maritime environment. The system allows the retrieval of weapons from the main magazines to the hangar and flight deck using only a third of the personnel associated with a traditional manual approach. The c.680 core complement of *Queen Elizabeth* is approximately the same as *Invincible* despite the significant increase in size and capability. Aircraft retrieval from the hangar is facilitated by the use of twin, US-style deck-edge lifts, each of which is able to accommodate two F-35Bs.

The *Queen Elizabeth* design retains the familiar ski-jump first introduced in *Invincible*, which permits a higher take-off weight for a given runway length. Moreover, the new ships' longer, c.280m flight deck allows extended take-off runs. A particular problem with first generation STOVL carrier operations was the inability of aircraft to recover to

A cutaway of the Queen Elizabeth *class. The twin island configuration maximises the size of the flight deck, whilst implementation of integrated electric propulsion allows the ship's main gas turbines to be located immediately below the islands, allowing shorter exhausts and easier maintenance. Other noteworthy features include the large lifts, which are capable of handling two F-35Bs or a Chinook helicopter with rotor blades extended. The hangar is relatively small compared with the total size of the ship but is capable of stowing a wide range of aircraft types. (Ross Watton, Crown Copyright 2010)*

Queen Elizabeth *in the course of being floated out from her building dock on 19 July 2014. She had been formally named by HM Queen Elizabeth II some two weeks earlier on 4 July.* (Aircraft Carrier Alliance)

their host ship with a full payload in less than ideal weather conditions, leading to the jettisoning of expensive unused munitions. This weakness is also present, to a lesser extent, in the F-35B and the extended flight deck length has permitted consideration of a new landing technique to address the issue. The proposed implementation of Shipborne Rolling Vertical Landing (SRVL) will see aircraft approach the ship from astern at low speed and on a relatively steep glide path, using only their brakes to bring them to a stop. A new landing reference system, the Bedford Array, has been developed to facilitate an accurate approach, particularly in rough sea state conditions.[15] Whilst a significant step forward, SRVL will still impose operating limitations in the absence of an angled deck, as a full-length flight deck will need to be kept clear in case of brake failure or other incidents.

Many other technologies implemented in the *Queen Elizabeth* class design are carried over from previous Royal Navy ships. For example, the main volume search radar is the long-range S1850M that was developed from the Thales Nederland SMART-L array and which is also found in the Type 45 destroyer. This is supplemented by a BAE Systems Type 977 Artisan medium range surveillance radar that forms an important part of the Type 23 frigate mid-life modernisation programme and will carry out key air traffic control functions on the new carriers. The integrated electric propulsion (IEP) system also has similarities with that found in the Type 45 destroyers. A power plant comprising two Rolls Royce MT-30 gas turbines and four Wärtsilä diesel generators can supply up

to 110MW of electricity to a distribution network that fulfils both propulsion and shipboard 'hotel' requirements. Propulsion is provided by four GE Converteam advanced induction motors. Two drive each of the ship's twin shafts to permit speeds of over 25 knots. In contrast to the *America* class's hybrid system, there is no direct mechanical linkage between the engines and the shaft lines. One advantage of this arrangement is that it has allowed the gas turbines to be positioned high in the ship, beneath the islands, facilitating both exhausting and maintenance requirements.

The *Queen Elizabeth* class programme has not been without its critics, particularly given its high cost in an age of financial austerity. The project's budget has increased steadily since it was first conceived and now stands at £6.2bn (c.US$10bn) or around US$5bn for each ship. Reductions in the overall strength of the British armed forces have also resulted in plans to broaden the class's utility beyond the carrier strike role, not least because likely purchases of F-35B jets are unlikely to support a fixed-wing air group of the size originally envisaged.[16] Instead, the evolving concept of Carrier Enabled Power Projection (CEPP) envisages the new ships serving as rapidly re-configurable joint operating platforms that can, for example, serve as readily in the amphibious assault as in the strike role. In the latter configuration, the carriers would embark a force of Royal Marines as well as supporting helicopters from all three services, including Royal Navy Merlins, Royal Air Force Chinooks and British Army Apaches and Wildcats. Studies are underway to increase the current six helicopter landing spots to as many as ten in support of this concept, while troop accommodation is likely to be enlarged when the ships first refit. To some extent, therefore, the *Queen Elizabeth* class will exhibit similar multi-role flexibility to the US Navy's *America* class, although the strike mission remains their primary *raison d'être*.

India: Vikrant Class

The fourth and final new carrier type under construction is India's Project 71 air defence ship, which has been named *Vikrant*. Steel cutting for the new ship started in 2005 in advance of formal keel laying in 2009. She was subsequently launched from Cochin Shipyard Ltd on 12 August 2013. Current plans envisage sea trials commencing in 2016 prior to a 2018 commissioning date. This schedule looks overly optimistic in the light of the many delays that have impacted the project.

A general-purpose design intended for strike, air defence and anti-submarine missions, *Vikrant* has adopted the STOBAR system first implemented by the Soviet Navy towards the end of the Cold War. STOBAR carriers incorporate a ski-jump to allow aircraft to launch under their own power, with arrester wires being used to allow a conventional recovery. The system is therefore capable of use with non-STOVL aircraft that are equipped for barrier-assisted recovery without the expense and complexity of installing a catapult launch system. However, it is only suitable for aircraft with a high thrust-to-weight ratio and is often associated with limitations on maximum payload. To date, only Russia, China and India have adopted STOBAR, all using former Soviet-era carriers and aircraft based on the Russian SU-33 and MiG-29K types.[17]

Vikrant's key design characteristics are set out in Table 1. In contrast to STOVL carriers, CATOBAR-equipped ships have to be reasonably large so as to allow a sufficient take-off run. This is reflected in a total length of c.260m and a full load displacement in excess of 40,000 tons. Both take-off and landing operations take place at an angle to the ship's axis, with one of the two aircraft launch positions set close to the stern so as allow fully loaded aircraft the maximum length possible for launch. A notable feature of the design is the two narrow aircraft lifts set to starboard, which appear to be based on the minimum requirements of the MiG-29K. This could present a difficulty if there is a desire to operate larger types in the future. A total air group of up to thirty aircraft is envisaged, although a normal complement is likely to be a squadron of twelve MiG-29Ks and an equivalent number of anti-submarine and airborne early warning helicopters. No information has been released on the required SGR.

As is common with many other recent indigenously-constructed Indian warships, *Vikrant's* design represents a mix of Russian and 'western' practices. Although the STOBAR concept is Russian and that country has been heavily involved in providing technical input into the aviation facilities, Italy's Fincantieri has also been heavily involved with the project under a contract signed in 2004. The Italian company has had particularly heavy involvement with the design of the propulsion system, which is based on a combined gas and gas (COGAG) arrangement of four GE LM2500+ turbines driving twin shafts. This power plant is similar to that installed in Italy's smaller STOVL carrier, *Cavour*, and there are a number of similarities between the two ships.

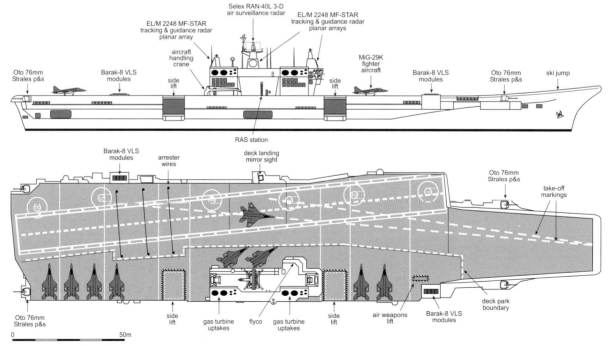

Provisional profile and plan views of Vikrant. There are two take-off positions depending on the weight of the aircraft, with fully-laden aircraft needing to use as much of the flight deck as possible. There are also six spots for helicopter operations. One other notable feature is the relatively narrow size of the aircraft lifts. (Drawing by John Jordan)

Other design elements have apparently been revised in the course of construction and, given that fitting out has yet to commence, must be regarded as speculative. Israel is another country that India has cooperated closely with in recent years and it appears likely that *Vikrant's* air defence system will have a strong Israeli influence. For example, computer-generated images that have been released of the new ship show four fixed arrays for Israel Aerospace Industries' Elta subsidiary's MF-STAR active phased radar arranged on top of the island structure. This will be used to control the Barak 8 medium range surface-to-air missile system in India's new Project 15A destroyers and it would seem that this pairing will also be adopted for *Vikrant*. Further use of Italian technology is also likely. This may include the Oto Melara 76mm gun system, possibly in the new Strales configuration with radio-guided munitions, and the Selex RAN-40L long range surveillance radar.

A key objective behind Project 71 has been to develop a local capability to construct the largest and most sophisticated ships; indeed the original 'air defence ship' designation for *Vikrant* was changed to 'indigenous aircraft carrier' in 2006. This approach has undoubtedly helped India to gain valuable insights into the construction of large warships, for example in fostering the development of modular techniques and leading to the development of a local capability to manufacture the required high-tensile

An impression of the new Indian aircraft carrier Vikrant, *which is currently under construction by the Cochin Shipyard in Kochi. A STOBAR design, she features a ski-jump and angled landing deck.* (Indian Navy)

steel. Against this, it seems that the extent of the challenge has been much greater than first-envisaged, with the planned delivery date subject to considerable delay. It could also be contended that reliance on the capacity of local industry and historic industrial partnerships, partic-

Vikrant *was floated out on 12 August 2013 in a condition suggesting that considerable amounts of further work will be required before sea trials can take place; a planned 2018 commissioning date therefore looks challenging. A key rationale for the carrier project has been the development of a local capability to construct the largest and most sophisticated ships, but this may have come at the cost of overall capability.* (Indian Navy)

ularly with Russia, has unduly influenced design choices, leading to a less flexible and capable ship. Reports certainly suggest that different choices will be made with respect to planned future construction, possibly extending to adoption of the US Navy's EMALS. Meanwhile, overall costs for *Vikrant* are likely to exceed US$4bn, little less than the much larger *Queen Elizabeth*.

Helicopter Carrier Designs

In addition to these four classes which are specifically intended – at least in part – for fixed-wing operation, other ships are currently under construction to act as helicopter carriers. Some of these, most notably the French *Mistral* class amphibious assault ships, have little or no potential to embark fast jets. At the other extreme, there are others that have been designed with the option of fixed-wing aviation firmly in mind. Amongst these, the Spanish *Juan Carlos I*, which entered service in 2010, has the greatest potential. Intended primarily to conduct amphibious missions, she was equipped with a ski-jump and lengthy flight deck to support Harrier and possible future F-35B operations at times when the now-decommissioned STOVL carrier *Príncipe de Asturias* was unavailable.[18] She is therefore somewhat similar in configuration to the US Navy's *America* class, although she retains a well-deck. Two sisters are currently in the final stages of construction as the Royal Australian Navy's *Canberra* class. Although these ships were originally ordered solely to support helicopters, the Australian government has recently announced that purchase of a small number of F-35Bs is being considered to operate from them. It is possible that a smaller variant, recently ordered by Turkey, might also use the American jet in due course.

The advent of the F-35B might see other nations join the fixed-wing naval aviation club, particularly in Asia. For example, South Korea has already built one through-deck amphibious assault ship, *Dokdo*, and plans more. These could be adapted for STOVL operation with relative ease. Neighbouring Japan has already completed a pair of through-deck helicopter-carrying destroyers of the *Hyuga* class intended mainly for anti-submarine missions, and the first of two larger variants, *Izumo*, was launched in August 2013. Indeed, any restraint on Japanese naval fast jet operations is as much political as technical, as the current, strict interpretation of the post-war constitution has resulted in the prohibition of 'offensive' weapon systems such as aircraft carriers.

Conclusion

The successful construction and operation of fixed-wing aircraft carriers remains a challenging objective from both a financial and a technical perspective. Few countries have sufficient resources to support fixed-wing naval aviation, while the technical barriers to entry for those wishing to establish the capability are immense. For example, it is likely to take India some fifteen years or more from the start of *Vikrant's* construction to deploying her in a meaningful operational role. Similar planned

timelines for the *Queen Elizabeth* class are only a little shorter. Whilst the development of the F-35B might support an expansion of naval aviation to new countries, the costs involved in such a process should not be underestimated. High hopes for the Harrier's potential as a carrier aircraft in the early-1980s produced few tangible sales outside of established carrier operators in spite of the clear success of the type in the Falklands War.

For those navies able to overcome the financial and technical hurdles the rewards are substantial. Although much has been written about the vulnerability of large ships to modern missiles and torpedoes, there are good reasons why no aircraft carrier has suffered material damage from enemy action since the end of the Second World War. It should be noted that very few countries outside of the major powers possess anti-shipping weapons in sufficient quantities to pose a significant threat to a carrier group. Even those that do would find it difficult to penetrate the layered defences such a group would adopt. Discovering and tracking a fast-moving carrier group would also not be an easy proposition. In turn, the recent focus on enhancing sortie generation rates and sustaining flexible operations against a range of targets provides the current generation of carriers with a capacity unmatched by earlier generations of ships. Indeed, there are few land-based air forces that would be able to match the capabilities of the air groups proposed for a carrier of the *Ford* or *Queen Elizabeth* classes. Despite the predictions of the sceptics, the modern aircraft carrier looks set to remain the queen of the oceans in the first half of the Twenty-First Century.

Acknowledgement:
The author thanks David Hobbs for commenting on a preliminary draft of this chapter.

Sources:
This chapter has been researched from contemporary industry and government marketing literature, as well as press releases and news reports. The following sources provide further reading material:

David Architzel, 'The US CVN 21 Aircraft Carriers Programme: Capability Requirements, Concepts and Design', *RUSI Defence Systems – Summer 2006*, pp.44-46, Royal United Services Institute, London 2006.

Charles Oldham (Editor in Chief), *HMS Queen Elizabeth*, Faircount LLC, Tampa FL, 2014.

Norman Polmar, *The Naval Institute Guide to the Ships and Aircraft of the U.S. Fleet – Nineteenth Edition*, US Naval Institute, Annapolis MD 2013.

Ronald O'Rourke, *Navy Ford (CVN-78) Class Aircraft Carrier Program: Background & Issues for Congress – 31 July 2014*, Congress Research Service, Washington D.C. 2014.

Scott Truver, 'US *Makin Island* (LHD-8)', *Seaforth World Naval Review 2012*, pp.128-147, Seaforth Publishing, Barnsley 2011.

Footnotes:
[1.] As of late 2014, Brazil, China, France, India, Italy, the Russian Federation, Spain and the United States all routinely deploy fixed-wing aircraft at sea. In addition, the United Kingdom is building the new *Queen Elizabeth* class with the intention of resuming aircraft carrier operation by c.2020. Since the end of

the Second World War, Argentina, Australia, Canada, the Netherlands and Thailand have all commenced – but subsequently abandoned – fixed-wing carrier aviation.

2. The US Navy is currently required by law to retain a set number of operational aircraft carriers, but this number is steadily falling. The requirement was first established by the FY2006 National Defense Authorization Act, which set the total at twelve ships; the number was soon reduced to eleven carriers. Subsequently, the FY2010 National Defense Authorization Act permitted a temporary reduction to ten ships between the decommissioning of *Enterprise* (CVN-65) and the delivery of *Gerald R. Ford*. Even this total may not be sustainable, as there is currently considerable debate within the United States as to whether the mid-life refuelling and refit of the *George Washington* (CVN-73) is affordable.

3. CATOBAR is also frequently referred to as conventional Catapult Assisted Take-Off But Arrested Recovery.

4. At the time of writing, the composition of the ten US Navy carrier air wings (CVWs) has largely been standardised around a c.70-strong structure comprising:
– four strike fighter squadrons (VFA) with a total of c.44 F/A-18 Hornets and Super Hornets;
– one electronic attack squadron (VAQ) with five EA-18G Growlers;
– one airborne early warning squadron (VAW) with four E-2 Hawkeyes;
– one helicopter sea combat squadron (HSC) with c.8 MH-60S Seahawks;
– one helicopter maritime strike squadron (HSM) with c.11 MH-60R Seahawks.
A couple of C-2A Greyhound carrier on-board delivery aircraft are also often embarked on forward-deployed ships. It is worth noting that both the *Nimitz* and *Ford* classes are capable of supporting much larger numbers of aircraft; during the Cold War era complements in excess of 70 fixed-wing aircraft plus additional helicopters were common.

5. This is a simplification. The flexibility offered by current multi-role jets allows them to be rapidly reconfigured to different roles; the F/A-18 has certainly been successful in air-to-air combat.

6. US Navy documents suggest the CVN-78 design is intended to sustain a minimum sustained SGR of 160 sorties per day, with a higher objective of up to 220 sorties per day being targeted. The equivalent surge SGRs are 270 and 310. In practice, there is some scepticism that even the minimum requirements will be met.

7. In general terms, higher-frequency radars produce a sharper beam for a given size of antenna but have a shorter range. The DBR therefore combines the precision of the Raytheon X Band radar (operating in the 6,200-10,900MHz frequency) with the greater range of the Lockheed Martin S-Band radar (operating in the 1,550-3,900MHz frequency) to obtain the best of both worlds.

8. Undertaking accurate cost comparisons of modern warship programmes is notoriously difficult, with long programme times, the impact of inflation, and different accounting methodologies all serving to confuse. As a result, various figures are quoted both for the total cost of *Gerald R. Ford* and for that part of the cost contributed by non-recurring development expenses. At present (2014), it appears that it requires around US$12bn to construct a *Ford* class ship.

9. A debate over whether the US Navy's supercarriers could be supplemented or even replaced by smaller types has been ongoing for many decades. For example, a 60,000-ton full load displacement, conventionally powered CVV medium aircraft carrier equipped to operate around 50 conventional and STOVL aircraft was seriously considered in the 1970s in lieu of continued *Nimitz* class construction. Several Vertical/Short Take Off and Landing (VSTOL) designs for sea control (rather than strike) duties were also examined at the same time. Whilst the big carrier lobby has continued to hold sway, the STOVL capabilities incorporated into the US Navy's amphibious assault ships arguably reflects the continued influence of the alternative point of view.

10. The 'Lightning II' Joint Strike Fighter is being built in three variants which enjoy significant design commonality. These are the F-35A for conventional, land-based operation; the F-35B STOVL variant; and the F-35C carrier-based CATOBAR aircraft. In spite of the shared basic design, the different types still exhibit material variations in range and payload.

11. Both Ingalls Shipbuilding and Newport News Shipbuilding are currently divisions of Huntington Ingalls Industries Inc., which was created in March 2011 from Northrop Grumman's shipbuilding business.

12. Reports suggest that hangar space in the *America* design is around 40% greater than in the preceding *Makin Island*. Stowage for aviation fuel has also been more than doubled to 1.3m gallons. However, the dimensions of the new-generation aircraft are larger than those they are replacing.

13. The relatively high sortie generation rate of the F-35B reflects the inherently flexible nature of STOVL aircraft operation compared with conventional aircraft types. By way of comparison, the F-35A land-based and F-35C CATOBAR-compatible variants of the Lightning II both have a sustained SGR of only two sorties per day, increasing to three each day during a surge.

14. The design selected for the *Queen Elizabeth* class was based on a proposal by Thales UK in association with British Marine Technology (BMT). This was preferred over a rival design proposed by BAE Systems in a decision announced in 2003. However, partly reflecting the political implications of awarding such a significant contract to a French-owned company, the decision was accompanied by an announcement that the programme would be taken forward through an alliance approach in which the UK MoD would also participate. The alliance was enlarged to include Babcock at a later stage.

15. To a certain extent, the Bedford Array is a modern development of the mirror landing aid invented by the Royal Navy's Nicholas Goodhart in the 1950s.

16. Recent UK MoD announcements suggest that *Queen Elizabeth* will normally deploy with an air group comprised of just twelve F-35Bs, as well as other rotary assets.

17. Other fourth-generation aircraft are reportedly suited for STOBAR operation if suitably equipped, including the Dassault Rafale, Eurofighter Typhoon and Saab JAS 39 Gripen. Of these aircraft, the naval variant of the Rafale could be used without further modification as it is already equipped for arrested recovery.

18. Both the *Mistral* and *Juan Carlos I* designs were described by the author in an earlier article in this series entitled 'Modern European Amphibious Assault Ships', *Warship 2011*, pp.80-93, Conway, London 2011.

POSTWAR WEAPONS IN THE ROYAL NAVY

In the second of a series of articles on technical developments in the Royal Navy during the post-war era, **Peter Marland** describes the Navy's efforts to produce effective weapons systems for its ships.

At the end of the Second World War the RN owned a collection of legacy gun mountings; there was work in progress to meet new construction, plus wartime thinking about the future place of guided missiles. Plans are captured by the DNO *Titbits* and annual Progress in Naval Gunnery (PING) reports held by TNA, and I IMS *Excellent* XP files that catalogue legacy and new projects, which included:

– studies for an improved 6in Mk 24 and 25, in advance of the fully automatic Mk 26;[1]
– the 5in Medium Calibre Dual Purpose (MCDP) gun, intended for the new Cruiser-Destroyer;
– the new 3in Mk 6 and 6in Mk 26 for the *Tiger* class cruisers;
– concept work on the 4in Mk 25 for DEMS, and the Vickers private venture 4in Mk N(R);
– work on the DA Fused Close Range (DACR), Bofors 40/70, and Coastal Forces System Mk 1 and 2, plus thinking which led onto what would later become the Seaslug and Seacat surface-to-air missile systems.

The overall timeline for the projects and their outcomes are shown in Fig. 1.

Organisation: At the end of the war there were a number of disparate organisations involved in naval weapons systems, embracing aspects of policy, research, acquisition, and trials acceptance. These are listed in the author's previous article about fire control (see *Warship 2014*, p.148), but also added the Ministry of Supply, responsible for the tri-service development of guided missiles.

Technologies

The principal wartime data transmission system was the M Type 'step-by-step' system, using DC switched between +24v/0v/-24v as the input shaft rotated. This was replaced by the Magslip, an AC system developed before the war and used to drive either oil servos or electric power drives. Post-war, magslips were supplemented by the similar (but smaller) US synchro.

Remote Power Control (RPC): This included RP 10/15 and 40 series hydraulic drives, or the RP 50 series electric drive incorporating metadynes; the amplidyne was a US equivalent. The design issues changed across the period. In the pre-war period, hydraulic RPC was dogged by non-reversible worm drives in the power trains of older gun mountings; this was overcome by the later electric RP50 drives and short stiff gearing trains. Transistor module amplifiers and thyristor power drives eventually arrived in the 1970s.

After the war, the sheer mass of the mountings became the concern, and more energetic RPC follow (particularly at the 'end of roll') began to demand large peak powers. This drove the search of feed-forward schemes, off-mounting training motors (to limit rotating mass, and hence inertia), plus re-circulating energy from the gun recoil to power the loading cycle in 6in Mk 26.

Feed Systems: Over the period, power hydraulics evolved from 1940s VSG engines to the 1950s Vickers radial or chain conveyers, with long movements, rotating scuttles and tilting buckets. Post-war systems encountered significant reliability problems due to wear & tear among the highly stressed mechanical components and large numbers of microswitches. Finally, by the late 1960s Seadart, Ikara and 4.5in Mk 8 adopted modern hydraulics with shorter motions, for reduced complexity at lower speeds.

Shell Fuses:
– Direct Action (DA): on impact with the target in wartime surface and SAP shells, or as a reversionary (or selectable mode) in later shell fuses.
– Time Mechanical (TM) Fuses 206, 207, 211: a clockwork fuse for AA, also retained longer-term for Radar Echo (RE) and starshell as Fuse 215; replaced by more modern Fuse N7 (see BR932/45).
– Continuously Adjustable (CA): an early post-war time fuse giving better accuracy with the fuse capacitor charged at the gun muzzle via rods, fingers, wires or wipers, as the shell was fired; Fuse 711 had a Time of Flight (ToF) up to 10.5 sec., the longer-range Fuse 717 up to 40 sec.
– Variable Time (VT): wartime proximity fuses were supplied by the USA as Mk 56 and Mk 60 fuses, with the same nose profile as Fuse 211; US fuses were replaced by British fuses in the N80 to N98 series. N97 Mk 8 added selectable sensitivity and DA modes via fuse paralysing gear, but a notional N99 multi-role fuse with 5 modes was not successful.

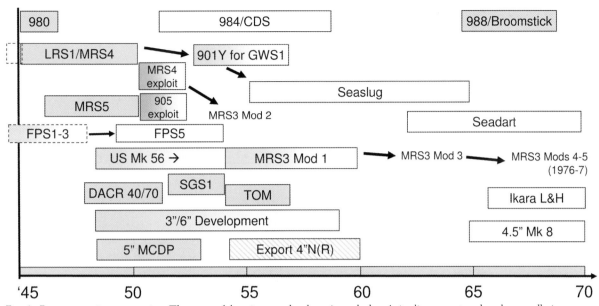

Fig. 1: Post-war project sequencing. The successful projects tend to have 'stretched out' timelines, compared to the cancellations (darker-shaded boxes).

In contrast to the US Navy, the UK never adopted an infra-red (IR) shell fuse, though several of the RN's missiles used such fuses.

Warheads: Most of the early AA missiles used a Continuous Rod (CR) warhead, which worked well against aircraft, but required critical fuse timing. It was replaced in later missiles (and Mod 1 upgrades) by a simple blast/fragmentation warhead with greater HE content and pre-fragmented or tungsten cubes.

Close Range Armament: After the end of the war, the RN had an inventory with a wide variety of gun mountings and calibres. Post-war, 20mm and 2pdr were run down, and most ships retained into the 1950s adopted uniform 40mm close-range batteries.

40mm mountings included the: Mk 1 (US twin), Mk 2 (US quad), Mk 3 manual single (derived from land service), Mk 4 (twin Hazemeyer, based on Dutch

system), Mk 5 (UK twin), Mk 6 (UK sextuple mount), Mk 7 single with hydraulic drive, Mk 8 abandoned, Mk 9 single with electric drive. The Baffin (or Boffin) was a single 40/60 barrel installed on the former power-driven twin 20mm mounting, and was most often seen on Canadian service.

Buster Mk 1 and STAAG Mk 2 were much more elaborate tri-axial or biaxially-stabilised twin 40mm mountings, with onboard centimetric fire control radars, predictors and power supplies.

4.5in Mk 4 to Mk 6 Mountings: Captain de Jersey described destroyer main armament development in RNE Oct 1953/Jan 1954 (Vol.6 No.4/Vol.7 No.1). Although advancing UK practice significantly, these mountings faced far fewer problems than the 3/5/6in described later. The Mark 4 twin mounting was developed from the aircraft carrier mounting, and was trialled in HMS *Savage*, then fitted in all the 'Battle' class

TABLE 1: DNO R&D BUDGET PROJECTIONS 1949

DNO Vote 6 Expenditure

Project:	Est Total Cost	Spent to 48/49	Estimates 49/50	50/51	51/52	Future Trends 52/53	53/54	54/55
MCDP (twin and single)	652,000	52,000	30,000	30,000	100,000	170,000	170,000	100,000
3" Twin	250,000	32,500	45,000	70,000	80,000	17,500	5,000	–
3" Single	100,000	–	10,000	8,000	30,000	40,000	10,000	2,000
6" Mk 26	470,000	100,300	80,000	120,000	100,000	50,000	19,700	–
DACR	25,600	600	10,000	15,000	?	?	?	?
RPC Progress	770,500	125,000	134,500	136,000	128,000	119,000	112,000	16,000
Stabilisation	85,600	37,600	15,000	25,000	8,000	?	?	?
LRS1	600,000	182,000	78,000	80,000	100,000	100,000	60,000	–
MRS3	1,201,000	82,000	235,000	340,000	300,000	200,000	44,000	–
MRS4	600,500	22,500	50,000	50,000	100,000	150,000	150,000	78,000
MRS5	881,000	176,000	172,000	157,000	162,000	160,000	40,000	14,000
GW Launchers & Control	280,000	15,000	25,000	36,000	64,000	50,000	50,000	40,000
Totals:	5,916,200	825,500	884,500	1,067,000	1,172,000	1,056,500	660,700	250,000

destroyers. The Mk 5 single was a conversion of the 4.7in Mk XXI mounting with a 4.5in barrel, to give a single overall calibre in *Savage* and the later 'Battles', albeit limited to 55° elevation rather than 80°. The Mark 6 mounting was initiated in September 1942 and originally intended to achieve 12rpm per gun, with fixed ammunition, swinging arms and an auxiliary shell tray for an automated transfer. The decision was made in April 1943 to aim for 18rpm per gun, and to use hand transfer of separate shell and cartridge case into the gun loading tray. In order to minimise dead time for AA fire, fuse setting was as close to the gun as possible (at the top of the hoist).

Planning for the Postwar Period

The Gun Fire Control Symposium of September 1949 (in X.900/12 Fire Control Policy) listed DNO's Vote 6 research & development budget for weapons and fire control projects. Table 1 shows the relative shares, and the degree to which the programme was delivered successfully. Smaller projects were not listed, and DNO noted the considerable costs for ammunition carried elsewhere in the vote structure. The seven-year programme totalled £5.92m, of which £2.86m was subsequently cancelled (48%). The actual 'sunk' cost was £1.45m (or 25% of the original total). MRS3 was the single largest programme; however, the gun mounting element was £1.50m, of which £0.78m was cancelled. The briefing also shows the need for savings, and cancellations therefore reflect financial prioritisation, not necessarily project failure.

The immediate post-war period (1945-55) covered a significant degree of flux, and there are numerous references to difficulties with shortages of skilled technical staff, particularly electrical draftsman, which severely slowed overall progress. In hindsight, there were simply too many projects, and this may account for the significantly greater attrition compared to later periods.

Weapon Projects: Guns

Mountings were categorised as either Upper Deck (UD, eg 4.5in Mk 5) or Below Deck (BD, eg 4.5in Mk 6). Below Deck mountings were either short trunk down into the gun bay (3in Mk 6) or long trunk down to the main magazine (6in Mk 26). DNO *Titbits* for 1947 identified work in progress on 16in triple mountings, 6in Mk 24 and Mk 26, on a new 5in MCDP, and on 4.5in Mk 6. Post-war research work on new gun mountings included a new automatic 5in weapon in the February 1951 Cruiser/Destroyer design. This remained a paper feasibility study that died with the ship in the 1953 review and does not feature in Notes on AWW; nor does the DACR close-range mounting. Naval gunnery trials also included a new L70 version of the Bofors, but this was not taken forward, and fleet fits remained the venerable L60, as the 40/60.[2]

Notes on Above Water Weapons chronicle a prolonged acceptance process for the new 3in Mk 6 and 6in Mk 26 mountings in the trial cruiser *Cumberland*, and then the *Tiger* class cruisers. The 6in Mk 26 was a disaster: a large complex turret weighing 152 tons that rarely achieved the gun functioning burst-fire requirement. The 4.5in Mk 5 and Mk 6 were barely adequate (due to build-up of errors, slack hydraulic servos, and slow firing rate. In contrast, the 3in Mk 6 was an outstandingly good AA weapon. The ammunition was common with the US Navy, and the Mk 6 mounting was also in widespread Canadian service.

Vickers 4in Mk N(R): The Vickers 4in Mk N(R) mounting with Mk Q gun (see the author's Note in *Warship 2013*, pp.174-77, for detail) was a successful export weapon, building on an Army prototype; it was offered to the RN in late 1953 as part of the approval for export to Chile but was turned down, largely on the grounds of the large stockpile of other mountings already available. In actual fact, Vickers produced a very sound design with a 62-calibre barrel for better range, fed from twin hoppers, allowing one man to conduct up to three burst engagements without an exposed crew on the upper-

Fig. 2: Overall DACR weapon concept: four- and two-barrel inclined axis versions.

deck. The feed system was much less complex (and hence more reliable) than either the 3in or the 6in. It would have made a very capable RN weapon, and presaged many of the later improvements.

The sketch design for a Type 42 East Coast Gunboat showed a Mark 25 single (DEMS) gun, not the Vickers Mk N(R). Subsequently, in November 1955, MoD rejected the 4in Mk 19 for the new 'Tribal' class frigate, selecting instead the 4.5in Mk 5 and citing problems with 4in rates of fire at high angle, better 4.5in surface fire, and the wish to concentrate on 4.5in as the new MCDP (ADM 1/26040).

Direct Action Fused Close Range (DACR): A project was initiated in 1947 for a close range AA gun system with overhead 'zenith' cover. Most of the design study options used two or four 34mm L70 gun barrels in a frame with roll and training axes (rather like Mortar Mk 10) allowing a very wide range of cover through the direct overhead, but giving a small null ahead or astern (countered by a quadrantal layout, with 2, 3 or 4 mounts in ships from frigates upwards). The weapon was fired at 600rpm per gun, and was principally intended to be used against high diving 'missile' targets such as the Hx293 guided bomb or the Japanese *Baka* suicide weapon. The options study[3] also included 'scarecrow' alternatives with between seven and 30 barrels around a common axis and fired in sequence. The system was fitted above decks or in a well. The images show the general design intent, though there was a wide range of alternative feed (belt, fan feeder or magazine) methods. The favoured option represented in ship sketch designs used the $X_R Y$ axis set, with the base of the mounting tilted forwards. DACR did not include a fire control system, which would have had to be of CRP2 or MRS3 Mod 2 accuracy, although an-mount optical sight was mooted.

Bofors 40/70: Bofors 40mm L70 calibre barrels (40/70) were to upgrade WW2 mountings. Initial trials of new Bofors N4 barrels and a 9-clip autofeeder were intended to upgrade Mk 5 and 6 mountings to Mod 1. New design (Mk 11 twin and Mk 14 single) mountings were intended to have battery-backed RPC for defensively equipped merchant ships (DEMS). Only the single 40/70 entered land service with the Army and RAF light AA regiments. Naval usage was dependent on a cut-down MRS3 fire control to give high accuracy pointing, and ultimately died due to cost (sunk investment in 40/60) and uncertainties over actual performance.

Coastal Forces System (CFS) Mk 1 and 2: CFS1 prototyped full radar control but failed, and the subsequent CFS2 used a radar ranging input from Type 974 to the lead computing optical gunsight. This gave a very well-stabilised 17pdr (3.3in) gun with a semi-automatic feed, for use in a seaway. The early trials gave exceptionally promising results, and the weapon was intended for the 'Bold' class FPBs, but the project was cancelled when coastal forces were run-down in 1956.

5in MCDP Gun: The post-war Medium Calibre Dual Purpose (MCDP) programme was intended to arm the

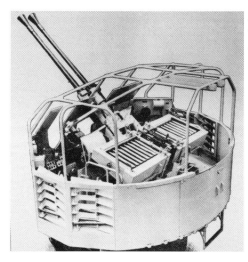

Fig. 3:
40/70 Mk
5 Mod 1.

Fig. 4: CFS2.

new cruiser-destroyer designs, but was eventually cancelled in September 1953.[4] There was a series of designs for 5 inch guns and mountings, with automatic feed mechanism and water cooling. The complete round would have weighed 130lb. Fire control was originally going to be LRS1, but following its cancellation in 1950, the assumption was that MRS3 would provide the capability, though it lacked the required range.

5in Mark 1 Mounting: The Mark 1 mounting design used fixed ammunition and became too complex and heavy, driven by a requirement for a high rate of fire (60rpm) and catapult ('flick') rammers for the fixed ammunition.

5in/70 QF Mark N1 Gun: The 1948 Vickers-Armstrong (Barrow) proposal for a twin 5in/70 mounting had a revolving weight of 189 tons, while Vickers-Elswick's proposal for a similar mounting weighed 113 tons (both figures excluded ammunition).[5] There was also a single mounting with a maximum elevation of 90° and a weight of 74 tons. Cyclic rate of fire for all of these designs was about 66rpm, although higher figures have been quoted.

5in Mark 2 Mounting, with 5in/56 QF Mark N2 Gun:
From 1952 until its cancellation in September 1953, the Mark 2 mounting was developed as a twin gun turret, firing at 40rpm per gun using separate ammunition. Based on a Vickers design for a land anti-aircraft gun, this navalised version was essentially a shorter and lighter version of the Mark N1. The single and twin mountings weighed about 55 and 90-95 tons respectively; both had a maximum elevation of 90°. The high rate of fire was only sustainable for the first minute; subsequent firing was limited to no more than 10rpm in order to extend barrel life. Shell weight was set at 58lb, muzzle velocity was reduced from 3350fps to 3200fps, but the propellant temperature increased from 1900°K to 2100°K. The lower feed system used an endless chain hopper carrying shell and cartridge alternately. The upper feed was an articulated gun chain that had some similarities to the 3in Mk 6 radial conveyor. Each feed system held 20 rounds in the hopper and 20 in the gun chain, via 90° fans to the upper sprocket.

The requirement included AA fire with 5-6 bursts each of 20 seconds duration, with 10-15 second intervals. The Mk 2 mounting also stressed SU fire, with a continuous burst of up to 100 rounds. Only one nature of ammunition was in the feed system, and it could take between 1½ and 5 minutes to change-out to another load. Outfit was 500 rounds per turret.

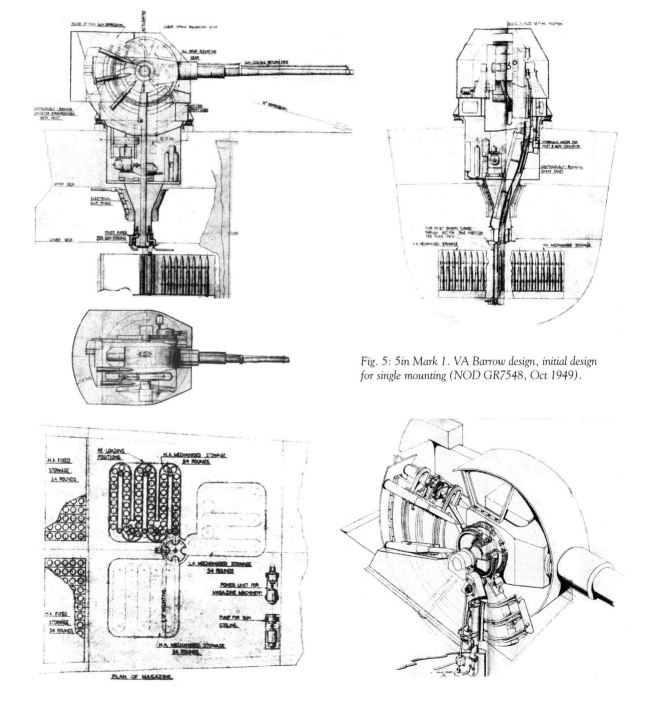

Fig. 5: 5in Mark 1. VA Barrow design, initial design for single mounting (NOD GR7548, Oct 1949).

The 4800-ton Cruiser-Destroyer: an artist's impression of Design Study I dating from February 1951, with three 5in Mk 1 mountings.

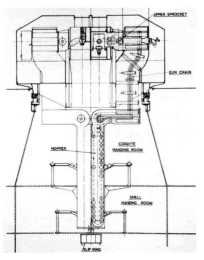

Fig. 6: 5in Mk 2 mounting. (PING, 1953 edition)

TABLE 2: MCDP AMMUNITION STUDY

H is modelled as best from parametric cases A-C.
Units are: length in inches, MV in feet per second, weight in lbs.

Round:	Calibre	Round Length	MV	Shell Weight	Burster Charge	All Up Round length	weight
A Full Calibre	4.8	23.0	3360	44.2	8.9	59	111
B Full Calibre	4.8	31.0	2845	66.4	13.7	67	133
C Full Calibre	4.8	38.0	2515	88.5	18.8	74	154
D *Littlejohn*	4.36	33.5	3129	54.0	13.4	70	121
E *Littlejohn*	4.0	28.4	3460	41.6	8.4	65	109
F *Littlejohn*	3.69	25.0	3770	32.7	5.6	61	100
G FSDS	2.68	44.5	3700	30.8	4.7	61	122
H Full Calibre	4.8	23.0	3360	44.2	8.9	59	111

5in Ammunition: Reports from Fort Halstead cover the internal ballistics of the proposed Naval 5in MCDP gun. These were UK-US collaborative studies that also contributed to the post-war USN 5in/54 calibre programme. The study considered eight types of projectile: four full calibre designs, three 'Littlejohn' (using squeeze bore), and one fin stabilised discarding sabot (FSDS) round. The choice was between AA performance at maximum range (where FSDS was the preferred choice, ranking above Littlejohn and Full Calibre) and surface performance; this was sensitive to range, and FSDS did not achieve the best results against surface or land targets. The report recommended the Full Calibre round as an interim solution,[6] then to progress onto the more exotic rounds. This may account for the choice of an HE Common shell for AA, and a separate HE Piercing round against cruiser-sized surface targets. The modelling calculations were based on a 70-calibre long barrel at 4.87in smooth bore or 4.8in rifled. Full calibre round H was the best of parametric cases A-C, of increasing length and weight (see table).

A fixed charge of 36.8lb of relatively cool propellant gave a barrel life of 765 rounds (or 1543 rounds of FSDS). The study covered AA fire out to 15,000yds Range Future (Rf) and surface fire out to 30,000yds. 5in MCDP was much more energetic than other guns, with an 18 sec. time of flight to 15,000yds (FSDS), increasing to 29 sec. for the full calibre round. In contrast, 6in N5 took 35 sec. to reach the same range, whilst 3in and 4.5in required 42 sec. Despite the higher velocity, accuracy of long range fire would have been dominated by the rate measuring technology in the predictor, plus the RPC performance to stabilise the very heavy mounting.

The recommendation may have been influenced by the Littlejohn requirement for a barrel that would have been incompatible with HEP, whilst FSDS had a unique chamber design that would not have handled the other natures. The study also listed the competing designs for the Mk 1 twin mounting as Vickers-Armstrong (Barrow) weighing 180 tons, V-A (Elswick) at 105 tons, or ADE/V-A Elswick at 130 tons.

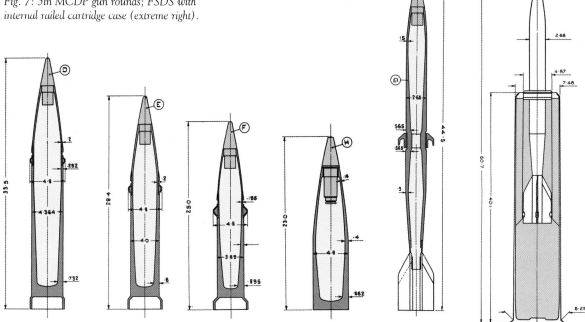

Fig. 7: 5in MCDP gun rounds; FSDS with internal railed cartridge case (extreme right).

Tiger Class Weapons: Whilst the 3in had a very complex high-speed ammunition feed, the 6in weapon rarely achieved its designed rate of fire of 20 rounds per minute per gun due to mechanical failures in its highly stressed feed system. Initial firings were successful,[7] but by later life the 6in system had become an embarrassment.

3in Mk 6 Mounting (3in Mk N1 Gun):. The mounting was developed by Vickers between 1946 and 1959, with firing trials at Eskmeals and at sea in HMS *Cumberland*. The UK fitted nine mountings in *Tiger* class cruisers, while Canada fitted it to eleven frigates (total of 25 production systems). The 70-calibre gun barrel and the ammunition were common with the USN, and the firing rate of 90rpm per gun (reduced from 120rpm) required water cooling. The mounting used metadyne-based RP53 electric power

drives for both motions; the combination of a long barrel, high MV and rate of fire, a flat trajectory, and the stiff servo drives, gave an outstandingly good AA weapon.

The mounting necessitated a complex feed system (anecdotally derived from a milk bottling plant), with seven transfer points between a hopper and the gun loading tray. When fully loaded, the feed system held 322 rounds:

Small hoppers (A and B, 32 each)	64
Large hoppers (C and D, 90 each)	180
Small hopper conveyors (6 each)	12
Large hopper conveyors (10 each)	20
Outer feed ring	12
Inner feed ring	10
Radial conveyors (12 each)	**24**
	322

Also involved in the transfers were a middle feed ring (with shell scuttles), and intermediate hoists and conveyors. Each round weighed 38lb, and the outfit was 1882 rounds per mounting (1600 HE, 72 SUP and 210 AAPF). The rotating mass was 37 tons.

Original plans included a wider fit with dual mounts in *Leopard* class AA frigates and a sided fit in aircraft carriers, with a very long articulated belt conveyor feed, or endless chain hoists, from a deep magazine out to the gun sponsons.

6in Mk 26 Mounting (6in Mk N5 Gun): In contrast to the 3in Mk 6, the 6in Mk 26 was problematic, due to the high torques in the feed system; particular problems were the scuttles and tilting buckets, the three-part feed tray, and complexity caused by a Recoil Energy Power System (REPS) used on the elevating mass of the gun. Overall mounting weight (including armour) was 170 tons; shells

Fig. 8A: 3in Mk 6 mounting: overall layout.

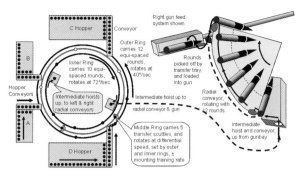

Fig. 8B: 3in Mk 6 mounting: feed system (gunbay left, and turret right).

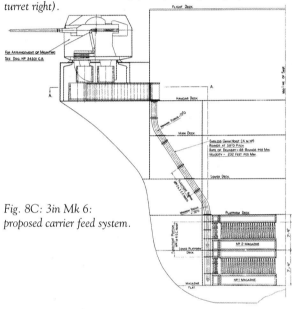

Fig. 8C: 3in Mk 6: proposed carrier feed system.

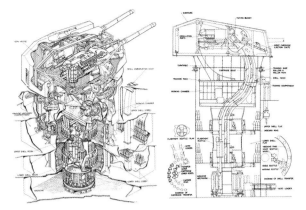

Fig. 9: 6in Mk 26 mounting: feed system.

were 130lb, cartridges 77lb, the total outfit 1098 rounds. The feed system is shown in Figure 9.

4.5 inch Mk 8: A January 1965 project study led to endorsement of the SR in Jan 66. This was a new gun mounting derived from the 105mm Abbott which included a muzzle brake and fume extractor. It used a low maximum angle and lower rate of fire (c.25rpm), for better reliability. The feed system allowed the initial rounds loaded into the feed ring to be fired from the Ops Room without the gun quarters closing up, but retained a 180° index option to allow different rounds (starshell or chaff) to be rapidly fired, despite the remainder of the feed-ring being loaded with HE. Mk 8 entered service in the Iranian *Zaal* in 1971, then *Bristol* in 1973, followed by the Type 42 destroyer, the Type 21, Type 22B3 and Type 23 frigates, and finally the T45 destroyer.

The fixed ammunition weighs 37.2kg (82lb), a

TABLE 3: GUN MOUNTING FEED SYSTEM STRESS

The table shows the feed system throughputs (round weight x rate of fire) for the post-war gun mountings, as an indication of the relative stresses involved. Colour coding is white (low), light grey (intermediate), darker grey (high, by weight/feed velocity or complexity):

Gun/Mounting	4.5" Mk 6	4.5" Mk 8	4" Vickers	3"Mk 6	6"Mk 26	5" Mk 1
All-up round weight lb	55+38.5	81	66	38	130+77	130
Rounds/min (per gun)	18	24	50	90	20	60
Feed system load Lb/min	1683	1944	3300	3420	4140	7800
Ton/min	0.75	0.87	1.47	1.52	1.85	3.48
Rd+Ctge Transfer points	2+2	4	2	7	5+5	4

TABLE 4: RANGE TABLES

The key aspects of gun performance that influence fire control are: initial muzzle velocity (MV), projected time of flight (ToF), average projectile velocity, and the effect of the shell's shape, expressed through a Ballistic Coefficient. This information is captured in range tables that also include the effects of: tenuity, drift, earth's rate, and Equivalent Constant Wind. The AA ceilings are limited by fire control.

Gun/Cal	Shell		Max LA Range			AA Fire		
	MV	Weight	Range	ToF	Elev'n	Height	Range	ToF
6"/50	2450	130	24,500	73	80°	47,500		51
5.25"/50	2600	80	23,400	74				
4.5" Mk 8/55	2850	46	23,800	77	50°	29,500		38
4.5" Mk 6/45	2350	55	19,500	62	80°	39,000		46
					55°	27,000		36
4"/45	2600	31	17,000	62	80°	34,500		41
3"/70	3420	15	19,200	65	80°	42,200		45

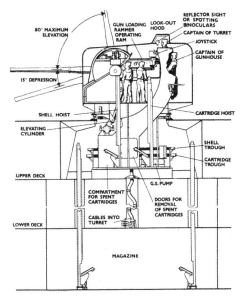

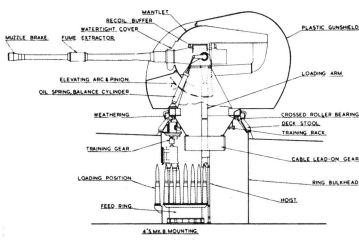

Fig. 10: 4.5in mountings: Mk 6 (left), 37 tons ; Mk 8 (right), 22 tons.

maximum set by hand-loading in a moving seaway. The original staff requirements for 4.5in Mk 8 and its GSA1 fire control system called for Surface (SU) and Naval Fire modes, but the AA capability was dropped in the 1990s. There have been two principal upgrades: a Mod 1 gun mounting, and Improved Ammunition. The Mod 1 mounting uses electric drives in place of hydraulics to reduce the fire risk, and a faceted shield (nicknamed 'Kryten') to reduce the radar signature, while the Improved Ammunition has base bleed for extended range.

Close Range Weapons: The Malaysian conflict forced reinstatement of single 20mm Oerlikons for surface fire ('junk bashing'). Fig. 11 shows the changes in the mounting from the wartime Mk 1 to the post-war Mk 7A (the basic gun remained unchanged). The wartime mount was higher (7 feet to the top of shield), balanced and allowed the gunner to reach higher elevations for AA fire. The Mk 7A was primarily for low-angle fire; it had a shorter pedestal (5ft 6in overall) with a counterbalance to give reduced inboard length. There was a twin (Mk 12A), fitted aft in 'Ton' class minesweepers, which was resur-

rected during the Falklands for ships taken up from trade.

The Falklands also led to a major fitting programme to add close-range guns for AA fire against manned aircraft, including:

– modern belt-fed mountings: single 20mm GAM-BO1, or 30mm twin BMARC GCM-A03;
– 20mm Phalanx CIWS using closed-loop spotting, initially with depleted uranium ammunition – subsequently updated as Block 1B with revised barrels and an IR sensor;
– 30mm Goalkeeper (with tungsten ammunition);
– the most recent single 30mm DS30B, and Automated Small Calibre Guns.

Surface-to-Air Missile Systems

Wartime thinking included a conceptual LOPGAP (Liquid Oxygen & Petrol Guided AA Projectile) and post-war guided missile planning included the 'X', 'Y' and 'Z' weapons. The January 1947 *Titbits* listed Seaslug

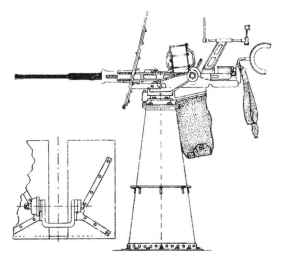

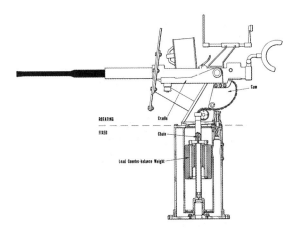

Fig. 11: 20mm mountings: Mk 1 (left) and Mk 7A (right).

(medium range GAP), Popsy (close range GAP), Expert (ship-to-ship low trajectory with underwater terminal phase), and Yodel (ship-to-ship with high trajectory, for plunging fire). The post-war torpedo 'Z' weapons are outlined by Kirby,[8] and included: Zonal, Zorster, Zombie, Zeta and Dewlap, all cancelled in 1949. There was some overlap between Zonal and Expert for an air-flight weapon with a final underwater approach to the target.

Seaslug (GWS1/GWS2): Development via LRS1 and Type 901 to GWS1 spanned a period of 12 years through to 1961. Seaslug was a contemporary of the RAF Bloodhound and Army Thunderbird, except that it was solid-fuelled rather than using ramjets. In addition to the eventual DLG, the system featured in sketch designs for cruisers, converted carriers, or slow convoy AAW escorts (like *Girdleness*) where it was fed from a deep hold via a lift. Seaslug was a large missile stowed horizontally in a long 'hangar' magazine high up in the ship.

Seaslug was a 'beam rider', and though the launcher had two 'barrels' it represented a single channel-of-fire via the sole Type 901 guidance radar. In addition to the basic line-of-sight beam riding (LOSBR), the updated GWS2 system had extra modes: up-and-over, plus two for low-angle or surface engagement (Micawber and CASWTD) using Type 901M's TV camera. The radar was developed from LRS1, and used a 9ft diameter microwave lens, with a peak power of 750kW at I band to give a range of 65,000yds. The conical scan system had a beam-deflecting unit able to separate fine beam pointing from the director's coarse motion.

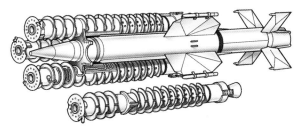

Fig. 12: Seaslug 2 missile. The corrugated fins were designed to ensure clean separation of the boosters from the dart.

Seaslug Launcher & Handling (L&H) system: The prototype launcher & handling system was originally developed in HMS *Girdleness* (see Jon Wise, *Warship 2007*, pp.9-28). This included a 'deep hold' stowage, with missiles held horizontally in trolleys which were raised via a lift, up to a ready-use space in line with the triple barrelled launcher. The magazines had elaborate ventilation and protective plate 'sumps' to cater for potential leaks of the red fuming nitric acid fuel used in early rocket motors, but happily the service rounds adopted solid-fuel boost and sustainer motors. *Girdleness* stowed up to 60 rounds in three holds, and the ship's design was considered for a slow convoy AA escort carrying 16 missiles in a single hold.

The DLG design evolved between May 1955 (concept) to June 1958 (final design) to include Seaslug Mk 1 (first four hulls) and Mk 2 (second four). GWS1/2 adopted a single deck magazine layout with a long 'hangar' that overlaid the machinery spaces on 2 deck (akin to the minedeck in the wartime *Abdiel* class), and led to a twin launcher aft on the quarterdeck. Capacity changed from 24 (first two hulls) to 39 in DLG03-08, using a mix of ready-use and crated stowage. This linear magazine required frequent blast doors in order to avoid a potential chain reaction along the 'load line'. The system was built by Vickers and was broadly contemporary with 6in Mk 26.

In DLGs missile handling was all on one level (2 deck) except for embarkation via the flight deck hatch from 1 deck.[9] The magazine layout was essentially a long 'tube', where missiles could only be transferred aft at the traverser between left and right lanes, side-lanes, discard spaces or the loader. At the forward end there was a smaller check room traverser.

Sketch plans note up to four 'special' (ie nuclear) rounds, and early NAWW from 1959 to 1962 describe alternative HE and W warheads for Seaslug Mk 2, to be changed by ship's staff in the discard bay (rather than being held in the side lane as an all-up round). The design of the Mk 2 included beacon tracking for range coincidence fusing/command detonation, and changes to control stiffness which extended range. There are TNA references to closed files on AWE feasibility studies for nuclear warheads.[10]

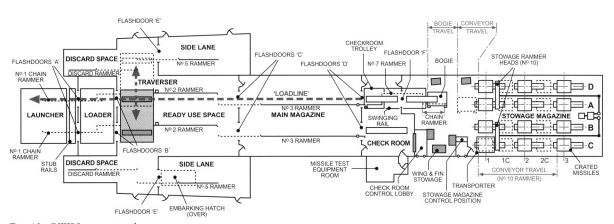

Fig. 13: GWS2 magazine plan.
Note: not to scale: the length has been compressed.

(© John Jordan 2014)

Magazine System: The missile slid inside four guide rails (top/bottom/left/right) mounted on space frames, all mounted on lower deep beams for rigidity and with upper fixing to the deckhead. Each missile had six shoes (four at the rear, and two at the front left & right), all as part of the boost motor attachment rings. The rails were interrupted by flashdoors (both horizontally sliding and a scuttle 'barrel' that rotated upwards). Fig 14A shows the space frames; the pole rammers worked alongside the bottom rail and pushed the missile's lower shoe. The left & right lanes were relatively close (c.3ft apart), and the space frames on each side were coupled together to build a 'raft'. Loading was automated from the Missile Quarters Position (MQP) for motions aft of the check room, but required efflux deflector plates between the missiles to be removed manually.

Missiles were shunted by pole or chain rammers, with small gaps in the rails to accommodate sliding flashdoors; the shoes were long enough to bridge the gaps. The long run of the rails effectively gave a 'linear tube' stowage with reduced ability to shuffle missiles, except at the traverser (moving the missile nearest to the launcher across to the discard bay or in/out of a sidelane). The Mk 2 missile was slightly larger (by about 1in in diameter), but there were contingency plans for GWS2 to embark the smaller Mk 1 missiles using extended shoes.

When under remote control by the MQP, the L&H system required significant supervision within the magazine itself, and ship's staff often chose not to move long strings of missiles simultaneously, and would move one missile at a time into the next gap, like a child's sliding tile game. (Contrast with the later Seadart, where index

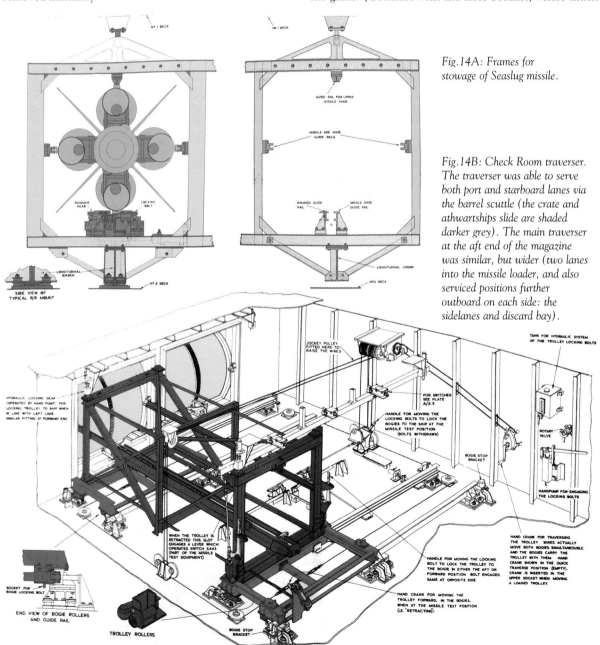

Fig.14A: Frames for stowage of Seaslug missile.

Fig.14B: Check Room traverser. The traverser was able to serve both port and starboard lanes via the barrel scuttle (the crate and athwartships slide are shaded darker grey). The main traverser at the aft end of the magazine was similar, but wider (two lanes into the missile loader, and also serviced positions further outboard on each side: the sidelanes and discard bay).

movements around the magazine were fully automatic.)

The missile was 19ft 6in feet long, and therefore demanded relatively long motions from the loading system. This was achieved using 'pole rammers' with a 22ft stroke; the longest run was No 3 rammer, serving up to four missiles in line in the main magazine. The pole rammer was an articulated metal bar, sliding in the lower rail, with a head that engaged the missile shoe. This was driven by a multi-sheave wire rope system powered by a hydraulic press (similar to wartime heavy gun turrets, or carrier arrester wires). The handbook indicates that the pole rammers could move from one to four missiles simultaneously, through a 22ft pitch length, before the motion was reset. Chain rammers were used in a few positions like the loader, and engaged the top shoe. Pole rammers were similar to pusher hoists, using a stroke movement to 'index', with rounds then held by latches, until the next stroke movement upwards.

Hydraulics: The Seaslug handling system was developed by Vickers-Armstrong; it worked at a moderate pressure (1000psi) but required a high volume of oil, large bore pipework, plus a sizeable hydraulic plant room with three VSG pumps, whilst the launcher had RP53 electric drives. The later Seadart, Ikara and 4.5in Mk 8 used a largely common range of modern hydraulic components including a packaged General Hydraulic Unit, all operating at 3000psi. The design intent was to maximise commonality and hence reduce development & spares holdings, given that many platforms had two (out of the three) systems fitted.

Seacat: PING 1957 introduced the manually-guided Green Light missile, with development starting in 1957, for a possible in-service date of 1961. The concept was

Fig.15: Green Light and Seacat missiles.

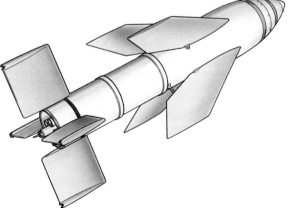

originally known as Popsy. Figure 15 shows Green Light, recognisable as Seacat except for the ring-shaped tail. This was expected to have 74% Pk against a jet fighter, against 14% for a Bofors over the 1200-4000yd range bracket. The system was intended to fit on 40mm Mk 5 foundations, and would have either a two-man manual director, or a possible CRBFD fit (later GWS21).

Seacat was accepted in 1962 against a requirement for a short-range weapon to replace Bofors mountings on a similar foundation. The Short's missile was manually guided by an aimer who tracked the missiles flares visually, using thumb joystick commands (left/right/up/down). The missile was controlled by a UHF link from the launcher aerial, with commands generated by Outfit MAA (frequency set by matching crystals in ship and missile). The four-round launcher was reloaded by hand from the Ready Use magazine, itself replenished from a deep magazine. The missile pad in use (and launcher in a dual fit) was selected at the Launch Control Console Mk 20 in the console space.

The Seacat GWS went through several iterations:

- GWS20: Initial manual director for clear-weather firings; two-man crew (aimer and the director officer, who pushed the director round to the target bearing); fitted in 'Ca' and *Daring* class destroyers, some Type 61 frigates, *Rothesay* class frigates, *Eagle*, and *Fearless/Intrepid*.
- GWS21: Early dark-fire system, using CRBFD with Type 262 radar to track the target; aimer in the director; fitted in 'Battle' class destroyers, *Eagle*, DLG 01-4, and 'Tribal' class frigates.
- GWS22: Later MRS3-based system, in *Leander* class frigates and *Hermes*; variants were 22A in *Tigers*, 22B in Ikara *Leanders*, and both 22C and 22D in Batch 2 Exocet *Leanders*; later, TVA(1) was added for automatic gathering.
- GWS24: In Type 21 frigates using the aft Type 912 and TVA(2), with the aimer below decks for auto gather and autoguide.

The Mod 0 missile had valve electronics, while Mod 1 had solid-state with a bigger warhead (44lb) with an IR nose fuse and graze fuses in the wings. Seacat was used operationally in the Falklands, and post-war changes added a Low-Level Height Cushioned missile. The UK did not adopt the lightweight 'triple' export launcher.

Seadart: The project was initiated in 1960 as the CF299 missile and successor to Seaslug; it was to be fitted in both CVA-01 and the Type 82 destroyer, but sketch plans also included: aft in frigates, forward in an AA version of Type 19, and an export to the Netherlands. It became GWS30 Mod 0 in *Bristol* (38 missiles), and Mod 2 with a lightweight launcher in Type 42 and CVS (22 missiles), both with dual channels of fire. The system used the Type 909 (initially known as Desertcar), an I-band monopulse radar, to track the target and also to provide J band illumination. The missile was a semi-active homer on the reflected signal, but included proportional navigation, a rear reference link, and jamming assessment via Type 909. GWS30 used vertical 'deep-hold' stowage, based on

Fig. 16: Seadart missile.

Vickers launcher & handling (L&H) machinery, and incorporating Solenoid Actuated Changeover (SACO) valves, Honeywell microswitches, relay logic, and short piston movements. The system had much in common with Ikara and the 4.5in Mk 8, being generally reliable except in the case of 'stops' caused by microswitch failures, where most of the subsequent damage was caused by ships staff cycling the magazine manually, one valve at a time. Early sketches allowed the warhead to be changed in the checkroom, for an alternative (SAP) payload to be used against surface targets.

The Seadart GWS30 Mod 1 magazine in the Type 42

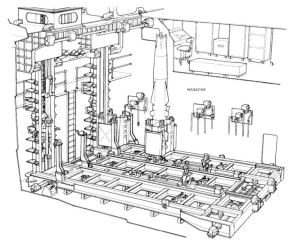

Fig. 17: GWS30 magazine machinery. There were three rows in the Type 42 destroyer (Mod 1 – shown here), vice four rows in the Type 82 (Mod 0).

destroyer featured three lanes, (7, 6, 7 missiles); it could index the left and centre **or** the centre and right lanes to load the lower hoist, then the intermediate hoist position.[11] This was a smaller version of the *Bristol* GWS30 Mod 0 which had four lanes (10, 9, 9, 10 missiles) and was able to index left and right sides independently (plus separate check room space). The missile could be replenished at sea (RAS) via the N15 shipping container.

GWS31 would have been a comprehensive improvement, including a Mk 2 missile, but was abandoned in the wake of the 1981 Nott Review. Post-Falklands improvements were known as the 'famous five': ops room and ADAWS enhancements, plus missile warhead, guidance unit and fuse changes, and separate improvements to Type 909M, under the ADIMP programme

Seawolf: The project was initiated in 1963 as the Confessor feasibility study, becoming Seawolf (PX430) under NSR6522. Seawolf uses command to line-of-sight (CLOS) guidance, with the radar tracking both target and missile to generate steering commands. Early systems also had a TV mode for multipath conditions or surface targets. GWS25 used the Type 910 tracker plus the Type 967/ 968 surveillance package and a 6-barrelled launcher.

Later fits shifted to the Type 911 tracker, but plans for a 4-barrel launcher as a Type 42 retrofit were abandoned, and Phalanx was fitted in lieu. The most recent fits in Type 23 frigates are the vertical-launch GWS26 (32 missiles in silos) with Type 911 trackers and the Type 996 surveillance radar. There have been additional improvements, for example replacing the TV camera by a thermal imager. GWS25 and 26 represent single 'channels of fire' per tracker, but a proposed GWS27 with a Marconi ST1805 'multifire' tracker would have introduced phased-array technology for multiple engagements over a sector. There have also been upgrades to the missile fuse, and further system improvements as the Seawolf Mid-Life Update. The system variants are shown in the accompanying table.

Later Missile Programmes: In the second half of the 1980s, the MoD pursued a Support Defence Missile

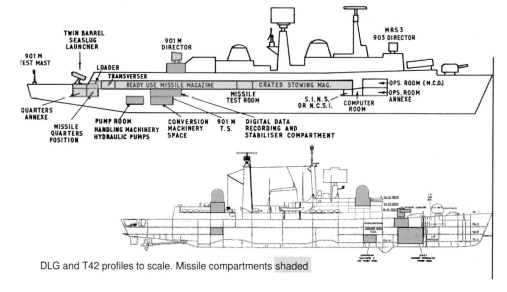

Fig. 18: Seaslug/Seadart magazine layout. DLG 01-08 stowed 24 (rising to 39) missiles with partial crated stowage in a linear magazine. The impact of this scheme on the ship is shown below in profile, compared to the later (and much neater) Seadart.

DLG and T42 profiles to scale. Missile compartments shaded

TABLE 5: **SEAWOLF SYSTEM VARIANTS**

The greyed cells denote projects which were cancelled/abandoned.

System	Ships		Surveillance	Tracker	Launcher
GWS25 Mod 0	T22-01 to 06, Leader 3A		967/968	910	6 barrel
GWS25 Mod 1		Cancelled	967M/968	910M	6 barrel
GWS25 Mod 2			967M/968	VM40	6 barrel
GWS25 Mod 3	T22-07 onwards		967M/968	911	6 barrel
GWS26 Mod 0	T23 fallback	Cancelled	996(1)	911	6 barrel
GWS26 Mod 1	T23, AOR		996(1)	911	32 VL
GWS26 Mod 2	T42B2/B3, CVS	Cancelled	996(3)/(4)/(5)	911	4 barrel
GWS27	T23B2	Cancelled	996(1)	ST1805	32 VL

The early 6-barrelled trainable launcher for Seawolf on the forecastle of the converted Leander class frigate Hermione. The photo was taken in August 1985. (John Jordan)

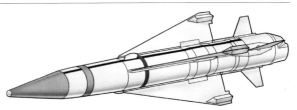

Fig. 19: GWS25 Seawolf missile.

(OTH) Targeting. After repairs to ships damaged in the Falklands, the remaining capital spare Exocet system was trailer-mounted as LABELS and deployed to Gibraltar.

The most recent SSGW was the American AGM-84 Harpoon, initially acquired for submarines (as the Block 1B RN Sub-Harpoon) after the failure of Sub-Martel, then fitted to RAF Nimrods for the Falklands, with an updated Harpoon Block 1C-4 finally selected for Type 22 Batch 3 and Type 23 (as GWS60).

System (SDMS) on the basis that, following the bruising cancellation of GWS31 by James Nott, the UK could not attempt a major missile project alone. SDMS emphasised multiple channels of fire but a more limited range requirement, and effectively killed-off GWS27. The logic led to PAAMS, where the prime contractor (MBDA) built on their existing Aster missile, which had a significant range capability. The 'modern' missile systems about to enter service are:

- Sea Viper (also known as the PAAMS system) in the Type 45 destroyer, using the Aster missile fired vertically from the Sylver canister, and directed by the Sampson radar (Type 1045).
- Sea Ceptor in the Type 26 frigate, potentially using the Common Anti-Air Modular Missile (CAMM), and directed by the Medium Range Radar (Type 997).

Surface to Surface Guided Weapons (SSGW)

The RN acquired the French MM38 missile as a counter to Soviet 'tattletail' tactics, given that there was no prospect of mounting a large-calibre gun (6in to 8in) that would equate to the Exocet SAP warhead. GWS50 was fitted initially to the 'County' class (DLG05-08) from 1973, then to Leander Batch 2 and 3A, Type 21 and 22 frigates (four per ship). Targeting was initially carried out using organic sensors (Type 992 or 993 radar, plus UA13), but swiftly incorporated voice reporting by the ship's Lynx helicopter using its Seaspray radar for Over-The-Horizon

Underwater Weapons

The limitations of the traditional depth charge – which was nevertheless retained into the post-war period in the 'Ford' class of seaward defence vessels – led to a focus on ahead-throwing weapons, and the introduction of both Hedgehog and Squid during the later part of the Second World War. Hedgehog used 24 small contact-fused charges fired out to 275 yards, and was supplanted by the heavier depth-fused Squid. Squid was roll stabilised, and fired a triangular pattern of projectiles (or two patterns in double-mount ships) about 400 yards directly ahead of the attacking ship. Depth setting was electric, and the mountings were re-loaded by hand.

Squid was replaced by the post-war Limbo (A/S Mortar Mark 10), controlled by Sonar Type 170 and MCS10. Limbo fired similar projectiles to Squid, but used much longer barrels with a variable range bleed valve, able to fire between 400 and 1000 yards. The mounting moved in roll and pitch to give 360-degree training. Loading was automatic, with several salvos of weapons ready in the handing room, which was replenished from a deeper magazine. Projectiles were the A/S Mk 6 with a hydrostatic fuse, and the later Canadian NC22 projectile which added a magnetic proximity mode. Light projectiles were fired for training. The control system allowed dual fits to achieve a 'sandwich' effect, intended to burst around the target

There were plans to introduce the Bidder ASW weapon, and several Type 15 conversions, and the early Type 12 and 14 new-build frigates had multiple fixed and trainable torpedo tubes for full-length A/S torpedoes, However, the Mk 20 torpedo failed to deliver the predicted performance and was dropped about 1960,[12] though it was retained in the shorter stern tubes of SSK submarines as an anti-escort weapon.

Surface Torpedo Weapon System (STWS): The last Mortar Mk 10 was fitted to HMS *Bristol*. Contemporary *Leander* conversions (Batch 2 and 3A) and the new Type 21 frigate and Type 42 destroyer were unable to accommodate the weight (and required a larger flight deck for Lynx), while its range (<1000 yards) was uncomfortably close in the context of a fast nuclear-powered submarine. STWS was an anglicised version of the US Mk 32 triple torpedo tube for lightweight 12.75in diameter torpedoes. The Royal Navy initially adopted the electric Mk 44 built under licence from the US, then the Otto-fuelled Mk 46; these would be superseded by the UK Stingray weapon (NASR7511 of June 1968). The new Type 23 frigates adopted a more elegant Magazine Torpedo Launching System, with double tubes inside the ship's structure, loaded from within the air weapons magazine by power-assisted handling gear, and with silo 'flaps' over the tube muzzles.

Ikara: Ikara was introduced as a force weapon, able to deliver torpedoes (Mk 46) at short notice from a guided missile, and updated in-flight on the basis of information from any escort (or helicopter) in contact with the target submarine. The feasibility studies evaluated the Australian Ikara, French Malafon and US ASROC systems, and the staff requirement was raised in 1964 for fits in CVA-01, the Type 82 destroyer and the proposed Type 17 ASW escort. The specified payloads were Mk 31, Mk 44, Mk 46, NASR7511 and HE 600 Nuclear. The UK was critical of the original RAN magazine scheme, which stowed missiles nose to tail, quite tightly packed together; magazine safety trials showed ignition of a missile and venting of the efflux. The system finally went into *Bristol* as GWS40, and the Batch 1 Ikara *Leander* conversions as GWS41. Ikara used a hydraulic handling system to deliver missiles to an assembly room for winging and finning, before loading onto a trainable launcher:

Ikara Launcher & Handling System: The original Ikara magazine arrangements were intended for the Type 17 ASW frigate (fitted aft), Type 82 destroyer (fitted forward) and CVA-01 (starboard quarter), and are shown in Figs. 22A and 22B.

All the early schemes considered an alternative (nuclear) payload, held in a deep magazine, and exchanged in the starboard annex to the Ikara Assembly Room (IAR). After cancellation of the nuclear payload[13] the compartment structural layouts were retained in the *Bristol* installation (GWS40), but the scheme was simplified to work on a single deck level, with missiles held in stools secured to the deck, and lifted out by a single saddle and conveyor for transfer to the loading trolley. The main magazine now held 14 missiles, whilst the former payload exchange space became a reserve magazine, with simplified air-powered hoist allowing manual movement of a further 9 missiles.

After the HE600 payload cancellation many features (the payload umbilical, 'arm' command, and wiring) were left in place, offering a latent nuclear capability; however the fatter 16.5in diameter payload could not have been accommodated in the narrow 12.75in torpedo-sized stowage stools.

Ikara *Leanders*: Ikara fits in Type 17, Type 82, and CVA-01 were announced in 1964 under NSR7668.[14] The high-level decision to undertake the *Leander* conversions was announced in 1967 due largely to the reduction in the Type 82 numbers following the demise of CVA-01. The timeline for the Batch 1 refits to include Ikara is indicated in Whitwam & Watty,[15] with feasibility work carried out 1967-68. The Ikara *Leander* (GWS41) stowed missiles in a deep magazine (two rows, of 6 and 8) made from the former 4.5in magazine and shellroom, with a hoist up to the IAR which then fed the launcher on 1 deck. The launcher sat in a Zareba well, protected by a canvas Igloo. Loading movements were hydraulic, and missiles were fired at a fixed 55° elevation when ship's roll and pitch were within limits.

All the RN service missiles were the M4 variant, with a Mk 46 payload. Ships always carried a single test missile,

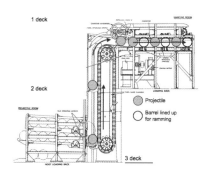

Fig. 20: *Mortar Mk 10 hoist and handing room. The feed arrangements provide an example of an endless chain hoist.*

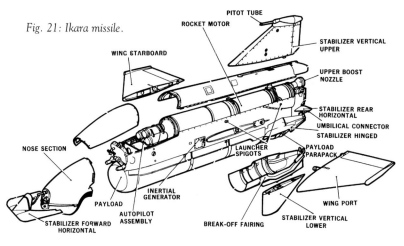

Fig. 21: *Ikara missile.*

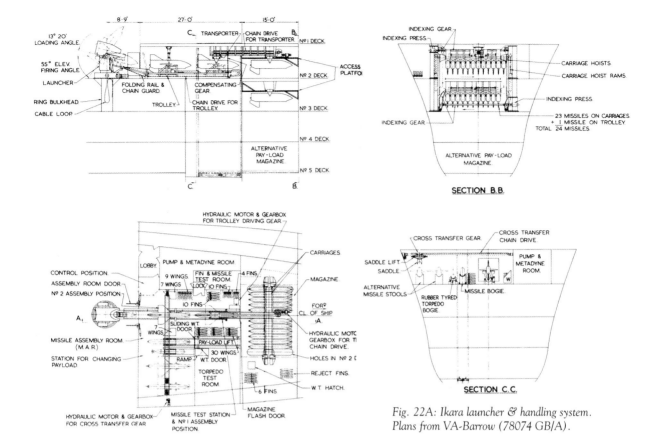

SECTION B.B.

SECTION C.C.

Fig. 22A: Ikara launcher & handling system. Plans from VA-Barrow (78074 GB/A).

necessary for daily functional tests, with the remainder of the outfit as operational missiles. Torpedo modes and settings were applied pre-launch by the ASW Director (ASWD) from the ops room.

System Software: Ikara was 'hosted' within the ADAWS 2 or 5 operational software and had no reversionary mode in the event that the parent computer was offline. System control was via the ASWD's console function to nominate a track for engagement. One innovative

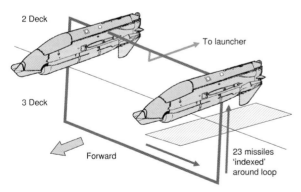

Fig. 22B: Type 82 Ikara magazine: simplified view. Missiles were hung below a carriage and stowed with the lower fin (SVL) fitted, but without the remaining wings and fins. This formed a vertical 'merry-go-round' running between two decks. This had similarities with the contemporary Seadart (albeit arranged horizontally, rather than vertically).

area was the Ikara System State & Command Panel (SSCP) and the associated Weapon Setting Panel at the ASWD's position in the ops room. The SSCP gave excellent visualisation, using a flowline for the whole engagement, colour coded for health, via a flat panel display. This gave a much better understanding of system status, compared to the somewhat 'clunkier' user interfaces of the contemporary Seadart and gun systems.

Note that 'fire' and 'cut down' required deliberate action by two parallel pushes for additional safety. Once fired, the missile flew at a height of c.1000ft, set by an aneroid barometer in the upper fin. The Tracking & Guidance system used a transponder in the missile that replied to the ship's guidance commands. This 'reply' pulse was tracked in azimuth by a monopulse tracker aerial, and the system measured missile range by timing around the loop. The parent ADAWS computer then generated steering commands to update the trajectory against the target submarine's future position derived by the SUBPREDA prediction algorithm. System range in standard conditions was in excess of 24,000 yards, but was significantly affected by wind.

There were proposals for simplified BASIK and BOXIK systems, and Ikara was mooted for both the Type 22 and Type 43 in a carousel magazine. Additional studies covered new variants: M5 (track whilst scan), M6 (Stingray), and M7 (airbreathing; the basis of the Turana drone). Ikara remained in RN service from 1973 to 1989, although towards the end of this 16-year period the emphasis in ASW had shifted across to towed array work

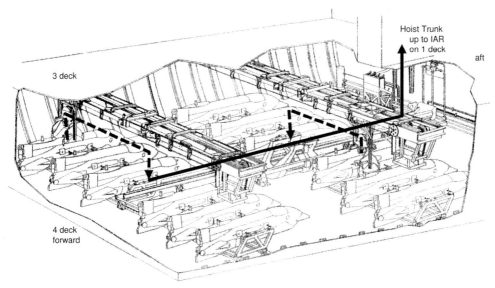

Fig. 23A: Leander GWS41 magazine layout.

3 deck

Hoist Trunk up to IAR on 1 deck

aft

4 deck forward

at longer range, with close-range ASW handled by MATCH with Lynx, or STWS torpedo tubes.

Discussion: The Ikara *Leander* (IKL) episode points out the difficulty faced by the Naval Architects:

– Ships designs were intended to include both Board and accommodation margins, for subsequent in-service growth and changes. The original (gun) *Leanders* had used up all the Type 12 margins. *Leanders* would still have had margins, but with a compact layout they were not in useful areas, so the margin wasn't flexible enough to support significant refits at the half-life point (Ikara, Exocet and Seawolf conversions).

– Ikara was a big-ship system, originally aimed at new 3500-tonne ASW frigates and the larger Type 82 DLG. It was not a happy fit in a 2800-tonne escort at the half-career point. The significance of this was lost during the transition from Type 17+82 to Type 82+IKL. The changes might have worked, but would have required

compromise on either the number of rounds to be carried and/or on keeping the Mortar Mk 10, Wasp/MATCH and the overstern Type 199 sonar rig.

– The irreversible sequence was begun in early 1962, once the UK decided it could do better than Australia and wanted a bespoke L&H system, initially for Type 82. This led to a complex double-height system. The components were re-engineered into the flat system seen in *Bristol*, but relied on a significant tween-deck height[16] that could not be accommodated aft in Leanders.

– There were concerns aired at Committee, but these were assuaged by emphasising: that Ikara was a **Force** weapon; that the IKL would not be a significant portion of the escort force; that AA arcs (for Seacat) would be improved; and that the only capability lost was bombardment. The consequence was a single-purpose ASW frigate with all the systems (Ikara, MATCH helo, mortar and Type 199 sonar), but one which had limited operational deployment capabilities.

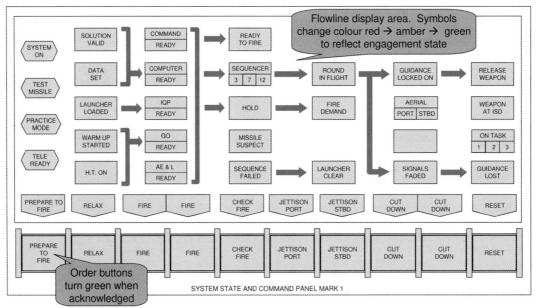

Fig. 23B: Ikara System State and Command Panel (SSCP).

Conclusions

Over the post-war period outlined in this paper, the RN did relatively well. A comparison with contemporary developments in the US Navy yields some interesting observations, which follow.

With LRS1 and FSDS ammunition, the 5in MCDP would have been a system of almost *baroque* complexity. After its cancellation, the RN then spent the next three decades trying to make 'a silk purse' out of the 4.5in Mk 6, via constant practices against very benign AA targets like the slow *Rushton* which was usually towed at constant course/speed and height.

The USN did better with its 5in/54 series of guns and ammunition, and innovated with Phalanx for anti-ship missile defence. The RN showed a fixation with heavy-calibre weapons, requiring 4.5in or larger, despite their mediocre AA performance. The potential AA effectiveness of the 3in Mk 6 or the Vickers 4in Mk N(R) was not fully recognised; in contrast, the French were content with a 100mm (3.9in) gun which offered more balanced benefits.

The RN did not have the reliability issues encountered by the USN with their '3T' (Talos/Terrier/Tartar) missile programme. However, each RN system **had only one** significant upgrade (Seaslug Mk 2, Seacat Mod 1, Seadart Mod 1, and Seawolf MLU). In contrast, the USN carried out a long series of incremental improvements which steadily transformed Tartar/Terrier into the latest block of Standard SM3 used for ballistic missile defence, while maintaining compatibility with a wide range of launcher configurations.

UK technical histories show the value of running back-to-back projects that allow 'lessons learned' to be carried forward. The UK showed strength in operational analysis and in trials, delivering relative value for money. There was greater in-house commitment and a creative partnership between Naval Officers, Scientists and Engineers. Seawolf, for example, was more innovative than Sea Sparrow in terms of meeting an emerging threat from the Soviet SS-N-7/8.

It is not clear the RN could have attempted anything as ambitious as Aegis; however the USN probably neglected the frigate part of its escort force and focused attention on its high-end units. The adoption of PAAMS reflects International collaboration, and also shows that the USN had 'de-risked' the concept (as with the atomic bomb, they proved it was possible, although they had a false start with Typhoon).

The RN Ikara *Leander* episode illustrates the law of unintended consequences. When the system components were re-packaged for *Bristol* after cancellation of the 600lb payload, the requirement to be able to hoist one bare missile across the others in the athwartships stowage

ABBREVIATIONS:

AAPF	Anti-Aircraft Practice Flash (shell)
AWE	Atomic Weapons Establishment (Aldermaston/Burghfield)
BR / CB	(Royal Naval) Book of Reference / Charge Book for classified subject
CA	Continuously Adjustable (early postwar electronic time fuse for shell)
CFS1/CFS2	Coastal Forces System Mk 1/Mk 2
CIWS	Close in Weapons System (especially the USN Phalanx)
CRP/CRS	Close Range Predictor/System
DA	Direct Action (shell fuse)
DACR	Direct Action fused Close Range gun mounting, able to fire through the zenith
DAMS/DEMS	Defensively Armed (or Equipped) Merchant Ship
DLG	Destroyer Light Guided Missile ('County', then Type 82/42 classes)
DNO	Director of Naval Ordnance (at Bath)
FSDS	Fin Stabilised Discarding Sabot, novel shell design, but widely used ashore
HE	High Explosive (shell)
HEP	HE Piercing (proposed shell)
L60, or /60	Gun barrel length, expressed as multiple of the basic bore calibre
L&H	Launcher and Handling (system)
LRS	Long Range System
MATCH	Medium Range Attack Torpedo Carrying Helicopter
MCDP	Medium Calibre Dual Purpose gun mounting (5in, later cancelled)
MQP	Missile Quarters Position (from which the L&H system was controlled)
MRS	Medium Range System
MV	Muzzle Velocity
NAWW	Notes on Above Water Weapons, annual report, superseding PING
NC	Nickel Chrome (grade of steel armour plate)
NGS/NGFS	Naval Gun Support/Naval Gun Fire Support (shore bombardment)
NW	Nuclear Weapon
PING	Progress in Naval Gunnery annual report in TNA, superseded by NAWW
QF	Quick Firing gun using metal cartridge, and automatic closing breech. Alternative would be Breech Loading (BL) gun with bag charges.
Rf / Rp	Range future (shell range after ToF) / Range present (current target range)
RP**	Remote Power (number), types of RPC
RPC	Remote Power Control
SACO	Solenoid Actuated Change/Over Valve, in hydraulic L&H systems
STAAG	Stabilised Tachymetric AA Gun (40mm Bofors with on-mount Type 262 radar)
STUFT	Ship Taken Up From Trade, especially during the Falklands
STWS	Surface Torpedo Weapon System
SUP	SUrface Practice (shell)
TM	Time Mechanical (shell fuse)
ToF	Time of Flight (for shell)
VSG	Variable Speed Gear (hydraulic pump)
VT	Variable Time (proximity fuse for shell)

meant that the system could not be fitted aft in *Leander*. This was the driving factor behind the forward fit, in lieu of the gun and a deep main magazine. It also illustrates the lack of flexibility in the board margin, eroded since the original Type 12 design.

There are different engineering cultures in the RN and USN; the RN rotated engineer officers between sea and shore postings, whilst the USN developed a shore-based Materiel Professional career stream. The RN did benefit from a more resilient departmental organisation with three layers (engineer officer, charge chief, and maintainer), compared to the USN with a non-specialist line officer as the head of department; an example of this vulnerability was a USN escort in a major Allied exercise in 1981 that used more than 1200 fuses to faultfind a tricky defect on a SQS-26 sonar, then asked for another box in order to complete the diagnosis!

The UK may well have enjoyed a more coherent acquisition and engineering R&D community due to its smaller size – the much larger US organisations faced greater overheads, compounded by the sheer physical size of the USA. Gadeken's papers (see Sources) make an interesting contrast between the different styles of the UK Procurement Executive and the US Materiel Professional, but reflect the position up to the late 1980s; these may not carry forward to DE&S, after the changes set out by Gray in 2009.

Acknowledgements: The author is grateful for the help of Lt-Cdrs. Bill Legg and Clive Kidd at Collingwood, and Lt-Cdr. Brian Witts at *Excellent* for access to their museum collections of BRs, journals and files.

Primary Sources:

Journal of Naval Engineering articles via http://www.jneweb.com/

Naval Weapons pages at http://www.NavWeaps.com, plus discussion boards.

HNSA website for USN (and some RN) handbooks, via http://www.hnsa.org/doc/

The National Archives (TNA) at Kew: (ADM files), NMM (P&P) at Woolwich (ships covers), HMS *Collingwood* (BR's and JRNSS journals), and HMS *Excellent* (XP series files and documents).

Books and Papers:

For postwar projects, see annual reports: CB04540 series Progress in Naval Gunnery (PING) 1952-57, held at TNA (ADM 239/493 to /765). PING was superseded by Notes on Above Water Weapons (NAWW) through to 1972-73 (ADM 256/149 to 165).

The RN text books on gunnery are the mid-1950s BR 1898 series Gunnery Manual; BR1898(2) dictionary, plus BR224/45 The Gunnery Pocket Book 1945, see also BR224 Introduction to Naval Gunnery 1960, and BR1096 Ordnance Engineering Notes.

For project management see: Jordan G, Lee I, Cawsey G, 1988, *Learning from Experience*, HMSO; Gadeken OK, 'Through the Looking Glass', JNE Dec 92 Vol 34 No 1, pp29-34; Gray B, *Review of Acquisition*, Oct 2009, Annex C.

Visits:

HMS *Belfast* in the Pool of London, with 6in, 4in and 40mm.

HMS *Cavalier* at Chatham, with 4.5in Mk 5.

HMS *Plymouth* at Birkenhead with 4.5in Mk 6 (since scrapped).

Explosion! museum at Gosport

Firepower museum at Woolwich

Footnotes:

1. Pre-war and wartime systems used Mark numbers in roman form (Mk VI), but later shifted to arabic format (Mk 6). Both schemes existed side-by-side in documentation. The original scheme used star * notation for smaller improvements, but became superseded by the US Mod numbers (the Imperial system started at Mk 1, whereas the US baselined at Mod 0). There were often different mark numbers for the gun and for the mounting, with the same barrel being applied to different mountings.

2. Post-war conservatism was due to the large legacy of 40/60 materiel (ammunition and barrels) that could not be re-used in a 40/70 programme. Other examples of conservation included re-cycling Army 6/17pdr cartridge cases as the charges for A/S Mortar Mk 10.

3. G.652 dated 1948: report of Panel on Zenith DA/CR Naval Weapon.

4. This section draws on the Navweaps website text, HMS *Excellent* and TNA documents.

5. For comparison, the twin 4.5in Mark 6 mounting weighed 44 tons.

6. ADE (Ministry of Supply) Report 22/48 Vol 1 and 2, Analysis of Requirements for a Naval Medium Calibre Dual Purpose Weapon, Nov 1948.

7. See Peter Parkinson at http://www.navweaps.com/Weapons/WNBR_6-50_mkN5.htm.

8. Development of the Torpedo, and Rocket Propelled Torpedoes papers at http://www. geoffkirby.co.uk.

9. For the GWS1 Launcher & Handling system see BR954(4A) in ADM234/851.

10. ES7/6 Designs of NW for Seaslug Mk 2, Jan-Dec 1965, and ES7/7 through /9 NW for Seadart Jan-Dec 1966, DEFE 69/467 NW for heavyweight torpedo. There is also a note DEFE 24/194 Dec 1966, Sec NS about the nuclear warhead for Seaslug being in abeyance since 1962, and at 2 years notice.

11. Uncertainty in the declared total (20 or 22) is due to the potential to hold two missiles at the IHP, with some penalties to operational flexibility.

12. See ADM 302/39, Operational and tactical value of Mk 20(E) torpedo, and ADM 239/552, Mk 20 (E) and (S) torpedo handbook, CB4835.

13. DEFE 24/91 for DS4 acquaint 1/67 dated 27 June 1967. Deletion of HE600 from Ikara M4- option under NSR 7668, due largely to the reduction in the Type 82 numbers following the demise of CVA-01.

14. ADM 333/2 for RNIK 10 feasibility study, dated July 1964.

15. Whitwam DF and Watty AJ, 1979, 'Modernising the *Leander* Class Frigates', Trans RINA 1979, pp.37-52.

16. Leander tween deck height was 7ft 6in, with both 1 deck and 2 deck cambered. In contrast, *Bristol's* deckhead height was 8ft 6in, rising to 8ft 9in on the centre-line, from a flat 2 deck.

THE NAVAL WAR IN THE ADRIATIC
PART 1: 1914-1916

Conflict in the Adriatic during the Great War has received little attention compared with the naval war in the North Sea, the Atlantic and even the Pacific and Indian Oceans. **Enrico Cernuschi** and **Vincent P. O'Hara** aim to correct this deficit with a two-part article detailing the running battles for supremacy in these narrow waters between Austria-Hungary and the allied forces of France, Italy and Great Britain.

English-language accounts of the First World War at sea have focused primarily on the actions in the North Sea and the wider activities of the German submarines, despite other important naval campaigns. In the Mediterranean, for example, the navy of the Kingdom of Italy, the Regia Marina, with assistance from Great Britain and France, faced across the Adriatic Sea the Imperial and Royal Navy (k.u.k. Kriegsmarine) of the Austro-Hungarian Empire, supplemented by two or three dozen German submarines. The principle of the decisive naval battle – the rationale for the dreadnought fleets of all the major naval powers – proved of little relevance in the narrow waters of the Adriatic; this was a theatre that encouraged and rewarded innovation. The Adriatic campaign fostered the development of expendable weapons such as the fast motor torpedo boat and manned torpedo. It was in the Adriatic that aircraft first sank a submarine. Mine warfare and massive antisubmarine barriers flourished there. Certain things worked and certain things did not. In the crucible of war the Adriatic navies of one hundred years ago forged principles for modern warfare in narrow waters that remain relevant today. This is evidenced by the story of the surface forces and the patrols, bombardments, raids, and battles which took place there.

The Stage

Geography dictated the nature of the naval war in the Adriatic. The sea is long and narrow; its shallow waters, particularly in the northern basin, are conducive to mining, torpedo boat, and submarine operations. The Italian west coast is open with few good ports. In 1915 only Venice could support a battle fleet. Ancona and Porto Corsini could base coastal flotillas, while Bari in the southern basin was exposed to the weather and had no naval infrastructure. Brindisi had a large anchorage, but work on making this excellent location into a cruiser base began only in 1913 and remained incomplete at the end

of the war. Taranto was home to the battle fleet but was outside the Adriatic, and forces could not rapidly intervene from there.

The geography of the east coast is more complex, with many inlets and coastal archipelagos. However, once again good ports were few. Austria-Hungary's fleet base was Pola in the far north, only 70 nautical miles from Venice. There was a minor facility at Sebenico midway down the coast, suitable for light forces. The only other military harbour was Cattaro in the far south near the Montenegrin border. From there the k.u.k. Kriegsmarine operated cruisers, destroyers, and submarines. Access to the open waters of the Mediterranean passed through the narrow Strait of Otranto farther south. Geography thus put the Austro-Hungarian Empire in the peculiar situation of having a high seas fleet of first-class dreadnoughts with no high seas on which to sail. The Austro-Hungarians themselves were first to demonstrate the hazards of operating large warships in these narrow waters when the k.u.k Kriegsmarine submarine *U 12* torpedoed the French dreadnought *Jean Bart* on 21 December 1914.

In the decades before the First World War, Italy and Austria-Hungary were allies and the presumptive foes of their joint fleets were France and, after 1909, Great Britain. However, given their history and natural rivalries,

U 12 damaged the French flagship Jean Bart *in December 1914, but was lost in August 1915 in an Italian minefield off Venice.* (Boris Lemachko collection)

both Rome and Vienna gave serious consideration to the possibility that they would fight each other. It was natural that Austro-Hungarian naval planners should consider their 1866 victory over the newly-minted Italian navy in the Battle of Lissa as a template for a renewed conflict. In this scenario the naval command envisaged a decisive battle with the Italian fleet to gain command of the Adriatic Sea. It believed this battle would quickly follow the outbreak of war. Should this plan fail, the Austro-Hungarian battleships did not have a coherent mission, other than maintaining a threat in being. Lost somewhere in the Mahanian construction programs adopted by Vienna and Rome was the fact that Lissa decided nothing. Other naval missions included protecting the long coast of Dalmatia and interfering with enemy traffic. Fleet support of the Imperial army and submarine operations in the broader waters of the Mediterranean were missions that evolved as the war developed.

The primary missions of the Italian Navy were to blockade the Austro-Hungarian battleships in Pola, to protect the kingdom's shipping and the maritime flank of the army, and to close the Strait of Otranto to enemy passage. Secondary missions included protecting traffic with Albania (and later Greece), and the harassment of enemy maritime communications. After the spring of 1916, when German submarines became more active, containment of these boats became another primary mission.

In 1915 Italy, as the stronger naval power, had the advantage over its foe and thus no reason to seek a fleet action in the Upper Adriatic through uncharted thickets of minefields, submarine ambushes, and nocturnal torpedo boat traps. In the south, Cattaro had limited facilities and the Austro-Hungarians could not base their dreadnoughts there for extended periods. This reduced the Habsburg navy to waging a war of harassment that stood no chance of wresting control of the Otranto Strait from the Entente powers and opening up the opportunity to operate in the wider Mediterranean. The makers of Italian naval policy, particularly Paolo Thaon di Revel, the Regia Marina's chief of staff, appreciated this dynamic and he advocated a type of warfare using expendable units that would be *audace e continua*, that is, audacious and continuous. The result was a complex and protracted guerrilla war that has been described as a stalemate but was, in fact, anything but.

The Actors

In August 1914 a Franco-British agreement assigned to France the supervision of naval operations in the Mediterranean. After Italy announced her neutrality on 2 August 1914, the French admiralty hastily dropped its long-planned offensive against Rome and ordered its Mediterranean Fleet to instead act against the Austro-Hungarians only. This task traded the anticipated fleet action for a campaign the Marine Nationale was ill-prepared to fight, lacking the doctrine, the infrastructure, or the types of warship required. France declared war on the Austro-Hungarian Empire on 12 August and the fleet entered the Adriatic to break the Habsburg naval blockade

TABLE 1: THE BALANCE OF NAVAL POWER IN THE MEDITERRANEAN, AUGUST 1914

	Austria-Hungary	Germany	France	Britain	Italy
Dreadnoughts	3	0	4	0	3
Battlecruisers	0	1	0	3	0
Pre-dreadnoughts	3	0	17	0	6
Coastal battleships	6	0	10	0	3
Armoured cruisers	3*	0	11	0	10**
Light cruisers	2	1	0	4	3
Protected cruisers	2	0	3	0	8
Destroyers	18	0	42	16	33
Torpedo boats	29	0	100***	16	100***
Submarines	6	0	15	0	18

*one obsolete; ** two obsolete; *** approximately

of Montenegro, which was being conducted by a flotilla of older vessels based at Cattaro. The French also hoped to lure the k.u.k Kriegsmarine's main battle fleet from Pola, where it could be engaged and defeated in a conclusive battle to be fought by overwhelming forces at ranges comparable to those at Tsushima, as all the Mediterranean powers lacked the sophisticated predictors and rangefinders of the British, American, and German navies.

On 16 August the French fleet, accompanied by British armoured cruisers, surprised the old cruiser *Zenta* and destroyer *Ulan* off the Montenegrin port of Antivari. The battleships unleashed 500 shells at *Zenta*, sinking her with heavy loss of life, although *Ulan* escaped. The French, however, suffered significant damage when three major guns exploded during the action, damaging the *Justice* (one 194mm gun) and *Condorcet* (two 240mm). Two other battleships collided after the action. The French set a bitter tone to the conflict by letting *Zenta*'s survivors drown.

While this action ended the Austro-Hungarian blockade, it did not spark the desired fleet action. The commander-in-chief of the k.u.k. Kriegsmarine, Baron Anton von Haus, had no intention of sailing south to challenge the superior French fleet, despite intense German pressure from the first days of the war for him to use the fleet 'offensively' in an effort to seize Albania (with its newly-appointed German monarch). The Germans believed that such a thrust would encourage

The October 1914 Italian landing at Saseno Island off Valona. (Enrico Cernuschi collection)

Greece to join the Central Powers and draw off Entente warships from the Dardanelles. Haus, however, argued there was nothing the Austro-Hungarian battleships could achieve by engaging in a gung-ho battle against a superior enemy, even should they be victorious. His foe of choice was Italy, and so he bided his time and made plans to deal with his archenemy when, as seemed inevitable, war erupted between Rome and Vienna. Following the same logic the French declined to risk their fleet up the Adriatic far from their base at Malta, the more because Greece allowed only a discrete use of its anchorages in the Ionian Islands for Marine Nationale destroyers and submarines until January 1916, when the French seized Corfu to use the island as a battleship base. Other than two battleship bombardments of Cattaro in September 1914, light forces and submarines conducted what fighting there was between the Franco-British forces and the Austro-Hungarians, while in the upper Adriatic traffic with Italy proceeded on a peacetime basis giving Germany, more than penniless Austria, precious food-stuffs cultivated in the peninsula beyond the limits of the Franco-British naval blockade.

Austro-Hungarian mines and raids inhibited half-hearted French efforts to use Antivari as a supply port for Montenegro and Serbia. An Austro-Hungarian mine sank the French destroyer *Dague* there on 24 February 1915. On 27 April the French armoured cruiser *Léon Gambetta* fell victim to the Austro-Hungarian submarine *U 5* while patrolling the Otranto Strait. Nearly seven hundred French sailors died in this disaster. Meanwhile, Haus remained in Pola steadfastly waiting for Italy to join the conflict.

Italy Joins the War

When, on 24 May 1915, Italy finally declared war against the Habsburgs (but not Germany), nearly the entire Austro-Hungarian fleet sortied to bombard Ancona and other Adriatic ports. Although this has been cited as evidence that the k.u.k. fleet was eager for a general action, the targets were, in fact, safely outside the inter-vention zone of Italy's dreadnoughts at Taranto, and the Regia Marina's old battleships and armoured cruisers did not emerge in angry swarms from Venice and Brindisi to be easily overwhelmed by the Austro-Hungarian dread-noughts.

In the course of these shore bombardments there was a minor encounter when a pair of Italian destroyers on patrol ran into the light cruiser *Helgoland* shelling Barletta. The Austro-Hungarians ran down and overwhelmed the *Turbine*, which was suffering from machinery problems. Otherwise the k.u.k. Kriegsmarine's grand sortie sparked no clashes at sea. The Austro-Hungarians returned to port claiming a moral rather than a material victory.

Within weeks Italy and her new allies were retaliating with bombardments of semaphores, light houses and railway lines on the opposite Adriatic coast. The military impact was minor but the price high. In the southern Adriatic the Austro-Hungarian submarine *U 4* torpedoed and seriously damaged the British light cruiser *Dublin* on 10 June, and the same boat sank the Italian armoured cruiser

The Italian battleship Regina Margherita *in 1915. (Enrico Cernuschi collection)*

Garibaldi on 18 July (see Zvonimir Freivogel, 'The Loss of the *Giuseppe Garibaldi*', *Warship 2012*).

For the remainder of the year the waters of the southern Adriatic were troubled by Austro-Hungarian raids and shore bombardments, and by the Italian occupation of the island of Pelagosa. The Duke of Abruzzi, commander of the Italian battle force, envisaged Pelagosa as a stepping stone to a bridgehead on the Sabbioncello Peninsula on the central Dalmatian coast, but the Italian army refused to release the men and artillery required. Predictably this pointless action provoked a series of minor engagements and then an unsuccessful Austro-Hungarian counter-landing before the Italians sensibly evacuated the small, waterless island. Nonetheless the short occupation of Pelagosa did serve to reinforce Admiral Haus' fears that Italian landings threatened his coast. In fact, the Austro-Hungarians worried about this throughout the war. In October 1918, the Imperial army maintained a division at Cattaro, and two infantry brigades and various minor units throughout Dalmatia for a total of 60 battalions and 800 guns, while Italy relied on 10,000 coastguardsmen to perform similar duties along its shoreline.

The major prize in the southern Adriatic was actually the sea lanes between Italy and the Balkans, not toeholds in the Dalmatian archipelago. After Bulgaria declared war in October 1915 and cut the route to Serbia from Salonika, the ports of Montenegro and Albania became major supply points for the beleaguered Balkan front. The traffic to these ports proved a tempting target, and the k.u.k. Kriegsmarine launched a series of raids against it starting in November, 1915.

Italian floating battery with 152mm/40 guns. (USMM)

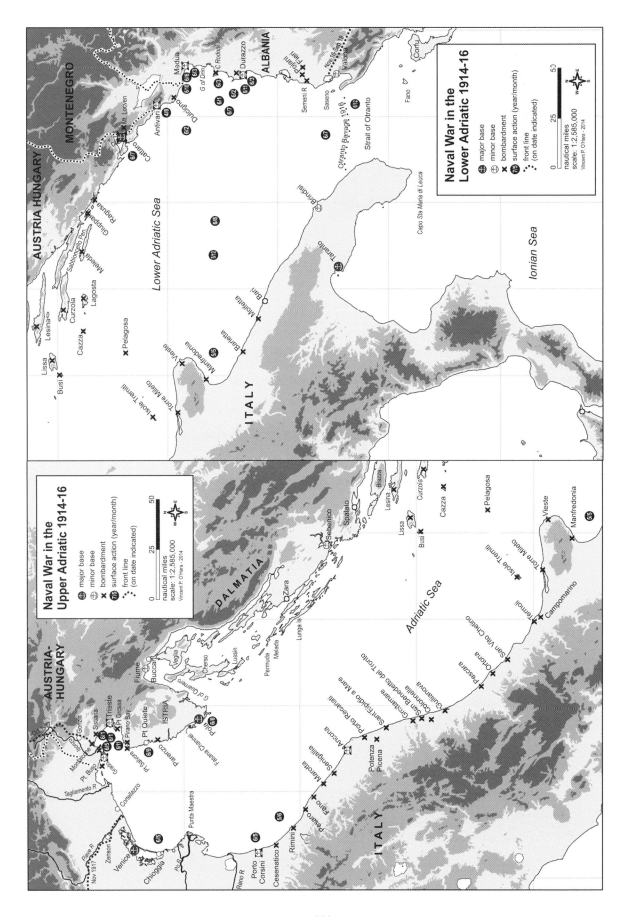

The Italian destroyer Irrequieto *in 1915.* (Enrico Cernuschi collection)

The Austro-Hungarian coastal battleship Wien. (Courtesy of Zvonimir Freivogel)

On the night of 22/23 November the scout cruiser *Helgoland* and six modern destroyers swept south and sank an Italian motor schooner and a small steamer. Four Italian destroyers sailed to intercept but did not make contact. On 5 December the Austro-Hungarian cruiser *Novara*, accompanied by four destroyers and three torpedo boats, sank a tug, a small steamer, and six motor schooners and finally, on the return home, the French submarine *Fresnel*. The following night *Helgoland* and six destroyers hit Durazzo and accounted for five small schooners. These raids caused an uproar. The Italians even temporarily suspended traffic to Durazzo because the Marine Nationale had reassigned to escort duty off Salonika the two French destroyers squadrons which were supposed to be supporting the Regia Marina in accordance with the convention Italy signed upon entering the war.

Following this success Admiral Haus sent *Helgoland* and her flotilla of modern destroyers to raid Duzzaro once again. The k.u.k Kriegsmarine force arrived off its target at dawn on 29 December and, although the two Italian destroyers that were the major objective of the raid were not present, sank a steamer and two schooners. However, while manoeuvring to evade fire from a shore battery the destroyer *Lika* struck a mine and sank, while another mine severely damaged her sister, *Triglav*. The raiders turned for home at six knots with *Triglav* under tow. Meanwhile, British, French, and Italian warships were departing base or raising steam.

The Royal Navy light cruiser *Dartmouth* and the Regia Marina scout cruiser *Quarto* sailed from Brindisi at 0700 followed by five French destroyers. Two hours later the Italian light cruiser *Nino Bixio* and the British *Weymouth*

The Austro-Hungarian light cruiser Novara. (Aldo Fraccaroli collection)

left Brindisi escorted by four Italian destroyers. Meanwhile, the armoured cruiser *Kaiser Karl IV* with four torpedo boats sailed south from Cattaro in response to the Austro-Hungarian commander's call for assistance. The French destroyers made first contact, forcing the Austro-Hungarians to abandon the *Triglav*. They sank the doomed cripple rather than maintaining the pursuit, but *Dartmouth* and *Quarto* were still between the Austro-Hungarians and Cattaro. A chase all the way to the Italian coast ensued. The Entente ships hit *Helgoland* and the destroyer *Csepel* several times but not decisively, and with darkness the Austro-Hungarians broke contact and escaped.

The repercussions of this action were significant. Coordination between the Entente navies had been poor, and the enemy's escape was a source of frustration to all. On the Austro-Hungarian side, the loss of two of their six best destroyers was a serious blow.

The Northern Adriatic

In the Northern Adriatic, flotillas of destroyers and torpedo boats fought a different type of war. The goal there was the initiative itself and the Regia Marina's need to contain the enemy's battle fleet of four dreadnoughts, three pre-dreadnoughts, and six coastal battleships in Pola harbour. The concern that k.u.k. battleships could appear off Venice or the minor Adriatic bases remained constant until November 1918, imposing upon the Regia Marina an on-going vigilance manifested by an average of eight destroyers and/or torpedo boats patrolling or laying mines in enemy waters on any given night, while an Austro-Hungarian force of about four small warships was doing the same. On average about thirty modern Italian warships of these types faced half their number on the other side. In this context Italy's seizure on 25 May 1915 of the little harbour of Grado was particularly significant. The town quickly become the Regia Marina's main base in the Gulf of Trieste for torpedo boats and the long-range gun-armed pontoons that were to prove so vital in supporting the army's coastal flank.

Submarines also extracted a toll, as when the German *UB 14* disguised as the Austro-Hungarian *U 26* (Germany

Austro-Hungarian torpedo boat TB 83F. These 250-tonne warships were the workhorses of the Habsburg fleet. (Aldo Fraccaroli collection)

was not at war with Italy until August 1916) sank the modern Italian armoured cruiser *Amalfi* on 7 July 1915. The four powerful and relatively fast ships of the *Pisa* and *San Giorgio* classes had been dispatched to Venice a few days before to support the torpedo flotillas. The move proved unsound, and in April 1916 the three survivors returned to Brindisi, confirming that the surface campaign in the Northern Adriatic was an affair for expendable units only. The two adversaries used their destroyers and torpedo boats for patrols, bombardments, minelaying, and as navigational aids for bombers and airships. The Italians also planned harbour-forcing missions while the Austro-Hungarians preferred hit-and-run bombardments of Italian coastal towns, although they left Venice alone as they considered its integrated defence system of shore batteries, minefields, and constantly patrolling torpedo boats and submarines too difficult a proposition for a direct assault.

More difficult to understand was the k.u.k. Kriegsmarine's lack of support of its frontline troops. The Italian Northern Adriatic command maintained a flank force based in Venice for this specific purpose. This collection of old warships was formed around the small pre-dreadnoughts *Saint Bon* and *Emanuele Filiberto* supporting the even older pre-dreadnought *Sardegna*, the ancient armoured cruisers *Carlo Alberto* and *Marco Polo* and the protected cruiser *Etruria*. Before the opening of hostilities Admiral Giovanni Patris, commander of this 'Rust Squadron', 'seeing that his warships were too big to operate effectively in the lagoons of Marano and Grado and at the mouths of the Timavo and Tagliamento rivers, decided to outfit pontoons and barges with old guns from decommissioned warships.

On 11 June the first convoy entered action off Grado; it comprised three pontoons, each armed with two 6in guns, towed by tugs and supported by a dozen small steamers, motor boats and barges. They could make only three knots, but their fire proved effective in supporting the taking of hills around the town. The bombardment continued during the following days, unchallenged by the Austro-Hungarian navy. Shore batteries replied but with little success against the pontoons, which were camouflaged and changed moorings every night. The Italian Army, with few big guns, appreciated their support and constantly requested more. On 24 October 1915, for

example, Italian navy pontoons fired 250 shells, recording 110 rounds in reply from enemy shore batteries. On 28 October the numbers were 113 and 29 respectively; on 4 November 150 and 57. By October 1915 there were 97 naval guns of 3in to 8in calibre between Grado and Monfalcone, a number which grew to more than 150 within a year. Long range, pontoon-mounted guns periodically shelled the Trieste shipyards and this harassment forced the Austro-Hungarians to abandon their most important industrial centre after the loss of Monfalcone on 9 June 1915, relying on Fiume's primitive facilities for new construction and for the fitting out of warships.

Complementing this fire support activity was a swarm of barges and small steamers that ferried munitions to the army, a vital traffic given the region's poor roads. In 1915 they delivered 61,900 tonnes of supplies without loss to enemy action. These deliveries grew to 524,956 tonnes in 1916, 769,500 the next year, and 1,381,900 by 1918. In the spring of 1916 the Austro-Hungarians began a similar traffic, ferrying approximately 10,000 tonnes in 1916 and 1917 and 50,000 tonnes during the last year of the war.

Italian forces also raided aggressively, seizing Austro-Hungarian self-propelled pontoons and small steamships sometimes by *coup de main*; an example was the 15 January 1916 capture of the small steamer *Timavo* taken in the upper Isonzo River under the cloak of fog. Other prizes included nine more small Austro-Hungarian steamers and five large pontoons. The Regia Marina converted all of these vessels into armed pontoons or auxiliary gunboats that gave useful service along the front line. Thus, control of the coastal waters off the Isonzo front paid Rome appreciable dividends, while the k.u.k. Kriegsmarine focused on low-risk coastal bombardments of minimal military value.

War in Albania

The main naval event in Albanian waters was the evacuation of the Serbian Army, which began in November 1915. On 27 January the Austro-Hungarian cruiser *Novara* and two torpedo boats sailed to raid Durazzo. The destroyers collided and returned to base, and a mixed Franco-Italian force intercepted *Novara* short of her destination. After a brief exchange of fire, the light cruiser escaped north. On 6 February there were two engage-

The self-propelled pontoon Padus *armed with a 152mm/40 gun.* (Enrico Cernuschi collection)

ments following an Austro-Hungarian attempt to strike an evacuation convoy which intelligence indicated was at Durazzo. In the first, the Italian destroyer *Bronzetti* and the British light cruiser *Weymouth* chased the Austro-Hungarian destroyer *Wildfang* to Cattaro. They never got within range before *Wildfang* reached the cover of friendly shore batteries. In the second, the British light cruiser *Weymouth* and a French destroyer intercepted *Helgoland* and six torpedo boats on their way south. Action opened at dusk, and range closed to 7,000 yards before the Austro-Hungarians turned north. After dark they unsuccessfully launched torpedoes and then broke contact.

Sailing mainly from Durazzo, 45 Italian steamers made 202 voyages supplemented by 25 French (101 voyages) and 11 British (19 voyages) ships. The Italian vessels ferried 112,268 men and the British and French about 70,000. The three Entente navies shared escort duties with 584 missions conducted by the Regia Marina, 340 by the Marine Nationale and 235 by the Royal Navy. Under the Duke of Abruzzi's command they completed the evacuation of the Serbians, their Austro-Hungarian prisoners, and many civilians by 9 February. After April six reformed Serbian infantry divisions arrived on the Salonika front, providing an important reinforcement to the Entente army fighting there.

The Southern Albanian campaign had one aftermath. Durazzo had been garrisoned by an Italian brigade. With the Austro-Hungarian XIX Corps advancing, this brigade was forced to evacuate on 26 February. It lost about 850 men to Habsburg artillery, but the k.u.k. Kriegsmarine's surface vessels did not interfere. The Regia Marina, on the other hand, conducted five bombardments of Austro-Hungarian troops around Durazzo in the week leading up to the evacuation, By November 1916 the Italians had regrouped around a new fortified line protecting Valona, and with each side fielding an army corps the Albanian front remained static until July 1918.

In the Northern Adriatic, skirmishes between Italian and Austro-Hungarian destroyer and torpedo boat flotillas and other small craft occurred on 4 January, 17 January, 3 May, 22 May, 24 May, 11 August, 13 September, and 30 November. These were all inconclusive affairs with little damage inflicted on either side. The smallest involved an Italian MAS boat against an armed motorboat off the Istrian coast on 22 May while the largest, off Port Corsini on 3 May, saw two Italian flotilla leaders and two destroyers chase four Habsburg destroyers and six torpedo

Italian naval officers of the destroyer Insidioso *after a successful 1916 raid in the Lower Adriatic which concluded with the seizure of an Austro-Hungarian flying boat.* (Enrico Cernuschi collection)

boats to the shelter of a minefield, inflicting only splinter damage on one of the destroyers.

Employment of the seven k.u.k. dreadnoughts and pre-dreadnoughts seemed unlikely even without the constant presence of torpedo-armed warships swarming the narrow waters of the northern Adriatic, given the superior Entente battle forces based at Brindisi, Valona, Taranto, and Corfu. The Entente dreadnoughts included five Italian at Taranto (six in 1916) and an average of six French at Corfu. As for pre-dreadnoughts there were six Italian, ten French at Corfu, and four British at Taranto. From this list the pre-dreadnought *Benedetto Brin* and the dreadnought *Leonardo da Vinci* can be subtracted. They were sunk by Austro-Hungarian saboteurs on 27 September 1915 and 2 August 1916 respectively. By January 1916 the Duke of Abruzzi decided the battle line would consist of only his five dreadnoughts and the four *Vittorio Emanueles* because the *Regina Margherita* and the four British battleships were too slow. French collaboration in a fleet action was questionable and no joint exercises and training were conducted until December 1916. The Entente margin of superiority over the Austro-Hungarian line of battle was thus constant, but narrower than suggested by a mere inventory of hulls.

During that same period Regia Marina warships conducted nine shore bombardments and three harbour forcing missions. Italian fast pre-dreadnoughts of the *Vittorio Emanuele* class often covered the cruisers and

The Austro-Hungarian Flying Boat K 30 seized and ferried to Brindisi in 1916. (Enrico Cernuschi collection)

MAS 6 *and* 9. (Aldo Fraccaroli collection)

TABLE 2: NAVAL SURFACE ACTIONS, BOMBARDMENTS AND RAIDS: 1914-1916

Year	Date	Nation	Zone	Units	Type/Mission	Comments
1914	8 Aug	AH	S	PC *Zenta, Szigetvár*; DD *Uskoke*; TB *Tb 72*	SB	vs Antivari.
1914	13 Aug	AH	S	BBOs *Radetzky, Monarch*; BBC *Wien, Budapest*; AC *Kaiser Karl VI*; PC *Kaiser Franz Joseph I, Szigetvár*, TC *Panther*; DDs & TBs	SB-D	vs Mt. Lovcen from Cattaro Bay. Various ships. Also 9, 12, 14, 28 Aug.; 6, 8, 9, 11, 16-19, 21, 24 Sep.; 5, 22-26, 30 and 31 Oct. and 28 Nov. 7 Jan, 18 May 1915.
1914	16 Aug	FR/AH	S	FR BB *Courbet, Paris*; BBO *Diderot, Danton, Vergniaud, Voltaire, Condorcet, Vérité, République, Patrie, Justice, Démocratie*; PC *Jurien de la Gravière*; DD FLOTx2; BR AC *Defence, Warrior*; DDx4. AH CL *Zenta*, DD *Ulan*	SE-D	off Antivari. *Zenta*+. *Condorcet* (turret explosion), *Justice* (turret explosion), *Démocratie* and *Justice* (collison).
1914	1 Sep	FR	S	BB *Courbet, Jean Bart*; 9xBBO; 17x DD	SB	vs Cattaro.
1914	2 Sep	AH	S	DD *Scharfschütze, Ulan*; TB *Tb 64, 66*	SB-D	vs Montenegro Coast.
1914	16 Sep	AH	S	TB *Tb 68, 72*	R-L	Medua.
1914	17 Sep	FR	S	AC *Ernest Renan*	R-L	Pelagosa.
1914	17 Sep	AH	S	BBO *Monarch*; TBx4	SB	vs Antivari.
1914	19 Sep	FR	S	BBO *Démcratie, Patrie*; AC *Léon Gambetta, Jules Ferry, Victor Hugo*	SB-D	vs Cattaro.
1914	19 Sep	FR	S	DDx6	SB-D	vs Stoncica lighthouse, Lissa Is.
1915	14 Feb	AH	S	DD *Csikos*; TB *Tb 15, 68*	SB-D	vs Dulcigno and Antivari.
1915	2 Mar	AH	S	DDs *Csikos, Streiter, Ulan*; TBs *Tb 66, 67*	R-L	Antivari. Royal yacht *Rumija*+.
1915	5 Mar	AH	S	TB *Tb 57*	SB-D	vs Antivari.
1915	24 May	AH	N	BB *Tegetthoff, Viribus Unitis, Prinz Eugen*; BBO *Habsburg, Arpád, Babenberg, Erzherzog Karl, Erzherzog Ferdinand Max, Erzherzog Friedrich*; DD *Dinara, Reka, Csikós, Velebit*; TB *Tb 50 E, 51 T, 53 T, 54 T, 55 T, 57 T, 58 T, 60 T, 62 T, 63 T, 64 F, 67 F, 69 F, 70 F, 72 F, 74 T, 75 T, 76 T, 77 T*	SB-D	vs Ancona. GE MV *Lemnos*+ (3,129 GRT) GK MV *Barbara*, IT MV *Città di Tripoli*, *Concettina*; tug *Filippo*.
1915	24 May	AH	N	BBO *Radetzky*; TB *Tb 56 T, 73 F*	SB-D	vs Potenza Picena, Termoli and Campomarino.
1915	24 May	AH	N	AC *Sankt Georg*; TB *Tb 1, 2*	SB-D	vs Rimini and Pesaro.
1915	24 May	AH	N	CLS *Novara*; DD *Scharfschütze*; TB *Tb 78 T, 78 T, 80 T, 81 T*	SB-D	vs Porto Corsini. SBat returns fire. *Novara*(1), *Scharfschütze*(1), *Tb 80 T*(1).
1915	24 May	IT	N	DD *Bersagliere, Corazziere*	SB-N	vs Grado.
1915	24 May	IT	N	DD *Zeffiro*	SB-N, R-L	vs Porto Buso.
1915	24 May	IT	S	PC *Libia*, AuxC *Città di Siracusa*	L-Rcn	vs Pelagosa.
1915	24 May	AH	S	CLS *Admiral Spaun*; DD *Wildfang, Streiter, Uskoke*	SB-D	vs Manfredonia, Vieste and Barletta RR stations and lighthouses.
1915	24 May	AH	S	CLS *Helgoland*; DD *Csepel, Tátra, Lika, Orjen*	SB-D	vs Barletta &Tremiti Is.
1915	24 May	AH/IT	S	AH force above. IT DD *Turbine*	SE-D	*Turbine*+ *Csepel*(1), *Tátra*(1).
1915	24 May	IT/AH	S	PC *Libia*; AuxC *Città di Siracusa*. AH force above	SE-D	Brief long-range action. *Helgoland*(splinters).
1915	29 May	IT	N	DD *Bersagliere, Lanciere, Artigliere, Garibaldino*	SB-D	vs Monfalcone yard.
1915	1 Jun	IT/BR/FR	S	IT AC *Pisa, Amalfi, San Giorgio, San Marco*; BR CL *Dublin, Dartmouth*; IT CLS *Quarto, Bixio*; DD *Animoso, Ardito, Ardente, Audace, Nullo, Impavido, Indomito, Insidioso, Intrepido, Impetuoso, Granatiere, Irrequieto*; TB *Centauro, Clio*; 3xFR DD	SB-D, L-R	vs Lissa and Curzola signalling and wireless stations.
1915	5 Jun	IT	N	DD *Bersagliere, Lanciere, Corazziere, Artigliere, Garibaldino*	SB-D	vs Monfalcone. Repeated 7 June.
1915	5 Jun	IT/BR/FR/AH	S	IT AC: *Garibaldi, Varese, Ferruccio, Pisani*; BR CL *Dublin*; IT CLS *Quarto, Bixio*; IT DD *Animoso, Ardito, Ardente, Audace, Nullo, Irrequieto, Impavido, Indomito, Insidioso, Intrepido, Impetuoso*; FR DD *Cdt. Rivière, Bisson, Bouclier, Cdt Bory, Protet, Magon*	SB-D, L-R	vs Ragusa, Vecchia, Capo Rodoni, Lissa, Lagosta, Meleda, Busi, Maligrado, Oste, Glavat, Cazza, and Sant'Andrea islands.

Year	Date	Nation	Zone	Units	Type/Mission	Comments
1915	9 Jun	IT/BR	S	IT AC *Ferruccio, Varese*; CLS *Bixio*; DD *Nullo*. Covering force: AC *Garibaldi, Pisani*; BR CL *Dublin*; IT CLS *Quarto*; DD *Impavido, Indomito, Insidioso, Impetuoso, Intrepido, Irrequieto, Animoso, Ardito, Ardente, Audace*	SB-D, L-R	vs Medua, Punta Semana and Capo Rodoni. AH MSch3+ CL *Dublin* (TT) by *U 4*.
1915	10 Jun	IT	N	Aux MS *Timavo*	SB-D	vs Duino. *Timavo*(1) by PBat.
1915	18 Jun	AH	N	CLS *Novara, Admiral Spaun*; DD *Scharfschütze*	SB-D	vs Tagliamento, R lighthouse.
1915	18 Jun	AH	N	AC *Sankt Georg*; TB *Tb 57, 58, 63, 67*	SB-D	vs bridge near Rimini.
1915	18 Jun	AH	N	DD *Szigetvár*; TB *Tb 64, 69*. Covering force: CLS *Saïda, Helgoland*; 3xDD; 5xTB	SB-D, SE-D	vs Colonnelle. IT MV *Grazia*+ (1,373 t), 2xMSch+ off Rimini in SE after SB.
1915	11 Jul	IT/FR	S	IT AC *Garibaldi, Varese*; CLS *Quarto, Marsala*; DD *Animoso, Ardito, Ardente, Audace, Strale*; AuxC *Città di Palermo*; TB *Clio, Cassiopea, Airone, Astore, Arpia, 34, 35. 36, 37 PN*; FR DD *Bisson, Bouclier, Cdt Rivière, Magon*	SB-D, L-R	Pelagosa-L; Curzola, SB. L-Rcn. Lagosta. Italians occupy Pelagosa.
1915	13 Jul	AH	S	DD *Tátra*	SB-D	vs Pelagosa.
1915	18 Jul	IT	S	AC *Garibaldi, Varese, Ferruccio, Pisani*; CLS *Quarto, Marsala*; DD *Intrepido, Irrequieto, Animoso, Ardito, Ardente, Strale*; TB *Alcione, Airone, Astore, Arpia, Cigno, Clio, Calliope, Centauro*; FR DD *Bisson, Bouclier, Cdt Rivière, Cdt Bory, Protet*	SB-D, L	vs Ragusa, Gravosa and Giuppana Is. *Garibaldi*+ by *U 4*.
1915	23 Jul	AH	N	CLS *Saïda, Helgoland*; DD *Velebit, Reka, Dinara, Csepel, Tátra, Balaton*; TB *T 74 T, 78 T*	SB-D, L	vs San Benedetto del Tronto, Ortona and Termoli. *Dinara* (bullets) An AH landing party cut the telegraphic underwater cable on Tremiti.
1915	28 Jul	AH	N	CLS *Admiral Spaun*; DD *Uskoke*	SB-D	vs Fano RR works.
1915	28 Jul	AH	N	CLS *Novara*; DD *Scharfschüze*	SB-D	vs Ancona.
1915	28 Jul	AH	S	CLS *Saïda, Helgoland*; DD *Lika, Tátra, Triglav, Balaton Csepel, Orjen*	L	Pelagosa. Landing repulsed. *Helgoland*(6).
1915	17 Aug	AH	S	CLS *Saïda, Helgoland*; DDs *Lika, Orjen, Velebit, Dinara*	SB-D	vs Pelagosa.
1915	3 Nov	IT/AH	N	IT TB *13, 15 OS*. AH Aux MSx2; PBatx1	SE-D.	MS flee behind SBat; pontoon+ by IT TBs.
1915	22 Nov	AH/IT	S	CLS *Helgoland, Saïda*; DD *Tátra, Balaton, Csepel, Orjen, Lika, Triglav*	Rd	Otranto barrage. IT MSch *Gallinara*+, MV *Palatino*+.
1915	5 Dec	AH	S	CLS *Novara*; DDx4, 3xTB	Rd	IT MSch *Benedetto Giovanni*+, MV *Thira*+, Albanian MSchx5+, tug+; FR SS *Fresnel*+.
1915	6 Dec	AH	S	CLS *Helgoland*; DD *Tátra, Balaton, Csepel, Orjen, Lika, Triglav*	Rd	vs Durazzo. IT MSch *Carmelitano, Gelsomino*+. Albanian 3xMsch+.
1915	7 Dec	IT	N	TB *2, 3, 6 PN, 30 AS*	SB-D	vs Sistiana. Isonzo Armee High Commd.
1915	29 Dec	AH/IT/ BR/FR	S	AH CLS *Helgoland*; DD *Tátra, Balaton, Csepel, Lika, Triglav*. IT CLS *Quarto, Bixio*; DD *Abba, Nievo, Mosto, Pilo*; BR CL *Weymouth, Dartmouth*; FR DD *Casque, Bisson, Renaudin, Cdt Bory, Cdt Lucas* R.	SE-D	vs Durazzo. IT MV *Palatino*+ *Unione*+ *Triglav*+ *Lika*+ Chase after raid. *Helgoland*(5), *Csepel*(1), *Balaton* (splinters); *Bixio*(1). *Pilo*(splinters).
1916	4 Jan	IT/AH	N	IT TB *14, 15, 18 OS*. AH Aux MS	SE-D.	G of Trieste. MS flee to cover of SBat
1916	7 Jan	AH	S	AC *Kaiser Karl VI*; PC *Kaiser Franz Joseph I, Aspern*; TC *Panther*	SB-D	vs Mt. Lovcen. Also on 8, 9, 10 Jan. Various ships.
1916	17 Jan	IT/AH	N	IT TB *19, 22, 23 OS*. AH Aux MS	SE-D	Gulf of Trieste. MS flee to the cover of SBat.
1916	27 Jan	AH/IT/F	S	AH CLS *Novara*; 2xDD. IT PC *Puglia*; FR DD *Bouclier*	SE-D	Raid on Durazzo. AH DD collided and dropped out before action. AH CLS intercepted short of Durazzo, brief exchange of fire.
1916	3 Feb	AH	S	AC *Sankt George*; CLS *Helgoland*; DD *Wildfang*; TB *83F, 87F, 88F*	SB-D	vs Ortona and San Vito Chetino.
1916	6 Feb	IT/BR/ AH	S	BR CL *Liverpool*; IT DD *Bronzetti*. AH DD *Wildfang*	SE-D	Inconclusive chase Durazzo to Cattaro.

Year	Date	Nation	Zone	Units	Type/Mission	Comments
1916	6 Feb	BR/F/ AH	S	BR CL *Weymouth*; FR DD *Bouclier*. CLS *Helgoland*; TB *Tb 74, 78, 80, 83, 87, 88*.	SE-DN	Interception north of Durazzo. ***Tb 83*** and ***74*** collided.
1916	19 Feb	IT	S	DD *Bronzetti, Schiaffino*	SB-D	vs AH troops encircling Durazzo to cover evacuation.
1916	23 Feb	IT/BR/FR	S	IT flank force: PC *Libia, Puglia*; TC *Agordat*; AuxCx3; 7xDD. Cover force: BBO *Regina Elena, Napoli*; CLS *Marsala*; BR CL *Weymouth, Liverpool*; IT & FR DD flotillas	SB-D	vs AH troops encircling Durazzo to cover evacuation. Repeated 24, 25, 26 Feb. AuxC ***Città di Siracusa***(1) by FBat on 25th.
1916	14 Mar	FR/AH	S	FR DD *Faulx* and *Cdt. Renaudi*. AH MS *3* and *4n*	SE-D	Off Durazzo. Brief chase to cover of SBat.
1916	15 Mar	IT/AH	S	IT DD *Animoso, Insidioso*. AH DD *Orjen*	SE-D	Brief chase in Drin Gulf to cover of SBat. AH 1xMV.
1916	18 Mar	IT/AH	S	IT DD *Insidioso*. AH MV	SE-D	Brief chase to SBat in Durazzo Gulf.
1916	3 May	IT/AH	N	IT DDL *Rossarol, Pepe*; DD *Missori, Nullo*. AH DD *Velebit, Scharfschütze, Pandur, Csikós*; TB *Tb 76 T, Tb 92 F, Tb 93 F, Tb 98 M, Tb 99 M, Tb 100 M*	SE-D	off Porto Corsini. AH retreat behind minefield. ***Csikos*** (splinters).
1916	9 May	IT	S	DD *Corazziere, Aquilone*	SB-D	vs Semeni R mouth (Albania).
1916	22 May	IT	N	TB *15 OS*	SB-N	vs Punta Salvore.
1916	22 May	IT/AH	N	IT *MAS 19*. AH armed Motor Boat *Leni*	SE-D	Gulf of Trieste. ***Leni***.
1916	24 May	IT/AH	N	IT TB *21, 22 OS*. AH DD *Velebit, Scharfschütze, Dinara, Reka*; TB *Tb 89 F, Tb 92 F, Tb 98 M, Tb 99 M, Tb 100 M, Tb 75 T*	SE-N	off Chioggia. Brief action, ***Tb 75T***(1), ***21 OS***(1).
1916	24 May	AH	N	BBO *Zrínyi*; TB *Tb 4, 7*	SB-D	vs Senigallia and Porto Recanati.
1916	28 May	IT	N	TB *24 OS*	HF	Penetrates Trieste launching two torpedoes against the steamer *Iskra*. ***24 OS*** (splinters).
1916	31 May	AH	S	DD *Orjen, Balaton*; TB *77T, 79T, 81T*	R-D	Otranto barrage. BR drifter+ *Beneficient*+ Target was troop convoy.
1916	6 Jun	IT	S	MAS *5, 7*	HF	Penetrates Durazzo, MV *Lokrum*+ (924 GRT).
1916	12 Jun	IT	N	DD *Fuciliere, Alpino, Zeffiro*; TB *40 PN, 46 OS*	SB-N. L	vs Parenzo. ***Zeffiro*** (splinters)
1916	15 Jun	IT	S	MAS *5, 7*	HF	Medua.
1916	16 Jun	IT/AH	S	IT DD *Pilo, Bronzetti, Mosto, Audace*. AH DD *Wildfang*	SE-N	Brief action off Medua. ***Wildfang***(1).
1916	23 Jun	AH	N	DD *Uskoke, Streiter*	SB-D	vs Giulianova.
1916	25 Jun	IT	N	TB *19, 20, 21 OS*	HF-SB	Pirano Bay. Unsuccessful.
1916	25 Jun	IT	S	MAS *5, 7*	HF	Durazzo; MV *Sarajevo*+ (1,100 GRT). ***MAS 5, 7*** (both bullets).
1916	27 Jun	IT	N	TB *1, 3, 6 PN*	SB-D	vs Trieste. ***1 PN*** (splinters).
1916	9 Jul	IT/AH	S	IT DD *Impetuoso, Irrequieto*. AH CLS *Novara*	SE-D	Brief inconclusive chase.
1916	9 Jul	IT/AH	S	IT DD *Bronzetti*. AH MSch	SE-D	MV sunk off Capo Laghi, near Cattaro.
1916	9 Jul	AH	S	CLS *Novara*; TB *73F, 54T, 87 F*	R, SE-N	Otranto barrage. BR drifters *Astrum Spei*+, *Clavis*+ ***Frigate Bird, Ben Bui***.
1916	11 Jul	IT	N	DD *Alpino, Fuciliere, Carabiniere, Zeffiro*. Cover force: DDL *Pepe, Poerio*; DD *Missori, Nullo*; TB *1, 3, 4, 6, 8, 10, 11, 12 PN*. TB *19, 20, 21, 22, 24 OS*	SB-N	vs Parenzo ***Zeffiro*** (splinters). TBs lay minefield.

An Italian Navy-armed train in 1916. (Enrico Cernuschi collection)

destroyers of the inshore squadrons. The Austro-Hungarians, in the meantime, conducted shore bombardments against towns in the northern sector on 3 February, 23 June, and 5 November. The damage was generally insignificant, and during the first attack the Italian navy-armed train *N. 2* with its four 4.7in guns arrived within minutes, validating in this first test the mobile defence system conceived by Thaon di Revel the year before. It was a good dividend, at least on the propaganda front, giving the coastal inhabitants the feeling they were not defenceless. In the 5 November attack, when three torpedo boats shelled the railway station of Sant'Elpidio a

Year	Date	Nation	Zone	Units	Type/Mission	Comments
1916	2 Aug	IT	S	MAS 6	HF	Durazzo, no results.
1916	2 Aug	AH	S	DD *Wildfang, Warasdier*	SB-D	vs Molfetta.
1916	2 Aug	FR/IT/ BR/AH	S	AH DD *Wildfang, Warasdiner*. Reinforcements: AC *Aspern*, TB 80 T, 85 F. FR DD *Cdt. Bory, Bisson*; IT DD *Ardito, Ardente, Impavido, Abba*; CLS *Bixio*; BR CL *Liverpool*	SE-D	The units escorting *MAS 6* engaged the AH DDs returning from SB of Molfetta. The *Aspern* force comes up in support ending the action. Entente cruisers never close range. *Wildfand* (1), *Warasdiner* (splinters).
1916	5 Aug	IT	N	TBs *24, 46 OS, 40 PN*; Aux MS *Timavo*	SB-D	vs AH front lines.
1916	10 Aug	IT	N	*40, 41 PN, 46, 58 OS*; MASx2; Aux MS *Timavo*	SB-D	vs AH front lines.
1916	11 Aug	IT/AH	N	IT TB *1, 3, 4 PN, 24 OS*. AH TB *Tb 91 F, 94 F, 98 M*	SE-N	Off Pola. Italian TBs chase. *3 PN*(splinters).
1916	13 Sep	IT	N	IT TB *40, 41, 42 PN, 46 OS*	SB-N	vs Punta Grossa.
1916	13 Sep	IT/AH	N	IT TB *1 PN*. AH 2xTB; 3xMV	SE-D	Off Porto Quieto. The AH convoy reached cover of SBat.
1916	16 Sep	IT	N	2xTB FLOT	SB-D	vs Punta Salvore.
1916	8 Oct	IT/AH	S	IT DD *Bronzetti*. AH *Tb 68*	SE-N	Off Medua. Brief chase to cover of SBat.
1916	2 Nov	IT	N	TB *PN 9*; *MAS 20*	HF	Fasana Channel. BBOC *Mars*(two duds).
1916	3 Nov	IT	S	MAS 5, 7	HF	Durazzo. No results.
1916	4 Nov	IT/AH	S	DD *Abba, Nievo, Pilo*; TB *34, 35, 36 PN*. AH TB *83 F, 87 F, 88 F*; DDx2	SE-N	Brief encounter.
1916	5 Nov	AH	N	TBs *Tb 83 F, 87 F, 88 F*	SB-D	vs Sant'Elpidio a Mare.
1916	30 Nov	IT/AH	N	IT TBx?. AH Aux MSx?	SE-D	Gulf of Trieste. MS flee to cover of SBat.
1916	22 Dec	AH/FR/ IT/BR	S	AH DD *Scharfschütze, Reka, Dinara, Velebit*. FR DD *Casque, Protet, Cdt Rivière, Cdt Bory, Dehorter, Boutefeu*; IT DD: *Abba, Nievo, Pilo, Impavido, Irrequieto*; BR CL *Gloucester*	SW, SE-N	Otranto barrage. *Cdt Rivière*(5), *Casque*(1), *Scharfschütze*(3), *Reka*(2) *Dinara*(2) in night engagement. *Abba, Boutefeu* and *Casque* collided. AH forces escaped.

Table Abbreviations

National:

AH	Austria-Hungary
AU	Australia
BR	Great Britain
FR	France
GE	German
GK	Greek
IT	Italy
US	United States

Ship Types:

BB	Dreadnought battleship
BBO	Pre-dreadnought battleship
BBC	Coastal battleship
BM	Monitor

AC	Armoured cruiser
PC	Protected cruiser
C	Cruiser
CL	Light cruiser
CLS	Scout light cruiser
DDL	Large destroyer/flotilla leader
DD	Destroyer
TB	Torpedo boat
MS	Minesweeper
MAS	Motor torpedo boat
SC	Submarine Chaser
SBat	Shore battery
PBat	Pontoon battery
MV	Merchant vessel
MSch	Motor schooner
TC	Torpedo Cruiser

Mission Types:

SB	Shore Bombardment
R	Raid
L	Landing
SW	Sweep
E	Escort
SE	Surface Engagement
Rcn	Recon
P	Patrol
D	Day
N	Night
HF	Harbour Forcing

Ships in **bold italics**: damaged (number of hits in parentheses)

Ships followed by +: sunk

Mare, the intervention of the navy's *Treno Armato Numero 1* ended the bombardment, expending twenty-five 4.7in shells against the attackers.

After its occupation Durazzo became a main Austro-Hungarian supply terminal, and Entente forces immediately began to harass maritime traffic heading there. Italian and French destroyers conducted sweeps on 14 March, 15 March, 16 June, 9 July, 2 August, and 8 October. Most of these actions involved Entente forces chasing lighter Austro-Hungarian units to the cover of shore batteries. In the 2 August action, however, an Entente force consisting of a British light cruiser, an Italian scout cruiser, four Italian and two French destroyers out to support a harbour forcing mission against Durazzo encountered two Austro-Hungarian destroyers returning from a bombardment of Molfetta. In a chasing action the Austro-Hungarian ships were lightly damaged before an armoured cruiser and two torpedo boats sortied from Cattaro in support, causing the Entente squadron to turn away. Although they caused little damage, these skirmishes along with Allied submarine patrols forced the Austro-Hungarians to escort their convoys with torpedo craft. This constant action became an appreciable strain on the k.u.k.'s southern squadron and Cattaro's primitive

The Italian torpedo boat 45 PN at Taranto. In the Italian Navy torpedo boats performed a multitude of missions, serving as escorts, offensive patrol boats, minelayers, minesweepers, and for shore bombardment and special operations. (Enrico Cernuschi collection)

facilities, as the machinery of the destroyers and torpedo boats was not designed for such sustained employment. The valuable flotilla craft thus required more frequent maintenance, and their crews began to grow fatigued.

Harbour Forcing Actions

The practice of forcing enemy harbours was a long-established tradition; it was a tactic the Italians quickly embraced in an effort to expand the ways they could strike the enemy. Even on the first day of the war the destroyer *Zeffiro* penetrated the small anchorage of Porto Buso, sinking a pair of customs boats and landing a party that captured the port's garrison of 48 men. In a more ambitious effort on the night of 28 May 1916, the torpedo boat *24 OS* slipped into Trieste harbour under the cover of bad weather and launched two torpedoes at the steamer *Iskra*. They exploded against a mole, leading the Italians to believe the attack succeeded. The small warship escaped with only a few holes in her side.

On the night of 6/7 June the recently arrived MAS 5 and 7, a new type of fast, miniature warship conceived by Thaon di Revel in 1914 to attack enemy harbours, crept inside the boom protecting Durazzo and sank the Austro-Hungarian steamer *Lokrum*. Despite increased Austro-Hungarian vigilance, Commander Costanzo Ciano led *Zeffiro* and two torpedo boats into Parenzo on 12 June. The raiders seized a squad of customs guards and shelled a newly-completed seaplane station as two other destroyers

bombarded the nearby island of San Nicolò. Shore batteries near-missed *Zeffiro* causing splinter damage to the destroyer.

In the meantime, MAS boats harassed enemy harbours on the nights of 15/16 June, 25/26 June, and 2 August. During the second June incursion, MAS 5 and 7 sank the steamer *Sarajevo* at Durazzo. Also, during the night of 24/25 June the torpedo boats *19*, *20*, and *21 OS* tried to capture the small steamer *Narenzio* from inside the northern Adriatic port of Pirano. Discovered at the last moment, they cut the tow cables and escaped undamaged, despite the reaction of a battery and some Austro-Hungarian auxiliary minesweepers that tried to engage.

These pinpricks caused little damage but created dissension among Habsburg commands, with the army complaining about poorly-defined responsibilities for coastal defence and the absence of the Imperial Navy along the front line where the Regia Marina was increasingly active. There the self-propelled and towed pontoons continued to support Italian army efforts with their artillery. Important actions occurred on 14-16 May (1,600 shells fired); 28-29 May (380 shells); 14-17 June (830 shells); and 28-29 June (1,218 shells). The last bombardment helped repulse an Austro-Hungarian offensive against Monfalcone.

The Austro-Hungarian Navy was impressed by the MAS boats and began to credit them with unrealistic characteristics. The Regia Marina also appreciated their potential and ordered them in great numbers. However, only the best crews – at best two dozen – could perform anti-shipping missions, while the remainder of that mosquito armada was used, for lack of anything better, as antisubmarine craft along the Italian coast now threatened by German submarines.

Small numbers of German U-boats achieved great results in the Mediterranean, and Cattaro became an important base for them, especially after Italy declared war on Germany on 28 August 1916. The Mediterranean submarine campaign outside the Adriatic is beyond the remit of the present article; however, the containment of the Central Power submarines operating out of Cattaro became an important mission of the Entente navies; likewise, the k.u.k Kriegsmarine was tasked with facilitating their passage into the wider Mediterranean. A primary consequence of this containment effort was the expansion

Italian torpedo boats at Gardo. (Rivista Marittima)

British drifters at Taranto, 1916. (Enrico Cernuschi collection)

The Italian battleship Leonardo da Vinci, *Taranto 1916.*
(Enrico Cernuschi collection)

A pontoon of the Ranocchio *type armed with a 4-inch gun. All the pontoons were unique and were modified and fitted out in the Venice Naval Dockyard.* (Enrico Cernuschi collection)

The Austro-Hungarian destroyer Balaton *at Cattaro on 14 March 1916.* (Aldo Fraccaroli collection)

of the Otranto barrage, leading to frequent Austro-Hungarian raids against it. In fact the main activity of the Austro-Hungarian surface forces from Cattaro between April and December 1916 was against the drifters patrolling the Strait of Otranto and the traffic between Italy and Albania. Of eleven raids conducted, those of 31 May, 9 July and 22 December resulted in surface actions. In the first two the raiding forces sank three drifters and damaged two. In the last a British light cruiser leading five Italian and six French destroyers intercepted four Austro-Hungarian destroyers. In a wild night engagement three French, one Italian and three Habsburg destroyers were damaged. The action confirmed the on-going tensions and lack of coordination between the Entente navies.

The Regia Marina attempted a more elaborate harbour forcing action, which was three months in preparation, on the night of 1/2 November against the Fasana Channel where the Austro-Hungarian battleships trained. Supported by an escort force off the channel entrance, the torpedo boat *PN 9* (Commander Domenico Cavagnari, a future Italian naval chief of staff) depressed the booms using a pair of large anchors. This allowed *MAS 20* to slip in. In the darkness the motor boat, sailing slowly using a silent electrical engine, searched for a target. She finally launched against the old ironclad guard ship *Mars*. The two weapons hit, but did not explode and caused only limited flooding.

On the night of 3/4 November *MAS 6* and *7* forced Durazzo once again. No results were obtained for lack of targets. A brief and inconclusive surface action followed between the Italian escort force of three destroyers and three torpedo boats and a k.u.k. Kriegsmarine flotilla of two destroyers and three torpedo boats.

The conduct of the Adriatic naval war in 1916 confirmed the strategic limitations of the Austro-Hungarian harassment campaign. With the k.u.k. Kriegsmarine battle fleet port-bound in the upper Adriatic and the sea lanes to Albania contested only by sea denial actions, submarine warfare (conducted mainly by a few dozen German boats) was the only way for the Central Powers to accomplish any significant naval activity in the Mediterranean. This elevated the support of the submarine campaign to a strategic imperative for the Austro-Hungarian navy. Nonetheless, the Italian home front was still quiet and well-nourished by Christmas while, from the harsh winter of 1915/1916, time was working against Vienna. At this point, the respective losses inflicted in the naval war to date were very much in Austria-Hungary's favour. In the Adriatic the k.u.k. Kriegsmarine had lost only the old cruiser *Zenta*, two destroyers, and four submarines. On the Entente side the count was one dreadnought, two pre-dreadnoughts, three armoured cruisers, three auxiliary cruisers, five destroyers, two torpedo boats, and eleven submarines.

Editor's Note: Part 2 of this article, dealing with the years 1917 and 1918, will be published in *Warship 2016.*

WARSHIP NOTES

This section comprises a number of short articles and notes, generally highlighting little known aspects of warship history.

FAIRFIELD'S CANCELLED CAPITAL SHIPS

A visit to the Govan shipyard of BAE Systems prompted **Ian Johnston** to investigate the capital ship orders placed with the former Fairfield Shipbuilding & Engineering Co. Ltd.

BAE Systems' Govan shipyard has a key role in building Britain's new aircraft carriers, being responsible for the construction of two of the largest hull blocks for *Queen Elizabeth*, LB03 and LB04, and blocks LB03, LB04, LB05 as well as both superstructure islands for her sister *Prince of Wales*. These carriers will be the largest warships ever constructed for the Royal Navy. However, the Govan yard has a long association with other famous capital ships of a bygone era, including some which were ordered but never built. In the latter category was a carrier dating from 1944 which was close in dimensions to the *Queen Elizabeth* class.

The list of capital ships that did make it into the water begins with the *King Edward VII*-class battleship *Commonwealth* launched in 1903. She was followed by six others: *Indomitable* (1906), *New Zealand* (1909). *Valiant* (1914), *Renown* (1916), *Howe* (1940) and *Implacable* (1942). The subject of this article is the four remaining ships, which for a time were real enough, but which were cancelled for reasons that underline the vagaries of naval procurement. Between 1888 and 1965, the Govan yard was known famously as the Fairfield Shipbuilding & Engineering Co. Ltd. The Director's Minute Books of this company, long since archived at the Mitchell Library in Glasgow, offer an interesting if cryptic commentary on the fortunes of the yard, and from them it can be seen that Fairfield's

capital ship contracts had a three to two chance of making it into steel.

The first of the cancelled ships was the *Hood*-class battlecruiser *Rodney*, the first reference to which was at a meeting held in the Board Room on 12 May 1916, the minutes stating simply that the Admiralty had placed orders with the company for a battlecruiser, a light cruiser and a torpedo boat destroyer. *Rodney*, one of four *Hood*-class ships, was laid down on No.1 berth at Govan on 9 October 1916. However, the catastrophic loss of three battlecruisers at the Battle of Jutland on 31 May and the consequences for battlecruiser design had by this time ensured a significant reworking of the armour scheme. *Rodney* could not rise much above her double bottom while this redesign was underway, although the erection of engine and boiler room bulkheads gave some indication of the ship she could have been.

By the time the design issues had been resolved, the upper limit of ship-building capacity, fully stretched with new construction and repair work, allowed only one of the *Hood* class to be given the green light: this, of course, was *Hood* herself, under construction at Clydebank. At Fairfield, several thousand tons of *Rodney* was sterilised on the berth in the hope that she would eventually be restarted. And there it would remain while the Admiralty juggled ship-building priorities, never quite finding the manpower resources to restart the three other *Hoods*, although their design continued to evolve. As early as December 1917, the shipyard wrote to the Admiralty in respect of 'the financial loss owing to the occupation of the most important building berth in the yard by HMS *Rodney* upon which vessel under Admiralty instructions no work is being done'. The situation was

largely unchanged during the following year, mainly because of insufficient labour. It was not until February 1919 that the Admiralty finally made the decision to terminate the contract, allowing the building slip to be cleared. This decision was undoubtedly met with relief at the shipyard, which had plenty of merchant keels to lay down.

One point of interest outside the present narrative concerns a warship that flickered briefly as a prospect in the record of the meeting held on 18 May 1917, which states simply that 'the Admiralty have intimated their intention to place an order with the Company for a seaplane carrier'. One month later, at the meeting held on 22 June, this intention came to an abrupt end when the meeting noted that 'the Admiralty have postponed the order for the seaplane carrier'.

The second of Fairfield's 'unbuilt' contracts was for a G3 battlecruiser, one of four contracts placed post-war which provided much hope to a beleaguered British armaments industry now shorn of naval work. The minutes for 27 October 1921 simply note that the Admiralty have placed the 'order for the hull and machinery for a battlecruiser'. The order was actually placed by letter of 24 October.

The vast capital ship construction programmes then underway in the USA and Japan required a response if Britain was to retain her position among the leading navies. The Great War had accelerated warship design to the point where most of the British battlefleet, although of recent construction, was obsolescent, and in the design of the G3s the hard-won lessons learned resulted in formidable warships which were technically far in advance of *Hood*. However, in November, with the Washington Naval Conference on the limitation of naval armaments in prospect, shipbuilders were instructed to suspend work on the G3s pending further notice. The agreement reached among the powers in February 1922 was to result in their cancellation; it was further stipulated that battleship construction be halted for a period of ten years. In response to these momentous events, the directors' meeting held at Fairfield on 22 February 1922 noted that the Admiralty had 'definitely decided not to proceed with the hull and machinery provisionally ordered for a battlecruiser'. Ironically, at the same meeting, the board discussed compensation claims against the Admiralty for 'losses due to cancellation of contracts', primarily *Rodney* of the *Hood* class.

Although Britain was permitted by the Treaty to construct two 16-inch-gun battleships (they became *Nelson* and *Rodney*) to counter the latest American and Japanese construction, the 10-year 'battleship holiday' agreed at Washington forced the contraction of the armaments industry, which had been greatly expanded to meet the threat from Germany. When rearmament began in 1936, there were fewer shipyards capable of battleship construction, fewer armour mills and fewer skilled men. When the intention to build five battleships of the *King George V* class was announced, it

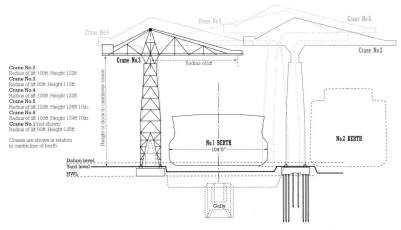

**Position of
ELECTRIC TOWER CRANES
at Berth No.1**

Crane No.2
Radius of lift 100ft. Height 122ft.
Crane No.3
Radius of lift 90ft. Height 113ft.
Crane No.4
Radius of lift 100ft. Height 122ft.
Crane No.5
Radius of lift 120ft. Height 126ft 10in.
Crane No.6
Radius of lift 100ft. Height 134ft 10in.
Crane No.1 (not shown)
Radius of lift 90ft. Height 125ft.

Cranes are shown in relation
to centre line of berth

Although Rodney *was laid down on the slip that had just constructed and launched* Renown, *the* Hood-*class ship was bigger, so this drawing was prepared to show clearances on either side of the hull. Fairfield had also embarked on a major upgrade of berth cranes, replacing simple 3-ton derricks with fixed electric tower cranes capable of lifting 12 tons. This drawing also shows the vertical clearance between crane jibs.*

was an odds-on certainty that Fairfield would pick up one of the five. As early as October of that year the Admiralty advised the yard to prepare for the ship, but it was not until the meeting of 22 June 1937 that the Fairfield Board noted that the Admiralty had accepted the Company's tender for the battleship HMS *Beatty* (later *Howe*).

This was followed sixteen months later, on 12 October 1938, by a note

that the tender for the fleet carrier *Implacable* had been accepted. Across the UK, shipbuilding capacity was once again being pushed to the limit, with predictable results. The more impressively gunned successors to the *King George V* class, the *Lion* class, were announced in 1938 with the first two, *Lion* and *Temeraire*, ordered in February 1939. These were followed by *Conqueror* and *Thunderer* in August of the same year, the latter

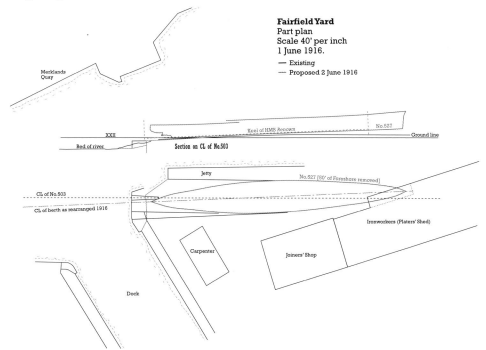

Fairfield Yard
Part plan
Scale 40' per inch
1 June 1916.
— Existing
-- Proposed 2 June 1916

This drawing, prepared at the beginning of June 1916, shows the realignment of No.1 berth to accommodate Rodney. *The drawing shows the line of the berth as it was when* Renown *was built. As* Rodney *was to have been longer, the berth has been realigned to provide a longer launching run without the risk of hitting the opposite side of the river. The hull has also been positioned farther up the berth than that of* Renown, *and this has required the demolition of part of the platers' shed to accommodate the bow of the ship.*

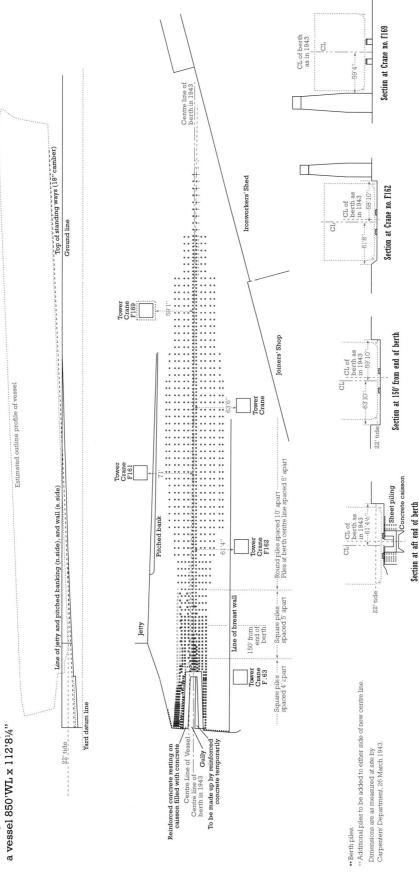

No.1 Berth.
Arrangements for laying down
a vessel 850'WL x 112'8¼"

Section at Crane no. F169

Section at Crane no. F162

Section at 150' from end of berth

Section at aft end of berth

This drawing shows the arrangements for laying down the Malta-class carrier Africa at Fairfield; its purpose is to show the clearances of such a large hull on the fixed structure of the slipway and surrounding tower cranes. The launch of the ship is also the subject of careful consideration, and the realignment of the berth's centre line is recommended to facilitate this. This realignment shows that additional piles would have to be driven into the ground at the bow and stern to ensure that the hull was properly supported during construction at all times. Hull and superstructure sponsons would be left off until after the hull had been launched, as the width between the fixed tower cranes on the berth was limited to 120 feet. The Gully was where the forefoot dipped into the river as the ship finally left dry land during launch; the new centre line required additional concrete work here to ensure symmetry on either side of the forefoot.

Lengthy notes, twelve in total, describe all of the above in detail including how the ship would be taken into the fitting-out basin after launching and, eventually, how the vessel would be turned in the river when making her journey to the sea. It is clear from this drawing, which is undated (although likely to be mid to late 1943, possibly early 1944), that Fairfield has been provided with provisional dimensions only, and that detailed information on the final form of the vessel is awaited. The notes state that overall there is no obstacle to accommodating this ship on No.1 berth – it was incumbent on all shipbuilders to demonstrate to the Admiralty that the arrangements for supporting and protecting the ship at all stages of construction were adequate. (All drawings by Stephen Dent, based on originals at BAE Systems Govan Shipyard)

being allocated to Fairfield as noted in the minutes of 12 September. The outbreak of war in Europe one month later forced a re-evaluation of ship-building priorities against the realities of manpower, armour capacity and main armament production, particularly as the KGV class was in full production alongside other urgently-required warships. In October 1939 all four *Lions* were suspended for one year with completion of the first two, *Lion* and *Temeraire*, pushed back to March and September 1944, rather than early 1943 as initially intended. It was expected that *Conqueror* and *Thunderer* would not be laid down until January and April 1941 respectively. As with the *Hood* class 25 years earlier, suspension did not stop the design process, which was now energised with much real data from operational experience with the KGVs. However, the first two *Lions* were never restarted, the other two never laid down, and all four were cancelled in 1944.

Fairfield's final 'unbuilt' capital ship was the fleet carrier *Africa*, fourth ship of the *Audacious* class, two of which later became *Ark Royal* and *Eagle*. The Fairfield Board meeting of 11 August 1943 announced the order for this ship as a 'fleet aircraft carrier' without mentioning a name or class, simply referring to it as Ship No.722. What happened next is at present unclear. Some published sources state that *Africa* became the fourth unit of the very large *Malta* class fleet carriers while others state that only three *Maltas* were ordered (ie not including *Africa*). The only other reference to *Africa* in the Fairfield minute book, with brevity uppermost in the mind of the secretary, notes on 13 November 1945 that 'the light fleet carrier *Monmouth* and the fleet carrier *Africa* have been cancelled'. However, based on evidence shown in the caption opposite, there is every reason to believe that Fairfield's *Africa* was indeed a carrier of the *Malta* class.

Thereafter Fairfield would build relatively few warships in line with the rapidly shrinking post-war Royal Navy. Probably the best known was the cruiser *Blake*, completed to a revised design in 1961. Fairfield's last warship was the 'County'-class guided missile destroyer *Antrim* completed in 1970. Thirty years would elapse

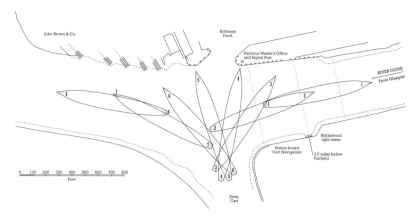

Because the Clyde is a relatively narrow river, very large vessels like the G3 couldn't be turned at the shipyard. The first available space where this could be done was at the confluence of the Clyde and Cart opposite John Brown's shipyard. The drawing shows this procedure, which would be managed with great care, a minimum of six tugs being required. Soundings of the river were taken about every 400 feet; these are shown on the original drawing but for reasons of clarity are represented here as dotted lines. The channel was 26ft deep at low water and 37ft at high water.

before the hull for the amphibious assault ship *Ocean* was contracted during the Kvaerner years. Since the demise of the Fairfield Shipbuilding & Engineering Co. Ltd. in 1965, the turbulent history of British ship-building has witnessed a depressing slide into statistical irrelevance with the closure of one yard after another. At Govan, six different management teams have taken control since 1965, culminating in BAE Systems in 2000 and the full-time resumption of warship construction.

This article was prompted by a visit to the Govan yard by the author to see if any old yard plans existed for use in *The Battleship Builders* (Seaforth 2013, co-authored with Ian Buxton). Since the Fairfield era, successive new managements had put their stamp on the company, sweeping away traces of past incumbents, resulting in old company records being deposited with the City of Glasgow Archives. It appears, however, that some things couldn't simply be thrown away. A number of old, folded technical drawings relating to shipyard facilities and infrastructure had been preserved by Tommy Vaughan, Plant Maintenance Manager at the Govan yard. Stored in brown cardboard boxes, they remained alongside current computer-generated drawings neatly stored on Dexion shelving, as if still in front-line service.

Some of the drawings dated back to the 1910s including, remarkably, a

proposal for a large shipyard to be built at Dartford, Nova Scotia, in anticipation of warship orders for the then-newly-created Royal Canadian Navy. Other drawings show the impact that large ships would have had on yard facilities, launching clearances, routes to be taken when leaving the yard as well as detailed river soundings all the way from Fairfield down to the open sea. Four of these plans have been specially redrawn to illustrate this Note.

Sources:
Primary documents:
At Glasgow City Archives in the Mitchell Library:
UCS2/1/4 Directors Minute Books for 1908-17.
UCS2/1/5 Directors Minute Books for 1918-33.
UCS2/1/6 Directors Minute Books for 1933-46.
Drawings from the Plant Maintenance Department at BAE Systems Govan yard.

Articles:
Ian Sturton, 'Cancelled Sisters: The Modified *Hood* Class', *Warship* 2010, pp.96-102.

Thanks to:
BAE Systems.
Tommy Vaughan, Plant Maintenance Manger at BAE Systems Govan yard.
Paul Sweeney, Operations Strategy Manager, BAE Systems.

WARSHIP PREFIXES

In a kind of warship parallel to the old 'How should you correctly address a Duke?'[1] question, **Stephen Dent**, with the help of some of the annual's regular contributors, takes a look at the surprisingly knotty question of national prefixes.

In 2013, while working on another project, the Assistant Editor was struck by the frequency with which published secondary sources use erroneous (and in some cases entirely fictitious) prefixes for the names of warships of nations other than the United Kingdom and the United States. While it can be argued that these help to clarify the nationality of vessels, especially when the work in question is aimed at the non-specialist reader, the simple fact is that many of these are wrong, and yet in time they can become accepted as correct, simply through repetition and the resulting familiarity. So here, presented in no particular order, is a collection of what the correct prefixes should be for the ships of various nations' navies, together with notes on how, when and why they came about.

United Kingdom – Royal Navy: HMS – His/Her Majesty's Ship. The origin of this famous group of letters goes back to the late seventeenth century, an era of numerous (if often rather piecemeal) reforms in the British navy (along with the accompanying civilian administration and industrial support infrastructure). It was Charles II, after the restoration of the monarchy, who not only adopted the formal title of the Royal Navy, but also that of His Majesty's Ship. There is a certain degree of irony in this since, unlike some of the ships that had taken on the Spanish Armada, which had actually belonged to Queen Elizabeth I, the ships were now owned by the state, with Charles the titular head of a constitutional monarchy. Given what had passed in the preceding decades (and indeed would take place in the coming few as well), the relationship between Crown, Parliament and people was somewhat uncertain, to say the least, and this form of words helped to

secure one aspect of the situation, firmly re-stating the bond in the case of the navy. Nevertheless, the ships were His Majesty's only inasmuch as he stood at the head of the country, to which they really belonged.

However the abbreviation HMS did not come into use for another century, the earliest example of it as a prefix being for the otherwise unremarkable 5th rate HMS *Phoenix* in 1789, prior to which the custom was to refer to a vessel by the abbreviation 'His Ma[ties] Ship'. During the nineteenth century the abbreviation HBM, standing for His/Her Britannic Majesty's [ship] was also in widespread usage, though only by those from overseas. The phrase '<u>The</u> HMS so-and-so', commonly used today in the mainstream media (and, disappointingly, in some more specialist sources as well) is, of course, completely incorrect.

America – United States Navy: USS – United States Ship. At first American warships were referred to on the basis of individual type, for example 'United States Frigate', in a deliberate effort to take a different approach to that of their recently cast-off colonial masters, the British. The simpler prefix we know today seems to have come into use gradually, around the beginning of the nineteenth century, though it only became widespread during the War of 1812. Although similar to British practice, it was not *too* much so, and was merely a reflection of a greater confidence in the new nation's cultural identity. However even then the older version continued to be used for many years, only finally being discontinued in January 1907 by way of an Executive Order from President Theodore Roosevelt.

The obvious major departure from this basic formula was the use of the slightly anomalous CSS (Confederate States Ship) for vessels in the service of the southern states during 1861-65. Others, more recent, include USNS (United States Naval Ship) for the civilian-manned auxiliary and transport vessels of the Military Sealift Command (before 1970 the Military Sea Transportation Service), while Coast Guard cutters over 65ft in length are prefixed by USCGC.

The addition of a type classification

and number (eg DD116) after the ship's name was introduced in 1921. This was also applied retrospectively to vessels which had been lost, though not entirely consistently.

France – Marine Nationale. The French navy in the modern era, with no royal family to worry about, has not bothered with any kind of prefix. The letters FS, standing for 'French Ship', resulted from Admiralty Memo 1616/11/7/40 in July 1940 and applied to French warships serving under RN operational control. (At the same time the decision was made that they were to fly both the White Ensign and the French ensign.) The subsequent NATO use of this designation has been in use for many years but is strictly unofficial.

Italy – Regia Marina. By some distance the most complex prefix convention of any of those used by the major navies, that employed by Italy would make a Warship Note in its own right (and perhaps will...). Officially, the prefix RN, meaning Regia Nave (Royal Warship), with the word Nave using a capital 'N' instead of a lower case 'n' since it was referring to Italian warships only, was used for battleships and aircraft carriers, known respectively as Nave (pl. Navi) da Battaglia and Nave (pl. Navi) Portaerei. The same prefix was used for some important auxiliary warships too, such as the Royal Yacht *Savoia* and sloops *Eritrea* and *Diana* prior to and during the Second World War. Following on from that, similar type-specific prefixes were used for other vessels, for example RI, meaning Regio Incrociatore (Royal cruiser), for cruisers (with no difference between the various types – heavy, light, protected, colonial etc.), and so on. However RN followed by a type name was used for auxiliary (non-combatant) vessels, eg RN Idrografica for survey ships, and indeed RN on its own was also used for very minor craft such as lighthouse tenders. Having said all that, in reality RN simply followed by the ship's name became the widespread practice.

Since the formation of the post-war republic things slowly changed, first to type-specific prefixes without the 'Royal' and then, since the 1960s, the overall generic 'Nave' for all types.

(In a further variation, while in theory the wording on sailors' hat bands followed the same rules, in reality a certain amount of freedom was allowed, based on the preferences of some commanding officers. Perhaps not surprisingly this practice was discontinued during the Second World War and generic hat bands were introduced instead, though since then the practice has occasionally resurfaced.)

Imperial Germany – Kaiserliche Marine: SMS – Seiner Majestät Schiff (His Majesty's Ship). The first German 'national' fleet, the Reichsflotte or Federal/Imperial Fleet ('Reich', like the Dutch 'Rijk', has no direct equivalent in English), was founded in 1848 but dissolved four years later. Two of its ships joined the Prussian Navy (Preußische Marine), which in 1867 became the Norddeutscher Bundesmarine (North German Confederal Navy), and then in turn the Kaiserliche Marine (Imperial Navy) in 1871. In addition to the above prefix, the following were also used in particular cases:

SMY – Seiner Majestät Yacht (His Majesty's Yacht – the Emperor's yacht)
IMY – Ihrer Majestät Yacht (Her Majesty's Yacht – the Empress's yacht)
SMF – Seiner Majestät Feuerschiff (HM Lightship)
SMH – Seiner Majestät Hilfsschiff (HM Auxiliary Ship)
SMW – Seiner Majestät Werkstattschiff (HM Depot/Support Ship)
SMU – Seiner Majestät Unterseeboot (HM Submarine – ie U-boat)

No official prefix has been applied to the names of German warships since 1918, although since 1956 FGS (Federal German Ship – in English!) has been used for NATO administrative purposes (see also France, above), although not a formal part of the ship's designation in the manner of 'HMS'. In addition to the four different names used during the nineteenth century, there have been no fewer than eleven different titles applied to Germany's various navies (including a number of short-term organisations – in both East and West – in operation during the years imme-

diately after the Second World War) during the twentieth century: a remarkable total of fifteen which reflects the country's numerous changes in form, status and regime. Since 1995 the force has been called simply the Marine, although colloquially known as the Deutsches Marine.

Netherlands – Koninklijke Marine. (Royal Netherlands Navy). Hr Ms, which literally translates as 'Her Majesty's' [ship]. This was in use throughout the twentieth century, during which the Netherlands had as head of state three successive queens: Wilhelmina from 1898 to 1948 (including the Second World War period, when she was in exile), then Juliana until 1980, and then Beatrix until 2013. The prefix HNlMS (His/Her Netherlands Majesty's Ship) is commonly used internationally.

Norway – Kongelig Norsk Marine (Royal Norwegian Navy). The formal prefix, very rarely used, is HMS, for 'Hans Majestets Skip' (His Majesty's Ship[2]), but normally a ship is simply referred to by its name and nothing more. However KNM, meaning 'Den Kongelige Norske Marines Skip' (Ship of the Royal Norwegian Navy) has also been used widely since 1946, though not prior to that. The well-known HNoMS (His Norwegian Majesty's Ship) most likely dates from sometime after April 1940, when Norwegian ships operated with other Allied ships around Britain. While common elsewhere this is never used in Norway.

Japan. Japanese official sources, such as those produced by the Navy Ministry Secretariat or former naval architects, are consistent in giving ships' names only, with no prefix (though occasionally also class/type). The likes of 'HIJMS' sometimes found in secondary sources are therefore entirely fictitious.

Poland – Marynarki Wojennej: ORP – Okret Rzeczypospolitej Polskiej (Ship of the Commonwealth of Poland). The term dates back to the seventeenth and early eighteenth centuries when the 'Commonwealth of Poland & Lithuania' was a major European power with a sizable navy,

before being dismembered under the 1st, 2nd and 3rd partitions (1772, 1793, 1795) between Russia, Prussia and Austria. After the end of the First World War Poland was reborn as a republic, and the historic term for the navy's ships was brought back. This has stayed the same throughout the ensuing upheavals, applying to ships of the inter-war navy, to Free Polish ships during the Second World War, to ships of the navy of the communist period, and on into the post-communist era right up to the present day. The only change has been to the flag, where under the communist regime the crown over the Polish eagle was omitted. In many ways the terminology is comparable to GB, Britain and the UK, all of which effectively mean exactly the same and have done ever since the Act of Union of 1707.

Éire (Republic of Ireland) – Irish Naval Service (*Seirbhís Chabhlaigh*): LÉ – Long Éireannach (Irish Ship). The use of Gaelic terms by the Irish navy is both because it is the country's official language (if less widely spoken than English), with all state institutions so named, and also – like the naming of many ships after famous women in Celtic mythology – a reflection of a sense of pride in this particular aspect of the country's heritage.

Russia. There was no official prefix for warships of the Imperial Russian Navy. Typically in reports and documents of the period the ships are generally designated simply as 'Cruiser *Variag*', 'Battleship *Sevastopol*' etc. Any prefixes assigned to ships of the Imperial Russian Navy (eg IRNS for 'Imperial Russian Navy Ship') have simply been made up and have no official standing. This fits in well with the old Russian navy in general, with nomenclature of all sorts being rather slap-dash and inconsistent, including the names of ship classes and types, designations for guns and mountings, and so on. During the Soviet era things changed in this (as in so many areas), but the acronyms used were for individual types of vessel (which, to this day, are frequently designated in a very different manner from those in other navies – eg Rocket Cruiser, Large Anti-submarine Ship, etc.).

Latin America. Of the major navies, neither Brazil nor Chile officially use prefixes, although both sometimes use particular designations for certain types of ship (as does Paraguay). Argentina, however, uses ARA (Armada República Argentina), while for the smaller fleets the following apply: Bolivia – ARB; Colombia – ARC; Ecuador – BAE; Honduras – FNV; Mexico – ARM; Peru – BAP; Uruguay – ROU; Venezuela – ANBV (formerly FNV but changed for political reasons).

The above listing is clearly not comprehensive, nor is it intended to be definitive. It is instead meant as much as anything as a starting point, placing this seemingly minor but actually quite fundamental subject before *Warship*'s wide and knowledgeable readership as an invitation to further debate and contribution. We would therefore be pleased to hear from any readers who can add to (or indeed correct) any aspect of this. A follow-up Warship Note will be published in a forthcoming edition of the annual.

Sources:
A wide range of primary and secondary sources have been consulted in the course of compiling this Warship Note, in addition to which the help and input of the following is gratefully acknowledged: Enrico Cernuschi, Aidan Dodson, Rob Gardiner, Geirr Haarr, Martin Hazell, John Jordan, Andrew Lambert, Stephen McLaughlin, Vincent O'Hara, Ian Sturton, Sergei Vinogradov, Henk Visser, Conrad Waters, Jon Wise.

Footnotes:
[1] 'My Lord Duke' or 'Your Grace', except in the case of Royal Dukes, when the correct formal address is 'May it please your Royal Highness'.
[2] Since Norway's independence in 1905 the country's three monarchs have all been kings: Haakon VII (1905-57), Olav V (1957-91) and Harald V (1991-present).

FALLEN EAGLE: THE ACTION OFF SAN JOSÉ, 26 DECEMBER 1944

Using Japanese primary sources to challenge aspects of the accepted version of events, **Michael Williams** looks into one of the lesser-known actions of the Second World War in the Pacific, which took place off San José on the coast of Mindoro on the night of 26-27 December 1944.

The Japanese operation which led to the action off San José has generally been dismissed as a hopeless and futile sortie by a hastily-cobbled-together force of warships, the primary objectives of which were never close to being achieved, and which resulted in the loss of one irreplaceable destroyer and damage to the remaining ships in the force, all to no avail. However, an alternative viewpoint is that its execution in the light of seemingly overwhelming Allied aerial and naval superiority marks it out as an audacious raid which deserves further scrutiny.

When looking at the Japanese perspective on *Operation Rei* (otherwise known as the 'San José Intrusion'), two original accounts left by Japanese participants are of value in determining what actually occurred. The principal one is that of Lieutenant Tsutomu Makoto, whose battle station was on the bridge of the heavy cruiser *Ashigara*, while further details come from the observations of Lieutenant Oikawa Hisao on board the light cruiser *Oyodo*.

Following the successful conclusion of the Leyte Island campaign, on 13 December 1944 an American amphibious assault struck Mindoro, an important staging post prior to the invasion of Luzon. Japanese Imperial General Headquarters felt that it could not let this go unanswered, and ordered General Yamashita to instigate a counter-attack. Given the limited resources then available following the debacles of the previous months, there was not much to call upon, but through perseverance and various redeployments a naval response was eventually put together.

Rear-Admiral Kimura Masatomi's force consisted of the cruisers *Ashigara* and *Oyodo*, and the destroyers *Kasumi* (Kimura's Flagship), *Asashimo*, *Kiyoshimo*, *Sugi*, *Kashi* and *Kaya*. It departed Camranh Bay for Mindoro on the morning of 24 December, successfully making an undetected passage across the South China Sea under cover of the prevailing poor weather. As it approached Mindoro, *Ashigara* launched her two Aichi E13A ('Jake') reconnaissance floatplanes to scout ahead, after which they were to head for Manila. The force arrived off the north coast of Mindoro late on the 26th without its presence becoming known to the enemy.

The first officially credited sighting of Kimura's Force was by Lieutenant Warren Michael Cox, who was flying his Martin PBM Mariner flying-boat on a reconnaissance patrol mission when at 1600 (Japanese time used throughout) he spotted eight suspect warships. After making a sighting report, he found that his bombs would not release and, after losing an engine, he landed his aircraft in Mangarin Bay on the west coast of Mindoro; it was then sunk by gunfire from an enemy plane, with one man mortally wounded and the surviving crew members spending the night in the water before being picked up the next morning.

A number of scouting aircraft were directed to the location of the sighting, in fading light and poor weather conditions, over the hours following Cox's initial sighting report, and the Japanese surface force was again spotted by a Consolidated B-24 Liberator (or in US Navy terminology, PB4Y Privateer). News of the sighting was soon confirmed by another Privateer landing at Hill Field, the crew of which, having reported their news, hurriedly refuelled, bombed up and set off again to shadow the enemy. The USAAF had a number of North American RB-25 Mitchell medium bombers (71st Reconnaissance Squadron, 5th Air Force) based at San José, and it was decided that it would be prudent to investigate this increasingly serious threat.

At Hill Field, all available aircraft and crews were quickly mustered to attack with whatever ordnance was available. The forces opposing the Japanese comprised primarily 13 B-25s and 92 assorted fighters: Curtiss P-40 Warhawks, Republic P-47 Thunderbolts, and Lockheed P-38 Lightnings, along with eleven PT-boats inshore and eleven more offshore. The US 7th Fleet was not close enough to intervene in the brief period of daylight remaining, although a powerful cruiser and destroyer group under Rear-Admiral Chandler nevertheless sortied from Leyte Gulf.

Seen from *Ashigara* the number of shadowing aircraft increased to three, at maximum range. They were shortly joined by a formation of the distinctive twin-tailed P-38's, which circled out of range during the hour or so of twilight after 1730. Emergency food rations were distributed to the men at their action stations on board the cruiser, while they watched the enemy aircraft.

For the Americans, as the sunset changed to a three-quarter moon illuminating the scene, every aircraft on Mindoro's strips was committed to attack the warships. B-25s took off with full (500lb) bomb loads from Hill Field; the runway did not have illumination, but jeep lights marked its boundaries, and coupled with the bright moonlight this was deemed sufficient to enable planes to take off and land. The sky above San José was soon thick with bombers and fighters heading out to meet the enemy, with red and green navigation lights twinkling.

Above the Japanese formation, one of the first P-38 pilots on the scene, Lieutenant Herald Lowery, circled over the ships with his landing lights on as a prominent navigation beacon, thus exposing himself to anti-aircraft fire, while his colleagues deployed to attack, aiming to halt or delay the naval strike with their cannon and machine guns before the bombers arrived.

On board the Japanese ships, exposed anti-aircraft gunners and bridge personnel donned their protective steel helmets and bullet-proof vests as speed was increased to 28 knots, while in the distance the enemy aircraft test-fired their guns; anti-aircraft battle stations were ordered. As the aircraft finally came in low, the rangefinders tracked the incoming wave.

Oyodo sustained strafing damage,

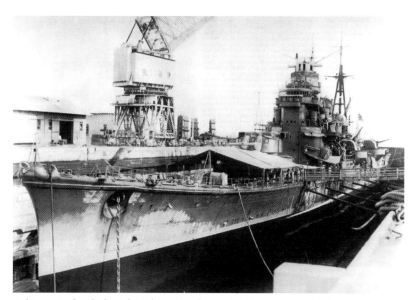

Ashigara in dry-dock at the Seletar Naval Base, Singapore, possibly in late December 1942. She had been fitted with twin 127mm dual-purpose guns on her weather deck amidships during the mid-1930s. Following her September 1943 refit at Kure she mounted 48 25mm MG in triple, twin and single mountings, which though poorly served by rudimentary FC directors could still unleash a formidable wall of fire at any attacker under 2,000m distant. (IJN Department of Naval Aeronautics)

and at 2101 was hit by two 500lb bombs dropped by a B-25. One penetrated to her No.2 boiler room but did not explode (it was finally extracted while at Cap St. Jacques on 30 December); the other hit the upper deck and exited through her port side leaving a 70cm diameter hole above the waterline, again without detonating. The damage was slight and limited to No.1 and No.3 single 25mm mountings, which were put out of action; only one man was wounded.

The B-25s were skip-bombing from 100ft, strafing at the same time. At about 2115 two direct bomb hits crippled *Kiyoshimo*, leading to her eventual loss (to a PT-Boat); she would be the only Japanese ship lost that night. *Asashimo* rescued 167 survivors; casualties were 82 dead and 74 wounded.

On *Ashigara*, above the roar of battle, a warning of low-level bombers approaching was heard. An emergency turn to port was executed as the bombs were released and, after a tense few seconds, they detonated away from the ship, throwing up great water columns. Now *Ashigara* was under strafing attack, bullets striking the ship and splashing alongside. At 2124 a number of aircraft carried out a concerted attack, during which the lightly-armoured gun shields and superstructure were penetrated and crew members hit.

Now comes the crucial point of contention. All official and secondary-source accounts state that at around 2130 *Ashigara* was hit on her port side amidships and seriously damaged by a single bomb dropped by a B-25, which tore a hole in her side and started heavy fires. However, first-hand personal accounts from those on board the Japanese ships state that *Ashigara* was in fact struck by a crashing fighter, which was carrying out a close-in strafing run from off her port quarter. These attacks were brave, carried out relentlessly and at point-blank range in the face of the ship's massed anti-aircraft fire, and in this instance the aircraft, a P-38, or its pilot was fatally hit, the machine crashing in the vicinity of No.4 12.7cm mounting.

The impact opened up a 2m gash in the hull, with fuel and ammunition starting a serious internal fire in No.3 crew compartment. This was on the middle deck immediately below the torpedo flat with its outfit of twenty-four 'Long Lance' torpedoes, each with their volatile oxygen fuel and 490kg explosive warheads; the situation quickly became critical. To make matters worse, a ten-strong damage control party stationed in the

A P-38 Lightning. This distinctive twin-boom land-based fighter was armed with a single 20mm Hispano M2 cannon and four Colt-Browning MG53-2 0.5in machine guns, all of which were located in the nose of the aircraft. (USAAF)

compartment had been wiped out. As the fire began to bear upon adjacent compartments, water was played over the torpedoes from above, while strenuous efforts were made to prevent the blaze spreading to the oxygen fuel compartment. But choking smoke and fumes inexorably spread into other sections, and although the principal 35mm armoured deck over the machinery had not been penetrated and speed was unaffected, preparations were now made to jettison the torpedoes.

Despite the damage *Ashigara* and *Oyodo* still embarked on their planned bombardment. At approximately 2300 *Ashigara* opened fire, and during the following 23 minutes she fired 158 common and 68 illuminating 20.3cm shells at the San José anchorage and harbour area, while *Oyodo* expended 98 15.5cm rounds. *Kasumi* fired four torpedoes at troop transports and reported one hit, while *Kashi* and *Kaya* fired two torpedoes each. The Japanese claimed to have sunk four transports, but this was an overly optimistic assessment; only the freighter *James S. Breasted* was damaged, although when she was later bombed her cargo of gasoline ignited and she was abandoned.

Apparently a lone Japanese aircraft followed a returning B-25 in and dropped its bombs just off the end of Hill Field. Since no co-ordinated

diversionary or supporting Japanese air strike was included within *Operation Rei*, it is possible that this aircraft was one of the two 'Jakes' launched during the approach. However, the presumed loss of these aircraft during subsequent operations from Manila means that this cannot be confirmed.

As the Japanese force retired at maximum speed, the fire on board *Ashigara* was finally contained and gradually brought under control. She had been peppered with machine gun fire, and several 25mm mounts had been destroyed. Reports of the battle damage amidships now reached the bridge: the floor of the gutted crew compartment had an accumulation of 30cm stagnant black water washing over it, with personnel killed and wounded still trapped within. To Lieutenant Makoto it appeared that a large number of the dead and wounded were horribly burned, and there was an acrid smell below; many crewmen were occupied in cleaning up, carrying the dead to the temporary morgue in the seamen's washplace, the wardroom being used for the treatment of the many wounded. All was now comparatively quiet, however.

On the catapult deck part of an aircraft wing with visible national markings was identified as coming from a P-38, while the pilot's remains

(only the upper torso being found, terribly burnt) were also recovered from the scattered debris.

Late on 27 December, as the squadron retired west at 20kts over a calm sea, members of the crew not on duty lined up on the quarterdeck, and the 47 casualties were wrapped in canvas shrouds (after hair and nail clippings had been taken) with a 20cm practice shell weight enclosed. In the glow of the setting sun, the band played, a volley of rifles rang out at the committal ceremony, and the name of each fallen crewmate was called as one after another the bodies slipped over the stern. The last body was that of the unknown enemy fighter pilot. Makoto confirms that the pilot's remains were handled like those of the others killed in action onboard the ship, with the same military honours as were given to their fallen crewmates. Later that night two of the seriously wounded died and were also buried at sea, bringing fatalities to 49 Japanese and one American.

With the new information extracted from Japanese sources, and through the good offices of the P-38 National Association, the identity of this lost pilot can now be determined. He was Lieutenant John Joseph Grillet (Service No. 0-763170), born 18 April 1923, who enlisted in Louisiana and was credited with one victory on 14 November 1944. Missing Air Crew Report No.11657 conveys the loss of P-38L-5 (tail No. 44-25352), from the 8th Fighter Group, 35th Fighter Squadron. Lieutenant Grillet is listed on the Manila American Cemetery (Philippines) tables of the missing; his life is also commemorated at Franklin Cemetery, St. Mary's Parish, Louisiana, with a memorial marker.

While the exact configuration of Lieutenant Grillet's P-38 on the night is impossible to determine, an operational weight of approximately 7,940kg, travelling at or near its maximum speed of 414mph, would have given the crashing aircraft an immense kinetic energy, resulting in the widespread damage to *Ashigara's* unarmoured upperworks. The crucial component appears to have been the nearly 400 US gallons of 100 octane aviation fuel unleashed onto the ship – with the short flight to the target area, little fuel will have been expended – together with the remaining ammunition which would have been cooked off by the intense heat.

The ineffectual nature of the Japanese intervention was confirmed on the 27th with the arrival of fighter cover from Leyte, followed by a task force of three cruisers and six destroyers, while a battleship and a couple of carriers were on the horizon. On the other hand, Kimura's successful escape is surprising. The undetected initial approach of the Japanese force might be explained through the poor weather conditions, but after the bombardment its general location in the South China Sea, well within the range of American aircraft, should have

resulted in a massacre, effectively a repeat of the 'Battle of the Bismarck Sea'. An overall emphasis on neutralising Japanese land targets appears to be primarily responsible for the failure of the Americans to sink Kimura's ships. While P-38s with 1,000lb anti-shipping bombs had taken off in pursuit of Kimura's force on the morning of the 27th, they had unaccountably returned without finding them.

In conclusion, two key aspects of this little-known action can now be firmly established. The *Ashigara* was impacted and seriously damaged by a P-38 fighter and not by a bomb, and the identity of the pilot responsible, Lieutenant John Joseph Grillet, previously recorded as missing, presumed dead, can be confirmed.

Sources:

Dull, Paul, *A Battle History of the Imperial Japanese Navy 1941-1945* (Naval Institute Press, Annapolis, 2003).

Lacroix, Eric and Wells, Lynton, *Japanese Cruisers of the Pacific War* (Chatham Publishing, London, 1997).

http://www5f.biglobe.ne.jp/~ma480/ senki-1-bankanoumi-ogawa1.html – Tsutomu Makoto (*Ashigara*).

http://www5f.biglobe.ne.jp/~ma480/senki -1-kumanonosaigo-sakonjyou.html – Oikawa Hisao (*Oyodo*).

http://www.combinedfleet.com/ashigara_ t.htm – *Ashigara*'s overall history.

Ms Dayle DeBry, Vice-President and Director of Public Relations, P-38 National Association.

WARSHIP NAMES AND THE COMMEMORATION OF THE SECOND WORLD WAR

Kenneth Fraser looks at the contentious subject of the different attitudes of the former Axis powers to naming new warships commissioned in the decades since the end of the Second World War.

There is a substantial academic literature discussing the problems of commemorating the Second World War in the defeated countries. This has not been much of a issue in the victorious nations, whose governments have been able to take it for granted that they were fighting in a good cause; but post-war Germans, for example, have inevitably had considerable difficulties with the question of what they were fighting for and how (or indeed whether) the war ought to be commemorated. This controversy has sometimes involved the names given to warships, and the successor regimes of each of the three principal Axis powers have taken quite different perspectives on this.

Italy

Italy was the only one of the three whose navy continued an uninterrupted career. It will be recalled that the royal government became a 'co-belligerent' after the Armistice of September 1943, and, although a

virtual Italian civil war continued until 1945, the great majority of the navy rallied to its cause. As far as names were concerned, all that had to be done was to change the few overtly Fascist ones, notably the battleship *Littorio* (referring to the Roman officials such as magistrates who carried the *fasces* – bundles of rods and an axe which symbolised their authority) which became the *Italia*.

Post-war names were usually uncontroversial, and followed traditional Italian patterns. It was even possible to repeat names from the Fascist era of a generally nationalist character. The first pair of helicopter-carrying cruisers in the early sixties, the *Caio Duilio* and *Andrea Doria*, repeated the names of a pair of earlier battleships, and the same principle was to have been followed for the second pair, the *Vittorio Veneto* and *Italia*, although the second ship was not laid down. In 1983, the aircraft carrier *Giuseppe Garibaldi* was named, like her cruiser predecessor of 1937, after the country's pre-eminent national hero.

However, many destroyers, frigates, patrol vessels and submarines were named after naval personalities of the Second World War, who in nearly every case had been awarded Italy's highest decoration, the Medaglia d'Oro al Valor Militare (Gold Medal for Valour), and these are worthy of a closer look.

Not many of the destroyers have

been named after individuals, but two of these were completed in 1993. The *Luigi Durand de la Penne* honoured the pioneer of human torpedoes who led the attack on Alexandria harbour in 1941, and who had died the previous year. His skill and courage could not be doubted, but nevertheless, he was exercising them in the service of the Fascist regime. The *Francesco Mimbelli* was named after a destroyer captain who had distinguished himself in an action off Crete in 1941, again during the Fascist period. However, the two latest destroyers, *Andrea Doria* and *Caio Duilio*, take their names from earlier eras, and both were formerly borne by battleships which served in both World Wars.

Of the fourteen frigates and patrol vessels named after individuals only one, *Luigi Rizzo* bore the name of a First World War hero, and three (two successive ships named *Carlo Bergamini* and *Virginio Fasan*) honoured sailors who had died on the Allied side. The other ten were all named after officers who had won their medals – and in most cases died – while fighting for the Axis.

All the new Italian submarines acquired since 1945 have been named after individuals. Those so honoured in the 1950s and 1960s all date from earlier periods of history, from *Enrico Dandolo* in the thirteenth century to *Enrico Toti* in the First World War, and in many cases their names had been used for earlier vessels. But from the early 1970s onwards the majority have borne the names of officers who served, or died on the Axis side. Some of these are at present being used for a second time. A particularly instructive example is that of Carlo Fecia di Cossato, who, after a successful career as a submarine captain, came over to the Allied side in 1943, but not long afterwards, apparently doubting that he had been right to do so, committed suicide. One of the latest boats is even named *Scirè*, after the submarine which carried Durand de la Penne and his comrades to Alexandria – the crew was collectively awarded the Gold Medal; however, that boat had been named, like the rest of her class, after a battle during Mussolini's Ethiopian campaign in 1936; an unusual choice for the twenty-first century. It seems that the Italian authorities have no inhibitions about commemorating the wartime activities of their predecessors in office.

Germany
A different approach prevailed in West Germany, whose armed forces were re-established in 1955. The first significant warships were some reconditioned minesweepers dating from the Second World War, which received the names of insects, first used for nineteenth-century gunboats, though *Bremse* ('Horsefly') and *Brummer* ('Bluebottle') had been given to ships of the 1930s. Some destroyers transferred from the U.S.A. had only numbers (as was the traditional practice), but a group of small destroyers and frigates transferred from Britain in 1958/9 all received the names of military and naval heroes which had been used before. Two of them might be considered uncontroversial: the *Brommy* (named after the commander of the first German navy of 1848) and the *Raule* (for the organiser of the navy of Brandenburg in the 1670s). But the others, the *Scharnhorst*, *Gneisenau*, *Hipper*, *Scheer* and *Graf Spee* (two nineteenth century Prussian generals and three First World War German admirals) bore the names of major warships of the Third Reich. The Bundeswehr must have revised its ideas thereafter, as nearly every newly built destroyer and frigate since that time has had the name of a federal

state or an important town. A year or two after the acquisition of the British ships, the largest vessel yet built for the federal navy, a training ship, was given the significant name *Deutschland* (used several times before) but it too has not been repeated since, possibly because of its nationalist connotations.

There was, however, a remarkable exception to the prevalence of geographical names. Gerhard Schröder, Minister of Defence in 1966-69 (not to be confused with the later Chancellor) considered that it would be appropriate to commemorate military and naval heroes even if they had fought for the Third Reich (as he himself had). For the names of the destroyers of the *Charles F Adams* class, he accordingly – and controversially – approved the names of one distinguished representative from each service. Of these, Field-Marshal Rommel was certainly a victim of Nazism, though he had served its cause until nearly the end of his life. Admiral Lütjens, who went down with the *Bismarck*, was no enthusiastic Nazi (his wife was of Jewish descent) but his last act, in sending a message of loyalty to Hitler, allowed him to be portrayed as such. The air ace Werner Mölders had for long been considered to be an anti-Nazi on the basis of a widely circulated letter, but by the time the ship was named this had been revealed to be a British forgery. Many years later, the Federal Ministry of Defence, after a long investigation, decided to stop using his name as an honorific title, notably for the fighter squadron JG74. (It should be added that the former German Democratic Republic avoided any comparable problems by opting for the names of Communist or Socialist heroes.)

Japan
The names of Japanese warships have never been taken from individuals or battles, and the majority have been drawn from geography, from the natural world, or (uniquely to Japan) from poetic imagery. It might be thought, therefore, that no problems of political nomenclature could arise there; however, the position is not quite so straightforward.

Some of the earliest ships commissioned by what was now to be called the Japanese Maritime Self-defence

Force appear (as we might expect in Japan) to have been chosen with their symbolic associations in mind. The first pair of destroyers transferred from the United States in 1954 were named the *Asakaze* ('Morning Breeze') and the *Hatakaze* ('Flag-fluttering Breeze'), and a pair of destroyer escorts the following year received the names *Hatsuhi* ('First Sun of the Year') and – most significantly – *Asahi* (which was officially given as 'Morning Sun' but when applied to a late nineteenth century battleship had been translated 'Rising Sun' after the national ensign).

Nor were the post-war naval authorities at all reluctant to re-employ the names of earlier ships of the Imperial Navy. This principle had already been followed by some of the numerous ships of the Japanese Coastguard. For instance in 1951 the *Kuma* class of inshore patrol vessels were all named after rivers; but twelve out of the twenty shared the names of recent cruisers of the Imperial Navy, and there was even a *Shinano*. The JMSDF was soon to follow a similar path: the *Asakaze* and *Hatakaze* mentioned above both repeated the names of IJN destroyers, and the same was true of the first significant new warships to be laid down, the frigates *Ikazuchi* ('Thunder'), *Inazuma* ('Thunderbolt') and *Akebono* ('Dawn'). The number of similar names since then is too great to bear repeating.

The parallels became particularly significant when the JMSDF began to repeat the names of major units of the Imperial Navy. The destroyers *Kirishima*, *Kongou* and *Kurama* of the early 1980s all bore the names (derived from mountains) of previous battleships and battlecruisers. The submarines *Soryu* ('Blue Dragon') and *Unryu* ('Dragon in Clouds') take the names of previous aircraft carriers. Most remarkable of all, the large helicopter-carrying destroyers *Ise* and *Hyuga* of 2009, named after old provinces, share the names of the two IJN battleships which during the Second World War had been converted to carry aircraft. This cannot be coincidental. An even larger such vessel, launched in 2013, is to be named *Izumo*. She, like the previous two ships, is named after an old province; but the last ship to bear the name, an armoured cruiser of 1900, was the IJN's flagship on the

China station from 1932 to 1942, the period of Sino-Japanese conflict. Japan has certainly not shied away from reusing the names of famous ships of the Second World War. It is interesting to speculate how far the naming policies of Italy, Germany and Japan over the years reflect different official attitudes to the commemoration of the countries' roles in the conflict.

Sources:
Italy: the World War II personalities and the submarine *Scirè* are all described in: http://www.marina.difesa.it/storiacultura/storia/medaglie/Pagine/default/aspx.
Germany: the controversies surrounding the three World War II personalities are fully covered in http://de.wikipedia.org/wiki under the entries for Gunther Lütjens, Werner Mölders and Erwin Rommel. The entries in the correspon-

ding English-language site http://en.wikipedia.org/wiki are less detailed.
Japan: *Jane's Fighting Ships*, 1962-63 and 2012-13. Anthony J. Watts and Brian G. Gordon, *The Imperial Japanese Navy* (London: Macdonald, 1971) pp.114-17.

[*Warship* would be interested to hear from any readers who can shed more light on this intriguing though controversial subject.]

A's & A's

Warship Gallery 2011
On p.204 of *Warship* 2011 we published a photograph of various Royal Navy ships in an anchorage, date and location unknown. The accompanying caption suggested an approximate date of 1935-37, based on the ships present, which included HMS *Cairo* and HMS *Echo*.

Recently, as a result of a conversation between the Assistant Editor and a friend, came the suggestion that the location could in fact be Cromarty, a rather indistinct modern-day photograph providing evidence, albeit not terribly conclusive, for this. This in turn led to contact being made, via the Archaeology for Communities in the Highlands (ARCH) project in Dingwall, with the Invergordon Archive, run by Malcolm McKean, and definite confirmation of the location as being the inner Cromarty Firth, looking WSW from a position just off Invergordon. Beyond the ships in the photograph lies the airfield (and former naval mainte-nance depot) at Evanton (FAA up until 1937, later RAF, today an indus-trial estate), while the distinctive hill in the background is Fyrish – it is this that conclusively pins down the loca-tion – and beyond that is Ben Wyvis.

With the location now confirmed, checking the ships' logs of *Cairo* (Captain Henry Pridham-Whipple, Commodore (D), commanding Home Fleet Destroyer Flotillas) and *Echo* dates the photograph to between 25 September and 12 October 1936, this being the only period when both were at Invergordon. Both ships arrived there from Scapa Flow shortly after mid-day on Friday 25 September, securing to 'C' and no.9 buoys respectively.

During the three weeks they were based at Cromarty both *Cairo* and *Echo* were at sea on exercises during 29-30 September and 6-8 October, so the photograph was almost certainly taken during 25-28 September, 1-5 October or 9-12 October, during which time they were either anchored or tied up to their buoys within the firth. Exercises included gunnery and torpedo firing (during one of the latter *Echo* lost a torpedo, resulting in much of the following day being spent on a fruitless search for this); sub-calibre, pom-pom and machine gun firing; anti-submarine exercises and dummy depth-charge attacks; paravane work for *Cairo* and TSDS (Two-Speed Destroyer Sweep) for *Echo*; *Echo* and *Escapade* taking turns towing one another; a 'night encounter', as well as more mundane things like inclination and compass adjustment. Time in the firth was spent in the usual activities such as divisions, cleaning and painting ship, divine service, make & mend and so on. Other ships present included *Nelson*, *Rodney*, *Orion*, *Courageous*, the destroyers *Escapade*, *Encounter*, *Eclipse*, *Express* and *Stronghold*, the submarine *Swordfish* and oiler RFA *Prestol*. This confirms that the 'S' class destroyer in the distance is indeed *Stronghold*, while Phil Glover of ARCH has in addition suggested that the rectangular object faintly visible beyond her bow is one of three floating targets that were lined up in the firth for FAA pilots to practice their aiming skills on.

Sources:
The ARCH website (http://www.arch-highland.org.uk/) includes details of Evanton's wartime history and of the surviving remains, while the

Invergordon Archive (http://www.theinvergordonarchive.org/) contains a wide range of material relating to the Cromarty Firth's history as a naval anchorage, together with much else besides.
ADM53/95414 – HMS *Cairo* log, September 1936.
ADM53/95415 – HMS *Cairo* log, October 1936.
ADM53/96559 – HMS *Echo* log, September 1936.
ADM53/96560 – HMS *Echo* log, October 1936.
Smith, David, *Action Stations* 7 (Patrick Stephens Ltd, Cambridge, 1983).
Parkes, Oscar, *Ships of the Royal Navies* (Sampson Low, Marston & Co. Ltd, London, 1937).

Acknowledgements:
Thanks to Susan Kruse, ARCH Project Officer; Willie Fraser, Eddie Szymborski and Bill Anderson of ARCH; Malcolm McKean of the Invergordon Archive; Alastair Fyfe and Charles Blackwood.

Last of the Line: the German Battleships of the *Braunschweig* and *Deutschland* Classes (*Warship* 2014)
The author, Aidan Dodson, has written to correct the comparative range (ie twice radius) figures given for these ships and their UK and US contemporaries on p.49. The correct figures are: *Braunschweig* 19,200km, *London* 20,500km and *Virginia* 18,200km; accordingly, all three classes had similar endurance. In addition, it should be noted that the *Braunschweigs* were completed with twenty 8.8cm guns, reduced to eighteen by 1906, after a pair mounted in the bridge wings were found to interfere too greatly with the operation of the ship.

NAVAL BOOKS OF THE YEAR

Jonathan Coad
Support for the Fleet,
Architecture and
Engineering of the Royal
Navy's Bases 1700-1914
English Heritage, 2013; large format
hardback, 450pp, illustrated with 488
photographs, maps, plans and archive
prints, in colour and b/w; price £100.00.
ISBN 978-1-84802-055-9

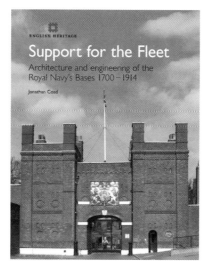

The subject of this massive and beautifully produced book is of arguably slightly peripheral relevance to the study of warships themselves, but those readers of *Warship* who are also interested in the history of engineering and architecture will find much here that will fascinate them. In seventeen chapters, Jonathan Coad deals with Royal Dockyards in the UK and overseas, bases in the Mediterranean, West Indies, North and South America and Australasia, hospitals, offices, barracks, ordnance and victualling yards, and even churches and chapels.

The Senior Service was in the forefront of innovation in engineering: the RN had a need for large roofs over its slips and developed complex timber roof trusses for them, possibly developed from medieval barns, but capable of greater spans and greater economy. There is a fascinating illustration of a brilliantly conceived metal shoe used to replace traditional timber jointing in the roof structure of the sawmills at Chatham Dockyard, a design associated with Marc Brunel. Timber gave way to iron as that became practicable; the metal shoe and those buildings that used iron columns with timber joists illustrate an interesting transitional stage. The Navy needed boat stores, with smaller spans than the slips, and developed iron structures of columns and arched beams, some even with

tension bracing, that rival the factories and warehouses of the period. One photograph of several individually well-known slips at Chatham deserves to be included in wider histories of modern architecture, showing grouped-together designs from 1837 (timber-framed and wonderfully curvilinear) and 1847 (with arched iron framing.) The Navy also needed dry docks, and the Rennie brothers developed structures of brickwork inverted arches carried on timber piling where the subsoil required it.

The service seems to have stuck with a classical simplicity for most of those buildings that did need outward show, avoiding the Victorian and Edwardian styles that look over-elaborate to the modern eye, although the 1887 Admiralty building in Whitehall and some of the overseas buildings seemingly intended to impress the locals do occasionally fall into the trap of tasteless exuberance.

Machinery was needed too: from rope-laying machines for the sailing navy, shown here in 19th century drawings, to the biscuit-making machinery in Chatham shown in a

photograph of 1901, with much else between. The machinery had to be housed: the naval bakery in Valetta (1844, now the Maritime Museum) was an extraordinary building with a steam-powered flourmill, the whole set-up designed for efficient use. This is just another of the buildings described here that can fairly be said to foreshadow modern architecture in terms of putting efficiency of use ahead of style, although without being able to entirely free itself from stylistic expression.

Housing built by the Navy at home tended to use typical civilian designs of the time, but the strict hierarchy of rank was preserved in officers' housing. The 1829 housing 'for inferior officers' at Sheerness must be extremely desirable today. It would be interesting to know whether the 'long service wings' to the rear of the 1720s officers' housing in Chatham represent an officer-servant relationship that is different from the contemporary civilian 'upstairs, downstairs' household. There is much still not understood about how the classic Georgian house actually 'worked' in either civil or military mode. Overseas, the need to cope with different climates and the opportunity to use local materials led to fascinating and elegant designs for barracks and housing, such as those at Garden Island, Sydney and Halifax, Nova Scotia. The imaginative use of corrugated iron roofing over verandahs foreshadows the vernacular architectures of Australia and South Africa.

Primarily, though, we think of navies needing dockyards. By the use of plans and archive illustrations, this book shows the quite staggering scale of the engineering work required to build so many of them, in the UK and all over the world. One photograph shows five steam excavators working at Devonport, another five piledrivers at Chatham Dockyard, while engravings from 1871, also of Chatham, show convicts man-hauling stone and excavating docks by hand, apparently a normal practice, but one this reviewer had never come across before.

At £100, this book is undeniably expensive. However, it should be seriously considered not only by warship buffs but also by anyone interested in the history of engineering and architecture. Almost every page contains something wonderful, from the unexpected (but not 'accidental') abstract sculpture of an access staircase diagonally crossing the curved, stepped inner face of a dry dock, to the flanged columns of the bakery at Stonehouse, designed to allow grain bins to be formed by the slotting-in of boards, and much, much else besides.

John Harris

Arthur J Marder
From the Dreadnought to Scapa Flow

Seaforth Publishing, Barnsley, 2013-14; paperbacks, B&W photo plates, maps; price £16.99 each.
Volume I: The Road to War 1904-1914 (488 pages) ISBN 978-1-84832-162-5
Volume II: The War Years: to the Eve of Jutland 1914-1916 (460 pages) ISBN 978-1-84832-163-2
Volume III: Jutland and After: May to December 1916 (383 pages) ISBN 978-1-84832-200-4
Volume IV:1917: The Year of Crisis (381 pages) ISBN 978-1-84832-201-1
Volume V: Victory and Aftermath January 1918–June 1919 (425 pages) ISBN 978-1-84832-203-5

This classic five-volume history of the Royal Navy during the years 1904-1919 was met with considerable acclaim when it was first published by OUP during the early 1960s. After many years of being available only from second-hand booksellers, it has now been reprinted by Seaforth in a new moderately-priced paperback edition.

Marder was fortunate enough to be undertaking his research at a time when a number of the naval officers who served during the First World War were still alive. He also conducted an extensive trawl of private correspondence, as well as delving into personal archives. At times this results in a jolt to our modern sensitivities, as when, at the beginning of Volume II, Marder assesses the British admirals of the day largely on the basis of what their fellow officers said or wrote about them! In other respects, however, the books have hardly dated, and Marder's narrative is always compelling.

Marder is fascinated by the four great men who stamped their mark indelibly on the Royal Navy during the early twentieth century: Fisher, the zealous reformer and slightly unhinged prophet; Churchill, the thrusting young politician whose knowledge of naval affairs was just sufficient to make him a danger to himself and others; Beatty, the dashing cavalry officer whose natural impetuosity would later be moderated by the heavy responsibility which came with command of the most powerful fleet in the world; and Jellicoe, the meticulous technocrat whose natural inclination towards tight central control was reinforced by his lack of trust in the abilities of his subordinates. Marder treats all of them with respect and no little affection; he praises their 'drive' and mental acuity, while at the same time making no attempt to conceal their personal shortcomings.

As for the issues and controversies thrown up by the naval events of the First World War, all receive comprehensive coverage. Marder is even-handed throughout and presents all the arguments; there is no polemic or taking sides, and he refuses to be drawn into the 'blame game' beloved of some modern writers. *From the Dreadnought to Scapa Flow* is history at its best, and Seaforth are to be commended for making the series available to the modern reader. The paintings by the distinguished maritime artist William Wyllie which feature on the jackets are atmospheric, and the new edition benefits from an Introduction by Barry Gough, author of *Historical Dreadnoughts: Arthur Marder and Stephen Roskill and the Battles for Naval History*. The production is everything one could wish for, and the original maps, which have necessarily had to be reproduced at a relatively small scale, are now available for full-size download from the Pen & Sword website.

John Jordan

James C Rentfrow
Home Squadron: The US Navy of the North Atlantic Station

Naval Institute Press, 2014; 240 pages, 16 B&W photographs; price £38.95. ISBN 978-1-61251-447-5

For the US Navy the later nineteenth century, between the end of the Civil War and the Spanish-American War, could be considered its dark age. How it evolved from a small predominantly coastal defence and constabulary cruising force attempting to represent both the country's interests worldwide and meet the demands of domestic duties has never been comprehensively examined until now. The Atlantic Fleet of 1874 was no more than a loose collection of individual ships which spent hardly any time working as a cohesive force and was barely capable of the simplest coordinated manoeuvres under steam; even in loose formation it could only achieve a derisory squadron speed of four knots. By 1897 the North Atlantic, or Home Squadron as it became known, was a fledgling battle fleet consisting of modern warships organised and exercised in manoeuvring and fighting in close-order.

In *Home Squadron* Commander James Rentfrow, a serving United States Navy officer, provides a detailed analysis of how this transition to the New Steel Navy occurred. Using the developments that took place on the North Atlantic Station between 1874 and 1897 as a case study, he demonstrates that rather than remaining idle and waiting for Mahan to kick-start the revolution in naval operations, the US Navy had over a number of years been developing the tactics of battle fleet operations even when for the most part it lacked the ships befitting a first class naval power.

The transition did not follow a coherent plan, with progress often hampered by conflicting operational demands. Initially Fleet exercises under steam were infrequent and utilised existing wooden cruising vessels. However, from 1889 the wooden cruisers were decommissioned to be replaced by new steel warships. In turn ad-hoc assemblies of vessels gave way to a more permanent combat force capable of routine exercising and developing the necessary fighting capabilities, tactics and manoeuvres. Rentfrow shows that the US government had an interest in developing an offensive naval combat capability as early as the 1870s. However, the process of change often resulted in the appearance of capability without the rigorous exercising necessary to deliver the required effect.

This book provides a wealth of detail on squadron activities that will more than satisfy anyone interested in the warships of the period. The author brings to light the complexities of operating a war fighting fleet, a skill that cannot simply be learnt overnight but must be developed and exercised regularly. Along the way he reveals those critical personalities who struggled to balance traditional cruising duties with the desire to maintain a fleet in being, and who by dint of personality and drive made the transition possible. He gives an insight into some of the tensions that existed between individual commands until clear organisation was imposed, and the unifying process that enveloped everything from signal books to paint schemes which set the conditions for the emergence of a world-class navy.

The book draws on significant primary sources, is extensively referenced and is supported by an exhaustive bibliography. However, there are a few minor editorial errors: USS *Metacomet* is referred to as the *Metacoma*, and the island of Faial in the Azores where the gunboat *Yorktown* put in for repairs is referred to as Fusal. Additionally, at one point the unique Harvey towed torpedo is referred to as a 'spar' weapon; when the towed nature of the weapon's actual deployment is understood it reinforces the point that cruising ships would need to regularly practice its use. However, these very minor criticisms do not detract from this excellent book.

Rentfrow has a fluent writing style and he sets out his account in an engaging and entertaining way. He must be congratulated for filling a critical gap in the understanding of the evolution of the New Steel Navy and for giving the topic the depth and insight it deserves.

Philip Russell

Ed. Eric Wertheim
Combat Fleets of the World, 16th Edition

US Naval Institute Press, 2013; hardback, 1008 pages, copiously illustrated with line drawings and B&W photographs; price £215.00/$295.00.
ISBN 978-1-59114-954-5

The Naval Institute Guide to Combat Fleets of the World, to give it its full title, was first published in 1977 as an off-shoot of the French-language *Flottes de Combat*. It became a biennial publication under the editorship of A D Baker III until 2002. Since then only two editions have been published, in 2006 and 2013, and A D Baker III has been succeeded as editor by Eric Wertheim, a defence consultant, columnist and author specialising in maritime and naval affairs. The current 16th Edition is therefore the first to be published for seven years.

The strengths of *Combat Fleets* have traditionally been the sheer quantity of detailed technical data provided, using a compact formula which makes extensive use of standard acronyms and abbreviations, and price – only 30% of the RRP of the current book version of *Jane's Fighting Ships*. In these respects the new edition does not disappoint. Coverage of the world's navies is particularly comprehensive, with greatly expanded entries on up-and-coming navies such as those of India and China. The Introduction has a concise regional survey of the navies of Australasia/Asia, Europe, the Middle East/Africa and the Americas; it is objective, to the point, and mercifully free of any 'political' agenda. It is followed by the standard metric/imperial conversion tables and a section on the terms and abbreviations employed throughout the book, using the entry on the UK's Type 45 destroyer as an exemplar. The entry for each country begins with data on personnel, bases and naval aviation and, in the case of the major navies, marines/naval infantry, coastal defence and weapons & sensors (again comprehensive, up-to-date and particularly useful).

There are multiple monochrome photographs of all the major classes of submarine and surface ship; these are reproduced across a single column, but

are generally sharp enough to show any differences between the ships of a class. The line drawings are something of a mixed bag. Many have been inherited from previous editions or are taken from sister publications such as *Flottes de Combat* and *Ships of the World*; artists include A D Baker III, Lucien Gassier, Robert Dumas and Jean Moulin. Most of the older drawings are waterline profiles; weapons systems and sensors are clearly numbered with a key beneath. Unfortunately, many of these older drawings appear to have been reproduced using photocopies rather than the originals, and some of the linework is 'smudgy' and uneven. Those from *Ships of the World* (many of which are used to illustrate the USA section) are also fairly basic. However, the latest two editions of *Combat Fleets* benefit hugely from the contribution of two younger illustrators, Tomasz Grotnik and Ivan Zajak, who have supplied numbered profiles *and* plan views of many of the most recently-completed ships using computer graphics. These are of the highest quality; as older ships decommission and their replacements enter service, future editions of *Combat Fleets* will undoubtedly benefit from a steady renewal of the line drawings.

At £215 per copy, one suspects that the new *Combat Fleets* will be more attractive to libraries than individual readers, many of whom will prefer to surf the net for information on the new types of ship. However, as a one-stop printed reference for the world's navies the new edition represents excellent value for money.

John Jordan

Philippe Caresse
Les cuirassés de la classe *Charlemagne*

Lela Presse, Outreau, 2013; large format hardback, 126 pages, copiously illustrated with maps and B&W photographs, plus an 80-page supplement with plans of the ships; price €45.00.
ISBN 978-2-914017-74-9

Readers will be familiar with the work of Philippe Caresse through his articles published in *Warship*. His articles on the loss of the battleships *Iéna* (2007) and *Suffren* (2010) were subsequently expanded into a book which was reviewed in *Warship 2011*.

A third article on the battleship *Gaulois* in *Warship 2012* has now been followed by a book on the three battleships of the *Charlemagne* class, of which *Gaulois* was a member.

Charlemagne, *Saint-Louis* and *Gaulois* constituted the first homogeneous class of battleship built for the French Navy for more than twenty years and were the first French battleships to have 12-inch (30.5cm) guns in twin mountings fore and aft – already a standard feature of British battleships of the period. Completed during the late 1890s, they were extraordinarily powerful ships for their size, but their protection systems quickly became dated and stability was an increasing concern. Placed in reserve shortly before the First World War, they were reactivated on mobilisation and saw active service in the eastern Mediterranean, particularly during the Dardanelles campaign. *Gaulois* survived severe damage at the Dardanelles only to be sunk by a German U-Boat in 1917.

The book follows the traditional French format, with an introduction outlining the development of the design leading on to a detailed technical study of hull, armament and machinery. A 70-page historical section then deals with construction and trials, peacetime activity and, finally, participation in the First World War. A production 'glitch' resulted in the omission of the official plans of the ships from the book, but these have now been published as an 80-page supplement which is despatched with all book orders – it is not available separately.

Coverage of the ships and their careers is extraordinarily comprehensive. The photographs are often stunning, and they have been used to complement the text: the technical section makes extensive use of close-ups and on-board shots, while the photos which illustrate the historical section show the ships at every stage of their service lives. Captions are informative, and the author has been able to provide approximate dates and places for most of the less-well-known images from private collections. The book design makes excellent use of the large page format, and shows a maturity not always evident in French publications of this nature.

The supplement comprises full sets of the official plans of all three ships, together with colour artwork to show livery and configuration at various stages of their careers. Some of the larger plans have been reproduced across the double-page spread, but care has been taken that no detail has been lost in the 'gutter'. The plans have naturally had to be reduced from their original scale of 1:100, so that many of annotations can be read only with a magnifying glass, but the reproduction is admirably 'sharp', and it is good to have all the plans together in a single source.

Despite the slightly elevated price this is an excellent purchase for anyone interested in the French Navy at the end of the 19th century.

John Jordan

Richard Johnstone-Bryden
HMS *Belfast*, Cruiser 1939

Seaforth Publishing, 2013; softback, 128 pages, 233 colour and B&W photographs and 5 line drawings; price £14.99.
ISBN 978 1 84832 155 7

One of Seaforth's 'Historic Ships' series, this book takes the form of an illustrated guide to the *Belfast*. A general introduction is followed by a 10,000-word history of the vessel which follows the basic series format: a section on design and construction, a further eight sections on her active career, and a section dealing with the efforts taken to preserve *Belfast* for the nation; each section is appropriately illustrated with photographs, paintings and reproductions of Admiralty drawings. The photographic section is the central focus of the book; it is organised to follow the tour of the ship a visitor would expect to experience.

The photographs were mostly taken by the author – where not, the photographer is separately credited. This means that all the main photographs are new, and each has been given an informative caption that guides the reader in a 'virtual journey' around the ship. There is the occasional small error: the item captioned 'engine order telegraph' on p.119 is almost certainly a boiler order telegraph, used by the engine room to tell the boiler room what steam is required, including such commands as 'make smoke'; the engine order telegraph is in fact depicted on p.120.

It is clear from these photographs that *Belfast* presents a sizable problem for her support team. In quite a few of the shots there are clear signs of rust streaks forming and of corrosion marks on fixtures and fittings. It is worth bearing in mind that when the ship was in commission, maintenance of the hull and equipment would have been performed by some 700 men, and even then the outboard paintwork would often have suffered rust stains and impact damage. Experience from the USA seems to suggest that a healthy volunteer group is vital to the ongoing maintenance of preserved naval vessels, with the successful and continuing restoration of USS *Slater* being a classic case. Whilst it must be recognised that the United States has a far larger pool of ex-servicemen and enthusiasts to call on, it is to be hoped that *Belfast's* support group continues to grow from its current figure of 39 to ensure the survival of such an historic ship.

So much more than a picture book, as with all this series, this title is an admirable guide to the vessel, one which can be enjoyed in the living room as much as onboard.

W B Davies

Geirr H Haarr
The Gathering Storm: The Naval War in Northern Europe, September 1939 – April 1940

Seaforth Publishing, 2013; hardback, 550 pages, illustrated with B&W photographs and maps; price £35.00.
ISBN 978-1-84832-140-3

This, the third of Geirr Haarr's books for Seaforth, is effectively a 'prequel' to his earlier works covering the German invasion of Norway (see *Warship* 2010, p.193), and continues his trademark approach of combining meticulous, wide-ranging research with balance, objectivity and an absorbing narrative. Compared to his previous volumes the treatment here is largely thematic, rather than strictly chronological, but this approach has been dictated by the broader scope of the coverage.

Haarr's greatest strength as a writer is arguably his ability to switch seamlessly from the broader (strategic) picture to the narrower (tactical) one and then to the most intimate of all –

the personal, individual account – and in the process drawing all of these together to provide an all-encompassing tale of events. The chapter on the Northern Patrol is a particularly good example. Throughout, the first-hand accounts are chosen from a wide range of sources, and then carefully incorporated so as to illustrate events with genuine clarity. Much the same applies with regard to the choice of photographs, while there are numerous maps – the lack of which was the major criticism of *The German Invasion of Norway*.

In the opening chapter the coverage of the RN's hardware and the inter-war treaty system is slightly sketchy and occasionally in error (eg there were four *Arethusa* class cruisers, not three). However, this section of the book simply sets the scene, and as soon as Haarr moves on to actual *events* his touch becomes sure. In his account of the earlier phases of the war Haarr argues that while the Royal Navy was much the better equipped, the *Kreigsmarine* was far better organised. However, the RN responded most impressively, with speed and with thoroughness, in particular in terms of organisation, while the *Kreigsmarine* ran aground on a combination of Germany's underlying lack of resources and the rigid and counter-productive Nazi system. Even by the spring of 1940 this failure to adapt to changing circumstances was starting to prove a real problem.

Haarr is not afraid to make some controversial assertions. He claims that arming merchant ships with defensive weapons was not only counter-productive because it made them targets, but also a huge waste of resources which would have been better used elsewhere. On a much more fundamental level, he also puts forward the idea that during these opening eight months of conflict Germany lost her single opportunity of genuinely challenging Britain's supremacy at sea, when the numerical disparity between the two fleets was at its smallest (though still very considerable). The losses incurred during the ensuing Norwegian campaign to all intents and purposes finished the *Kreigsmarine's* chances of reaching this position ever again.

One unexpected and frustrating omission is an almost complete lack

of any reference to the French *Marine Nationale*. While the latter had a quiet opening eight months of the war compared to the navies of the other two major combatants, the impression given here was that it did little other than send out the occasional ship to annoy the RN by getting in the way, and its numerous activities – escorting troop ships and convoys, submarine patrols in the North Sea, the hunting groups formed to counter German surface raiders – pass largely unmentioned.

Having taken a largely thematic approach to most of the book, in the final quarter Haarr reverts to a chronological one, as he moves on to the impact of the conflict on Scandinavia, culminating in a dramatic, uncompromising retelling of the *Altmark* affair (also depicted in Anthony Cowland's splendidly atmospheric jacket painting). The author contends that this event, seemingly so minor in itself, in fact sealed the fate of Norway (and hence Denmark) by focusing the attentions of both the German Führer and the British First Lord on what had hitherto been a relatively peripheral neutral country. The narrative ends with the opening moves of the German invasion and the coincidental Allied operations, and in so doing leads neatly into *The German Invasion of Norway*.

Minor quibbles aside, this is a top-notch addition to Geirr Haarr's stable of Seaforth titles, and is highly recommended.

Stephen Dent

Lars Hellwinkell
Hitler's Gateway to the Atlantic: German Naval Bases in France 1940-1945

Seaforth Publishing, Barnsley, 2014; 234 pages, 158 photographs and drawings; price £25.00.
ISBN 978-1-84832-199-1

Originally published in German in 2012 and based on extensive archival research, this book focuses on an aspect of the Second World War that has been little treated in print. During the First World War, the activities of the German Navy were heavily circumscribed by the fact that all its bases were on the Baltic and North Sea. As the author points out

in his first chapter, the lesson was fully understood by the interwar German admiralty, which frequently discussed the possibility of acquiring a base beyond the North Sea.

The French port of Brest was particularly coveted. Initially it was felt to be unattainable; however, the rapid advance of the German army in 1940 meant that by that summer the French Atlantic coast was in German hands. The dockyard installations at Brest had been sabotaged by the French prior to the Armistice, with only one dry dock serviceable and no functioning cranage. It was nevertheless decided to make it the principal German naval fleet base. The process of creating a fully-effective establishment was long and difficult, and relied heavily on French labour and expertise. Thus, when the first big ships began to arrive at the beginning of 1941, only limited facilities for overhaul, repair and support were available, with much work having to be done by ships' own crews. Brest was also within range of British bombers, and the battleships *Scharnhorst* and *Gneisenau* were damaged on a number of occasions while undergoing maintenance and repair, as was the cruiser *Prinz Eugen*. The constant air raids led to the big ships being returned to Germany in the 'Channel Dash' of February 1942, ending the dream of basing the principal part of the German fleet on the Atlantic.

More effective was the use of the French ports, in particular Lorient, as submarine bases, vastly increasing the vessels' operational reach, and a significant part of the book deals with the development of the supporting infrastructure, culminating in the construction of vast reinforced concrete submarine pens of the type also erected in Germany and Norway. The value of these was emphasised when the town of Lorient was all but obliterated by bombing raids at the beginning of 1943, while the German submarines, now safely ensconced in their new bunkers, were unharmed.

The book deals with the reality of life under the occupation, and in particular the contribution made by French workers to making the French bases operational and to the construction of the coastal defences which made up the Atlantic Wall between 1942 and 1944. This cooperation proved to be a double-edged sword, however, since it allowed Resistance members to be at the heart of the French naval bases, with consequent opportunities for espionage and sabotage.

As 1944 progressed, the surviving French-based German warships were gradually destroyed by air attack or in surface actions, while the ports themselves were declared fortresses against the prospect of Allied invasion, some (including Lorient) remaining as German-controlled enclaves until the very end of the war in Europe, despite the liberation of the hinterland. On the other hand, Brest was liberated in September 1944, utterly devastated and only gradually rehabilitated. The book concludes with a survey of the post-war history of the submarine bunkers, generally so massive that attempts to demolish them have been in vain; in many cases they remain in use, the bunkers at Lorient continuing to house submarines (albeit French ones) until 2005.

The book has been well translated, with only a few minor issues, and tells its story well. The author's interest is primarily in the 'people' side of things; on the naval side the focus is on the big ships and submarines operated by the Germans, with little on the operations carried out by destroyers and other smaller surface vessels. There is also hardly anything on the materiel left behind by the French, in particular the old cruisers which were employed by the Germans as accommodation vessels. A particularly interesting photograph on p.20, taken at Brest in 1940, mentions the patrol boats in the foreground but not the big armoured cruiser beyond. The ship in question is the *Gueydon*, which reappears on p.42 converted as a dummy *Prinz Eugen* in 1941. She would also feature in the end-game of the German occupation of Brest, when she and a number of other hulks were targeted by the RAF in August 1944 to prevent their use as blockships by the Germans (an aspect of the liberation of Brest not mentioned in the book). However, these issues are minor niggles; this is an excellent book which makes a real contribution to the history of the Second World War in European waters.

Aidan Dodson

Eds. John H. Maurer & Christopher M. Bell
At the Crossroads Between Peace and War: The London Naval Conference of 1930

US Naval Institute Press, 2013; hardback, 300 pages, 16 B&W photographs; price £45.50/$59.95.
ISBN 978-1-61251-326-3

At the Crossroads is a series of essays on aspects of the London Naval Conference of 1930, the most controversial of the interwar naval arms limitation treaties and the most difficult to negotiate. The editors are distinguished academics from the US Naval War College and Dalhousie University, Halifax respectively.

The first chapter, entitled 'A Turning Point in Anglo-American Relations?', is by John T. Kuehn, whose study of the US General Board, *Agents of Innovation*, was published by NIP in 2008 and reviewed in *Warship 2010*. Even if one accepts some of Kuehn's more bizarre claims for the agency of the General Board in matters of naval arms limitation, the chapter is a disappointment, being replete with errors, omissions and contradictions. The British position on the cruiser issue is presented in only the vaguest of terms, and there is no mention of the gun elevation controversy which surrounded the US Navy's proposal to modernise its older battleships, and which prompted formal British representations. Kuehn claims that Moffett's purpose in proposing the transfer of the *Lexingtons* to the 'experimental class' of carriers allowed by Washington was 'to try to retain the large ships while building even more of the small ones'. This is a serious misreading both of Moffett's intentions and of the Washington Treaty; had the *Lexingtons* been transferred to the 'experimental' category they could have been scrapped within their 20-year lifespan and replaced with more numerous smaller flight decks, but not retained.

Fortunately, the book improves markedly from this point. Christopher Bell's chapter on Britain and the conference is masterly in its grasp both of the 'technical' issues – notably the cruiser problem – and the political negotiation, much of which took place

between the British Prime Minister Macdonald and the US President Hoover prior to the conference. Perhaps the most striking claim here, backed by compelling documentary evidence, is that there was an informal agreement between Macdonald and the Admiralty that the total number of British cruisers could be reduced from 70 to 50 in return for a guaranteed building programme of three new cruisers per year for the duration of the treaty (ie until 1936).

Sadao Asada, author of the excellent *From Mahan to Pearl Harbor* (published by NIP in 2006 and reviewed in *Warship 2008*) provides the Japanese perspective, detailing the destructive internal battles between the civilians in the delegation and their naval advisers, which were aggravated by the regular communication of the latter with the hardline admirals of the naval staff in Tokyo. Asada's claim that 'All other naval powers developed the submarine for commerce destruction' is wide of the mark; however, in every other respect this is an admirably balanced and compelling account of Japanese participation in the conference.

Paul G. Halpern gives an account of the French and Italian positions prior to and during the London Conference. The French championing of 'global tonnage' as an alternative to limitation by 'categories' is particularly well explained, as is the detailed rationale put forward by the French for their overall naval requirements. The Italian position was far more straightforward (essentially: 'we don't care what we get as long as it is the same as the French'), but in the end this provided a much greater stumbling block to agreement than the more complex and nuanced French position. There are one or two small imprecisions and omissions; in particular, Halpern fails to deal with the difficult issue of how to accommodate the French *contre-torpilleurs* within the 'category' system favoured by the Anglo-Saxons. However, this is otherwise an exceptional study which fills a major gap in English-language accounts of the conference.

The chapter by John R. Ferris on the role of British intelligence in the conference reveals that the Government Code & Cypher School (GC&CS) was reading all communications between the capitals and their respective delegations. This intelligence proved a valuable resource in brokering the various deals; the British were aware not only of the 'bottom line' for each of the negotiating parties, but also of the dissension in the Japanese ranks.

Norman Friedman's chapter on Naval Strategy and Force Structure deals with the categories of ship which were the subject of the treaty. The author's analysis of the technical issues, in particular the very different British and American perspectives on the role of cruisers which were at the root of the parity problem, is exceptional, and there are some acute political observations (eg 'The US Navy exploited public anti-British feeling to get the forces they wanted while preparing to fight Japan'.)

At the Crossroads concludes with a Strategic Assessment of the London Conference by John H. Maurer which aims to put the London Treaty in its proper historical context. The ultimate failure of the treaty system is put down to two factors: the failure of the 'paper' agreement to satisfy the national aims and ambitions of all the powers represented at the conference, particularly Japan; and the emergence of other 'outsider' powers such as Soviet Russia and Nazi Germany, whose investment in naval armaments upset the delicate balance of power. Maurer sees the major positive result of the conference as the defusing of historical antagonisms between Britain and the United States. He also makes the astute observation that the ratios which were such a bone of contention at the conference 'bore little relationship to the actual strategic and operational problems that the American, British and Japanese navies would face during the Pacific War.'

John Jordan

Les Brown
British Destroyers: J–C and Battle Classes (ShipCraft 21)
Seaforth Publishing, 2013; softback, 64 pages, numerous photographs and drawings; price £14.99.
ISBN 978-1848321809

This instalment of the 'ShipCraft' series follows on from the same author's earlier work on the A–I and 'Tribal'-class destroyers, covering the new generation of two-boiler, single-funnelled vessels that followed the 'Tribals' and continued to be built down to the end of the Second World War. The book follows the usual pattern of the series, combining accounts and images of the design and careers of the vessels in question with reviews of available kits and images of models made both from some of these kits and by scratch-building.

The accounts of the design and modifications to the ships are comprehensive as far as their wartime careers are concerned, but their post-war changes are dealt with summarily in three paragraphs at the end of the book. Given the length of some of the ships' later careers and the interest of the modifications carried out, this is unfortunate, and the decision to exclude post-1945 detail is nowhere explained. Even if it was decided that covering the post-war era in detail would have extended the book beyond an acceptable length, surely at least a tabulation of key changes and some images could have been included? This rigid exclusion of any post-1945 detail also means that the FROG kit of *Undine* as rebuilt as a Type 15 frigate is not covered in the model section. Otherwise, the kit review section appears comprehensive and highlights the key issues with each of the models covered. The images of completed models give an idea of what can be achieved by the skilful modeller.

Photographs are provided for all classes, but line drawings are included for a selection only. There is also colour artwork showing a number of the camouflage patterns employed on the ships; while very helpful for modellers, it would have been good if *both* sides of the ships could have been provided, rather than just the starboard-side pattern in each case. Also, it would have been helpful if it could have been stated *which* ship of a given class is depicted.

Altogether, the volume will be of significant interest to anyone planning to model any of the vessels covered, but it is a pity that it suffers from the flaws in coverage noted above. While one acknowledges that the Second World War era is probably that most popular with modellers, the way in which ships built then were adapted in the 1950s to meet the challenges of the post-war world presents interesting modelling opportunities that should have at least been introduced in this volume.

Aidan Dodson

Duncan Redford and Philip D. Grove
The Royal Navy Since 1900
London: I.B.Tauris, 2014, 363 pages; 8 colour and numerous B&W photographs; tables, maps and figures; endnotes and bibliography; price £25.00.
ISBN 978-1-78076-782-6

Redford and Grove's work belongs to a series on the Royal Navy which has been published by I.B.Tauris in association with The National Museum of the Royal Navy and which currently numbers fourteen books. The series offers a less academic and cerebral alternative to Nicholas Rodger's much celebrated 'Naval History of Great Britain', the last part of which is currently in preparation.

There are ten chapters in this book. The first three cover the first two decades of the 20th Century leading up to the end of the First World War. A single chapter on the interwar years is followed by three on the Second World War, two on the Cold War and one which outlines events since 1989. This history is brought up to the date of publication with a description of the RN's part in Operation 'Ellamy', the military response to the Libyan Crisis in 2011, and a brief résumé of the hardware with which the RN will be equipped to meet the wars or crises of the near future.

It has to be said that there is little in this book which will be unfamiliar to the informed naval reader. However, this is a particularly accurate and generally well-written summary of events which also places the subject within the context of the wider world picture. The evaluation of the RN's key role in the First World War benefits greatly from this approach, given the current media fixation with the land war on the Western Front.

The book presents a reliable account of the way in which the RN has changed from being the largest force by some margin at the start of the 20th Century, powerful enough to exercise the so-called 'Two-Power Standard', to the much smaller, leaner navy it is today. Redford and Grove address the issues of end of empire, the impact of the coming of the nuclear age which initially threatened the very existence of conventional weapons, the never-ending battles with the Treasury – naval ships have always been extremely expensive to build and to maintain – and the dismal internal battles for status, recognition and supremacy with the RAF and the British Army.

Perhaps the only major criticism of this book is that the authors, both of whom are steeped in the traditions of the Royal Navy, indulge in rather too much 'RAF-bashing' in order to emphasise the importance of what used to be called the Senior Service. While it is unfortunately true that all servicemen and women are now frequently referred to in the media generically as 'soldiers', a rather more objective and sympathetic acknowledgement of the immense contribution of all three services to the protection of UK interests during this fascinating period of history would have been welcome.

Jon Wise

Thomas Wildenberg
Billy Mitchell's War with the Navy: The Interwar Rivalry Over Air Power
Naval Institute Press, 2013; hardback, 304 pages, 53 B&W photographs, 1 map; price £34.95/$34.95.
ISBN 978-1-087021-038-9

On 21 July 1921 US Army Air Service bombers sank the unmanned, stationary, target battleship *Ostfriesland* off the Virginia Capes, initiating a 'bomber versus battleship' controversy that continues to reverberate even into the twenty-first century. They did this by disobeying written orders and sinking the ship before Navy aircraft, which were due to bomb it in a series of scientific tests that were always intended to culminate in the ship being sunk. The fact that the ship could be sunk by aircraft bombs was never in doubt, but Brigadier General Mitchell turned the whole affair into an argument based on opinion rather than fact. Mitchell was the principal proponent in the USA for a unified air service, and when Congress rejected his proposals in 1920 he levelled increas-

ingly scathing criticism at the US Navy. He focused attention on the role of coastal defence, and increasingly used the press to further his arguments. To some contemporaries Mitchell was the prophet of strategic bombing, to others he was the 'stormy petrel' of aviation and a self-centred bigot who deployed other people's arguments to further his own ends in his quest to take charge of both the Army Air Service and a larger, unified air command.

Thomas Wildenberg has created a revealing 'pen portrait' of Mitchell's character in a well-researched book that is both scholarly and very easy to read; in fact I got so absorbed that I was unable to put the book down on several occasions. He describes a man who had commanded the operational US Army air units in France in 1918 with some distinction, planning and leading Allied air operations in the Battle of St. Mihiel in September 1918, and leading from the front by flying several missions himself. By 1921, however, he 'would twist the truth and distort reality in order to achieve his goals', eventually becoming 'a prisoner of his own megalomania who was court-martialled for insubordination'. It is undeniable that his bombers sank the *Ostfriesland*, but they had to be shown where she was, and if gunners on the ship had been firing at them they would have had to fly at altitudes that would have made accurate weapon delivery difficult. The test was meant to provide data, not to produce a showy demonstration of something that was already known to be possible. Hitting a ship that was already taking in water and listing was not difficult and this book explains that the myths had no real substance. The last chapter looks at the very limited success of US Army B-17 bombers against Japanese warships in 1942 to illustrate the difference between theory and practice. It underlines the fact that pilots have to be trained to attack ships effectively; you cannot expect land-based pilots to fly out over the sea, find an enemy warship and sink it without learning some very specialised skills

This is an excellent analysis of the events that took place 90 years ago off the Virginia Capes, and it lays bare the truth rather than the myths about the man who sparked the argu-

ment. It is sure to be the definitive work on the subject and is thoroughly recommended.

David Hobbs

John A Wolter, David A Ranzan & John J McDonough, eds.
With Commodore Perry in Japan: The Journal of William Speiden Jr, 1852-1855
Naval Institute Press, 2013; paperback, 256 pages, illustrated with B&W prints and maps, price $39.95/£30.50.
ISBN 13: 978-1-61251-238-9

William Speiden was just sixteen years of age when he joined the US steam frigate *Mississippi* in March 1852 as a purser's clerk. For the next three years (give or take a couple of months) he kept a detailed journal (actually two volumes) describing his experiences, and it is this that is reproduced here, edited with a carefully light touch by NIP as the first volume of their 'New Perspectives on Maritime History and Nautical Archaeology' series.

The book is not necessarily straightforward *Warship* readers' fare. While it casts a detailed and often fascinating light on everyday life on board a major vessel of the mid-nineteenth century US Navy, it also provides an equally interesting personal perspective on Commodore Perry's historic mission to Japan, an event of much wider than merely naval significance. As such this book should appeal to the student of international relations or of political, economic or cultural history.

Speiden's story begins quietly enough, with fishery patrol duties off Newfoundland, where there had been a long-standing dispute with the British. But then comes a visit from President Fillmore, and the *Mississippi* finds herself heading off to the far East. The first third of what follows is largely routine, reflecting what shipboard life was like: drills, Divine Services, setting sails, raising and lowering the smokestack, anchoring, coaling ship and so on. Looking back from 160 years on, the tendency is to think of the period of the transition from sail to steam as one of dramatic change. For Speiden and his fellow seamen, the constant switching from one motive power to the other and back again, with the associated evolutions (not to mention the frequent taking in tow of the sail-powered vessels when necessary), seemed completely normal.

Speiden is not one to reflect much on things: he sees them and records them in his journal. Initially he does show a youthful enthusiasm for just about everything, but this changes as the diary goes on: something which would have produced wide-eyed amazement early on is instead described in a straightforward, matter-of-fact manner. However, it is only once the squadron reaches Japan that the tale really starts to pick up. While Speiden did not attend all the major negotiations and meetings, he was well aware of the importance of what was taking place and made a point of getting an account from someone else who was present. The sheer novelty and exotic nature of so much of what he witnessed comes across well, although his account is coloured by some very mid-19th century attitudes towards people of other races.

The editorial endnotes are particularly comprehensive, arguably excessively so, as constant referencing of them has the effect of disrupting the narrative. Whether the serious student of Perry will learn much new here is hard to say, but to this reviewer, with little detailed knowledge of what took place, numerous intriguing details come to light, such as the Commodore's surprisingly bullish approach towards those he was negotiating with, and the fact that the Japanese were in fact already dealing with both the Dutch and the Russians. No sooner were Perry's negotiations complete and an agreement reached than assorted misunderstandings began to occur. From Speiden's account the impression given is that the Americans were much the more forthright here, and as a result tended to get their own way the majority of the time. It might well have looked different from a Japanese perspective, and this, of course, is the drawback of a first-hand telling such as this: it is entirely subjective. However, such accounts are the raw material of history. Taken on these terms, it is excellent.

Stephen Dent

Steven R. Schwankert
Poseidon: China's Secret Salvage of Britain's Lost Submarine

Hong Kong University Press, 2014; hardback, 219 pages, 33 B&W photographs, appendices, bibliography, index; price £15.00.
ISBN 978-988-8208-18-0

HMS *Poseidon* sank after a collision with a Chinese freighter a few nautical miles off the coast of Northern China in 1931. Twenty-one of her crew of 56 were lost. Five out of eight men who had been trapped in the forward torpedo compartment escaped by using the Davis Submerged Escape Apparatus (DSEA), a brand new form of equipment for which the crew had received very little training. Despite the loss of life and of his submarine, the commanding officer escaped with a severe reprimand, being found guilty of just one of three charges, that of hazarding his ship.

The account of the sinking of *Poseidon*, the court-martial which followed, and the subsequent fate of the surviving crew members occupies about half of this book. The remaining part explains how the story of the disaster was investigated by the author, a journalist and semi-professional scuba diver, who found out about *Poseidon* as a result of an internet search of wrecks off the northern coast of China, and discovered that the submarine had been salvaged by the Chinese in 1972. Schwankert was able to visit the city of Weihai (formerly Wei-hai-wei) from his base in Hong Kong and succeeded in locating the graves of two crew members who had been buried on a nearby island. He also wanted to see if was possible to find out what had happened to the remains of other men who would have been entombed in the submarine.

It is questionable whether the story merits its book-length treatment. Despite the tragic outcome, there is little to debate in the circumstances surrounding the sinking of the submarine. Schwankert does highlight minor controversies concerning the actions of some of the crew members following the collision. He also follows the lives and careers of some of the men after the event and tries to gauge the lasting effect of the experience on these survivors. However, the evidence he had to work with was limited and his research task was made more difficult by the passing of time.

In the second half of the work Schwankert is guilty of 'padding out' the story. Descriptions of his research include explanations about the requirements for obtaining a reader's pass at The National Archives (formerly the Public Record Office) in Kew and how to find the Royal Navy Submarine Museum at Gosport from Portsmouth Harbour railway station. His search for the graves on Liu Gong Island is painstakingly long and quite unnecessarily detailed.

One is left to question whether there is enough interest in this story to satisfy the general reader. Ironically, the salvage of the submarine removed the opportunity for Schwankert to use his expert skills and knowledge to good effect by investigating the wreck first-hand. Thus he was unable to forge a tangible visual link with the past. By the same token this is not a book for the specialist, who might also become irritated by the author's superficial grasp of naval technology and operations. Sadly, although Schwankert does provide some tantalising present-day impressions of the architectural remains of the former naval station at Wei-hai-wei, these are insufficient for those who might want to know more about an outpost of Britain's colonial past which is now largely forgotten.

Jon Wise

David Hobbs
British Aircraft Carriers: Design, Development and Service Histories

Seaforth Publishing, Barnsley, 2013; hardback, large format on glossy paper, 384 pages, copiously illustrated with plans and B&W photographs; price £45.00.
ISBN 978-1-84832-138-0

It is now 25 years since the publication of Norman Friedman's classic *British Carrier Aviation* (Conway Maritime Press, 1988), and comparisons are inevitable. However, this book is quite different in its conception and organisation. It also brings us to the present day, with coverage of the new *Queen Elizabeths* and the aircraft that will fly from them.

There are forty chapters, organised in broadly chronological sequence, and each class of aircraft carrier is allocated its own chapter. A section outlining the design rationale and development of the class, accompanied by useful data tables for the technical and aviation characteristics, is followed by individual service histories. Some types are grouped together for convenience, while other classes (eg wartime *Illustrious* class) are divided into their sub-groups to illustrate the important changes in thinking which dictated the modifications to the original design. The chapters on British carrier classes are interspersed with chapters which focus on contemporary developments abroad. The postwar reconstructions (eg the postwar *Victorious*, *Hermes* and *Eagle*) are accorded their own chapter as an acknowledgement of the new thinking which dictated their new flight deck, hangar and lift arrangements. All this works well, although in the final chapters the focus of the book becomes somewhat dissipated by the author's review of all current international developments in carrier aviation.

British Aircraft Carriers is illustrated with a wealth of photographs and line drawings, many of which are from the author's own collection. The photographs are not always of the highest quality, but have been carefully selected to illustrate points made in the text and are always interesting. The line drawings come from a variety of sources; many of them are flight deck schematics, again from the author's collection, and these are valuable in illustrating the progression in flight deck layout. There is a centre fold-out section with the official plans of many of the key designs, which are generally well-reproduced (if not always easy to read).

As a former Fleet Air Arm pilot, David Hobbs makes it clear from the outset that he is primarily interested in these ships from an aviator's point of view. The book is not only strong on the issues of flight deck, island and hangar design, but is particularly good on aviation logistics: the ability of the ships to stow an adequate quantity of aviation fuel (with the requisite level of protection), and the accommoda-

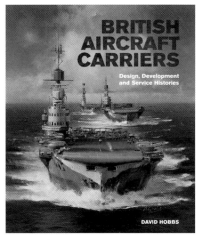

tion and movement of air weaponry. The allocation of a separate chapter to the 'maintenance carriers' *Unicorn*, *Perseus* and *Pioneer* makes its own statement.

The chapters on the early British and foreign carriers are generally competent and perceptive, although there are a few errors and inconsistencies between the data tables and the text, and the limited breadth of the source reading for the foreign ships results in the repetition of dated information, particularly on the IJN's *Hosho*. The central section of the book dealing with the carriers designed and built during the mid-1930s and 1940s contains some outstanding analysis. The author's (unfashionable) defence of the armoured carrier as the only way to go for a navy needing to operate in the Mediterranean before the advent of radar is particularly well expressed, likewise his demolition of the ships' successors planned during the Second World War when, following strong representation from aviators serving with the Fleet Air Arm, 'the Future Building Committee accepted that the requirements of aircraft operation dictated the design' (p.214). Unsurprisingly, David Hobbs expresses his unbounded enthusiasm for the light fleet carriers of the *Colossus* class, which featured an uncluttered flight deck, large aircraft lifts, and a single hangar with 17ft 6in clearance. These features enabled them to accommodate and operate all aircraft in service or projected, and made them attractive to other navies in the postwar era.

The author's account of British carrier aviation since the Second World War, and in particular since 1965, is a sorry tale. Initially obsessed

with revamping the carriers it already had in a misguided attempt to save money, the Navy became embroiled in a series of prolonged and mismanaged reconstructions which often cost as much as a new purpose-built carrier while delivering a ship which was inferior in capabilities and with ageing machinery. The cancellation of CVA-01 in 1966 as part of the British withdrawal from 'East of Suez' was followed by the discrediting of the strike carrier concept and an aversion to air-capable designs which looked 'too much like an aircraft carrier' (Admiral Varyl Begg). Hobbs is enthusiastic about the two new carriers of the *Queen Elizabeth* class, but sees them as a 'missed opportunity', being limited to operating short-range STOVL aircraft and helicopters when they should have been designed from the outset with 'cats and traps' for maximum effectiveness in power projection, air group flexibility and inter-operability. This entire section should make uncomfortable reading, not only for the politicians who have failed to understand the key principles of carrier aviation, but for the Navy, which has all too often failed to put its case in a coherent and persuasive way, leaving the key decisions to be made on the basis of commercial and industrial considerations, and which has also retained its predilection for 'gold-plating'.

John Jordan

Robert Gardiner
The Sailing Frigate: A History in Ship Models.
Seaforth Publishing, 2012; hardback, 128 pages, illustrated with 158 colour photographs; price £25.00.
ISBN 978 1 84832 160 1

In this book author Robert Gardiner uses models both from the National Maritime Museum and from American collections to illustrate the step-by-step development of the sailing frigate as a fighting vessel. Each of the book's illustrations is identified by the museum's unique reference number, while a link is given to the websites where this will produce information held by the museum on the particular vessel – an encouragement to further research, albeit initially on-line.

The first chapter deals with the fleets of Charles I and II and the intervening Commonwealth; each of the following five chapters covers roughly a 30-40 year period, culminating in the ironclad HMS *Warrior*. Each chapter deals with the structural developments, changes in armament and the variety of influences affecting the type. There is a bibliography, but unfortunately no index. Interestingly, in the chapter on the heavy frigate, the author concludes that the *Leda* class, of which *Trincomalee* and *Unicorn* are the only two vessels to have survived to represent their type in the UK, was perhaps not best suited to their intended task, despite the Admiralty ordering 47 of them over a number of years. This could explain in part why *Trincomalee* was reclassified as a corvette when finally commissioned for service in 1847.

Interspersed between chapters are several double-page spreads illustrating, for example, the development of armament or of bow/stern structure over the years, using close-up photographs of that part of the models. There are also four particularly interesting pages of half-block models, commissioned initially by Seppings, and kept up by Symonds, to illustrate the growth in size of the frigate from 1800 to 1850. This is followed by a small section on the last wooden frigates to be built in 1850; the largest, illustrated by a model of *Immortalité*, had a length between perpendiculars of 251ft, a full 130ft less than *Warrior*. If nothing else this illustrates the limitations of building in wood, even with Seppings' liberal use of iron wherever possible.

This claims to be the first in a series using ship models to illustrate development of various types. It will be interesting to see what comes next, and whether it manages to maintain the same standards of clarity and detail achieved by Robert Gardiner in this first volume. His choice of model is always appropriate and many of the models are in themselves works of art; however, he also doesn't hesitate to use a damaged or less-than-perfect model if it illustrates the point he is making. The result is a comprehensive description of the frigate's development made all the more lucid by the well-chosen illustrations.

W B Davies

Roger Branfill-Cook
X.1: The Royal Navy's Mystery Submarine

Seaforth Publishing, Barnsley, 2012; hardback, medium format on glossy paper, 192 pages, copiously illustrated with plans and B&W photographs; price £25.00.
ISBN 978-1-84832-161-8

The largest, most heavily armed, and deepest diving submersible of her day, *X.1* ('X' = experimental) was both a technology and a concept demonstrator. Commissioned for trials in mid-December 1923, *X.1* entered service only in September 1925; she was discarded in the early 1930s and broken up in 1936-37. Some elements of the advanced technology incorporated into the design (notably the 5.2-inch twin guns and their associated systems) were a success, but the high-powered 'composite' machinery was a disaster, and two years out of the three and a half *X.1* was in commission were spent in dockyard hands. Moreover, the basic concept, that of a submarine designed to fight on the surface, was inherently flawed; rather than being 'ahead of her time', as claimed in the foreword, she was effectively a dead end, and the Navy never proceeded with her planned successors.

The 'mystery submarine' of the title is something of a misnomer; the only mystery is how the Royal Navy would have made use of *X.1* had she been a technological success, given the constraints on submarine activity imposed by the naval arms limitation treaties. 'Secret' might have made for a more appropriate title; the author makes much of the unusual level of secrecy which surrounded *X.1*'s launch and much of her early career. Certainly the Navy was particularly anxious that foreign navies should not learn of her characteristics, not so much because it feared competition, but because there was a perception that such a submarine would be far more useful to a hostile power intent on posing a threat` Britain's seaborne trade.

The introductory chapter on the 'giant submarines' which preceded *X.1* is followed by five chapters on the design criteria and technical characteristics, then a further four chapters outlining the brief service history of the submarine, concluding with two chapters of analysis. The technical and historical chapters are extraordinarily detailed. Branfill-Cook has made extensive use of the archives at the Royal Navy Submarine Museum, Gosport, to conduct in-depth research, and every aspect of the submarine's construction and performance has been thoroughly investigated. Of particular interest is the description of the elaborate systems developed in relation to the guns, which were designed to be capable of opening fire within 90 seconds, the fire control solutions having been determined while the submarine was still submerged; *X.1* was fitted with Asdic and directional hydrophones for this purpose, and was also equipped with a director control tower and a 9ft rangefinder for use at periscope depth. The author is equally at home with the technical complexities of the 'composite' propulsion system. His well-researched account corrects claims made in earlier secondary sources that *X.1* broke both her shafts (see D K Brown, *Warship No.23*) by clarifying that the shafts in question were the overhead <u>cam</u>shafts in the 8-cylinder main engines, not the propeller shafts.

All of these chapters are extensively illustrated with the official plans of the various items of equipment and a series of beautiful internal drawings of the submarine by David Hill, together with a comprehensive set of photographs of *X.1* in service, some of which were taken by members of her crew. There is also a full set of the official plans of the submarine at the back end of the book; these have had to be considerably reduced in scale, but have come out well, despite the greyish linework.

The author's grasp of the broader technical and political issues is less secure. There is some confusion between 'fleet' and 'cruiser' submarines, both in the introductory chapter and in the chapter on foreign cruisers – the IJN KD type was a fleet submarine both in designation and function. References to the Washington and London 1930 treaties which governed the *modus operandi* of *X.1* and her foreign counterparts lack precision, and there is no detailed analysis of the implications of either the Root Resolution (Washington 1922) or the submarine protocol embodied in the London

Treaty (Part IV); in practical terms, the only 'convoys' that *X.1* could have legitimately attacked were ones comprising military transports, and these would almost certainly have had a cruiser escort. Branfill-Cook also understates the technical difficulties of re-engining a submarine (see his suggestion in Chapter 12 that *X.1* could have been retro-fitted with the large turbo-supercharged diesels developed for the later 'River' class). Unlike the capital ships the author mentions, a submarine is both weight- and volume-critical; new machinery would have to be accommodated into a pressure hull of strictly limited diameter, and any change in the overall weight of the machinery or in weight distribution would have impacted on buoyancy and trim.

Despite these weaknesses this is a remarkable book about a remarkable submarine. Although many of the author's conclusions are debatable, the enthusiasm with which he has embarked on this project and the depth and quality of his research are entirely admirable.

John Jordan

How to Pilot a Submarine

Amberley Publishing, 2014; paperback, 222 pages, 109 photographs, diagrams and illustrations; price £8.99.
ISBN 978-1-4456-3585-9

How to Pilot a Submarine is one of a series of 'How to' books that Amberley Publishing has recently produced based on various historical manuals and handbooks. (Others include *How to Fly a Battle of Britain Fighter*, based on the original Pilot's Notes, and *How to Survive an Atomic Attack* based on an advisory booklet published by the US Government during the Cold War.) Each book is essentially a facsimile of the original historical document; nothing has been added or altered in any way, and the contents here consist entirely of the original submarine training manual *The Fleet Type Submarine, Navpers 16160* which was produced in 1946 and based on the USS *Perch*.

The material contained in the book will be of great interest to anyone especially keen on submarines, and because the original document was produced by the US Navy as a training manual for submariners the information is, as you would expect,

comprehensive, detailed and precise. The book is divided into five sections spread over 21 chapters which cover Submarine History and Development, Construction, Submarine Systems, Operations and Training. After looking at the development of submarine technology it then moves on to look in detail at the construction of a modern submarine (as in 1946). It strips away the layers of components, equipment, systems and technologies and explains the workings of each; there are detailed diagrams and useful lists of definitions and phraseology which are always helpful to the armchair enthusiast. It goes on to describe the different operational manoeuvres of a submarine, explains the many procedures and duties aboard and covers the different aspects of submarine training.

The book is densely illustrated throughout with photographs and diagrams, and the appendix contains several detailed and potentially useful cutaway drawings of a submarine hull, though these lose some of their value from being scaled down so much to fit the small-format paperback.

Though not necessarily a book to read from cover to cover, *How to Pilot a Submarine* is a useful reference document for understanding some of the more technical aspects of submarine technology and contains a wealth of detailed information. It should be noted, however, that the material contained here is all readily available on-line.

John Peterson

Duncan Redford
A History of the Royal Navy: World War II

I.B. Tauris, 2014; hardback, 236 pages, illustrated with figures, maps, B&W photographs and colour plates;
price £20.00.
ISBN 978-1-78076-546-4

Published by I.B. Tauris in association with the National Museum of the Royal Navy, this book forms part of a major series of concise histories on specific wars and different aspects of the service, which already runs to 14 volumes, and is intended to present a comprehensive and readable history of the RN.

The Royal Navy's operations in the Second World War started on 3 Sept-

ember 1939 and continued until the surrender of Japan in August 1945. There was no 'phoney war' at sea and the Navy played a central role in the evacuation of the British army from Dunkirk, provided a sure shield against invasion during 1940-41, eliminated German surface raiders including the battleship *Bismarck* and protected convoys worldwide. Without the Royal Navy's defence of Britain's seaborne trade, and in particular the battle against German U-boats, there would not have been food for the country, fuel for the RAF's operations, or supplies to keep the army fighting in Europe, North Africa and the Far East. The author argues that Royal Navy made an outstanding naval contribution to Britain's survival and eventual victory, but that it came at a heavy cost in terms of ships and men. For the British Empire, the Second World War was a maritime war and it was the Royal Navy's war.

This slim volume contains a broad overview text supported by illustrations, maps and tables which support the easily readable story. The author makes a good case for greater public awareness that the war was a maritime conflict in which the RN played a dominant and pivotal role. However, a major weakness of this book is the minimal description of operations in the Mediterranean, East Indies and Far East. This limitation is significant because, in these theatres, it was the power of the British merchant marine protected by the Royal Navy which was decisive because of the former's ability to transport millions of service personnel plus their equipment and stores to key battle zones thousands of miles from the UK.

Thus, the author devotes 125 pages of the 205 pages to Home Fleet activities and the defeat of the attack on shipping. The Royal Navy's war in the Mediterranean is covered in 42 pages and is very much a broad-brush account with some important operations covered in just a few sentences. The war in the Far East is dealt with in just 28 pages, with a mere five pages devoted to the British Pacific Fleet, which was the most powerful British naval force deployed in the Second World War, and which supported the US Navy in its attacks on Japan. Similarly the vital Indian

Ocean convoys receive scant attention. One cannot help feeling that it would have been better to produce three volumes: one for the Home Fleet and the Battle of the Atlantic, one for the war in the Mediterranean and another for the East Indies and Far East. Despite these criticisms, this volume is a very readable introductory overview and provides a concise account of the Royal Navy in the Second World War. The book is nicely produced and represents good value for money.

Richard Osborne

Campbell McCutcheon
The Ships of Scapa Flow

Amberley Publishing, 2013; paperback, 96 pages, 139 photographs, 1 map; price £14.99.
ISBN 978-1-4456-3386-2

A quick on-line search of the words 'Scapa Flow' produces literally hundreds of results, proving both the widespread interest in the subject and the large number of books on the various significant events that took place there during the last century. *The Ships of Scapa Flow* is another title to add to this growing list, although it merely brushes the surface of each of the individual areas that the author has chosen to cover.

The slim paperback consists of an introduction followed by seven short chapters which in some cases contain just half a page of writing but which each feature several pages of photographs to accompany the text. The chapters cover the sinking of HMS *Hampshire* and HMS *Vanguard* during the First World War, Churchill's 'Phantom Fleet', the surrender, internment and scuttling of the German High Seas Fleet, and the massive salvage operation that followed. The last chapter jumps ahead to the Second World War and covers the sinking of HMS *Royal Oak* by *U-47* in October 1941. The subjects covered have all been written about in much greater detail elsewhere and here their stories appear in a highly condensed format. The sinking of both HMS *Hampshire* and HMS *Vanguard*, for example, is covered in less than two pages of text, The 'Phantom Fleet', which is probably the least-known subject and so the most interesting part of the book,

stretches to just five pages of text; this is the longest chapter (excluding the photographs). The longest overall is that on the salvaging of the High Seas Fleet which merits two pages of text but 29 pages of photographs, and so makes up almost a third of the book.

While the book is short on text it does contain a large number of very good photographs, some of which are particularly interesting or unusual and all of which are helpfully captioned, though in a book that relies so heavily on photographs it would have been useful to include source information for reference purposes. Also, while it is understandable that there is no index, a bibliography would have been useful for newcomers to the subject.

The Ships of Scapa Flow is a very quick read and gives a brief summary of some of the major naval incidents that occurred around the coast of Orkney during the last century. However it is well illustrated and offers a brief introduction to an interesting subject.

John Peterson

Jon K. Hendrickson
Crisis in the Mediterranean: Naval Competition and Great Power Politics, 1904-1914

US Naval Institute Press, Annapolis 2014; hardback, 219 pages; price $54.95/ £41.50.
ISBN 978-1-61251-475-8

The geopolitical situation in the Mediterranean before the First World War has often been ignored by historians. However, in the years before the conflict, evidence that the Mediterranean was shifting from British control to a wide-open and potentially anarchic state occupied the minds of many leaders in Austria-Hungary, Italy, France and Great Britain. This change was driven by three events: the weakening of the British Mediterranean Fleet to provide more ships for the North Sea; Austria-Hungary's decision to build a navy capable of operating in the Mediterranean; and Italy's decision to seek naval security in the Triple Alliance. These factors radically altered the balance of power in the Mediterranean in the years leading up to the First World War and thereby

forced Britain and France to enter into the *entente cordiale*. At the same time France undertook a rapid expansion of its naval forces to defend both British and French interests in the Mediterranean.

The key variable in this fluid situation was Italy, which was the weakest of the Great Powers and allied formally to Germany and Austria-Hungary, although the latter was also the Italian state's oldest and most feared enemy. However, at the same time Italy wanted good relations with her other regional neighbour, France, while also being completely dependent on the UK for coal and having coastal communications at the mercy of the British Mediterranean Fleet. Italian ambition to seize Libya from the Ottoman Empire necessitated improved relations with France, thereby increasing tensions with Austria-Hungary. The end result was the development of a dreadnought arms race between Rome and Vienna, and later Paris. These growing dreadnought fleets were capable of annihilating the pre-dreadnoughts that made up the British Mediterranean Fleet at a time when the Royal Navy's own growing fleet of dreadnoughts was being concentrated in home waters to counter Germany's increasing naval might. The scaling down of the Royal Navy's presence left the French with the problem of escorting its 19th Division from North Africa to France, and this in turn triggered the French dreadnought programme.

The author discusses Anglo-French naval co-operation, which depended upon unsigned secret agreements as well as the development of a joint command, a joint signal book, and plans to attack French convoys by the Austro-Hungarians and Italians. However he also demonstrates that the Italians could ill afford to risk their fuel supplies, shipping and new Libyan colony by going to war with Britain and France. Consequently Italy defaulted on her obligations to the Triple Alliance and joined the Allies in 1915 in return for promises of Austro-Hungarian and Ottoman territory.

The author has successfully explained the complex diplomatic and political situation in the Mediterranean in the two decades before the outbreak of the First World War; he has also discussed these events in terms of the underlying evolving technological bases of naval power in the region. However, the constant repetition of statistics should have been left to appropriate tabular indexes, and their inclusion in the body of the text of each chapter obscures important geostrategic issues. Another irritating feature is the overlong introduction to the beginning of each chapter, which is also concluded by a summary. In effect the same information is repeated three times in each chapter and this constant repetition adds nothing to flow of the essential narrative. Worse still, the lengthy introductory chapter is a broad-brush overview of the whole book and reduces the impact of the subject matter when it is presented in greater detail later on. Consequently, as the reader ploughs through the book he/she is left with the feeling of having read it all before – in the Introduction. While this is an interesting and well-researched book, the unnecessary repetition means that it is both overlong and over-priced.

Richard Osborne

Bernard D. Cole
Asian Maritime Strategies: Navigating Troubled Waters
Naval Institute Press, 2013; hardback, 320 pages, 1 map; price £22.49/$34.95.
ISBN 978-1-59114-162-4

Robert Haddick
Fire on the Water: China, America, and the Future of the Pacific
Naval Institute Press, 2014; hardback, 288 pages, 15 photos, 4 maps; price £22.39/$37.95.
ISBN 978-1-61251-795-7

In spite of the recent increase in tensions with Russia arising from the Putin regime's actions in the Ukraine, not to mention the impact of ongoing instability in the Middle East, it is the Asia-Pacific region that increasingly dominates current thinking within the United States' defence establishment. The Obama administration's so-called 'Pivot to the Pacific' has resulted in a steady growth in both diplomatic and military resources devoted to the region as it assesses

how best to respond to China's growing influence. Many academics and analysts have been contributing to this debate. The two books which are the subject of this review are just a small part of a significant body of research devoted to the subject.

In *Asian Maritime Strategies*, Bernard D. Cole, a retired US Navy captain and present-day lecturer at the National War College in Washington, D.C., provides a broad analysis of the strategic influences impacting navies in the Indo-Pacific region. After an introductory chapter setting the scene, he adopts a broadly regional approach. The major fleets of the United States, Japan, China and India are each accorded their own chapter; lesser navies are grouped together. A concluding chapter looks at areas of possible conflict – and of cooperation. Overall, Captain Cole takes a relatively sanguine view of the growth of Chinese military influence. 'The PLA [People's Liberation Army] remains neither quantitatively nor qualitatively capable of seriously challenging the United States, or perhaps even Japan, now or in the near term. U.S. naval and economic power remains unmatched...'

The book is strong in describing the geographical, historical and political factors that have influenced the various countries' fleet structures but occasionally falls short on its facts. For example, it mis-states the number of Aegis-equipped destroyers in South Korea's fleet and assumes that Japan will purchase the F-35B STOVL variant of the Joint Strike Fighter for its new helicopter-carrying destroyers. Errors of this nature are surprising given the otherwise high standard of scholarship displayed.

Robert Haddick, a military analyst and former US Marine Corps officer, is more focused on addressing the potential threat from China's military modernisation. In *Fire on the Water*, he explains why the Pacific is so vital to American interests and provides an interesting analysis of the strengths and weaknesses of Chinese and US military power in the region. In contrast to Captain Cole, he sees the PLA as providing a near-term threat to US naval dominance in the Western Pacific. He argues that China's possession of large numbers of relatively cheap but sophisticated

missiles (and associated targeting systems) would suffice to keep largely short-ranged US Air Force and Navy strike capabilities too far away to have a decisive influence in any future conflict. He also suggests the current response to Chinese anti-access/area-denial (A2/AD) capabilities, such as the joint USAF/USN Air-Sea Battle concept, tend to play to China's strengths. He argues for greater investment in assets such as submarines and long-range bombers to address his perception of current American weaknesses.

Neither of these books is necessarily aimed at *Warship*'s core readership. For example, there is little detail on the technological capabilities of the equipment supporting the various strategies described. Equally, the USNIP's rather austere publishing style, with the emphasis on text to the almost total exclusion of maps, tables or other visual aids, does not make for easy reading. Nevertheless, both books provide interesting and informative contributions to a debate that is likely to be a continuing theme in US maritime and political circles.

Conrad Waters

Norman Friedman
Naval Anti-Aircraft Guns and Gunnery
Seaforth Publishing, 2013; hardback, 399 pages, many plans and B&W illustrations; price £45.00.
ISBN 978-1-84832-177-9

The dust jacket claims that this book does for naval anti-air defence what the author's *Naval Firepower* did for surface gunnery: 'It is simply another superb contribution to naval technical history by its leading exponent.' Once inside, the scope is evident: a 'big' format, using high quality paper and binding, with the text broken up by a large number of photographs and drawings, at almost one per page. The book is well structured: an evolving threat, making AA fire effective, first steps, the inter-war period (with separate sections for the RN, USN, IJN and other European Navies), the Second World War (similarly divided), and post-war developments. The referencing, notes and bibliography are excellent.

The treatment of the subject is not without its problems. The author's style tends to blur the distinctions between sections; one notable example is the boundary between post-war and wartime narratives, where development began during the war but post-war illustrations are then pulled forward. The author also fails to flag-up the transition from the gun to the missile in late-war and post-war thinking. This problem is also present in the 'The Interwar RN' section, where the author's headings present a muddled chronology. His suggestion that the 'ideal system' came after HACS and the Naval Anti-Aircraft Gunnery Committee (NAAGC) of 1931 is in error; he then concludes with Commercial Fire Control, which was actually considered in 1931-32. The 'ideal system' was outlined by the earlier NAAGC in 1921, and again by the Admiralty Board in 1922, ie it pre-dates both the interim STS/SGS and HACS. NAAGC 1931 merely *restated* the concept of an 'ideal' system; its recommendations covered the fixes to HACS, the Landucci sight, and the diminutive Fuse Keeping Clock. NAAGC 1931 stated that an ideal system should be tachymetric (but not Flyplane!). The committee examined a number of candidate systems: Vickers -1 and -2 (viewed as the best), and one from Barr & Stroud (B&S) dated 1932, which the committee understood had not been built. The 'ideal' Tachymetric System Mk 1 (TS1) was not started until late 1937.

There is a strong sub-text, apparently influenced by the work of Jon Sumida on Barr & Stroud, that links B&S predictors with the retired Dutch Admiral Mouton, who was the firm's European representative until 1926. Any linkage through to subsequent German and Japanese AA systems based on Flyplane is tenuous at best: B&S merely tried to sell paper ideas between the late 1920s and 1932, when their fortunes were at a low ebb after the Admiralty picked AFCC for surface fire control, in preference to the firm's own Central Station Instrument Board design.

Whilst B&S had been 'initiated into HACS' in late 1926, there had been an earlier 'spat' with the Director of Naval Ordnance in 1922 over the potential for leakage of UK secrets via the company's export work. B&S developed reflector gunsights, rangefinders, and pendulum levels, but only manufactured HACS directors, AFCC and CRBFD as a 'build to print' activity. Their innovation was primarily in optical instruments and periscopes, not in gyros and stabilisers. This would tend to undermine the assertion that German systems built on B&S technology, because the Germans encountered major problems with stabilisation in their 1927, 1929, 1931 and 1937 systems – although these were apparently resolved in the later M42 version.

Crucially, Friedman fails to show <u>why</u> things happened in key areas like HACS or Mk 37. He doesn't really tackle 'rounds per bird', or the probability of kill, even though there was extensive theoretical work in the pre-war period and significant wartime analysis of real results. The book does, however, flag up the pre-war RN lead in gun direction, via visual sights and the Air Defence Officer, leading onto radar and target indication units; in this area, the RN led the USN in both concept and practical equipment through to the mid-1950s

On the immediate post-war exploitation of captured materiel, the reviewer found the author's views instructive. The UK evidently focused on 'V'-weapons, their inertial guidance, and the new submarines (fast battery-drive Type XX1 and the HTP-powered Type XXIII), but failed to undertake a comprehensive assessment of *Kreigsmarine* naval fire control. This contrasts with the US Navy's thoughtful assessment of Japanese AA equipment, which was the subject of a comparison with their own Mk 37. This may be a symptom of the fact that German surface forces were so badly worn down that the RN and RAF had no great experience of being savaged by naval flak, whilst in the Pacific the USN had to mount many carrier-borne attacks on Japanese surface units and would have had contemporaneous experience of the IJN's AA effectiveness.

As a minor niggle, the picture captioning is patchy: the Mk 67 is not named, Mk 60 and 61 are confused, and a number of captions of Bofors mountings describe 'Boffins' where they are clearly Mk 7 or Mk 9. Overall, the book is rather better on guns than on fire control; in 'The RN at War', the author skates over Flyplane (see the reviewer's own article in *Warship 2014*).

In summary, Norman Friedman's new book is well-written and is good in parts, but there are weaknesses in his approach and some significant errors. This is not the definitive reference for AA gunnery, rather a primer for additional research.

Peter Marland

Eds. Ian Johnston and Mick French
HMS *Ramillies*: The Final Salvo
Seaforth Publishing, Barnsley 2014; hardback, 256 pages, colour endpapers, 185 B&W images; price £25.00.
978-1-84832-211-0

Ramillies was the last of the 'R' class battleships to enter service and the last to be retired. Inadequately modernised between the wars, by 1939 all five were too slow for front-line duties and in 1942, when part of the Eastern Fleet, they were kept as far as possible from Nagumo's carriers. *Ramillies* was torpedoed by a Japanese midget submarine at Diego Suarez during Operation 'Dragoon', and after repairs provided supporting fire for the D-Day and South of France landings; one of her 15in guns is today outside the Imperial War Museum. She was the second British warship whose captain wore a *piupiu*, or Maori grass skirt, into action (the first was *New Zealand* at Dogger Bank and Jutland), the crew firmly believing this would save the ship from harm; certainly she survived the war without significant casualties.

The HMS *Ramillies* Association was formed in 1978 for old comrades to meet and discuss old times. By 2011, when numbers totalled thirty, including twelve former crew members, it was time to record oral memories, memories which with written narratives and a large photograph collection form the basis of this book. The foreword is by the Duke of Edinburgh, whose first ship she was.

From post-refit recommissioning to paying off, an unrivalled first-hand social history of lower-deck life in the days when Britain and battleships could still claim to rule the waves is provided; *Ramillies*, although obsolescent, badly ventilated and very wet, ploughing through waves rather than riding them, was always a happy ship. We are led through on-board activities by gunners, signallers, cooks, mariners and stokers; the description of cleaning water-tube boilers by climbing inside is remarkable. Spliced mainbraces, visits by King Neptune, runs ashore and brushes with the locals are not forgotten.

Although 'old men forget,' capable editing has ensured that few errors remain; the Free French were allies of Britain, not enemies, and the ship did not carry 4.5in or 4.7in AA guns. The comprehensive photographic coverage is excellent, but reproduction is poor – perhaps to be expected for old snapshots but disappointing for images from the Imperial War Museum – and all too many disappear into the 'gutter.'

An absorbing picture of a largely-forgotten era, this book is to be recommended as an account of life at sea in wartime, the antithesis of histories based on official records and archival searches.

Ian Sturton

Maryam Philpott
Air and Sea Power in World War I: Combat experience in the Royal Flying Corps and the Royal Navy
I. B. Taurus & Co, 2013, hardback, 210 pages, price £59.50.
ISBN 978-1-78076-151-0

This book evolved from the author's doctral thesis and I hoped, therefore, that it would offer new insight into the subject matter; I was bitterly disappointed to find that it did not. Worse, the author seems to have insufficient knowledge of the subject to make objective use of her sources and there are numerous errors: the American author AJ Marder, for instance, is referred to several times as the 'official Admiralty Historian'.

Problems begin with the breathtaking statement on p.1 that the contributions of the Royal Navy and Royal Flying Corps to the Great War 'have never been explored'. This is bad enough, but the author also finds difficulty comparing the RFC, that part of the Army that flew aircraft, with a Navy that operated vessels on and below the sea surface, a Royal Naval Division that included Royal Marines on land, and an RNAS with aircraft and airships operated from both ships at sea and on land. She frequently uses wild generalisations, referring to 'pilots and sailors', thereby omitting tens of thousands of mechanics and other non-flying branches of the flying services.

The book is divided into five sections entitled 'Training', 'Non-combat and Service Motivation', 'Technology', 'The Home Front' and 'Representations of War'. Despite the book's secondary title, none of these actually cover the experience of combat, and all suffer from the author's apparently pre-conceived notions of 'pilots and sailors'.

The section on training describes the wartime direct-entry scheme into the RFC for pilots and the pre-war 13-year-old cadet entry scheme for career seaman officers of the Royal Navy. The large number of officers who transferred to the RFC from other elements of the British Army are not mentioned. Perversely, the author fails to mention the direct entry scheme into the RNAS, thereby omitting men such as Wing Commander Raymond Collishaw DSO* DSC RNAS. No attempt is made to describe any other form of training, to compare reserves such as the RNR and RNVR with the regular naval cadet entry, or to mention the large number of outstanding pilots who joined the RNAS and RFC from Canada, Australia and New Zealand. The 'pilots' described are those who flew fighters, and little mention is made of the men who flew photographic and artillery-spotting missions, of those who flew from ships, or on long over-sea patrols carried out in flying boats and airships: all dull but often dangerous tasks that required different mind-sets. These omissions suggest that Philpott has only a tenuous idea of the purpose and capability of air operations in 1918.

No attempt is made to describe sea power as such, and on p.119 we are told that naval officers were 'unschooled in technical progress and relying on an eighteenth-century command structure' that produced an 'inability to wage war successfully' in 1914. There are other sweeping generalisations with little attempt to justify them, with the result that exemplars like Wing Commander JC Porte RNAS, who designed the world's most advanced flying boats, have no place in the book; nor have any of the other naval aviation pioneers, whose work was so remarkable that Captain GW Steel USN, who was sent to observe their work for the US Navy's General Board, stated in 1918 that 'so many ideas had been gained from the British that any discussion of the subject must consider their methods'. Of course a war fought with new and untried weapons deployed in huge numbers was bound to entail early mistakes and ideas that were ill conceived, but the way in which technology and tactics evolved to overcome them is a subject that deserves a better study than this, by an author who understands the subject.

The minimal coverage given to the RNAS is virtually all negative. The statement on p.145 that 'RNAS pilots eventually made it into action, only to spend their nights fruitlessly chasing the Zeppelins' ought to be balanced by mention of Flight Sub-Lt. RAJ Warneford RNAS, who won a VC for destroying a Zeppelin early on the morning of 7 June 1915. A more informed author would also have mentioned the innovative and successful strikes against Zeppelin bases and factories intended to limit their potential for raiding the UK, the first of their kind by any organisation. Much could have been made of the successful integration of RNAS fighter squadrons on the Western Front under RFC control in 1917-18, of the development of the world's first aircraft carrier, or of the plan to attack the German High Seas Fleet in its harbours by torpedo-aircraft, but they, too, receive no mention. The unfortunate amalgamation of the RNAS and RFC to form the RAF on All-Fools' Day 1918 is treated as the inevitable result that 'pilots' worked towards from the outset and 'sailors' failed to understand. The consequences for tactical aviation in support of naval and military operations are not mentioned, and I found no evidence that the author even understands that there were any. This book misses so many points, and misses them completely. I shall not be keeping my review copy and I emphatically do not recommend it.

David Hobbs

WARSHIP GALLERY

USS *North Carolina* (BB55)

Brooks Rowlett presents a series of photographs showing details of weapons and equipment on board the battleship, preserved at Wilmington, North Carolina.

USS *North Carolina* (BB55) was the first of the US Navy's fast battleships to be laid down. Her design was strongly influenced by the interwar naval treaty structures, which limited new battleships to 35,000 tons standard displacement. By the time of the London Treaty negotiations in 1936, the British government pressed for limiting gun calibre in new construction battleships to 14in (356mm) and the initial design for *North Carolina*, as with the Royal Navy's *King George V* class, featured three turrets each with four 14in guns. However, when the Japanese government refused to sign the London Treaty, an escalator clause was invoked by the US Government to increase gun calibre to 16in (406mm). The US Bureau of Ordnance was able to design a triple 16in turret to fit in the same space as the quadruple 14in. Therefore, contrary to the standard practice of designing a ship to be protected against guns of the calibre it carried, *North*

Carolina and her sister *Washington* (BB56) were protected only against 14in shellfire, as redesign against 16in weapons would have imposed unacceptable delays.

Like all warship designs the *North Carolina* class was a compromise, but a seemingly satisfactory one in many respects. However, the power requirements, shafting and propeller arrangements, and other structural aspects led the two ships of the class to both suffer from vibration problems. *North Carolina*, during her trials and early commissioning, embarked propellers of a different design several times; her frequent trips in and out of New York Harbor (having been built at the Brooklyn Navy Yard) led to her being compared to a tourist excursion craft, and she acquired the nickname 'The Showboat'. The vibration problems persisted at some speeds and reinforcements were worked in, particularly aft. Large external braces can be seen supporting the after main battery fire control

The forward 16in/45 turret. Unlike later classes the BB55 ships retained the long-base rangefinder and its characteristic extensions outside the turret. Note the doubling plates at the joints of hull plates. The BB55 class was of partially welded construction, mostly of the internal framing structure, while the external hull plates were still riveted. Also visible with their barrels pointed skyward are 20mm AA mounts, which are part of the typical large late WWII anti-aircraft batteries.(All photographs by the author)

The midships and superstructure showing the inclined armoured belt at the waterline. From left to right are the armoured conning tower, bridge, the forward tower topped by the forward Mk 38 Main Battery Director, the funnels, the port side 5in/38 DP secondary battery, the mainmast, the after superstructure (with the second Mk 38 director), and five of the 40mm quadruple Bofors AA mounts. Also visible are three of the four Mk 37 directors for the secondary 5in mounts. The radars atop the forward and midships Mk 37s are the early war Mk 4, but they have also been fitted with the late war Mk 22 'orange peel' antenna which would rock up and down, sweeping a radar beam that was wide in azimuth but narrow in elevation to determine target altitude.

A few changes since the original construction of the ship can be noted. The installation of a lookout platform about halfway up the forward tower in late 1942 remained a distinguishing feature of North Carolina; it was fitted at a level of the tower mast where lookouts were housed inside the tower, viewing out through small ports. The 40mm mounts and their Mk 51 directors were also fitted after the ship's completion, the superstructure mounts fore and aft having originally been 1.1in quadruple mounts. The 40mm quad abaft the midships Mk 37 director replaces a 36in diameter battle searchlight similar to the one remaining on the forward end of the same platform. Post-war modifications include whip antennae for radio communications, and the Mk 57 directors, visible as small dark dish antennas of radar Mk 34, mounted in tubs, one pair installed forward of the 40mm quad mount at the tower, the other pair installed outboard of the aft Mk 38 main battery director. The Mk 57s provided additional director capability for the 5in DP battery, allowing the battery to be further divided and engage more air targets; they replaced the Mk 51 directors for the 40mm previously installed in the same locations in smaller tubs, which in turn had replaced the MK 44 directors for the original 1.1in quadruple mounts. Vertical-stowed 20mm barrels in the platform extending from the aft deckhouse, below the aft Mk 37 director, are installed in positions used for additional searchlights when completed. Also visible, behind the base and vertical section of the boat cranes, is the external bracing applied to the aft director tower due to the vibrations experienced at high speeds. The photo shows the reproduction of the wartime Measure 32, Pattern 18d, which was applied to the ship in the 1990s to recreate history and improve the tourist appeal.

tower in some of the photographs reproduced here.

North Carolina saw action in the Pacific Theatre during 1942-45. She became the first fast battleship to escort an aircraft carrier task force in battle, being assigned to Task Force 16 built around the carrier *Enterprise* (CV6) at the Battle of the Eastern Solomons in late August 1942, where the unprecedented single-ship firepower output of her anti-aircraft battery led to other ships in the task group signalling *North Carolina* to enquire whether she was on fire! *North Carolina* was credited with shooting down seven Japanese aircraft; the claim was probably exaggerated, but these almost certainly did include one or more Aichi D3A dive bombers (Allied code name 'Val') from the Japanese

carriers *Shokaku* and *Zuikaku* from a group of four which diverted from USS *Enterprise* to target the battleship.

Just a few weeks later *North Carolina* suffered the less pleasant distinction of being the only US fast battleship to be damaged by a torpedo. Now in a task force built around USS *Saratoga* – *Enterprise* was under repair from the three bomb hits she received at the Eastern Solomons battle – *North Carolina* was hit by a torpedo from a spread of six fired by the Japanese submarine *I-19*. Three of the Type 95 21in (533mm) torpedoes struck USS *Wasp*, starting catastrophic fires that led to the carrier's eventual loss. Amazingly, two of the torpedoes continued several miles to *Saratoga's* task group, one striking *North Carolina*

on her port side just forward of No 1 turret and another hitting the destroyer USS *O'Brien* amidships. *O'Brien* survived that day, but her temporary structural repairs failed during her attempt to return to Pearl Harbor a month later, and she sank. *North Carolina* was repaired at Pearl Harbor and went back into action.

North Carolina served briefly into the post-war era and became a memorial for the US state of the same name in 1961. The photographs in this feature were taken during a visit to the ship in the spring of 2014.

Left: Taken from the platform around the top of the tower mast, just below the Mk 38 director, approximately 100 feet above the loaded condition waterline, this looks forward at the main battery turrets 1 & 2, anchor chains, forward single 20mm mounts and, near the bottom of the picture, the roof of the armoured conning tower. The circular plate on the main deck, with an arc section of circle aft, indicates where a wartime 40mm mount in its gun tub was removed in the 1946 refit due to excessive wetness. The BB55 class never carried a 40mm quadruple tub atop turret 2, unlike most of the South Dakota and Iowa class battleships. Behind the breakwater can be seen the paravanes for mine protection when transiting unswept waters. Note that the rangefinder housing 'ears' extending from either side of the turrets are not rectangular but wedge-shaped.

This is taken from the same platform as the previous photograph. It offers an overhead view of the 40mm quad mount in its tub on the first superstructure deck. A twin-mount version of the 20mm Oerlikon can be seen on the main deck. The variation in pattern of the deck planking reflects the replacement of many areas of the original teak deck by new wood, donated by the government of Myanmar. (Pieces of the original deck are offered for sale in the souvenir store for fundraising.) At the bottom left of the photograph is the top view of the Mk 57 director; forward of it is a signalling projector, and a pelorus is on the lookout platform below. Circular objects abaft the turret and on the next deck down are air ventilator 'mushroom' intakes. Museum ships, without active large crews to chip and repaint, are especially subject to rust, and some of this problem can be seen on the metal superstructure deck

The top of the forward tower, the port Mk 37 director, and the forward funnel. The SK-2 air search radar antenna is a modern replica rather than original installation. On the vacant small platform above it an SG-1 surface search radar antenna was mounted 1943-46. At decommissioning a Mk 13 fire control radar would have been atop the Mk 38 Director on the tower (see photo of aft tower); it was removed at some point late during the period when BB 55 was in mothballs, and again, at some point the antenna for an SG surface search radar was installed in its place. Visible on small x-shaped outriggers from sides of the upper observation platform are small radar jammer antennae, also installed in late 1944. Note the dark canvas covering the aperture where the rangefinder of the Mk 37 director protrudes from the director side; the rangefinder could rotate around its lengthwise access to view elevation, and could rotate to a limited extent in azimuth compared to the director housing. The cause of the dent in the funnel cap is unknown. Other small details of note are the aerology instruments on top of the Mk 38's rangefinder and on the yardarm. In 1944-45 a small radome was in place at the front of the forward funnel; this seems to have been removed at the time the ship was placed in mothballs; it probably covered a piece of countermeasures gear, possibly a TDY jammer.

The after deckhouse, with ship's bell visible just above the 40mm quadruple mount atop #3 turret. The square tub at the right of the photo is the Mk 51 director associated with the 40mm mount. The 40mm tub replaced an earlier tub installed in 1942 with three connected 'lobes' each housing a 20 mm Oerlikon light AA gun. A better view of the Mk 57 director (far left) and its Mk 34 radar dish antenna is also obtained from this angle. The after Mk 37 director appears to have the improved replacement for the Mk 4 radar, the Mk 12, along with the Mk 22 peel (the auxiliary antenna located in the center of the stacked troughs similar to the Mk 4 is a distinguishing feature between the Mk 4 and Mk 12). The diagonal external bracing for the Mk 38 director support structure can also be seen between the cylinder and the Mk 57s. The mockup radar housing for the Mk 13 main gunnery radar more clearly shows the airfoil-like shape. The actual antenna was an orange-peel type producing a beam wide in elevation but narrow in azimuth, that 'rocked' back and forth within the casing to scan around the target bearing.

This view from the starboard side forward looking back at the superstructure shows some of the matching details compared to the port views. The superstructure level with the closed-off scuttles over most of its length is the flag and signal bridge. The navigating bridge is the smaller structure above, with open scuttles. Some of the sliding covers of the vision slits in the armoured conning tower can also be seen. The topmost level of the conning tower is the gunnery officer's battle station, with repeaters for the main battery Mk 13 radar and indicators from the Mk 38 director; the lower vision slit level of the conning tower is the captain's battle station. Barely visible at the top of the conning tower where the rangefinder 'ear' of turret 2 overlaps is part of the antenna of the Mk 28 fire control radar, a backup for both the Mk 13s and the optical periscope, with its electronics also installed within the gunnery officer's station. The Mk 28 used the same antenna as the SJ surface search radar used in US submarines in 1943-45.

An internal view at the 2nd deck, below the main deck, showing an enclosed ammunition hoist path to one of the 5in/38 secondary battery mounts. Piping below the overhead is for the ventilation system, not liquids. Some details of the internal framing can be seen as well. This view is looking forward, facing slightly inboard, on the port side.

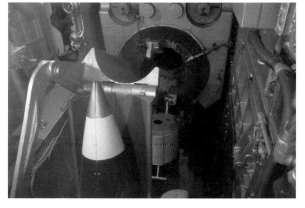

The after turret is open for visitors. This is the breech of the left gun, showing a 16in projectile sitting upright from the hoist, with the folding loading tray visible. The museum commission has arranged for the three guns in this turret to show three stages of the loading process (not pictured): the center gun shows the powder charges being loaded onto the tray, with the projectile already rammed into the breech, and the right gun shows the powder charges nearly completely rammed in prior to closing the breech. Sailor flat figures are used to show crew stations.

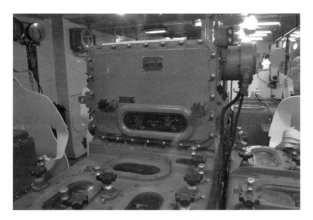

This view is taken in the Central Fire Control Station, below the waterline and behind the armour belt. The foreground equipment is an analogue computer for the 5in battery, with an attached starshell computer Mk 1. Both this and the following picture show the adoption of 'sailor shapes', more or less three-dimensional stick figures that show approximate positions of some of the operators of various systems around the ship in active service.

This is from the opposite side of the previous photo, showing a different portion of the secondary battery fire control computer. Note the target angle dial displaying an aircraft shape.

A view into the steering compartment, showing the steering machinery for the starboard rudder. Hydraulic rams are arranged in a pair on either side of the rudder post. The large tank at the rear of the compartment is a hydraulic fluid reservoir. One ram pushed and the other retracted to swing the rudder. Note the lights mounted in uprights; the overhead of this compartment is an armoured deck, and the steering gear itself is surrounded by an armoured box on all sides that is thicker than the belt armour of the main belt. Access to this compartment involves a slight ramp step up, as it lies in the underwater portion of the stern that doesn't match the elevation of the deck that extends the length of the ship. The rectangular plates on the deck are raised to provide traction for walking, as there were likely to be small amounts of leaked hydraulic fluid on the deck surface proper, which would be slick to walk on.

The two views above show part of the wide-base optical rangefinder mounted at the rear of turret 3. The two hoods are anti-glare covers over the lenses at the ends of the rangefinder. The rangefinder is actually free to move a few degrees around a vertical axis, somewhat to left or right of the actual direction of train of the turret, and the photo showing the base support at this end shows the rail-like structure and rollers that support this end of the rangefinder as it is trained. This also explains the wedge-like shape of the rangefinder 'ears' – the actual rangefinder can move a few degrees left or right inside the turret.

Each turret has a backup local fire control computer. Again in turret 3, this view looks down on the display, with indicator dials for own ship course, target course and angle, and dials and numeric indicators for own ship and target speed. Various hand knobs extend both upward and out to the sides to allow adjustment of the various inputs to the system.

Left: *A closeup of one of the Mk 51 directors with the Mk 14 optical gunsight. This director is apparently out of its original place to allow easy access to visitors; the director location for the 40mm quad mount in this area should have been in a higher tub on the superstructure. Based on drawings, the director is likely installed in a position occupied by a 20mm single during 1944-45.*

Above right and below: *The USN standard automatic heavy machine gun at the time of Pearl Harbor was the 1.1in mount designed by the Bureau of Ordnance. Unreliable and disliked in service, supposedly all 1.1in mounts were ordered scrapped in 1945. However, in recent years, both North Carolina and the museum battleship Texas have acquired mounts and have installed them on the ships. These views show some details of this mount. Compared to the later 40mm quad it was lighter, fired a smaller, lighter projectile with a smaller bursting charge, was slower to train owing to weak motors, harder to load due to closeness of the barrels, and suffered serious reliability problems due to projectiles jamming or misfiring. Gunner's mates stood by with mallets to dislodge jams and few of the users had anything kind to say about the mount, though the basic design was apparently reasonably sound and the problems could have been resolved. The overall superiority of the Bofors operationally led to the suppression of 1.1in mounts in favour of the Bofors guns. Note that the left gun appears to be in recoiled position – perhaps jammed in that position, a silent reminder of some of the problems with the gun mount during its wartime career. Despite its poor performance, shortage of the 40mm mounts resulted in several USN destroyer escorts completed as late as 1944 receiving a 1.1in mount in the after superfiring position in place of a 40mm Bofors twin mount.*